OECD Business and Finance Outlook 2015

OECD
BETTER POLICIES FOR BETTER LIVES

Please cite this publication as:
OECD (2015), *OECD Business and Finance Outlook 2015*, OECD Publishing, Paris.
DOI: http://dx.doi.org/10.1787/9789264234291-en

ISBN 978-92-64-23261-7 (print)
ISBN 978-92-64-23429-1 (PDF)

Foreword

This is the first edition of the OECD Business and Finance Outlook, *a new annual publication that presents unique data and analysis that looks at what might affect and change, both favourably and unfavourably, tomorrow's world of business, finance and investment. This year's edition focuses on how companies, banks, shadow banking intermediaries and institutional investors are trying to deal with a climate of very low interest rates and structural change in the global economy.*

The 2015 OECD Business and Finance Outlook *is the joint work of staff of the OECD Directorate for Financial and Enterprise Affairs. It has benefited from contributions from national government delegates and other parts of the OECD Secretariat.*

Table of contents

Tables

Figures

Follow OECD Publications on:

http://twitter.com/OECD_Pubs

http://www.facebook.com/OECDPublications

http://www.linkedin.com/groups/OECD-Publications-4645871

http://www.youtube.com/oecdilibrary

http://www.oecd.org/oecddirect/

This book has...

StatLinks

A service that delivers Excel® files from the printed page!

Look for the *StatLinks* at the bottom of the tables or graphs in this book. To download the matching Excel® spreadsheet, just type the link into your Internet browser, starting with the *http://dx.doi.org* prefix, or click on the link from the e-book edition.

Acronyms and abbreviations

ABS	Asset-backed security
ACWI	All country world index
ADV	Advanced economies
ALM	Asset-liability management
BEPS	Base erosion and profit shifting
BMD4	4th edition of the *OECD Benchmark Definition of Foreign Direct Investment*
BoP	Balance of payment
BRICS	Brazil, Russia, India, China, and South Africa
CAPEX	Company sales and capital expenditure
CAPM	Capital asset pricing model
CCP	Centralised clearing counter-party
CEO	Chief executive officer
CIP	Covered interest parity
CITR	Corporate income tax rate
CMU	Capital market union
COD	Cost of debt
COE	Cost of equity
COP21	UN Conference of the Parties to the UNFCCC (Climate Change Conference) 2015 in Paris
CPI	Consumer Price Index
CTA	Commodity trading advisor
DB	Defined benefit pension plans
DC	Defined contribution pension plans
DTD	Distance-to-default
EA	Age at which the individual began accumulating savings
EBITDA	Earnings before interest, taxes, depreciation and amortisation
ECB	European Central Bank
EECA	Eastern Europe and Central Asia
EIOPA	European Insurance and Occupational Pensions Authority
EME	Emerging market economy
EMIR	European market infrastructure reform act
EPS	Earnings per share

ESMA	European Securities and Markets Authority
ETF	Exchange traded fund
EU	European Union
FDI	Foreign direct investment
FED	United States Federal Reserve Board
FSB	Financial Stability Board
FVS	Future value of savings
GARCH	Generalized Auto Regressive Conditional Heteroskedasticity
GBI	Government bond index
GDP	Gross domestic product
GSIB	Globally systemically important banks
G-SIB	Global systemically important bank
GVC	Global value chains
GVCs	Global value chains
HF	Hedge fund
HFRI	Hedge fund research index
HQLA	High-quality liquid assets
IBI	International business investment
IBO	*Emissions Obligataires par Offre au Public* [Order Book for Retail Bonds (ORB)]
IC	Insurance company
ICMA	International Capital Markets Association
IEA	International Energy Agence
IG	Investment grade
IOSCO	International Organization of Securities Commissions
IPO	Initial public offering
LCRs	Liquidity coverage ratio
M&A	Mergers and acquisitions
MBS	Mortgage-backed securities
MCAP	Market cap to GDP as an equity bullishness valuation metric
MENA	Middle East and North Africa
MF	Mutual fund
MMF	Money market funds
MNE	Multi-national enterprises
MSCI	Morgan Stanley Composite Index
NAIC	National Association of Insurance Commissioners
NAV	Net asset value
NDF	Non-deliverable forward
NSFR	Net stable funding ratio

OECD	Organisation for Economic Co-operation and Development
OPEC	Organization of Petroleum Exporting Countries
ORB	Order Book for Retail Bonds [*Emissions Obligataires par Offre au Public* (IBO)]
OTC	Over-the-counter
P2P	Peer-to-peer
PE	Private equity
PF	Pension fund
PFI	Policy Framework for Investment (OECD) add to Ch 5 text
PMR	Product market regulation
PP	Private placement
PPP	Public-private partnership
QE	Quantitative easing
R&D	Research and development
RA	Retirement age
REIT	Real estate investment trusts
ROE	Return on equity
S-I	Saving and investment
SME	Small and medium sized enterprises
SOE	State-owned enterprise
SPE	Special purpose entity
SPO	Secondary public offering
SWF	Sovereign wealth fund
UCITS	Undertakings for Collective Investment in Transferable Securities
UIC	Ultimate investing country
VA	Value-added
WTO	World Trade Organization

Editorial

As we emerge from the crisis that peaked with the Lehman Brothers and AIG collapses in September 2008, an environment of very low interest rates seems likely to persist over at least the medium term. This will be good for debtors but generating returns on savings will be difficult. At the same time, advanced countries must confront the challenge of providing for ageing baby-boom populations by generating and mobilising more and more resources for medical care and pensions. While pay as you go (PAYG) systems will cover basic medical care and will carry some of the burden of providing pensions, much will have to be done privately and by relying on financial intermediaries to do their share.

Generating the necessary resources will require greater reliance on solid company investments that underpin productivity growth and therefore the fundamental value in equities and bonds. However, while very low interest rates have generated considerable financial risk taking, non-financial companies exhibit much more caution. Uncertainty appears to be holding back real investment in favour of share buybacks, cross-border asset divestments, and borrowing to finance such corporate activity in spite of significant cash hoarding in tax-effective zones. Nor does cash returned to shareholders appear to be finding its way into new productive investments. Instead, it often finds its way back into leveraged alternative products (including derivatives) as institutional investors search for yield in the attempt to avoid insolvencies. Public funding capacity, and private value creation to meet financial promises to future generations, depends on the strength of the economy. Policy will need to ensure both a better global allocation of resources to the most productive investments and a financial environment that is conducive for institutional investors to meet the income needs of ageing populations without taking excessive risk. Avoiding the rolling bubbles and busts in financial markets that have typified recent decades will be essential in achieving these objectives.

As we embark upon this endeavour, a few structural realities of the global economy and the challenges they pose will need to be addressed. First, the centre of gravity of the world economy has shifted during the past generation from the advanced economies around the North Atlantic to mostly-emerging economies in the Asia-Pacific region. Global value chains of large businesses have long been adapting effectively to this. But ensuring that the benefits are widely distributed in the advanced countries requires that (1) strong macroeconomic adjustment mechanisms are in place to encourage necessary resource reallocation and to sustain good job performance; and (2) returns on capital are attractive enough to encourage the necessary capital formation. This requires continued strengthening of the framework conditions which govern the environment in which businesses operate. Importantly, these include those relating to the cross-border flows in the international monetary system, financial intermediaries and competitive product markets.

Secondly, large numbers of retired baby boomers will have to be supported by smaller cohorts of younger workers, partly as beneficiaries of public transfers and partly by drawing on asset accumulations and their associated earnings. Inexorably, each member of the workforce will, directly or indirectly, have to support the well-being of high and rising numbers of retired people. This must create pressures that would be difficult to manage under any set of institutional arrangements. These range widely from extended family structures in economically undeveloped societies to the PAYG-financed public social security systems typical of modern advanced economies. OECD countries vary in the extent to which they depend on such PAYG-financed systems. But nearly all have also placed some of their trust in private financial intermediaries which fund long-term investment and rely on its returns to honour their obligations, or promises, to retirees who depend on them. These intermediaries, mainly pension funds and life insurance companies, face a challenge in generating the returns on their assets to enable them to meet their commitments in the low-return environment in which we now live. This reinforces the need to raise real returns on capital in advanced economies as a whole. But care must be taken to ensure that these institutions do not let their 'search for yield' lead them to such excessively high-risk investment strategies that their solvency, and their ability to deliver on promises, is threatened.

Thirdly, a resilient financial system is essential if our economic and social systems are to function well. While avoiding disrupting the macro-economy, it must mobilise credit efficiently and allocate investible resources productively, i.e. to where they will generate the highest prospective return while taking an appropriate account of risk. Common sense dictates providing support for the system in the event of crisis to avoid serious adverse macroeconomic consequences. But this implies an implicit guarantee and creates incentives to take risks on the assumption that gains are private but that losses will be covered by taxpayers. This implicit guarantee damages the ability of the system to carry out its allocative function well. In addition, the system remains exposed to instability since local problems are too easily spread, given the high degree of inter-connectedness. Much has been achieved in terms of reforming the regulatory and supervisory arrangements applying to financial institutions. But there is still more to be done to eliminate under-pricing of risk and to strengthen the ability of the system to absorb shocks. Importantly this includes ensuring strong capital bases and reducing inter-connectedness, either by separating shadow banking from more traditional deposit banking and/or via policies that limit critical leverage, re-investment, re-hypothecation and maturity transformation risks.

Finally, the post-crisis behaviour of much of the economic system poses a risk puzzle: why do so many people managing listed companies that carry out a large portion of the world's capital formation see so much risk on the horizon while so many major players in financial markets apparently see so little risk? Someone will inevitably be proved wrong. How do we avoid a crisis when this happens? This first number of the *OECD Business and Finance Outlook* examines many of the issues that OECD countries will have to address to ensure that the challenges can be handled smoothly.

Angel Gurría
OECD Secretary-General

OECD Business and Finance Outlook 2015

Executive summary

Keeping promises in a low interest rate environment

The first issue of the *OECD Business and Finance Outlook* looks at the way in which companies, banks, shadow banking intermediaries and institutional investors are trying to deal with a climate of very low interest rates and structural change in the global economy. The 'promises' of growth, employment and retirement income are seen to be at risk in the absence of policy actions.

Corporate investment and the stagnation puzzle

Following the easy monetary policies brought on by the crisis, financial markets have rallied strongly while companies that undertake capital spending do not appear to see the same value creation opportunities. Despite historically low interest rates, economic growth is stagnating in many regions due in part to the lack of investment. This is true of companies in the general industry, infrastructure and clean energy sectors. Bottom-up data of 10 000 of the world's largest companies listed in the Bloomberg World Equity Index for both advanced and emerging countries are used to explore this puzzle, enabling capital spending and matching financial data to be used over the period 2002-2014.

Trends, developments and policy concerns in financial markets

Policies and regulatory responses to crises tend to roll financial excesses into other sectors or regions. The response to the 2008 crisis has rolled the risk into the shadow banking and corporate bond sectors. Shadow banks intermediate credit between cash-rich and cash-poor investors in their bid to reuse securities and to gain access directly or synthetically to higher-yield and lower-risk alternative products in a world of low interest rates and rising longevity risk. At the root of the problem are a number of implicit promises that have been made to investors that are unlikely to be met in the absence of structural change and better regulation.

In this regard the outlook for the solvency position of pension funds and life insurance companies is of concern. Insofar as their promises are linked to evolving parameters or can be adjusted to the new environment of low interest rates, low inflation and low growth, these institutions may be able to weather the situation. However, there is a very serious concern for the financial outlook should these institutions become heavily involved in an excessive 'search for yield' in order to fulfil any fixed guarantee promises they may have made when interest rates were higher. Regulators and policy makers should remain vigilant.

Small and medium-sized enterprises (SMEs) are essential for the economic recovery from the current economic and financial crisis. The crisis has reduced bank lending and affected SMEs in particular because credit sources tend to dry up more rapidly for small firms than for large companies during economic downturns. Bank lending gaps have opened up since the crisis, and are especially pertinent outside the United States. Therefore, a two-pronged approach to fostering SME financing (in as far as it is a supply problem) is proposed: first, restoring banks' health to improve bank lending; and second, supporting the development of a broad range of non-bank financing for SMEs in debt and equity markets, the latter being especially well-suited for small dynamic, innovation-oriented SMEs. Owing to the diversity of the SME sector, financing remains complex and requires a variety of instruments and approaches. Policy makers can help by providing regulatory support and assist in the improvement of data transparency, standardisation, and raising awareness about available financing options.

Recent trends in global and regional cross-border financial flows involving multinational enterprises are reviewed using data on international mergers and acquisitions and foreign direct investment. Three main factors that are shaping the outlook going forward are examined. These are; broader economic trends, the growing involvement of governments in the governance of the global economy, and the sustainability of MNE investment from emerging market economies.

Strengthening market-based financing of corporate investment

During the last ten years, corporations' use of capital markets has changed in a number of important ways. These changes have partly been driven by macroeconomic events that have affected traditional sources of funds and shifted some of the corporate debt from traditional bank lending to corporate bonds. They may have been influenced by regulatory changes that may have contributed to a decrease in the use of public equity markets by small and medium-sized enterprises. Profound changes have also occurred in the functioning of secondary equity markets and trading practices during the last decade which raise important policy issues with respect to ensuring a level playing field among investors and efficient price discovery. Finally, in a low interest rate environment, where institutional investors are pressed to meet their client obligations, corporations have also had to respond to investor campaigns for higher dividends and share buyback programmes.

Pro-competitive policy reform for investment and growth

Promoting competition was declared to be a priority by the G20 in 2014, recognising that it is market competition between firms that provides them with an incentive to reduce costs and develop new and better products. The economic evidence shows that some of the most effective structural reforms to promote growth are those increasing product market competition. On the other hand the most damaging restrictions on competition often arise from protected state-owned enterprises (SOEs) or from regulatory policies that unnecessarily limit competition. Since state ownership is becoming more significant in the world economy, it is increasingly important to ensure that SOEs face similar competitive conditions, on equal terms, as do private sector firms. Identifying and redesigning the most damaging regulations can be difficult and, in many cases, politically challenging. Quantification of benefits and accounts of other countries' experiences can help explain and gain political support for reforms. Some cases are described here.

OECD Business and Finance Outlook 2015

Chapter 1

Overview: Keeping promises in a low interest rate environment

This chapter presents an overview of the OECD Business and Finance Outlook 2015. It looks at the way in which companies, banks, shadow banking intermediaries and institutional investors are trying to deal with a climate of very low interest rates and structural change in the global economy. The 'promises' of growth, employment and retirement income are seen to be at risk in the absence of policy actions.

The financial crisis that began in 2007 and peaked in September 2008 with the bankruptcy of Lehman Brothers and AIG's bail-out has passed, but some legacies remain to be addressed. The international banking system has undergone major repairs, as comprehensive reforms to the regulatory framework for banks have been substantially agreed and are in the process of being phased in. Balance sheets have been recapitalised and probabilities of major bank defaults have fallen; bank interconnectedness has declined, even if it still remains high. Most advanced economies have recovered from the recession of 2009, but recoveries have often been weak and uneven despite low interest rates for several years. Discouragingly, the business sector continues to display a subdued appetite for capital expenditure. Inflation remains too low for comfort, employment performance continues to be lacklustre and public finances remain a concern, constraining policy options in many countries. The business and finance outlook remains complex and the manner in which banks, shadow banking intermediaries, institutional investors, and companies in both emerging and advanced economies are trying to deal with it presents new risks. These challenges can put at risk growth, the recovery of employment levels and the possibility of workers having access to a reasonable retirement income.

The limits of central bank liquidity policies

The global financial landscape today reflects legacies of the crisis. Large amounts of public money were spent supporting the financial system at the peak of the crisis, leaving a legacy of high public indebtedness. Policy interest rates were reduced to near-zero in most advanced economies to fight recession and these persist even today. Cash injections and other measures to increase the liquidity of the banking system ('quantitative easing') were put into place partly to provide additional stimulus and avoid a 'freeze' in money markets triggered by concerns of counterparty risk. One of the outcomes of these measures is a world awash with liquidity, flattening yield curves and a reduction of risk premia as reflected in financial asset prices. This strategy has encouraged large players in the financial markets to pursue a 'search for yield' and to pay prices for assets in bond and equity markets that may not realistically reflect inherent risks.

A risk puzzle

The resulting disconnect in risk arises when listed companies, who conduct a large proportion of the world's capital formation, see considerable risk on the horizon while major players in financial markets seem completely unconcerned. This puzzling behaviour raises the spectre of a potential new crisis and the need to take appropriate measures to anticipate repercussions when one or the other of these views eventually proves to be wrong. The needed response must be built around three structural realities in the world economy:

- The centre of gravity of the global economy is shifting from the advanced economies around the North Atlantic to the Asia-Pacific region, in particular to a group of highly competitive and mostly-emerging economies. Financial claims on non-financial businesses in advanced economies operating in open competitive markets are thus underpinned by their ability to adapt global value chains to this reality.

- Populations in advanced economies, especially in Japan and in much of southern and central Europe, are ageing. They will be increasingly dependent on commitments from pension funds and insurance companies as well as on returns from their own savings managed as collective products by investment companies. Pension plans and retirement products such as annuities and mutual funds must meet customer expectations about returns, while being designed to take account of longevity risk in an environment of low interest rates.
- Notwithstanding large-scale financial reform designed to insulate taxpayers from the need to cover losses, local problems can easily become systemic in an interconnected system. This implicitly guarantees much more of the claims in the system than what is explicitly insured, creating potentially adverse incentives.

How can the system deliver on these promises? A number of priorities stand out.

Global value chains and investment

The global environment in which financial markets operate must include effective macroeconomic adjustment mechanisms. The issue is not just current account imbalances. The world has benefitted from the globalisation encouraged by open international trade and investment regimes. Business sectors in both advanced and emerging market economies have developed Global Value Chains (GVCs) that transfer technology and distribute production where it can be carried out most effectively. This behaviour has contributed to productivity gains in emerging markets, especially in Asia, prior to the crisis. Subsequently, however, while sales per worker (which includes foreign value-added) have continued to rise, the trend does not appear to have been matched by growth in domestic value-added.

This 'outsourcing' has also led to important shifts of production by multinational enterprises (MNEs) mostly away from advanced economies, which has resulted in weaker capital formation in these countries. Value-added per employee has not been rising in listed companies of advanced economies since the crisis. Transferring investment in this way may improve operational efficiency, but this should not be confused with investment in R&D and genuine productivity growth.

The tougher post-crisis environment is also leading to considerable divestment of international operations by MNEs. This suggests that restructuring and retrenchment continues to be a focus. Adjustment mechanisms need to work better to encourage compensating investment in other activities including R&D and social infrastructure, and to generate better employment performance. Unless this is done, 'secular stagnation' concerns will continue, protectionist threats to the open trade and financial system can be expected, and new doubts will emerge that resources for ageing populations promised by institutional investors like pension funds and insurance companies will be sufficient when called upon.

The international financial system

The currencies of most advanced economies float reasonably cleanly, facilitating adjustment, and for most of the post-Bretton Woods period this arrangement has worked well; but, the weight of emerging economies has risen to around half the world economy and these economies often manage their exchange rates heavily against the US dollar. Fiscal and monetary authorities in advanced economies may try to compensate while market pressures drive yields down. This encourages the creation of potentially higher-yield but riskier and potentially illiquid assets to satisfy the demand of longer-term investors in pursuit of returns to meet their long-term promises. At the same time, the lack of international competitiveness due to exchange rate overvaluation discourages new investment.

Declining company returns

International adjustment by itself is not enough. The returns on equity of listed companies have declined in much of the world, particularly in Europe and in emerging markets. These returns are now often below capital costs and even below the (low) cost of debt in emerging economies. This is a sign of potential over-investment, lack of competition and persisting inefficiencies. If performance is to improve, real returns on capital that will be reflected in returns on equity must be raised to make capital formation more attractive. In emerging markets this requires reducing over-investment and inefficiency and finding a better balance between consumption and investment, especially where financial repression and State-Owned Enterprises play a large role (the latter account for 45% of the listed sector in EMEs). There is a need to move away from replicative investment in manufacturing towards a greater focus on social infrastructure, the quality of labour and domestic demand linkages. In the advanced economies, it requires supplementing better international adjustment mechanisms with pro-competition policies, involving effective measures at the micro-economic level, that encourage innovation and investment.

Banks and shadow banking

As deleveraging ceases to be a priority, the supply of bank credit should improve and begin to ease financing constraints facing many businesses, especially small and medium-sized enterprises. It is important that new supervisory and regulatory regimes preserve the improvements that have been introduced to date, and ensure that past excesses are not repeated. Notwithstanding these reforms and improvements, banks still remain interconnected and vulnerable to rising exposures to each other, especially through large derivative positions and the collateralisation of borrowing, in the event that prices in financial markets suddenly and unexpectedly change. The best way to deal with this is clear separation of insured deposit banking from prime broking, custody and collateral services and derivatives trading so that losses in one segment do not absorb the capital of other lines of business. However, to the extent that the reforms associated with Volcker, Vickers and Barnier finally depart from this goal, it is all the more important to ensure strong bank capital bases which can act as shock-absorbers and contain local losses without damaging counterparties.

The strengthened regulatory framework that now applies to banks has increased their need for cash and high quality liquid assets, mainly government paper, and raised the costs of using repurchase agreements and derivatives. This has encouraged them to shift some activities to processes often referred to as shadow banking (alternatively, 'market-based financing')[1]. These do not primarily deal directly with non-financial lenders or borrowers but intermediate mainly between other non-bank financial institutions. These other institutions are generally either cash-short (such as pension funds and insurance companies), or cash-long (such as money market funds). In the low interest rate environment all of these funds need to improve their yields on investments. This incentivises them to reuse assets through securities lending and the buying of alternative assets with complex derivatives aspects. But, to engage in these activities also draws them into the need for cash for margin and collateral management according to the new regulatory rules. Shadow banking involves the main broker dealers, custody banks, lending agents and centralised clearing counterparties (CCPs) intermediating the needs of cash-poor institutional investors looking to reuse assets and cash-rich non-banks that are searching for greater exposure to securities given the low interest rates on cash. Shadow bank activities include securities borrowing and lending, trading and clearing of derivatives, custody services and collateral management.

While shifting these activities away from the banks moves certain risks it does not eliminate them. Rather it transfers them, at least partly, to the shadow banking world. These risks boil down to various types of market and credit risks, including counterparty risk, reinvestment risk, re-hypothecation risk, maturity transformation risk and clearing risk. It is precisely because of these risks that counterparties must provide collateral to insure exposed positions. Securities being lent to improve yields must be collateralised, and cash provided for margin payments are frequently reused ('re-hypothecated'). This allows a relatively small amount of cash to collateralise a large set of positions so long as these are well-hedged or balanced. But, in the event of a surprise in market developments, large net cash demands can materialise quickly which would put stress on the entire system allowing little time to work out problems.

So long as the system remains inter-connected, and especially if shadow bank activities are not separated from traditional deposit-taking and bank lending activities, the financial system remains exposed to unforeseen shocks. Some ways to minimise these risks include improving transparency, especially as regards data on derivatives and collateral; establishing minimum holdings of cash to address maturity transformation risks; limiting the reuse of cash in repurchase markets; establishing minimum capital requirements for CCPs; and providing last resort facilities to broker-dealers.

Corporate bonds

Low interest rates encourage borrowing in general, and the demand for higher yield products has encouraged companies in more speculative sectors and in emerging markets to issue higher-yield debt. Institutional investors in search of yield compete for this debt, which is often referenced in alternative products and used in securities lending and exchange-traded funds. The competition for yield has seen a dramatic fall in covenant protections, which reduces the liquidity of these bonds. In a period of stress, as might arise in a future normalisation of monetary policy, the illiquidity features may exacerbate price volatility and put pressure on collateral management in the shadow banking sector.

Dealing with longevity risk and pension and annuity 'promises'

The institutional investors who mobilise a large part of modern economies' savings and try to allocate these to uses which will pay the highest returns while managing risks face tremendous challenges. Pension funds and life insurance companies, which are the largest sectors, not only have to find ways to generate sufficient returns to keep their commitments to savers, but must also manage the longevity risk associated with defined-benefit pensions and annuities arising from uncertain mortality. Defined contribution pension plans and other savings vehicles managed by insurance and investment companies may protect these financial institutions from this risk, but only by shifting it to individuals who are poorly placed to manage it.

How do institutional investors do this in the current and prospective low interest rate environment, in which maturing fixed income assets can only be refinanced on less remunerative terms, or with alternative investments and high-yield corporate bonds that promise high returns but are generally illiquid and seemingly over-priced? This question points to the fundamental importance of strengthening the economic environment in ways that raise the real return on capital. This can ensure that new capital formation, especially in advanced economies is attractive and eventually delivers the returns that allow the institutions' promises to be met. Failing that, these institutions may face a challenge in delivering their commitments to retired savers dependent on them.

The rising share of assets invested in high-risk or potentially illiquid assets other than cash and marketable securities, such as leveraged hedge funds, high-yield corporate bonds, private equity and commodities, warrants vigilance by regulators and policy makers. There is a very real risk that the current trend for companies to return cash to shareholders via dividends and buybacks, as a way to boost short-term returns, will not be re-invested in more productive companies but instead into more leverage in alternative assets to which pension funds, in particular, are beginning to allocate more capital.

Small businesses financing

With banks adjusting to new regulatory arrangements intended to make activities other than traditional lending more costly in order to minimise systemic risks to the monetary system, external financing for investment will have to come increasingly from non-bank sources. For many large companies directly accessing the capital markets has always been the most efficient way to proceed and others have been gravitating there as universal banks become less responsive to their demands. For small and medium-sized enterprises the relationships they can establish with banks, and the collateral where they can offer it, make banks the best sources for most external funding for them, once the strains of deleveraging have passed. But capital markets are better placed to accept the risks inherent in providing long-term funding for dynamic and innovative small businesses in their start-up and early expansion phases. They are also better positioned to provide exit opportunities for angel investors and venture capital providers whose expertise is precisely with start-ups and who want to realise gains (rather than hold positions over long periods as the pension and insurance companies do). Thus, strengthening capital markets outside the banking system is a priority.

Capital market infrastructure

Strengthening capital markets involves more than bringing sources and users of funds together. It also requires building a strong institutional infrastructure which can handle the flows of money and information with transparency and integrity. The day-to-day operation of the markets must encourage price discovery that creates incentives to match providers and users of funds in ways that capital will be used most productively.

At the same time, risks must be borne by those best placed to bear them. The institutions and people that make markets function on a day-to-day basis, from the exchanges and the dealers to the accountants and the analysts, have had to adapt for many years to major changes ranging from the shift of the world's economic centre of gravity to the Asia-Pacific region to the move of financial activity online, as digitalisation has advanced. They have also had to cope with sudden shocks, from large oil price changes to recurrent financial crises. The regulatory environment has been changing in response to these forces. Several issues relating to incentives operating on key people who make illiquid markets function, the fragmentation of markets, high-frequency trading, complexity of investment chains and their implications have risen to the forefront. These may not have such high visibility as the other issues discussed above, but it is essential that policy makers do not lose sight of their importance for the financial sector.

Note

1. Some authorities use the term 'market-based financing' instead of shadow banking. Since "shadow banking" is used in official reports of the Financial Stability Board and is more common in the financial press, it is also used in this report.

OECD Business and Finance Outlook 2015

Chapter 2

Corporate investment and the stagnation puzzle

Following the easy monetary policies brought on by the crisis, financial markets have rallied strongly while companies that undertake capital spending do not appear to see the same value creation opportunities. Despite historically low interest rates, economic growth is stagnating in many regions due in part to the lack of investment. This is true of companies in the general industry, infrastructure and clean energy sectors. This chapter explores this puzzle from the point of view of bottom-up data of 10 000 of the world's largest companies listed in the Bloomberg World Equity Index for both advanced and emerging countries, which enables capital spending and matching financial data to be used over the period 2002-2014.

Main findings

- Assuming unchanged policies, the outlook is for lacklustre company investment, with general industry stabilising and infrastructure growing modestly, but certainly not sufficient to be a meaningful driver of world economic growth.
- Investment and innovation in the larger general industrial sector is essential, both for generating bankable returns for the infrastructure sector and for productivity growth.
- The perception of stagnating investment in advanced countries is due in part to the activities of multinational enterprises in global supply chains: the centre of gravity of world activity has shifted more towards emerging market economies (EMEs).
- Much large investment by multinational enterprises is associated with the transfer of intellectual property for participation in global supply chains. This has resulted in 'catch-up' of sales-per-employee in EME companies versus advanced countries (and profits for the latter) but value-added per employee is not catching up. By focusing more on operating efficiency and tax strategy, companies appear to have focused less on investment in R&D and innovation that is necessary to drive long-term productivity growth.
- Declining returns on equity and profit margin compression are evident in large companies, particularly in EMEs and Europe, due to this poor productivity growth and to over-investment in the general industrial sector of EMEs: their returns on equity have declined below the cost of equity and in some case below the low cost of debt (measures of over-investment).
- Over-investment and inefficiency appear to be more pronounced where financial repression policies are used to bottle up saving for investment in development strategies, and where tax incentives and state-owned enterprises play a disproportionate role. Evidence supports the idea that state-owned enterprises in EMEs do not share a level playing field (in commercial terms) with private industry in the infrastructure sector, compared with the more equal environment in advanced countries. Tax is shown to have a big impact on the location of investment.
- A theoretical global portfolio based on selling the highest quartile of heavier capital-spending firms to buy the bottom quartile that favours dividends and buybacks generates very strong positive return performance. This bias against investing companies may be due to increased uncertainty and the role of activist shareholders: it makes chief executives hesitate to invest for fear of a stock market attack.
- Operating cash flow is not sufficient in EMEs to cover capital expenditure, dividends and buybacks and the desired net acquisition of assets, resulting in borrowing to fund the gap. The opposite is true for advanced countries, particularly the United States where investment could be doubled at the expense of buybacks without borrowing or issuing any new equity.

- The combination of over-investment, inefficiencies and excessive borrowing in some parts of the global value chain while others invest less is not a sound recipe for productivity growth and the long-term value creation needed for the future support of ageing populations, and it also raises the risk of a new financial pressures centred on EME company debt.

Introduction

The greatest puzzle facing policy makers today is that, following the easy monetary policies induced by the crisis, investors in financial markets see little risk, while companies that undertake capital spending see so much risk. For some reason the 'hurdle' rate of return required to undertake new capital spending is so high that, despite historically low interest rates, economic growth is stagnating in many regions due in part to the lack of investment. On the other hand some parts of the world invest very heavily and have a strong presence of state-owned enterprises (SOEs). These divergences in investment intensity are occurring in the context of the rapid expansion of global value chains, particularly since the early 1990s, and the question arises as to whom this benefits, and whether the investment is generating the productivity growth needed to underpin the fundamentals of securities for the support of ageing populations in the future. This chapter explores this puzzle from the point of view of bottom-up data of 10 000 of the world's larger companies, which enables matching financial data (crucial to any proper analysis of company decisions with respect to capital spending) to be used. The equity and debt issued by these companies form the bedrock of investments by pension funds and insurance companies (topics taken up in more detail in Chapters 3 and 4). The related issue of small and medium-sized company financing of investment is taken up in Chapter 5.

Forces acting and investment projections

One part of the puzzle is that the very large general industrial sector includes most multinational enterprises (MNEs) which invest in various jurisdictions according to advantages perceived in global value chains and in different taxation regimes.[1] Outcomes in any one country are the net result of decision making by global firms where the macro policies of the parent country may have a diluted impact on what companies do locally as supply chains multiply and as transport costs fall. To understand how these decisions are made requires a focus on the company data, separating the larger general industrial sector where MNEs proliferate from infrastructure companies which are more capital intensive and have a greater domestic focus in the main. There are both structural and market impediments to global investment:

- Stock markets currently reward companies that favour dividends and buybacks and punish those that undertake more investment (shown below for a global portfolio) which creates higher hurdle rates for investment in the current uncertain environment.
- Past over-investment in large parts of the world economy and related inefficiencies are driving down returns versus the cost of both equity and debt, making it difficult for managers to add value.
- Over-investment is driven by: (i) financial repression[2] in some countries, including restrictions on cross-border flows that force high savings; (ii) the role of SOEs which benefit from monopoly positions, public procurement contracts, local content requirements,

cross-subsidisation, lower financing terms from state-owned banks, and conglomerate structures that allow for transfer pricing and related party transactions; and (iii) available low tax strategies.

- The easy earnings gains for advanced countries from intellectual property transfers within global value chains seem to be drawing to a close, but value-added productivity growth is stagnating.

The results of projections for general industry, infrastructure and clean energy (developed more fully below) are shown in Figure 2.1. These are based on a panel study of how the largest global companies behave according to returns on investment, expected earnings, the cost of equity and debt, banking system openness and tax factors.

Figure 2.1. **General industry, infrastructure and clean energy projections**

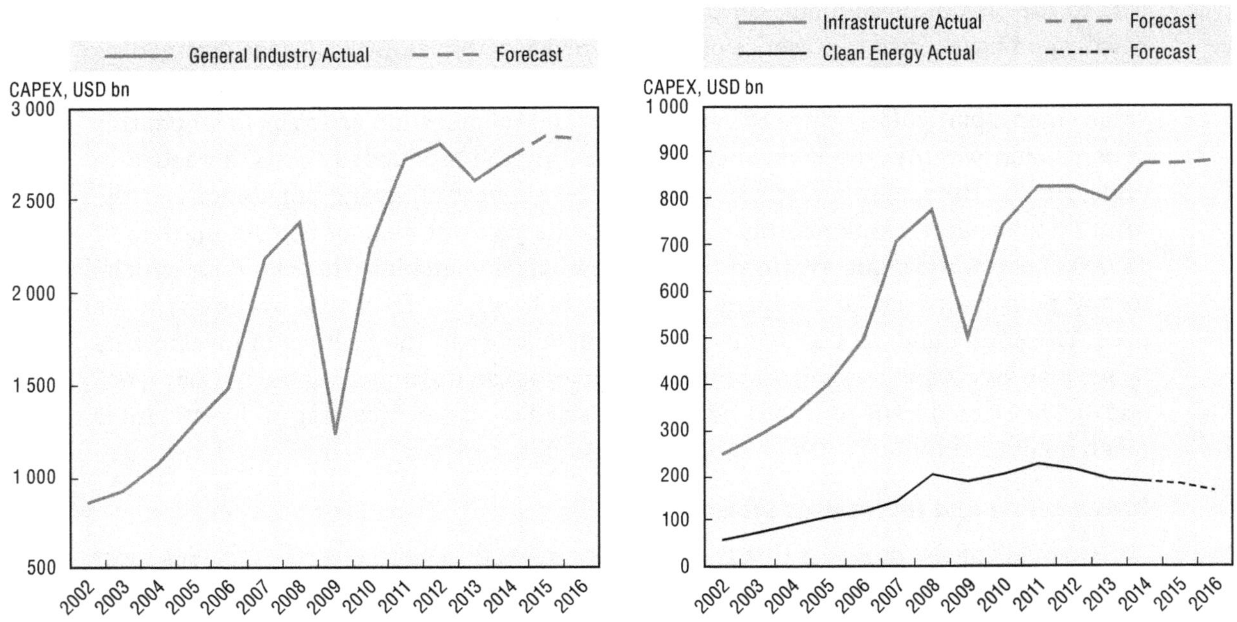

Source: Bloomberg, Datastream, OECD calculations.

StatLink http://dx.doi.org/10.1787/888933209159

With broadly unchanged policies, the outlook is for lacklustre company investment: general industry picks up modestly in 2015 but is flat in 2016, while infrastructure grows slightly and will require new policy initiatives if it is to become a more meaningful contributor economic growth. Clean energy investment appears to confront even stronger obstacles, making it an urgent issue in the run up to COP 21 in Paris (December 2015). Better investment performance will require policy changes that affect bankable returns, the cost of capital, tax, and productivity growth in all of the interconnected regions of the world economy.

Advanced versus emerging company sales, investment and employment

The 10 000 large companies included in the analysis are listed in the in the Bloomberg World Equity Index and cover some 75 countries over the period 2002 -2014.[3] The data are divided between companies in a fairly broad definition of infrastructure (including oil and related industries), the general industrial sector, and a separate group of clean energy companies.[4] These 10 000 companies are a large part of the world economy-company aggregated value-added is around 36% of world nominal GDP -and the matched financial data permits more precise analysis that cannot be undertaken using national accounts measures. The company data are nominal, and hence the aim is to look at what companies are doing with their dollars in a global context, given the policies they face in the jurisdiction where they are listed.[5] Where investment is concerned most of the following illustrations focus on the ratio to nominal capital spending to the company's sales.

General industry is more important than infrastructure

The shares of company sales and capital expenditure (CAPEX) for general industry, infrastructure and clean energy (as defined in Annex 2.A1) are shown in Figure 2.2 for advanced and emerging countries. Sales and investment in the general industrial sector (non-infrastructure) is by far the dominant part of economic activity in the large company world, so that without its growth less will be achieved for economic activity in the private sector. It is also evident in the chart that the sample of advanced economy companies invest much more in the capital-intensive infrastructure and clean energy sectors (around 32%) than do emerging countries (21%). EMEs tend to focus more on investment in the general industrial sector, where global value chains are important and where a focus on rapid development through export-led growth is commonplace.

Figure 2.2. **Advanced economies invest more in infrastructure**

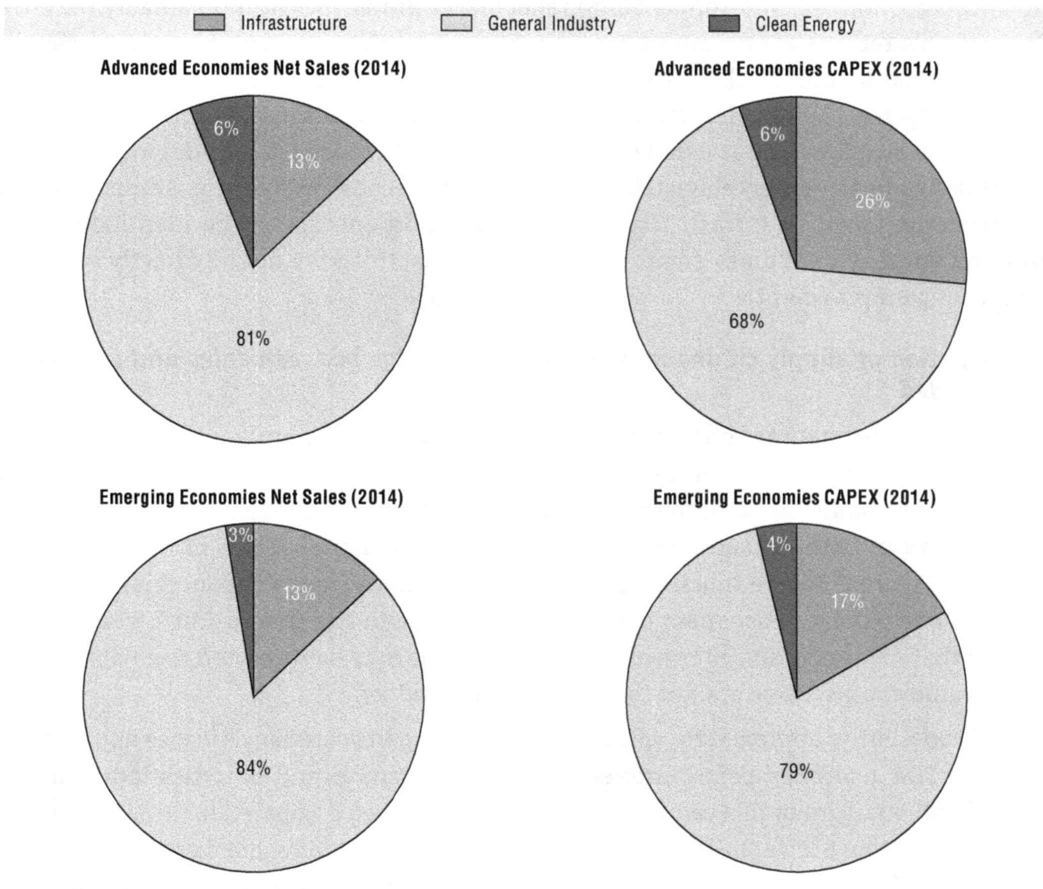

Source: Bloomberg, OECD calculations.

StatLink http://dx.doi.org/10.1787/888933209162

General industrial growth tends to lead infrastructure rather than the other way around

While infrastructure is a smaller sector, it is obviously critical to growth and development. General industrial development is quickly constrained by lack of infrastructure in the longer run. But where does the causality mainly lie? On average, does building infrastructure cause general industry to come? Or does the demand for infrastructure from a large growing general industrial sector create the returns that drive new infrastructure investment? Obviously both factors are at work, and simple statistical tests can never 'prove' anything. Figure 2.3 shows growth of net sales, capital expenditure and employment for the infrastructure and general industrial sectors. Sales and investment in the infrastructure sector are highly correlated with the general industry. The tentative evidence from a statistical test suggests that growth in the general industrial sector tends more to 'cause' growth in the infrastructure sector than the other way around (this point is demonstrated in Box 2.1). Private infrastructure investment is more readily forthcoming when the general industrial sector is growing strongly[6]. Policy action to facilitate infrastructure is highly desirable, but policy makers should not lose sight of the fact that promoting general industrial growth and an efficient allocation of capital should be the primary objective of policy for better growth and productivity.

CAPEX growth and sales are slowing in general industry in both emerging and advanced economies, and this is being reflected in infrastructure presumably because the bankable returns are becoming more problematic. Infrastructure is also more capital intensive, and so has weaker links with employment growth compared to the general industrial sector. The broadly-defined infrastructure industries in 2014 account for about 10% of total employment at listed companies in both advanced and emerging countries and this has been remarkably stable over the past decade[7]. While it is admirable that governments focus on infrastructure where clear bottlenecks can be identified, or as part of a strategy to address environmental concerns, this may not be directly effective for reviving employment.

Globalisation of supply chains may be driving a wedge between sales and company value-added

There has been some shifting of the centre of gravity of economic activity to emerging markets, and advanced economy companies are shifting technology as they participate in global supply chains. Up until the crisis, the rates of growth of EME sales, investment and employment in both infrastructure and the general industrial sector in the right-hand panels of Figure 2.3 were much stronger than those for advanced economies shown in the left-hand panels. Subsequent to the crisis sales growth has slowed. But it is important to note that sales contain intermediate products that may be imported from abroad via global value chains. Sales are not the same as value-added.

It is possible to approximate value-added by adding the company's wages and salaries to its EBITDA (earnings before interest, taxes, depreciation and amortisation). For the general industrial group this value-added growth rate is then compared to the sales growth in Figure 2.4. From a lower base, emerging markets sales and value-added growth were very strong in the first half of the 2000s, but began to separate from the middle of the decade: for the three years 2006 to 2008. Sales growth averaged 26% compared to 14% for value-added over the same period, (some 12 percentage points lower). For advanced countries a similar though more modest pattern is evident. As growth slows in the post-crisis environment, value-added continues significantly to under-perform sales in emerging countries. This separation is not evident in the post-crisis advanced country sales and value-added growth comparison: while slower, the growth rates are broadly in line with each other. This suggests that the benefit of MNE investment-led growth is diminishing over time for companies listed in emerging countries, for reasons that will be developed in subsequent sections.

Figure 2.3. **Investment in emerging economies is slowing rapidly post-crisis**

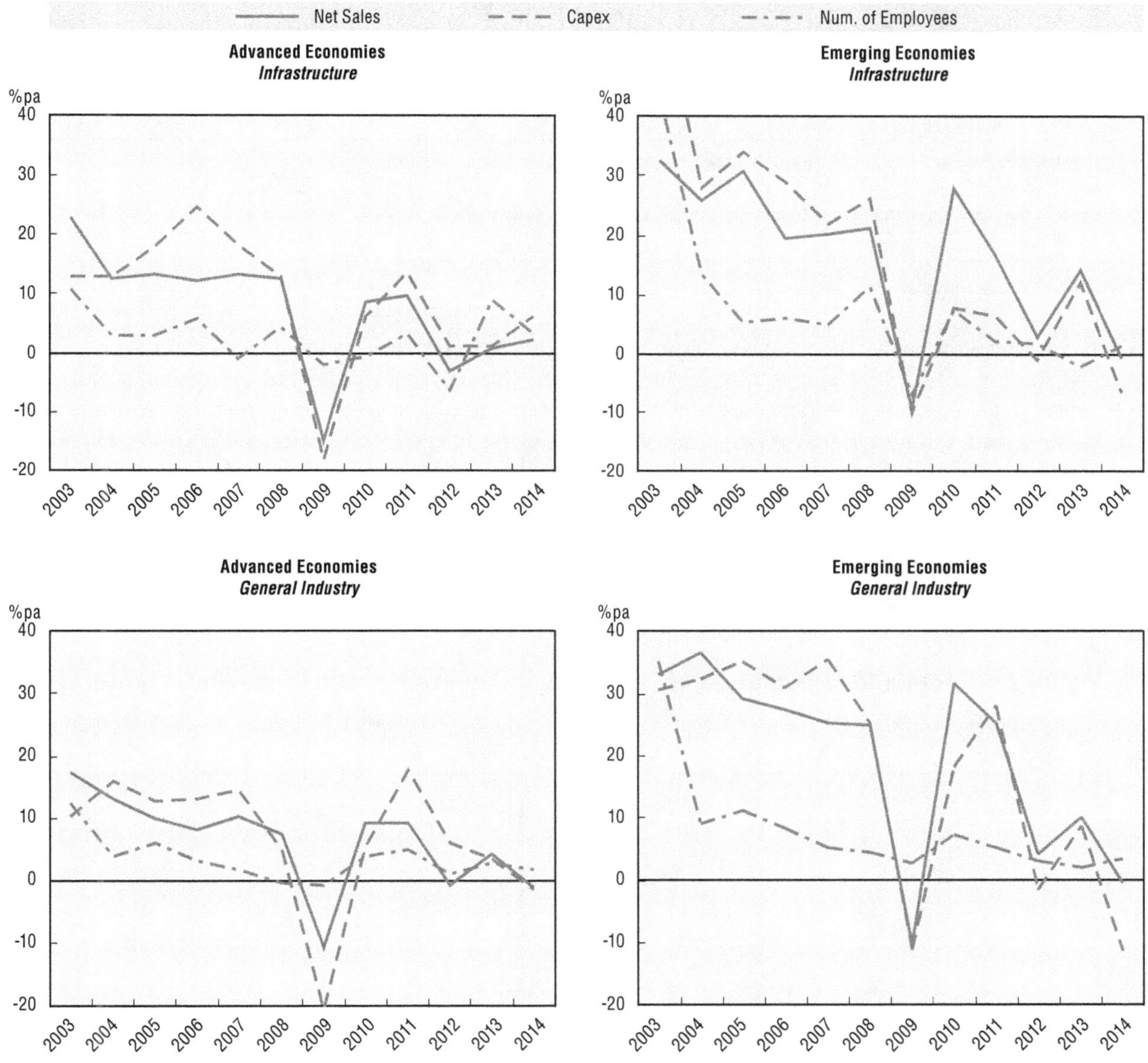

Source: Bloomberg, OECD calculations.

StatLink http://dx.doi.org/10.1787/888933209172

Box 2.1. **Causality between infrastructure and general industry activity**

Sales drive investment in the corporate sector. It is therefore of interest to know whether it is sales in general industry drive that of infrastructure in one-way causation, or whether two-way causation is present. Presumably if infrastructure investment were to be a locomotive in the growth strategy of governments then at least two-way causation should be present. This latter requirement does not seem to be present in the data.

To carry out some formal tests of the nature of causality between net sales in infrastructure versus non-infrastructure sector, a Granger causality test was performed using a sample of 73 countries over the period 2002 – 2014.[1]

The results of this test are shown in Table 2.1.

Table 2.1. **Causality between infrastructure and general industry activity**

Pairwise Dumitrescu Hurlin Panel Causality Tests (Lags: 1) Annual panel data from 2002 to 2014 including 73 countries All variables are expressed in logarithmic difference	W-Stat.	Zbar-Stat.	Prob.
Net sales of firms operating in General Industry do not homogeneously cause net sales of firms operating in Infrastructure	1.942	1.841	0.066
Net sales of firms operating in Infrastructure do not homogeneously cause net sales of firms operating in General Industry	1.055	-0.844	0.399

Source: OECD calculations.

StatLink http://dx.doi.org/10.1787/888933210309

The null hypothesis that the net sales of firms operating in non-infrastructure sector do not homogeneously cause the net sales of firms operating in infrastructure sector is rejected at the 10% probability level. However in the opposite direction, the null hypothesis of no causality cannot be rejected. These results are consistent with the notion that general industrial sales cause infrastructure sales, but not the other way round.

1. The Dumitrescu-Hurlin (2012) Granger Causality test with panel data does not treat data as one large stacked set of data but it allows all coefficients to be different across cross-sections. This test involves calculating standard Granger Causality regressions for each cross-section individually. The average of the test statistics is then taken: the W-bar statistic. The standardized version of this statistic, appropriately weighted in unbalanced panels, follows a standard normal distribution: the Z-bar statistic.

Figure 2.4. **Value-added versus sales is slipping in emerging economy general industry**

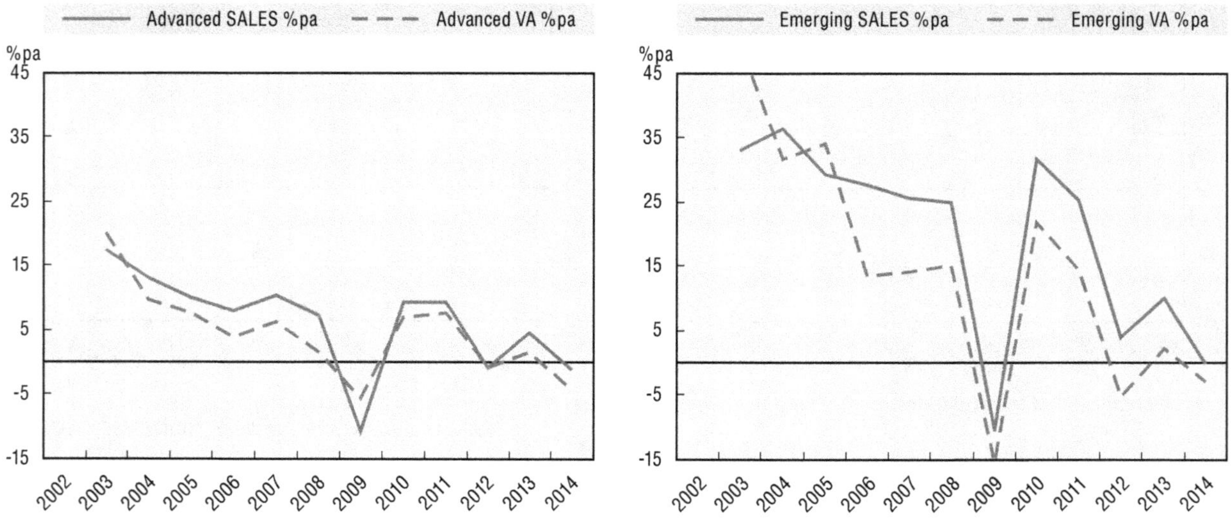

Source: Bloomberg, OECD calculations.

StatLink http://dx.doi.org/10.1787/888933209183

Is inefficiency affecting the allocation of capital spending in the global economy?

Economic growth requires investment and improvements in the efficiency of labour and capital (productivity). Such gains may come from the transfer of existing intellectual property under licence (technology 'catch-up') to other companies in different regions. But once these gains are exploited, innovation and research embodied in new capital spending is required to continue the growth process. How firms go about this and under what regulatory and competition environment is critical, because a given transfer of intellectual property is a one-off levels gain and not a permanent increase in productivity growth.

Private sector companies in market-based economies allocate capital spending according to shareholder value. Earnings may be retained for capital spending and growth, but only if the return on equity (ROE) exceeds the cost of equity. If this is not the case then value creation possibilities are not present for managers and firms will not carry out new capital spending[8]. They will choose to use their operating cash flow in other ways (by issuing dividends, carrying out share buybacks or, in certain cases when tax advantages are present, they may accumulate cash balances including in offshore locations). Alternatively, firms may exit or enter markets via mergers and acquisitions (M&A), and in the limit may close plants and shed labour. To operate effectively, companies need to make capital allocation decisions in an environment where competitive forces are allowed to work and the incentives to perform are there (an issue taken up in Chapter 8). When global supply chains shift there will be winners and losers, and local companies and jobs may be disrupted. In these cases the growth process requires macro-economic adjustment, which is facilitated by flexible exchange rates and open capital markets, adjustments in the cost of capital, the absence of trade protectionism, product market competition and labour market flexibility. Where policy creates impediments to the working of macroeconomic adjustment and competition economies will in general underperform in the face of global structural change. The question is: does the evidence bear out this proposition?

Gains via global value chains and operational efficiency appear to have run their course, but companies are failing to invest sufficiently in R&D and productivity enhancing innovation

In the past decade companies have increasingly participated in global supply chains and technology transfer has been an important part of this; a process that should help to level productivity between advanced and emerging country companies[9]:

- This typically involves large companies (particularly in the digital world) outsourcing tasks to other companies in emerging markets with very precise technical specifications required as to the components that they supply (e.g. an Apple or a Sony outsources to a Foxconn). Labour costs and tax incentives are often the motivation for locational decisions.
- Outsourcing involves intellectual property transfer under licence and may be associated with less investment in the parent company's country and more in the host country instead: i.e. the fabrication of components shifts to other locations in the value chain. Transport costs are less of a barrier to this process in the digital age; indeed most of the global value in trade is being transported by air (digital things) while most of the global volume (such as resources) is transported by ship.
- Where transport costs are a factor, or where capital controls and ownership restrictions would otherwise restrict access to large and growing markets, companies undertake joint ventures with affiliates in emerging economies, in addition to the tax and labour cost incentives for doing so.

However, while sales-per-employee appears to have equalised between emerging and advanced country large companies, this has not been reflected in value-added per employee.

Nominal sales and value-added per employee

For the 10 000 listed companies included in the sample, nominal sales per-employee (an approximation for productivity) was greater in advanced countries in 2002, especially for general industry (see the solid and broken lines in Figure 2.5). The gap for value-added per employee was much larger than for the sales-based measure. Heavy investment in EMEs (which for general industry is running at double the rate in advanced countries, as shown in Figure 2.6) has been associated with a convergence in sales-per-employee between advanced and emerging economies, for both infrastructure and general industry. However, this has not been reflected in much convergence of value-added per employee (shown in the columns of Figure 2.5).

Figure 2.5. **The global productivity catch-up in sales**

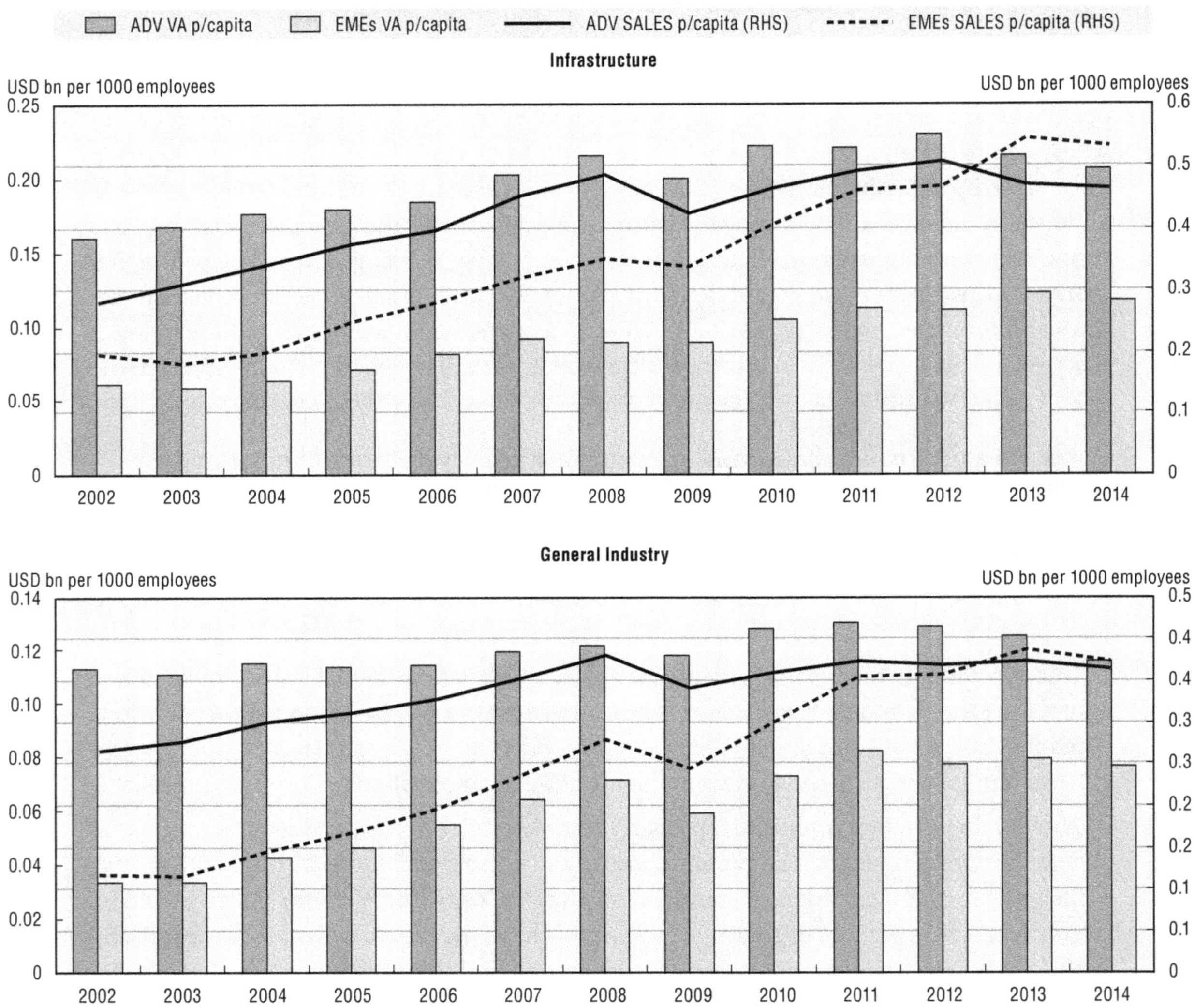

Note: ADV: Advanced Economies, EMEs: Emerging Market Economies, VA: Value-Added.

Source: Bloomberg, OECD calculations.

StatLink http://dx.doi.org/10.1787/888933209193

Figure 2.6. **Companies' capital expenditure rate greater in emerging economies**

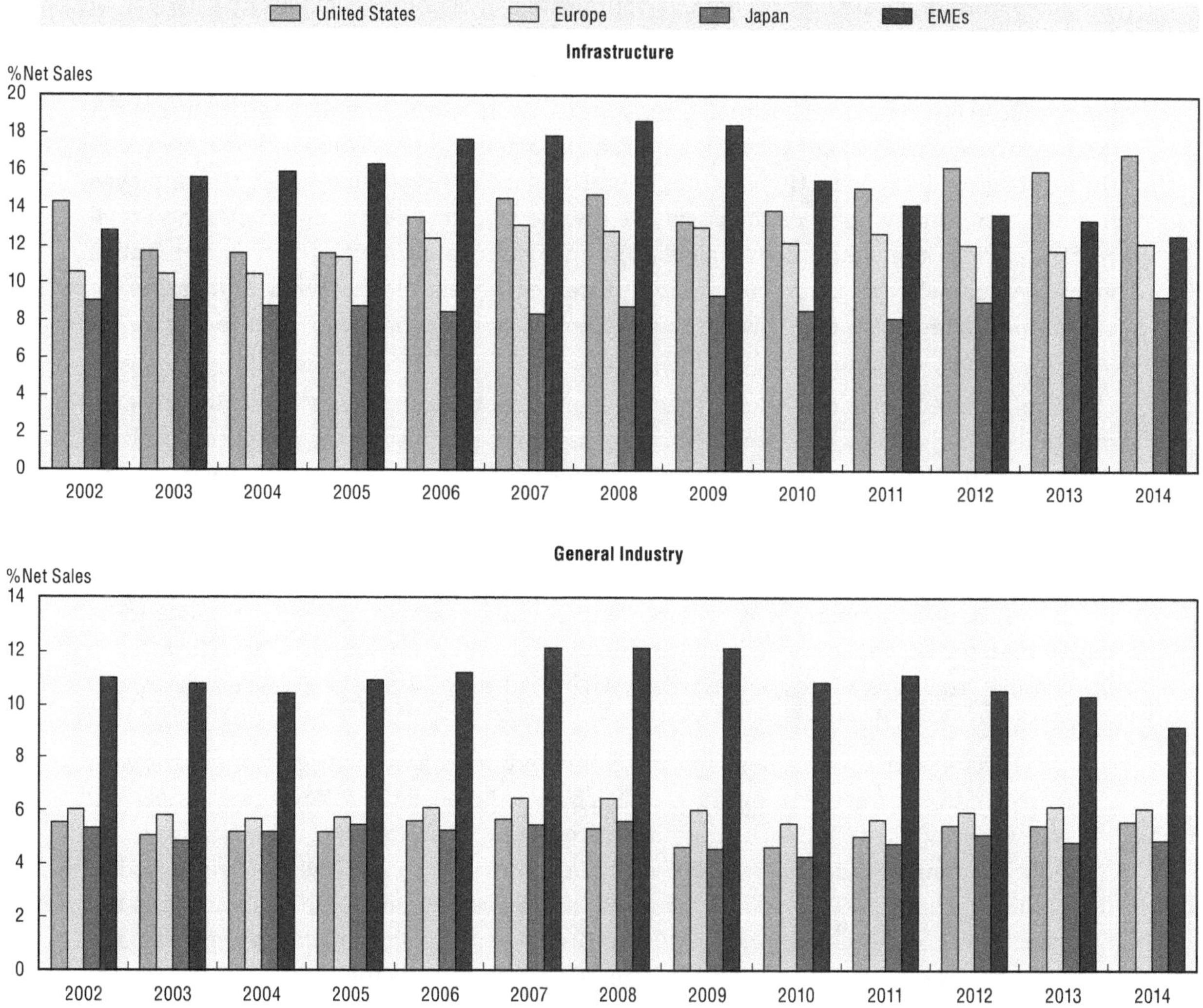

Note: Europe refers to the European Union and Switzerland.

Source: Bloomberg, OECD calculations.

StatLink http://dx.doi.org/10.1787/888933209207

This picture would appear to be consistent with improved advantages for advanced country cash earnings and profitability compared to emerging markets (while transferring investment risk to the latter). For example:

- Advanced company X transfers intellectual property to emerging affiliate Y, reduces its own higher cost labour and receives a cash royalty from the affiliate which uses the technology to produce components for the group (royalties may, via a more complex route, be held in a low-tax jurisdiction).
- The EME-based affiliate increases its employees (at a lower per capita wage) and its investment (plus related intermediate costs), allowing it to increase its dollar sales. But it must also pay the royalty to the advanced company or parent.
- Sales for the group may stay the same or indeed rise, but more of it is delivered from the company in the emerging country. Sales-per-employee may rise significantly in the latter, but value-added (wages plus its own EBITDA) per employee do not rise in line due to the investment and intermediate input costs and the royalties it must pay.

That sales-per-employee appear to have converged suggests that large MNEs have extracted most of the synergies from this optimisation of operational efficiency. Intellectual property transfer and re-arranging value chains is in some sense the 'low hanging fruit' for MNEs that does not require much investment in research and development (R&D) or new innovation. It is instead a reallocation of existing technology which, while contributing to the accumulation of cash in advanced companies, does not engender increasing permanently the rate of growth of productivity. In the general industrial sector value-added per employee has not been improving since the crisis in either advanced or emerging general industrial companies (see the columns in Figure 2.5). Innovation to improve productivity requires investment in R&D and strong competitive processes that see old inefficient companies die and new ones replace them. This does not appear to be happening on a sufficient scale for improving world corporate productivity growth.

The apparent absence of efficiency gains in global companies is not only being reflected in low growth of value-added per employee, it is also being reflected in falling ROEs in relation to the cost of equity and corporate borrowing rates—an issue explored in the following section.

ROEs are declining in emerging economies and Europe

The ROE of a company is very important for an investment project—it needs to be higher than the cost of equity if managers are to create value for shareholders. The ROEs in the country groupings of companies are shown in Figure 2.7. While the averages are around 10%, they vary over time and across regions.

- *The ROE for infrastructure*: is less cyclical compared to other industries. Consistent with the idea of over-investment during the tech boom and bust, the ROE was extremely low in the early 2000s in OECD countries, and recovers in 2004. However, in both Europe and emerging countries the ROE appears to have begun moving down even before the crisis of 2008-09. The US ROE, on the other hand, has moved up since the crisis towards the highest level of the period shown (to the 12-14% range, very far from the notion of a falling natural rate). In the energy-dominated infrastructure investment in the United States there appears to be no sign of stagnation in the most recent years, although falling oil prices may be expected to take some toll from 2014. Japan has improved somewhat.
- *The ROE for general industry*: is more cyclical, but also shows some broader downward movement in the emerging markets and Europe, whereas the United States has fully recovered to pre-crisis levels of around 14%. For Japan, a country known for over-investment in previous decades, the ROE sits well below that of other countries (though it has begun to move up consistently from 2011).
- *The ROE for clean energy:* This is a smaller sample (the listed clean energy index) and more volatile. Nevertheless, ROE is mostly lower compared to pre-crisis levels and is less than in other industries.

The cost of equity is generally higher in emerging markets

The cost of equity is shown in Figure 2.8. In advanced countries these lie in the main within the range of 8-14%. In each of the 3 sectors shown the cost of equity for EMEs is much higher, which may go part of the way to explaining their preference for debt (a risk to the outlook discussed later).

Figure 2.7. **Returns on equity are declining**

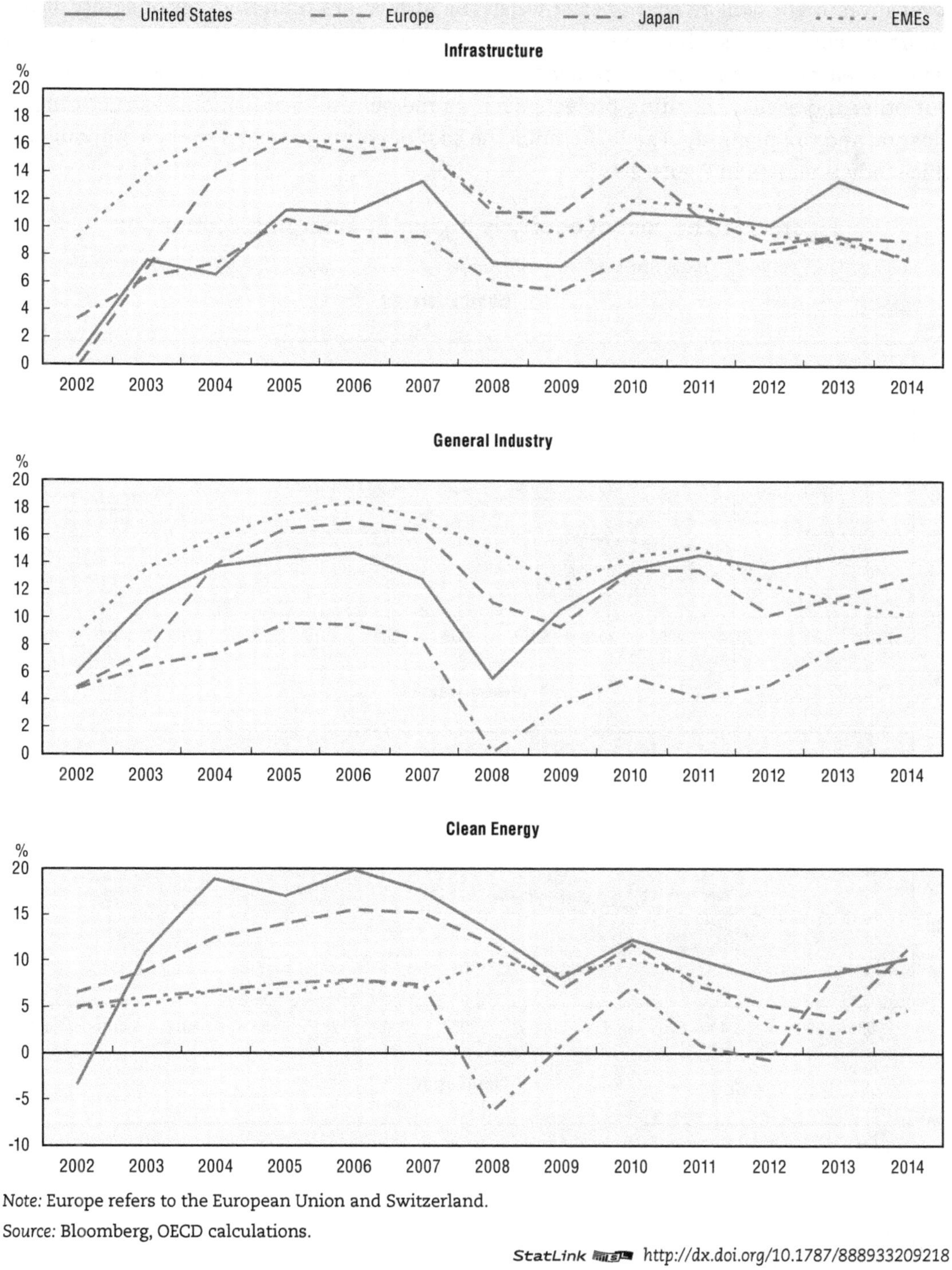

Note: Europe refers to the European Union and Switzerland.

Source: Bloomberg, OECD calculations.

StatLink http://dx.doi.org/10.1787/888933209218

The ROE versus the cost of equity is negative in emerging markets and Japan, a sign of over-investment

Many policy analysts focus on external funding as a constraint on investment (banks and institutional investors like pension funds and insurance companies). For larger listed companies in advanced economies this is on average not the case. Corporate balance sheets are strong, and the greatest source of funding for investment both infrastructure and general industry is retained earnings.[10] Consequently, for the purposes of this publication, 'over-investment' will be said to exist when the ROE is less than the cost of equity. If the return on equity is less than the cost of equity, managers cannot create value by investing retained earnings. It makes more sense to give money back to shareholders or to carry out other more value creating projects such as merger and acquisition, restructuring or closure, and tax planning. The ROE minus the cost of equity matched to the companies in this study is shown in Figure 2.8.

Figure 2.8. **The cost of equity is higher in emerging economies**

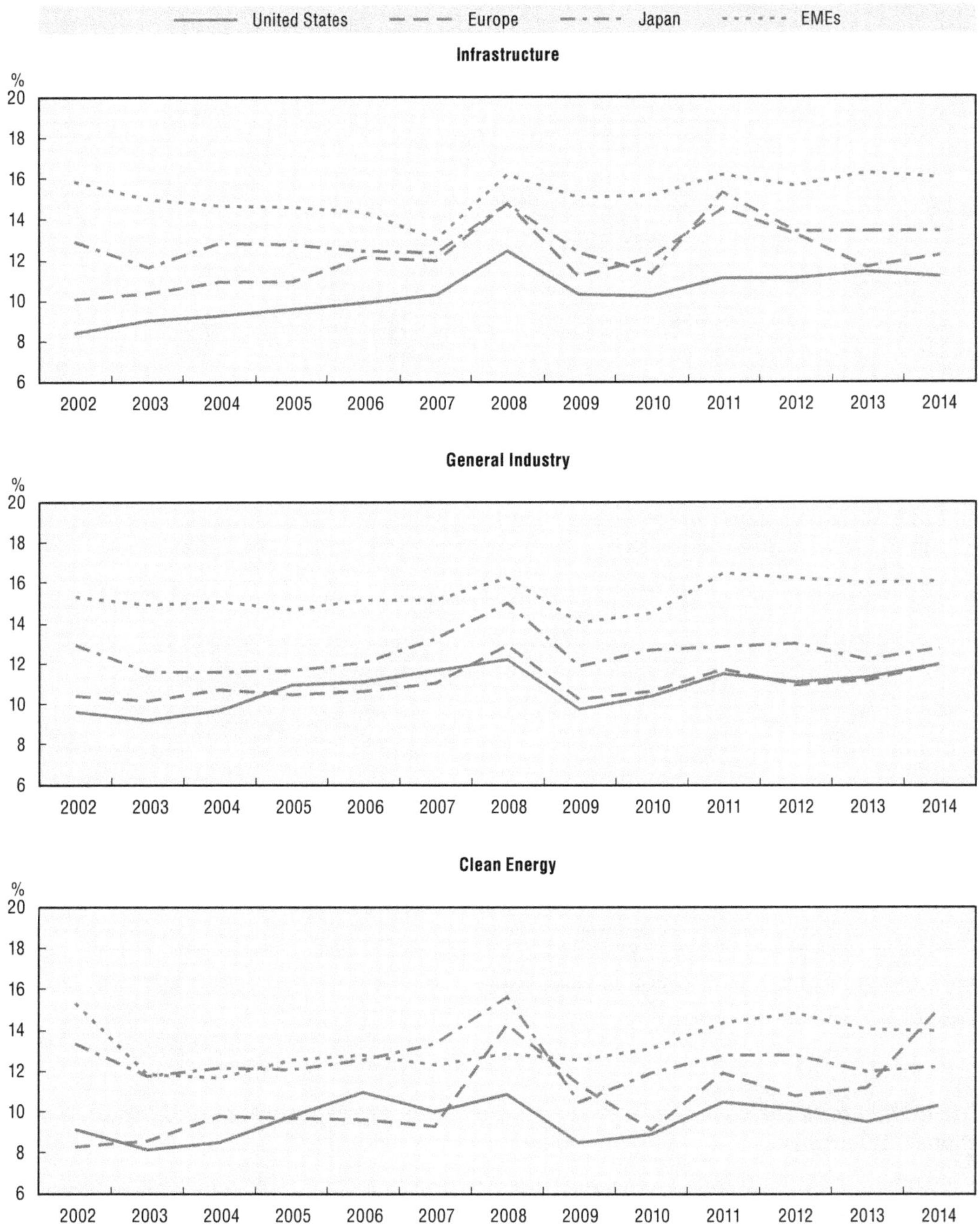

Note: Europe refers to the European Union and Switzerland.

Source: Bloomberg, OECD calculations.

StatLink http://dx.doi.org/10.1787/888933209227

Figure 2.9. **The value-creation gap: Negative returns on equity minus the cost of equity outside the United States**

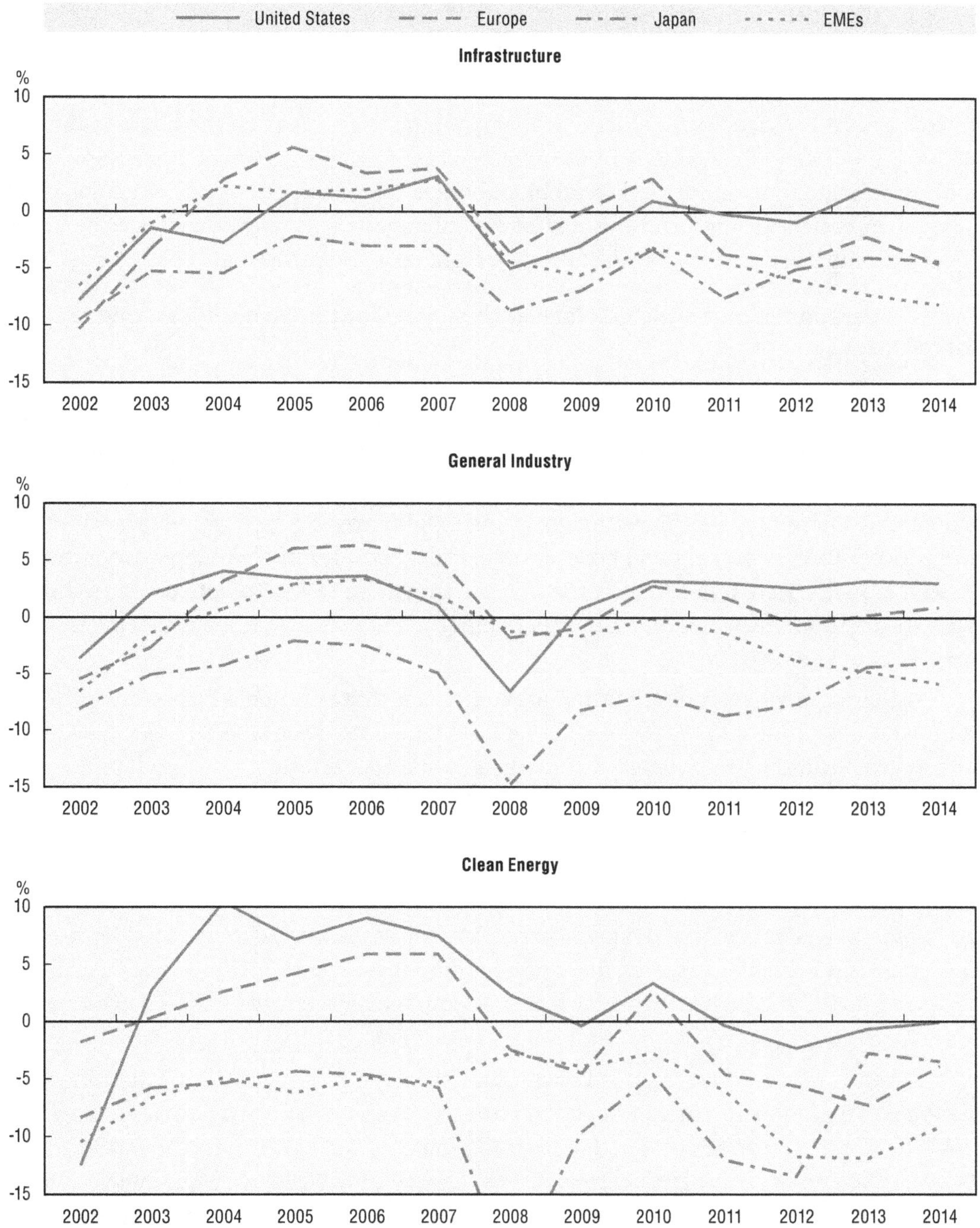

Note: Europe refers to the European Union and Switzerland.

Source: Bloomberg, OECD calculations. Based on a Bloomberg index of 10 000 companies in 75 countries.

StatLink http://dx.doi.org/10.1787/888933209239

- *Infrastructure*: The ROE minus the cost of equity has been falling in most regions, but remains slightly positive in the United States. Europe has declined to be in line with Japan (a past over-investment economy). For EMEs the gap is an order of magnitude worse than in other regions. This reinforces the notion that there may be over-investment or serious inefficiency problems related to financial repression, that make it difficult for private companies to add value.

- *General industry*: The picture is much better for this group of companies in the United States and in Europe. The decline in the value-creation gap for EMEs on the other hand began even before the crisis, and the heavy investment in this sector appears to be associated with value destruction according to this metric. Japan appears to remain beset by over-investment issues in this sector (though improving).
- *Clean energy*: For listed companies (except Japan) the value-creation gap has been falling. The United States has declined but remains broadly viable, whereas other regions are more clearly negative. Part of the problem here is that clean energy in particular relies more on project finance and the cost of equity may be less relevant. Hence the graph below comparing the ROE to interest rates might be a better metric.

The ROE versus the cost of debt is lowest in regions that have been less able to reduce rates

The picture is somewhat better if the ROE is compared with a measure of the cost of debt (Figure 2.10). This is because, due to unconventional monetary policy following the crisis, interest rates are at historical lows. However, for EMEs the fall in interest rates does not appear to have been sufficient to bring the gap into line with that of advanced economies. There is a step move down in the ROE-borrowing-rate gap versus pre-crisis levels in both infrastructure and general industry, though it remains more favourable for general industry. Here it has to be borne in mind that most EME corporate debt is in higher risk category than AAA, and for many companies the net present value of such investment projects could be negative.

Furthermore, where capital controls are so effective that a non-deliverable forward (NDF) market develops, the onshore rate may be held at higher rates than would be arbitraged with all sources of funding in open capital markets (see Box 2.2) (Blundell-Wignall and Roulet (2015).[11] This impact on capital controls on EME investment is considered further below. Thus the quoted onshore debt interest rates are higher than they should be compared to rates that would prevail with open capital markets. Implicit in such strategies are the beliefs that export objectives, together with the desire to achieve financial stability by influencing capital flows, will outweigh the higher cost of funding associated with financial repression. The empirical evidence however does not support these views[12]. There is a measurable negative impact of capital controls on domestic company investment (presented below).

For clean energy, the value-creation gap is still significantly negative for EMEs even when interest rates are used instead of the cost of equity. While the failure to price carbon given the current cost structure is a general explanation of poor global viability in the global economy, the greater problems for EMEs may stem from more local inefficiencies, competition from 'dirty' energy and SOEs, cost augmenting local content requirements and other regulations that cause reduced returns (see the policy discussion below).

Short-termism: the cash-flow, CAPEX and buyback puzzle

The last decade has seen the rising importance of activist investors who gain the support of other investors and proxy advisors to remove management, to gain influential board seats, and/or to make sure company strategy is in the best interests of shareholders (an issue taken up in Chapter 7). This may at times add to company efficiency when incumbent management is either lazy or pursuing plans that make less sense when compared to the better strategies of activists. The question arises as to whether the role of such investors is working to cause short-termism strategies at the expense of long-term investment, by effectively raising the hurdle rate (risk premium) associated with the latter[13]. Activists may have better strategies at times, but they may also favour the short-term gratification of dividends and share buybacks versus longer-term duration investment. Incumbent managers will certainly prefer giving in to shareholders' desire for more 'yield' in a low interest rate world than taking on the risk of uncertain long-term investments that might cause them to be punished in the share market.

Figure 2.10. **Improving returns on equity versus the cost of debt, but still low in emerging economies**

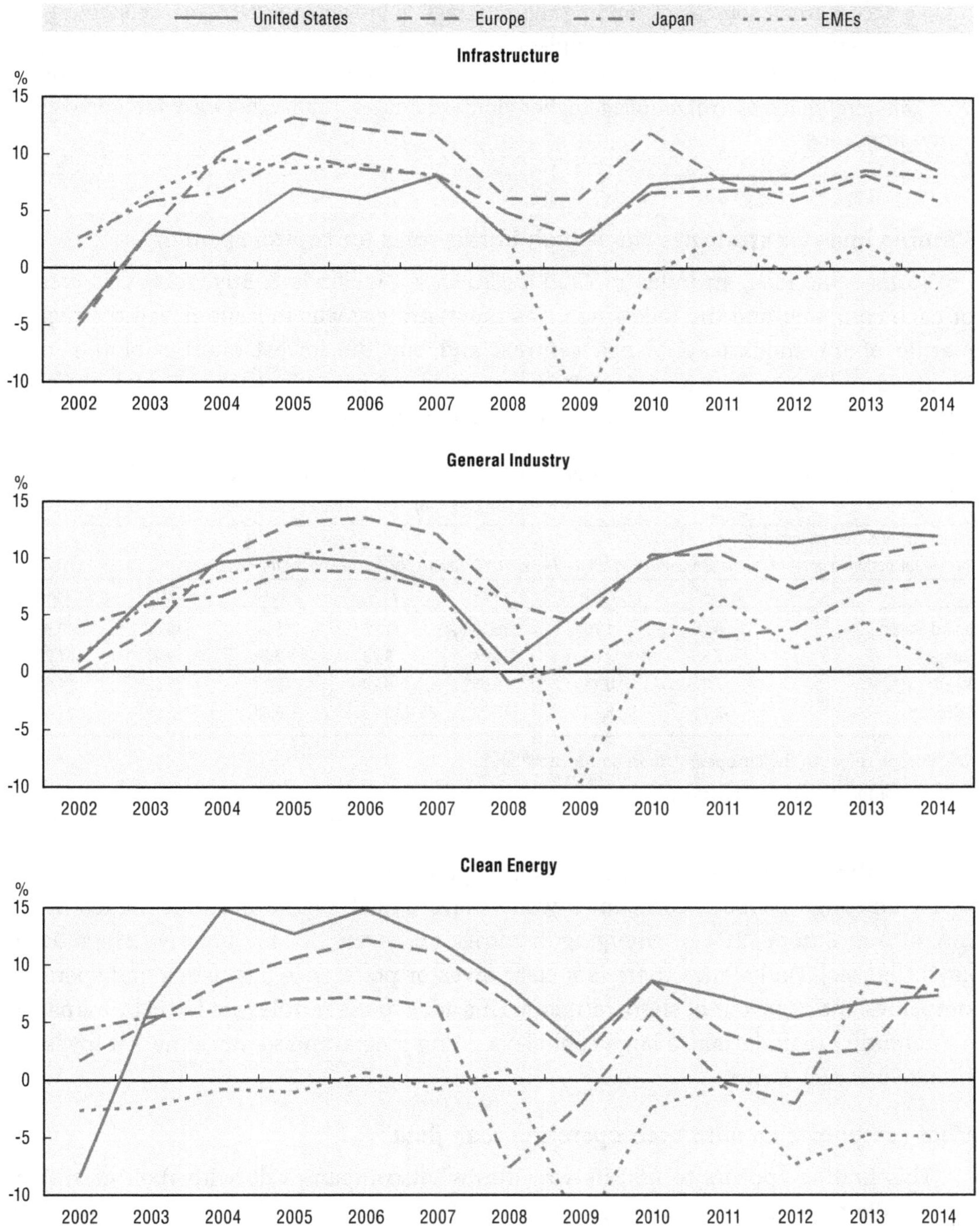

Note: Europe refers to the European Union and Switzerland.

Source: Bloomberg, OECD calculations.

StatLink http://dx.doi.org/10.1787/888933209248

Box 2.2. Non-deliverable forward markets

Countries with non-deliverable forward markets (NDF) are those where controls are so strong that an offshore market emerges to serve investor needs: a shadow market denominated in dollars that allows investors to hedge positions when they can't do so in domestic spot and forward markets in reasonable quantities and prices. The covered interest parity condition is written F=S(1+r)/(1+r$), where F is the forward rate, S the spot rate and r$ the offshore dollar rate. Hedged into the same currency yields are the same except for transactions cost. But where capital controls are binding, so that residents don't have access to all sources of funding the arbitrage is broken, and NDF markets emerge: NDF=S(1+i)/(1+r$), where i is the implied yield of the home currency offshore. A large positive differential of the onshore markets versus the implied rate on the home currency in offshore markets (r-i) implies higher domestic rates than otherwise for domestic investors.

Winning investor strategies cause high hurdle rates for capital spending

To test this idea, an index of CAPEX/(CAPEX + Dividends & Buybacks) was created for each company, and the following investment strategy was measured: sell the highest quartile of the index (capital heavy firms) and buy the lowest quartile of the index (Dividend and Buyback heavy firms). This strategy is compared for each year after the crisis in Table 2.2, and the cumulative gains are shown on the far right of the table.

Table 2.2. **Which market investment strategy outperformed?**

(percentage gain)

Infrastructure & General Industry
(buying the bottom quartile of companies CAPEX / (CAPEX + DIV & BUYBACKS) index and selling the top quartile)

	2009	2010	2011	2012	2013	2014	Cumulative
United States	0.56	1.70	16.18	11.98	3.84	15.55	49.82
Europe	-2.36	3.80	13.84	8.73	9.74	13.47	47.22
Japan	-7.27	0.45	9.63	9.29	2.17	-2.62	11.65
EMEs	-3.71	8.70	10.22	10.74	0.97	-5.52	21.40

Note: Europe refers to the European Union and Switzerland.

Source: Bloomberg, OECD calculations.

StatLink http://dx.doi.org/10.1787/888933210312

Over the six years shown, selling high capital spending companies and buying low CAPEX and high buyback companies would have added 50% to portfolio values in the USA, 47% in Europe, 21% in emerging countries and even 12% in Japan (where activists play little role). On balance there is a clear investor preference against capital spending companies and in favour of short-termism. This adds to the hurdle rate faced by managers in attempting to undertake a large capital spending programmes—stock market investors will likely punish them.

What companies do with their operating cash flow

This finding appears to find its way into what companies do with their cash flow: high hurdle rates alongside more problematic ROE trends augur against capital spending. While weaker investment is apparent across all regions, operating cash flow is stronger in the advanced countries[14]. Given the Table 2.2 finding, it would be fairly logical from a management point of view to return this cash to shareholders rather than undertake uncertain long-term investment projects that carry much more risk for managers in the market for corporate control. The risks instead would be born more by host-country investment in capacity and infrastructure. A summary of what companies have been doing in terms of the sources and uses of funds is set out below for the United States, Europe, Japan, and EMEs[15].

United States corporate financing flows show huge buybacks

- Operating cash flow as a share of sales is rising for both infrastructure (since 2005) and general industries (since 2008), and is more or less sufficient to cover both investment and buybacks.
- Borrowing was strong just prior to the crisis in both sectors and has been picking up again in infrastructure since 2010. For general industry this seems to be broadly correlated to the cycle of net asset acquisitions (which has weakened in the past 2 years). Infrastructure corporate borrowing is more correlated with the dividend and buyback cycle.

Figure 2.11. **US companies: Operating cash is rising and buybacks are huge**

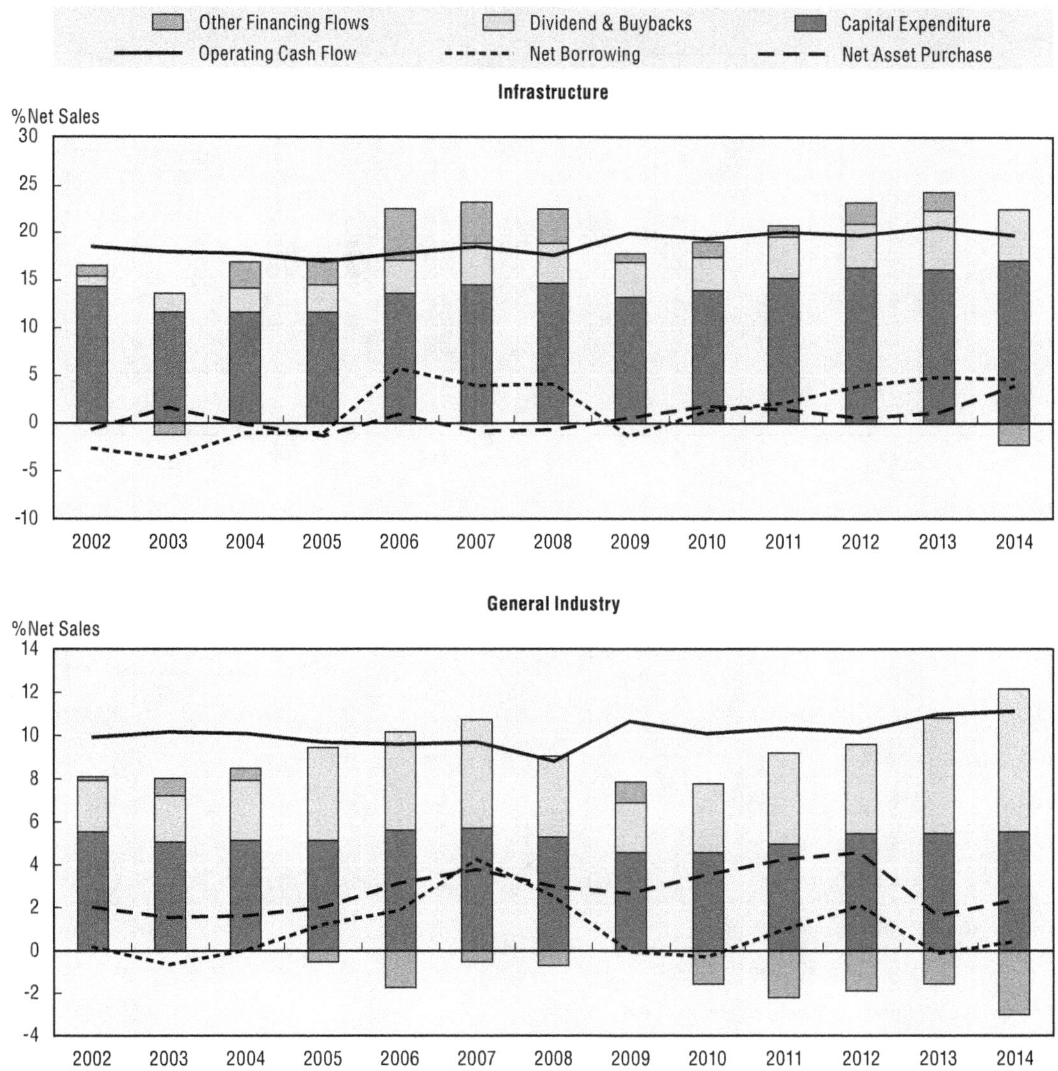

Source: Bloomberg, OECD calculations.

StatLink http://dx.doi.org/10.1787/888933209259

- Capital expenditure as a share of sales has been rising in both industry sectors, but not to the extent feasible given the funding flows. For infrastructure industries, dividends and buybacks show some sign of moderation in 2014. But for general industries dividends and buybacks are running at a truly remarkable pace; even faster than capital expenditure itself in recent years. There has been plenty of scope to increase capital spending, but instead firms appear to be adjusting to demands of investors for greater yield (dividends and buybacks).

European corporate financing flows

- In contrast to the United States operating cash flows in Europe have been drifting down for infrastructure and there is a marked downward post-crisis shift for general industry (following the aid provided via subsidies in 2009). These trends are consistent with margin pressure.

Figure 2.12. **Europe: operating cash is not enough to do it all**

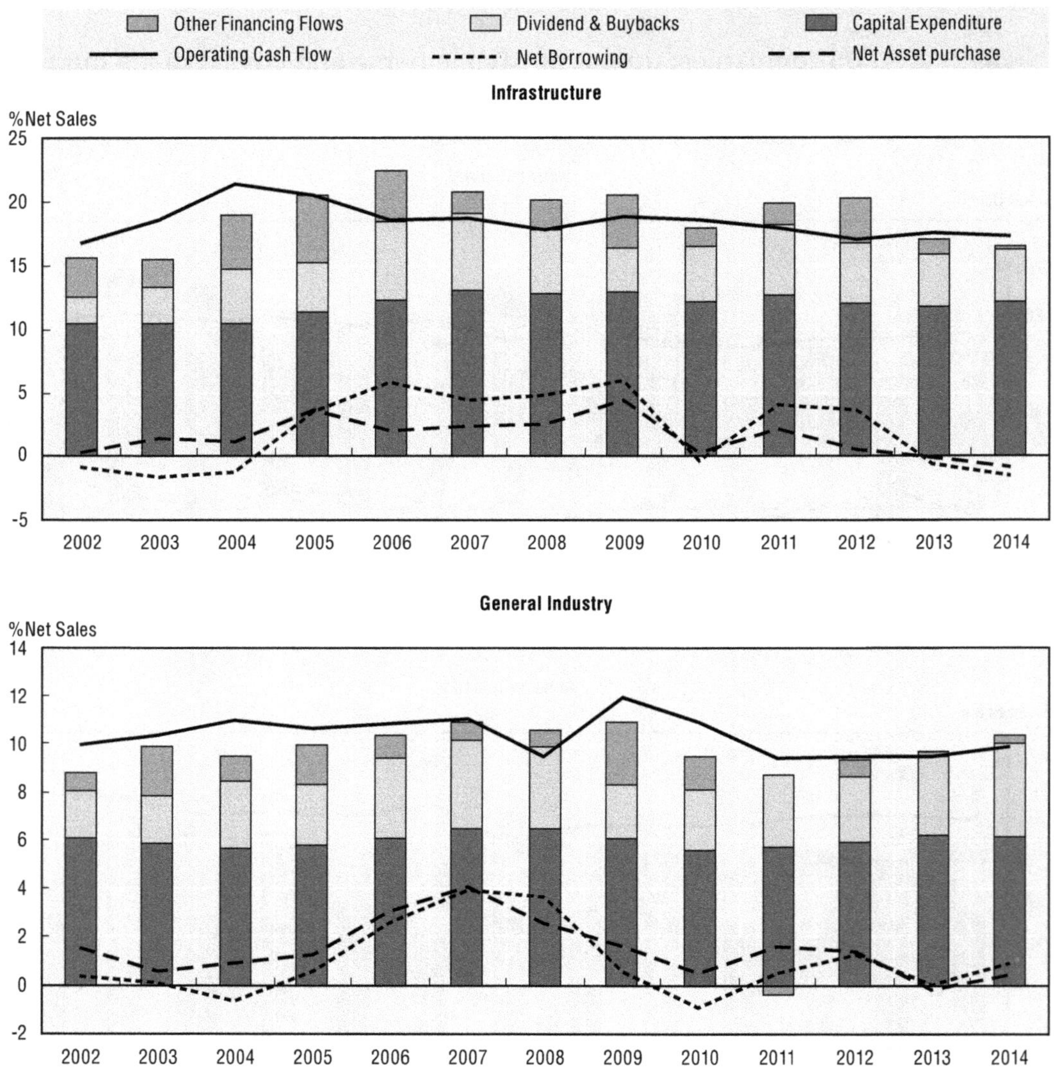

Note: Europe refers to the European Union and Switzerland.

Source: Bloomberg, OECD calculations.

StatLink http://dx.doi.org/10.1787/888933209267

- Borrowing rose modestly in 2011 and 2012, also possibly helped by crisis-related guarantees and interest rate subsidies, but has since fallen back in 2013 and 2014 due to banking supply and demand factors (particularly for infrastructure).
- Dividends and buybacks are only half of what United States companies pay (per unit of sales) in the general industrial sector. While there is no marked tendency for this component to rise in aggregate in Europe, companies in the United Kingdom and Switzerland (not shown) do indeed look very similar to the United States, with very strong growth in buybacks. The net acquisition of assets is much less than in the United States.

Japanese corporate financing flows

- Borrowing has been rising in infrastructure but is flat in general industry, as companies try to deal with restructuring from high debt-to-enterprise-value ratios from the past.

Figure 2.13. **Japan: No buybacks but acquisitions are firm**

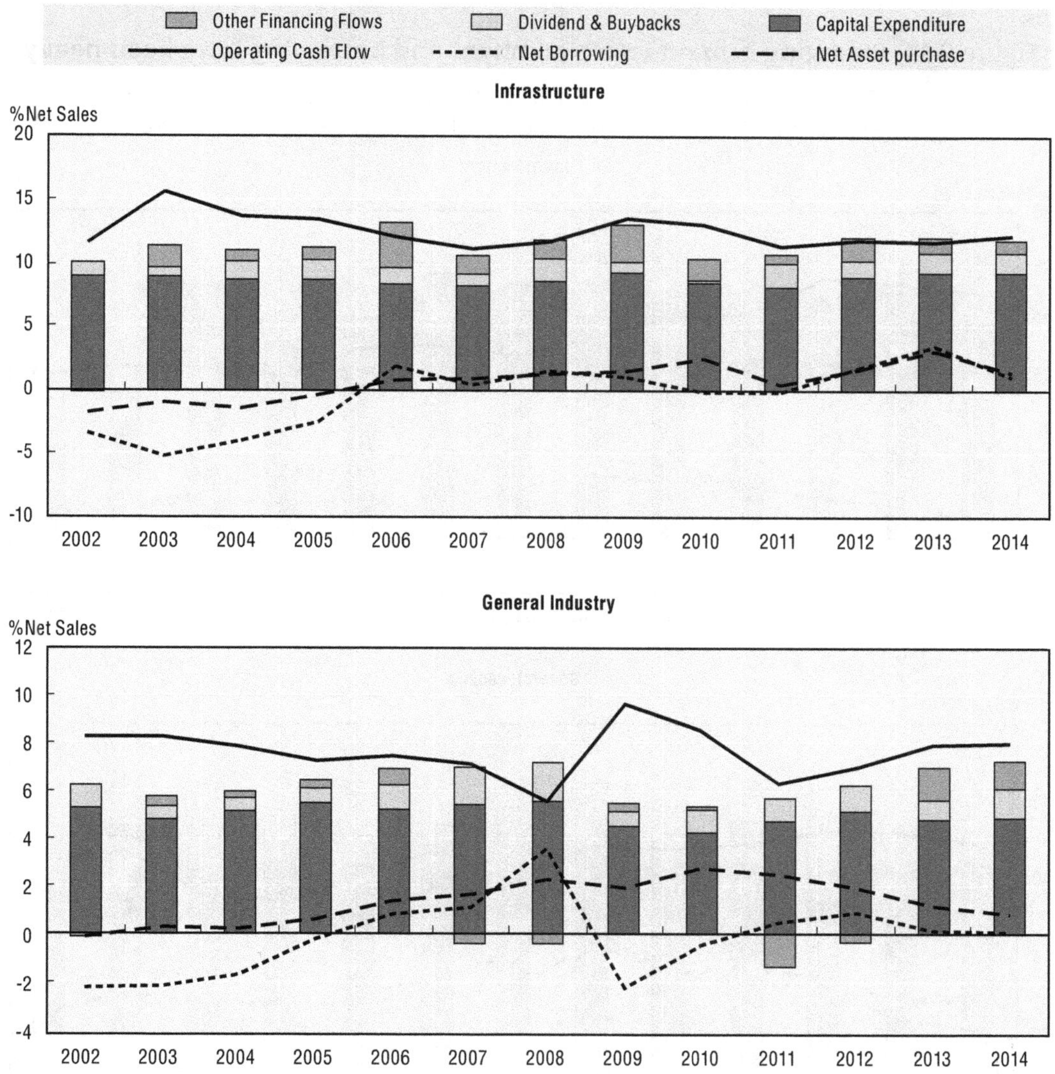

Source: Bloomberg, OECD calculations.

StatLink http://dx.doi.org/10.1787/888933209278

- For general industry operating cash flow is well in excess of any capital spending, which remains modest and flat, and dividends and buybacks are miniscule compared to companies in other countries. These companies appear to prefer acquiring 'other assets' such as shares in other companies.
- Tax rules appear to have a large impact on dividend repatriation from foreign subsidiaries. For general industries there is a sudden rise in operating earnings in 2009-10, presumably related to the tax reform at the time, which contributed to the corresponding drop in borrowing. A greater role for foreign dividends may explain some of the rise in operating earnings in recent years[16].

Emerging market corporate financing flows

Emerging market investment as a share of sales is much stronger than in other regions, but is declining since the crisis, consistent with earlier observations about ROEs and the cost of equity.

Figure 2.14. **Emerging economies: Investment and borrowing have been heavy**

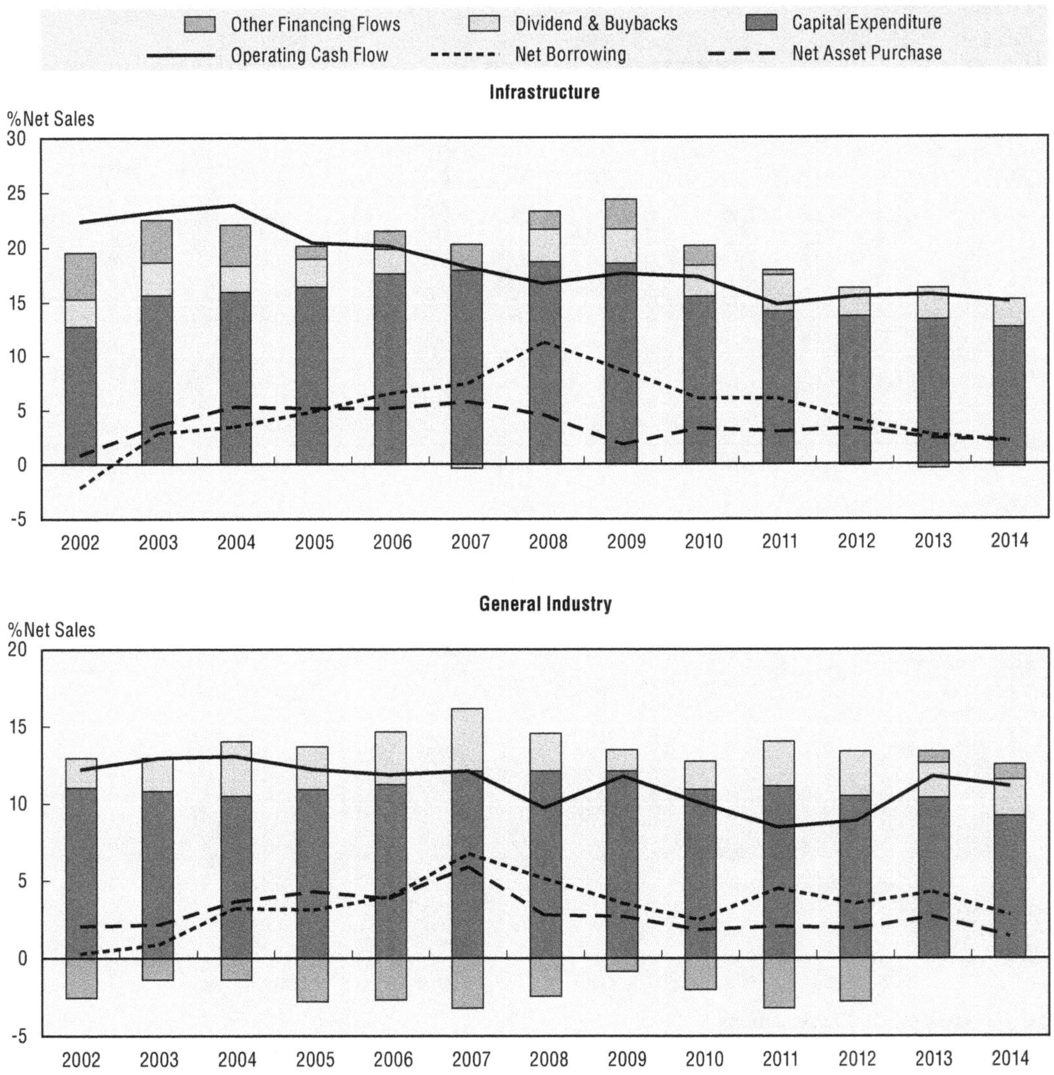

Source: Bloomberg, OECD calculations.

StatLink http://dx.doi.org/10.1787/888933209282

- For infrastructure companies, capital spending rose and peaked at 18.6% of net sales in 2008 (compared to 14.7% in the United States) and subsequently has fallen consistently to 12.6% in 2014 (while the United States has moved up to almost 17%). Prior to 2006 operating cash flow was high but falling and increased borrowing was needed to fund rising investment levels, dividends and buybacks and net asset acquisitions. Subsequently, the continued downtrend in operating cash flow is associated with falling capital expenditure levels and borrowing being cut back.
- For general industry capital intensity seems to be extraordinary compared to other regions. It peaked at over 12% of sales in 2008 (compared to levels in the range of 5-6% for the United States, Europe and Japan) and subsequently has moved down to a still high 9.2% (versus a 5 to 6% range elsewhere) in 2014. Net asset acquisitions continue following the crisis, but at a more moderate pace. Operating cash flow declined until 2011, but has improved in the past two years. This improvement was not reflected in capital spending but in a swing of other financing transactions from negative to positive.

Potential reasons for declining ROE and negative value creation gaps

Emerging market companies are more dominated by government shareholdings

One reason sometimes advanced for poor returns is the presence of SOEs that encourage over-investment, and/or put downward pressure on margins by operating on a non-commercial basis. In the listed MNE sectors there is a vast difference between advanced and emerging market countries in terms of government equity participation (see Figure 2.15).

Using a minimum 15% holding of the voting shares as the criteria for significant holdings, 39% of emerging market listed infrastructure companies fall within that category and 45% of non-infrastructure general industrial companies (where the coal mining, oil, gas, iron and steel sectors are mostly dominated by SOEs). There is also a high level of government involvement in the clean energy sector in emerging markets. The comparable figures for advanced economy companies are 13% for infrastructure and 8% for general industry.

It is important to note that while this chapter is aggregating company data to comment on trends, not all EMEs are so dominated by SOEs—as is the case in many Latin American countries. The Chinese SOE sector has quite a large influence on the aggregate picture, and over the past decade or so there has been a vast trend towards listing SOEs in China (a good first step for developing commercial principles), which is biasing upward the apparent trend in SOE share of EMEs.

ROEs in all advanced and emerging countries in the sample are compared in Figure 2.16 for those companies which are completely private and those which have significant government share holdings—the top panel shows infrastructure and the bottom general industry:

- *Infrastructure*: In advanced countries private ROEs have been stable at around 10% since the crisis, while SOEs have been moving down since 2005. Nevertheless, the average ROEs in state-owned and private companies are very similar. The averages are very different in EMEs: where the SOEs are significantly higher. Both private and SOE returns have fallen since the crisis, and both are well below their respective averages in the past

3 years. The fall in SOE infrastructure returns has been steeper in the tougher post-crisis environment; from being well above private for most of the period, they have fallen to slightly below in 2013-14.

- *General industry:* In advanced economies ROEs have been rising since 2008 and now sit above the period average. The reverse is true for SOEs. For EMEs, there appears to be little difference between SOE and private company returns. Both are declining, and both now sit well below the period averages.

Figure 2.15. **State-owned enterprises are dominant in emerging economies, 2014**

Percentage of net sales

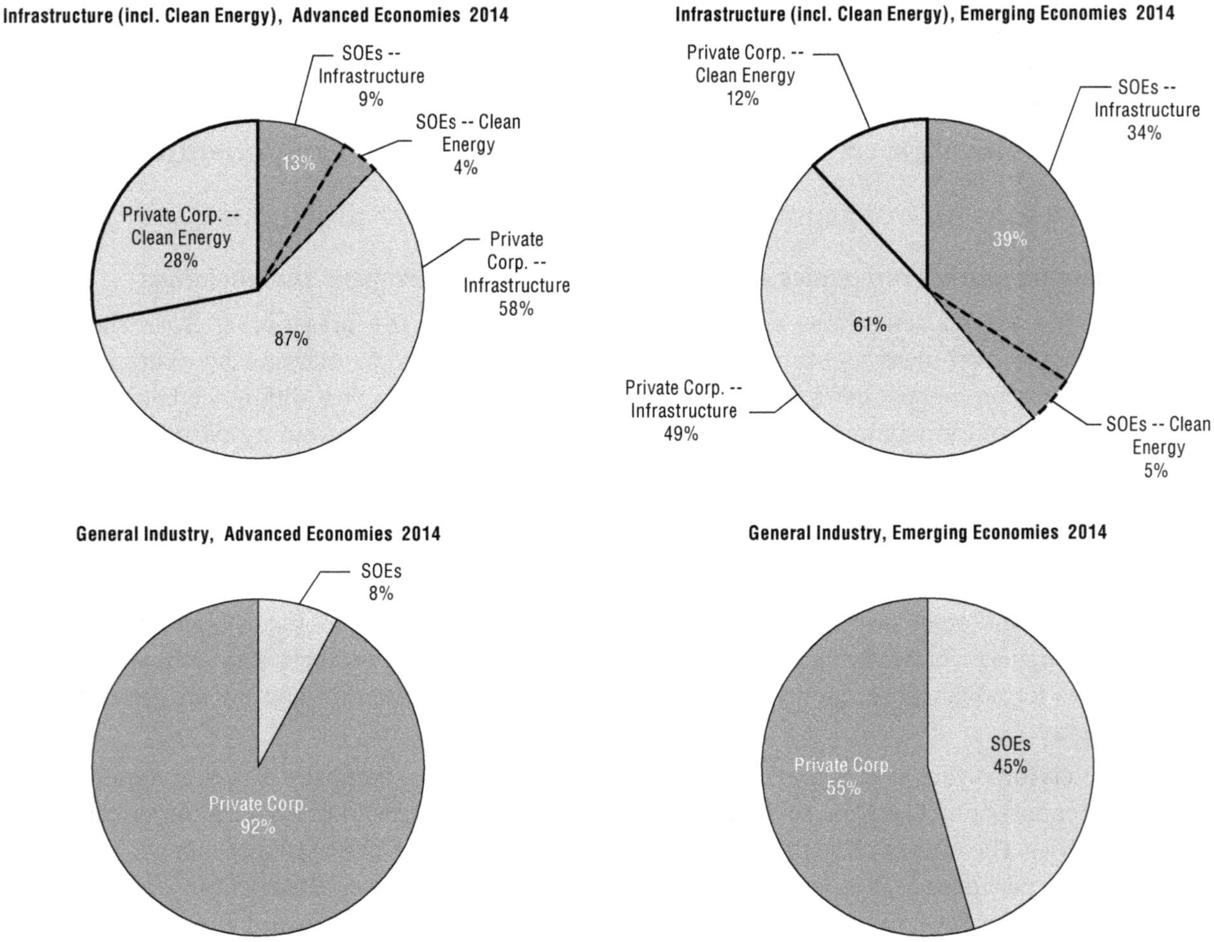

Source: Bloomberg, OECD calculations.

StatLink http://dx.doi.org/10.1787/888933209293

The stronger SOE returns over much of the period in EME companies with a significant state presence may have been due to factors that present non-commercial advantages (Christiansen and Kim, 2014).

- A favoured strong position in the domestic market with respect to: market access, concessions and contract terms; public procurement; preferential access to land; tariff structures in utility pricing; ownership restrictions (monopoly positions); and benefits of local content requirements (OECD, 2015)[17].
- Surrounding listed SOEs in some countries is a conglomerate structure, including up-stream and downstream industries and finance companies, where related party transactions may influence headline net profit statements.

- SOEs may be the recipient of cross-subsidisation, either in the form of subsidies for priority state objectives, via credits from state-owned banks at favourable rates, or because of implicit or explicit loan guarantees.

Figure 2.16. **Returns on equity, advanced and emerging economies, by company ownership**

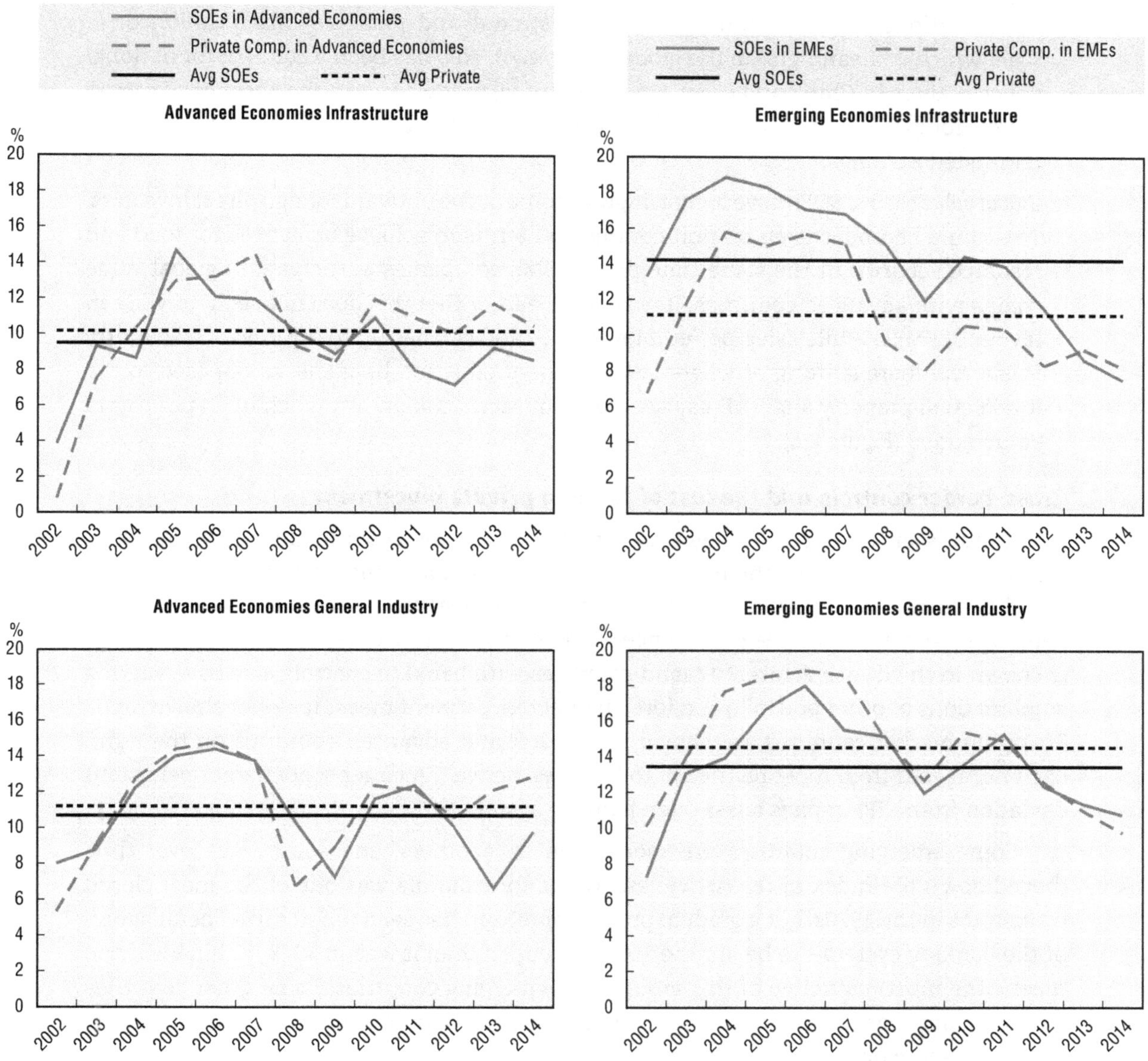

Source: Bloomberg, OECD calculations.

StatLink http://dx.doi.org/10.1787/888933209301

The role of the state or global value chains?

What is interesting is that despite such measures, the gap to fully private companies is falling in EMEs since the crisis, and this region appears to be subject to more general downward pressure on returns post the crisis in both sectors—much more so than in the advanced countries. There are two hypotheses worth exploring that explain this phenomenon.

- *Competition and the post-crisis world*: SOEs may not always operate according to the capital allocation model based on ROEs versus capital costs in a competitive market pricing environment, and inefficiency may be the result. This leaves them inflexible and less able to adapt in the tougher environment post the crisis. Where SOEs invest in activities unrelated to their core business inefficiencies and diminishing returns often arise. Such misallocations may contribute to over-investment and resource misallocation on a scale which is meaningful in the global economy[18]. This has been a concern for national policy makers in China and other Asian countries, partly because the absence of proper targets for capital structure and dividend policy has made a number of SOEs replete with reinvested earnings.
- *Global value chains:* SOEs have increasingly become active outward foreign direct investors. This could be undertaken on non-commercial terms to achieve objectives for food and resource security. At the same time private EME companies participate in global value chains with advanced countries. It was noted earlier that this does not seem to work in favour of EMEs. While sales-per-employee rises and catches up to the advanced country levels, the mere shifting of where some of the production happens, as opposed to the intellectual property and R&D aspects does not seem to allow any catch up in per-capita value-added (Figure 2.5).

Cross-border controls and the cost of funding private investment

Controls on cross-border flows can raise transactions costs in the capital markets faced by firms and reduce the breadth and depth of financial markets thereby leading to liquidity problems (particularly in crisis periods). A measure of openness of a country's banking system based on the persistence of its deviations from covered interest parity (CIP) is shown in the line in Figure 2.17 (and countries with banking controls also have varying combinations of other portfolio and foreign direct investment measures—not shown here). Emerging market countries are shown on the left and advanced countries on the right; each numbered from most restrictive to least restrictive[19]. A larger score (larger persistent deviation from CIP) implies a less open banking system.

Some emerging countries are more open than others, and some have over time moved down the index of restrictiveness. China for example was one of the most closed economies in the 1970s, but a gradual process of reform has seen progressive liberalisation of the banking system—to be around 50% more open than it was in 1978.[20] China is by no means the most restrictive of this grouping of emerging countries. Some other countries have actually been moving in the direction of more restriction. Advanced countries on the right have more open banking systems.

Also shown in Figure 2.17 is the average cost of equity for general industrial companies for the period 2010-2014 in the corresponding country. The cost of equity is equal to the onshore risk-free rate plus the equity risk premium. The cost of AAA corporate debt for the country is also shown. The averages of both measures for the emerging market and advanced countries as groups are shown in the broken lines. There is a strong tendency for countries with more open banking systems to have a lower cost of equity and debt. As noted earlier, countries with the strongest cross-border controls see offshore NDF markets form, and these are often associated with higher on-shore rates than would prevail in open financial systems (see Box 2.2). This, together with a high equity risk premium, raises the cost of equity. The EMEs of Figure 2.17 all have a relatively high cost of equity and debt and the first 15 of these all have NDF markets indicating quite strong controls[21]. In a separate recent study by the OECD it has been shown that the persistence of CIP deviations as an openness measure is negatively related to company capital spending once other determinants of investment are taken into account (See Annex 2.A2).

Figure 2.17. **Open capital markets reduce the cost of equity**

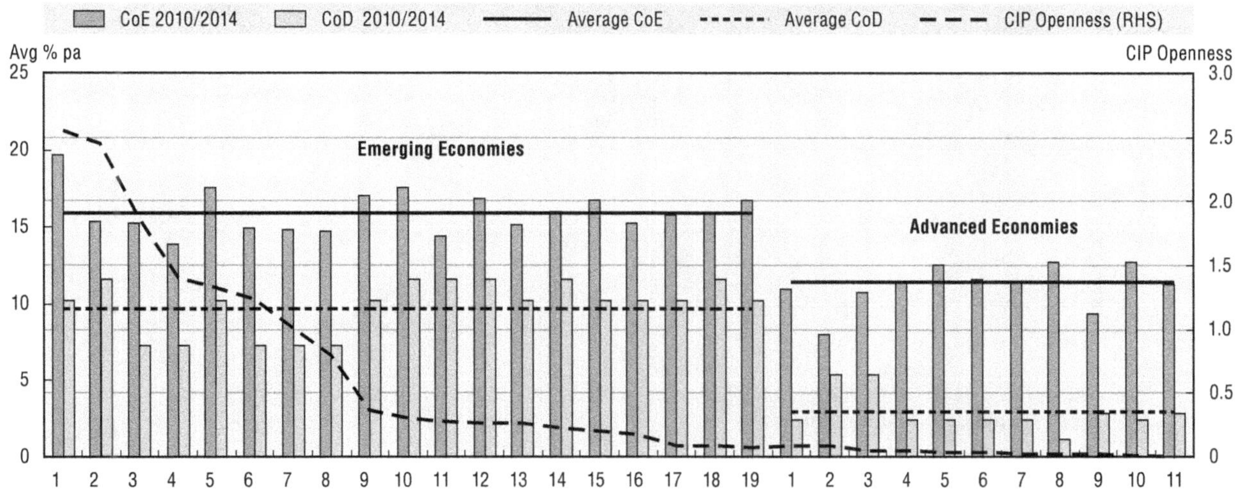

Note: Europe refers to the European Union and Switzerland.

Source: Bloomberg, OECD calculations. 2010-2013 averages.

StatLink http://dx.doi.org/10.1787/888933209312

Taxation incentives are driving more investment to emerging markets

Over-investment may also be encouraged by generous tax incentives. The OECD has surveyed the percentage of countries in various groupings that provide tax exemptions and/or tax holidays for foreign investors, and these are shown in Figure 2.18. The Middle East and North Africa (MENA) and Eastern Europe and Central Asia (EECA) are highly capital-intensive energy producing areas, and while they also use tax incentives they invest relatively more than other regions per unit of sales. For the group as a whole there is a positive association between tax incentives and capital expenditure. Tax incentives are particularly high in South Asia and East Asia and the Pacific, and if MENA and EECA are excluded (as they envelope the highly capital intensive oil producing countries), the positive slope of the trend line is particularly steep.

The ambiguous role of foreign direct investment: following global value chains and tax incentives

The aim of policy is to improve long-term investment, and of course foreign direct investment (FDI) can be a great contributor, creating jobs and adding value. FDI financial flows by purpose consist of mergers and acquisitions (M&A), capacity expanding investment ('greenfield' and extensions to existing affiliates), and financial restructurings, including for tax planning purposes[22]. An important component of FDI, reinvested earnings, may be particularly affected by tax planning. M&A is a large part of the FDI data, though it only changes the ownership structure of companies. M&A is also a way to expand global value chains (with intellectual property transfer as discussed earlier) without 'greenfield' investments.

Figure 2.18. **Asia is strong on tax holidays to boost investment**

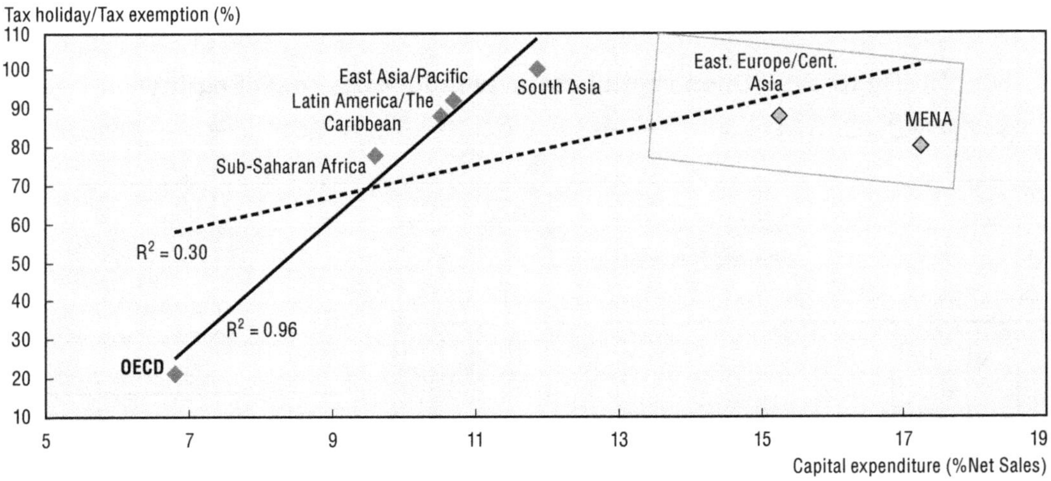

Source: Bloomberg, OECD Centre for Tax Policy and Administration. Percentage of countries in each group offering tax holidays or exemptions for foreign investors.

StatLink http://dx.doi.org/10.1787/888933209322

FDI data doesn't provide a breakdown of the M&A component, and data for the latter come from inconsistent sources, one based on financing transactions and the other on the acquiring company[23]. With this caveat in mind the total stock of FDI inflows is compared to trade in value-added in Figure 2.19, both as a share of GDP (OECD, WTO, 2011). There is a positive relationship. That is to say, that the further down a country is in the global value chain (the more its exports are foreign imports), the more foreign companies involved in the transfer of intellectual capital will have related FDI flows[24].

Chapter 6 takes up the issue of FDI and M&A developments, and some observations developed there are worth mentioning in the context of the investment themes in this chapter pertaining to global value chains:

- The current gap between (low) M&A transactions and (high) stock market capitalisation levels hints at the possibility of an increase of cross-border M&A transactions over the next few years in some regions. However, weakness in the emerging market economies and a sharp rise in international business divestment are factors pushing in the opposite direction.
- Cross-border investment has shifted gears from a pre-financial crisis growth trajectory to a post-crisis restructuring trajectory, with record levels of divestments of MNE assets being sold back into domestic ownership.

This may suggest that while initial phases of global value chain expansions are associated with increased inward FDI, the tougher post-crisis environment is seeing those assets being transferred back to the host country. The company may keep its place in the global value chain, but the associated risks are borne locally. Emerging market shares of both inward and outward cross-border M&A are declining in recent years.

Figure 2.19. **Inward foreign direct investment lines up with trade in value-added**

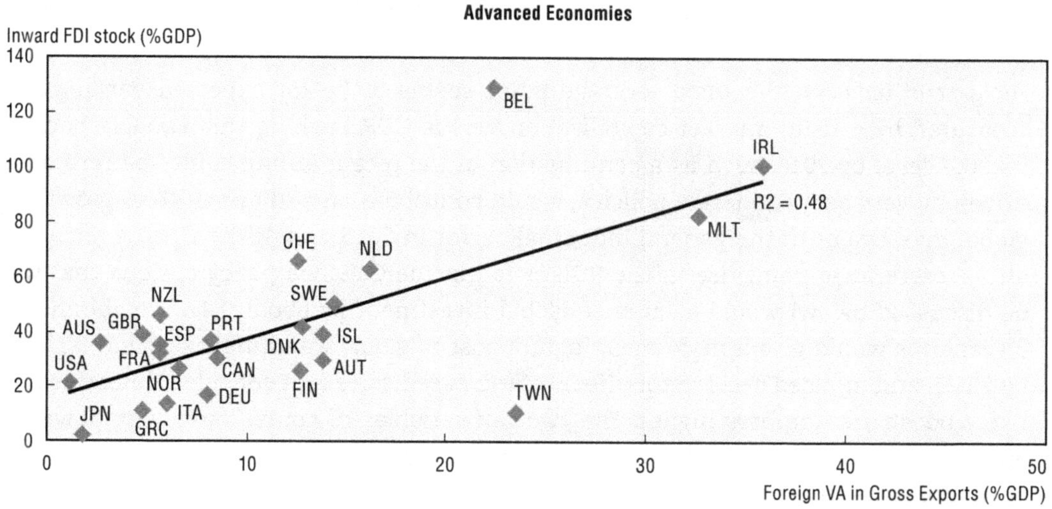

Source: OECD Trade in Value-Added (TiVA) Database, OECD International Direct Investment Database, UNCTAD Inward Foreign Direct Investment Flows Database, OECD calculations. Excluding Luxembourg, where flows are huge and GDP small. Averages 1995-2013.

StatLink http://dx.doi.org/10.1787/888933209334

The outlook for investment and sensitivity analysis

Many of the factors discussed above need to be thought about by policy makers and investors alike. There are signs of stagnation, over-investment, adverse incentives and returns that may make for a weak business investment outlook. To examine the broad empirical importance of some of the key variables, the OECD has tested them in a panel modelling exercise using the very large sample of company data on capital expenditure (with the matching financial data for each firm) on which the above analysis has been based (for general industry, infrastructure, and clean energy). The basic model results are set out and discussed in Annex 2.A2.

To gain a better understanding of where policy might have the best points of leverage to influence investment, the models are used to generate some projections of the aggregated outcomes and their sensitivity to different scenarios. Instruments are used to extrapolate the ROE, cost of equity (COE) and market-cap-to-GDP (MCAP) variables; while the tax and financial openness variables are held constant. As an example, the projected baseline assumptions for the (aggregated) ROE, COE and MCAP are shown for the general industrial sector in Figure 2.20 (the other sectors are treated in a similar way). The 'on-average' negative value creation proposition (ROE less than COE) begins to narrow over the forecast period, but remains negative due to the influence of EMEs. The market capitalisation variable moves broadly in line with GDP. Sales growth for the sectors in each country is assumed to be in line with OECD forecasts for nominal GDP growth. The base-case projections consistent with the US dollar numbers of Figure 2.1 are shown as growth rates in each of the three sector panels in Table 2.3.

Any general macro policy that accelerated sales would have an accelerator effect on investment (not included here). However, policies to push up investment independently of sales would need to influence the main explanatory variables found to be significant in the corporate decision making process shown in Annex 2.A2[25]. Some of the sensitivities of the projections to different scenarios for the independent variables are also shown in Table 2.3 for 2015 and 2016.

- *For general industry*: the main leverage point seems to be for expected earnings, as measured by a rising market capitalisation versus GDP. Pushing this variable back to its 2007 level by 2016, such as a continuation of the recent strong equity performance driven by very easy monetary policies, would contribute an additional 3% to growth of global investment in the general industrial sector in 2015 and 4% by 2016. A once-for-all 2.5 percentage point rise in the ROE or fall in the COE (via policy options that will be discussed below) would each raise global investment by about 0.4%. Combining all 3 scenarios would give a more meaningful boost to global investment (around 5.3% pa by 2016), and induced accelerator effects of increased sales (not considered here) would likely boost the numbers higher. The two tax variables of course have very powerful effects (see Annex 2.A2) and, fiscal room permitting, would be useful in the quest for even more investment.
- *For the infrastructure sector:* lowering the cost of debt spread (not the COE) provides the best leverage point for policy makers of the three scenarios shown, closely followed by policies that would raise the ROE (some of which are discussed below). Tax effects in infrastructure are even more powerful than for general industry and need to be considered by policy makers. The openness measure is also very powerful in this sector (Blundell-Wignall and Roulet, 2015)[26]: A 0.5-standard deviation fall in the capital controls variable in Annex 2.A2 would lead capital spending to rise by about 14 % in the long run (by improving access to finance and contributing to lower domestic capital costs).
- *For the clean energy sector:* the baseline projection is very challenging, and working on policy levers that affect all of the components of the model shown in Annex 2.A2 would be needed to turn the situation around (in the absence of a game-changing pricing of carbon at a high enough level).

Figure 2.20. **Returns on equity, cost of equity and market-cap-to-GDP assumptions for general industry projections**

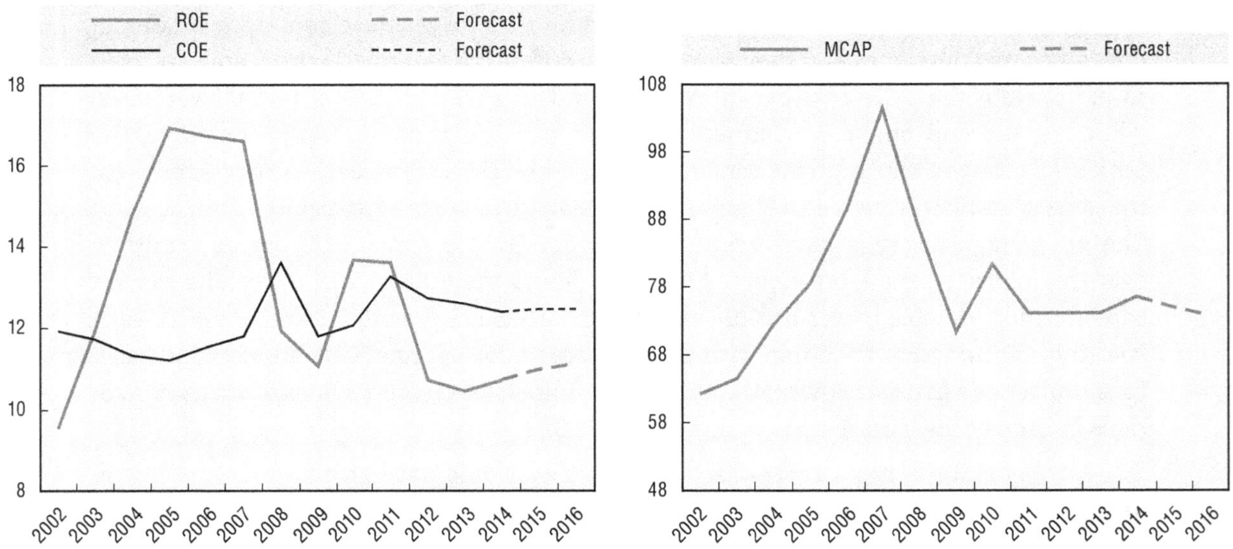

Source: OECD calculations.

StatLink http://dx.doi.org/10.1787/888933209342

This evidence-based research using micro data suggests that stagnation of investment is very likely to persist in the absence of meaningful policy measures of both a structural and cyclical nature applied consistently in all regions of the world economy. Such a broad-based approach is needed since MNEs invest in many regions (as global value chains spread) and there is a need to avoid *beggar- thy-neighbour* policy strategies based on exchange rate weakness (since everyone's net exports cannot rise as a global growth strategy). Some of these policies are discussed in the next section.

Table 2.3. **The outlook for listed business capital expenditure is weak**

	2003	2004	2005	2006	2007	2008	2009	2010	2011	2012	2013	2014	2015	2016
	Percent change													
	-	-	-	-	-	-	-	-	-	-	-	-	Forecast	Forecast
	General Industry													
Baseline Fcst	9.72	16.57	18.61	14.98	48.11	8.64	-48.30	81.56	21.92	2.84	-7.07	4.76	4.02	-0.07
ROE + 2.5 bps	-	-	-	-	-	-	-	-	-	-	-	-	4.54	0.49
CoE - 2.5 bps	-	-	-	-	-	-	-	-	-	-	-	-	4.45	0.50
Market Cap/GDP to 2007	-	-	-	-	-	-	-	-	-	-	-	-	6.97	4.37
All 3 scenarios	-	-	-	-	-	-	-	-	-	-	-	-	7.92	5.38
	Infrastructure													
Baseline Fcst	15.79	15.40	20.82	24.00	42.69	9.81	-35.27	47.06	11.55	0.48	-3.62	9.51	0.47	0.12
ROE + 2.5 bps	-	-	-	-	-	-	-	-	-	-	-	-	1.60	1.32
CoD - 2.5 bps	-	-	-	-	-	-	-	-	-	-	-	-	2.66	2.79
Market Cap/GDP to 2007	-	-	-	-	-	-	-	-	-	-	-	-	1.25	1.17
All 3 scenarios	-	-	-	-	-	-	-	-	-	-	-	-	4.59	4.98
	Clean Energy													
Baseline Fcst	25.40	22.63	17.55	11.65	18.31	44.82	-8.67	9.04	11.51	-5.27	-9.82	-2.49	-5.24	-7.56
ROE + 2.5 bps	-	-	-	-	-	-	-	-	-	-	-	-	-3.60	-5.98
CoD - 2.5 bps	-	-	-	-	-	-	-	-	-	-	-	-	-2.63	-3.74
Market Cap/GDP to 2007	-	-	-	-	-	-	-	-	-	-	-	-	-3.44	-3.74
All 3 scenarios	-	-	-	-	-	-	-	-	-	-	-	-	0.82	1.54

Source: OECD calculations. Projections are generated dynamically using the error-correction model based on the Engle 2-step procedure. Only the long-run co-integrating model is shown in Annex 2.A2.

StatLink http://dx.doi.org/10.1787/888933210324

Conclusions

Macro policies for general industrial MNEs

Policy considerations for general industry are quite different from infrastructure due to the dominance of MNEs in the group. Capital expenditure decisions in global value chains are affected by incentives created across multiple countries, so that monetary and fiscal policy effects in any one country are less powerful than before. Clearly weak global demand is an issue restraining sales and investment in the post-crisis environment. Since a large part of the world uses financial repression to maintain high savings and investment, global consumer demand for the products of MNEs is more restrained than otherwise as a consequence. While little can be done about this in the short run, longer-run policy needs to bear in mind that net export-led growth can't work for all countries.

The bottom-up company evidence presented here suggests there is still some considerable scope for monetary policy to work through the market factors identified independently of the important sales variable. The equity market capitalisation versus GDP variable (future earnings expectations) is particularly important in this respect, as are the

ROE and the COE. Easy monetary policies (including unconventional approaches such as quantitative easing) that serve to boost the equity market are a potential positive influence on capital expenditure. This is because a rising share price reduces the dividend yield, and hence the COE, while support of the central bank may also improve the investment climate and expectations for future earnings which causes market capitalisation to rise versus GDP.

Long time frames, activist investors and the buyback policy puzzle

It was noted earlier than capital expenditure by companies appears to have a higher hurdle rate than for financial investors. There are two fundamental reasons for this. First, real investors have a longer time frame compared to financial investors who believe (perhaps wrongly at times) that their positions can be quickly unwound. Second, managers of MNEs operate in a very uncertain world and the empirical evidence (see Table 2.3) suggests that equity investors 'punish' companies that invest too much and reward those that return cash to shareholders. If managers make an error of judgement they will be punished by activist investors and/or stock market reactions in general and hence they prefer buybacks. It is arguable that if managers do not have profitable projects, it makes sense to give the money back to investors so that they can reallocate it to those with better ideas. However, the evidence presented earlier suggests that the buyback phenomena is not associated with rising productivity and better returns on equity. A better use of cash requires an improved return environment would be encouraged by:

- Addressing structural reforms in both advanced and emerging economies.
- Reducing uncertainty about regulations, macro policy and taxation policy in the future.
- Encouraging a greater role in governance for long-term institutional investors, particularly in corporate remuneration which often drives the incentive for share buybacks (OECD, 2013).

'Zero rates' & 'permanent quantitative easing' are not reasonable assumptions

In terms of the uncertainty issue, it is unlikely that zero interest rates and quantitative easing will be perceived as stable long-lasting policies. Such policies will of necessity be reversed. However, before that, they will have a strong impact on exchange rates that may also lead to responses from other countries of a 'beggar-thy-neighbour' type that will actually increase uncertainly and hence the hurdle rate for investment. Until these issues are sorted out it may be perfectly rational for a company to hold back on investment and indeed continue to return cash to shareholders via share buybacks which gives investors short-term but more certain returns[27].

Corporate remuneration and the buyback puzzle

Buybacks benefit company executives and mutual fund managers (whose performance is measured over short periods), both of whom are rewarded with stock options and awards. A typical executive of a large firm has something like 80% of his or her compensation derived from equity participation (Lazonick, 2014). Buybacks enable executives more easily to meet quarterly and/or annual EPS (earning per share) targets on which their remuneration is based. Driving up the share price (or defending a fall) to push stock options 'into the money' (or keep it there) increases the personal gain of executives, while reducing the scope for investment. Where this is permitted to be carried through off-market share purchases at fixed price or via a Dutch auction tender process, there is a strong possibility of discrimination amongst shareholders[28]. The policy options to deal with this include:

- Revisiting executive option and share allocation schemes to align them with long-term investment objectives, as opposed to short-term EPS targets.
- Reducing the attractiveness of borrowing to carry out buybacks where the tax treatment of interest costs, capital gains and dividends are a factor.

Red tape and market infrastructure

Clear rules regarding reporting and disclosure and their effective enforcement are essential to assure savers and investors about the transparency and integrity of capital markets, without which they will not function well. However, there are many costs associated with regulations, listing requirements, risk controls and reporting that not all smaller companies can afford and this may keep them out of the IPO market. Market rules (such as tick sizes) and the increased use of new technology (electronic and dark exchanges, high frequency trading, exchange traded funds and other passive funds management strategies) have far-reaching implications for price discovery and hence for the allocation of investment and the ability of firms to carry out IPOs. These rules need further attention by policy makers. Some of these issues will be touched upon in Chapter 7.

Multinational enterprises and tax

Taxation, and particularly the corporate tax rates and the tax holiday and exemptions variables are very powerful influences on MNEs in the empirical evidence presented in Annex 2.A2. This means that domestic policy to boost investment in the home jurisdiction may be dissipated in the global economy according to the incentives provided by comparative tax regimes. South Asia and East Asia shown in Figure 2.18 are particularly advantageous in this respect. A number of European countries also offer tax advantages for cross-border investment activities. The elasticity of investment to home-country monetary policy is thereby weakened global tax competition. Tax reform (including the OECD's Base Erosion and Profit Shifting—BEPS—project) will ultimately be required to eliminate global distortions. Where relevant, however, tax incentives can be very useful, particularly in the area of R&D spending.

Incentives for research and development expenditure

The OECD notes that R&D expenditure was growing at only 1.6% per annum from 2008-2012 compared to double that rate for the years 2001 to 2008; while it has regained its pre-crisis growth more recently, this is off a lower base following the cuts of 2009-10 (OECD, 2014). Direct funding and tax relief represents 10-20% of country R&D spending but this, together with other measures, is evidently not doing enough. As noted earlier, since the crisis, the large sample of companies considered in this chapter show no meaningful growth in value-added per employee, either in advanced or in emerging economies since 2008. There are a number of policy areas worth considering.

- The model results show how effective changes in tax can be for attracting investment so that, if applied to R&D investment, the social pay-off could be greater in the longer run compared to non-targeted across-the-board company tax cuts.
- There is a need to address funding issues for smaller companies which may be more dynamic and survive or fail on the basis of their ability to innovate and find adequate funding (issues taken up in Chapter 5).

- The processes for grants, loans and guarantees need to be open, transparent and competitive.
- Competition policy more generally is also essential, particularly if there is a tendency for larger cash-rich companies simply to buy out smaller potential competitors (see Chapter 8).
- Venture capital is also particularly weak in Europe, and the liquidity and depth of this market needs further to be improved.

Policies for infrastructure companies

An examination of the data and causality testing suggests that sales of the larger general industrial sector may be quite important for infrastructure, so that the policies discussed above would if implemented improve 'bankable' returns to justify capital spending in this smaller sector. In addition, this section considers policies that raise the incentive to invest for private infrastructure companies in situations where SOEs compete with them.

- The role of the ROE is supported by the data in the results shown in Annex 2.A2. ROEs are declining in emerging markets and Europe (Figure 2.7), perhaps due to past over-investment and misallocation resulting from tax and various non-commercial advantages enjoyed by SOEs. Establishing level playing fields with competition policy and better governance principles for SOEs would help to improve ROEs for private infrastructure companies (an issue taken up in Chapter 8).
- SOEs in the infrastructure sector need to focus on core businesses, rather than conglomerate activities, and proper targets for capital structures need to be implemented.
- Interest rate spreads are important on the cost of funding side (due to credit risk). Lending on non-commercial terms for inefficient projects raises credit risk for all companies competing in the sector. Arms-length financial policies need to be implemented.
- Controls on cross-border fows are important in the more domestic-oriented infrastructure sector. These raise cost of financing compared with the risk free cost of debt. From Annex 2.A2 infrastructure and clean energy have highly-significant negative influences from the capital controls variable. A reduction in the index via deregulation programmes would reduce the cost of finance materially for private industry with positive effects on investment.
- Tax policy (from the results presented earlier) is likely to be a key lever for the sector[29].

Policies for clean energy

Clean energy returns are low versus the cost of funds (ROE versus the COE or the cost of debt), particularly in EMEs. This is possibly due to the absence of enabling policies, the role of SOEs, tariff design and the heavy use of local content requirements in the sector in many OECD and non-OECD countries. There is a need urgently to raise bankable returns in the sector:

- A first best policy would be to impose a price on carbon high enough to change the economics of the industry.
- Removing inefficient fossil fuel subsidies would help raise ROEs in the clean energy sector.
- Avoiding reversals of supportive measures including tariff structures and contract terms that deter future investors.

- Strengthening competition policy by designing open and transparent procurement processes, unbundling vertically-integrated network operators and establishing wholesale markets for electricity.
- SOEs should operate on a level playing field with private companies, and not enjoy monopoly or favoured market access.
- This will require coordinating supportive projects for grid development and access.
- Providing subsidies and tax advantages where relevant (the above empirical evidence suggests that company tax rates, tax holidays and exemptions have large effects); and
- Avoiding poorly-structured local content requirements which increase downstream cost for renewable-energy-based electricity generation.

A risk-case scenario for the company investment outlook

Debt-to-enterprise-value percentages are shown in Figure 2.21 for infrastructure (top panel) and general industry (bottom panel). Equity investment via company retained earnings is the prevalent form for investing by companies and is best suited for long-term sustainable growth: any failure of an investment project sees shareholders lose money and vice versa. Debt, on the other hand, while important at different times in the investment process and often useful for tax advantages, remains with the firm when investments fail. Debt-financed over-investment was a key characteristic of the Asia crisis of the late 1990s. Borrowing to pay dividends and buybacks, which is encouraged by the tax system, would also work towards a debt bias and against long-term investment.

A number of observations about debt-to-enterprise-value ratios stand out:

- *Investment in infrastructure is associated with higher debt ratios* than in other industrial groupings, due to: early stage financing needs; longer horizons for revenue benefits; and/or taking advantage of interest deductibility in the tax structuring of ownership and management rights. In emerging markets state-owned banks also play a large role in financing infrastructure and may operate with less-than-commercial terms. For all countries, debt-to-enterprise value on average is about 30% for infrastructure, and 20% for general industry.
- *The ratio for US companies* in the infrastructure sector has been trending down since 2008, and at 25% of enterprise value is below the global average. For non-infrastructure US companies there is no sign of an upward trend.
- *Japan (a country where stagnation has been at work for a long time)* has the highest debt-to-enterprise-value by some margin (42% average for infrastructure and 28% for other industries). For both infrastructure and other industries debt ratios post the crisis are falling though still generally higher than mid-2000 levels.
- *Europe is closer to Japan* in debt structure for infrastructure, and the post-crisis levels appear more challenging than before. Companies in the general industrial sector, on the other hand, do not appear out of line with US ratios.
- *The situation is very different in emerging markets.* The debt ratios were low prior to the crisis (13% for infrastructure and 9% for general industries in 2007). Subsequently, debt-to-enterprise-value ratios have been rising rapidly. For infrastructure the level has moved up quickly to over 30% of enterprise value, and for other industries to 25%, in both cases now approaching Japanese levels. Chinese companies (not shown) have a large impact on the EME ratio shown here.

Figure 2.21. **Debt-to-enterprise-value ratios**

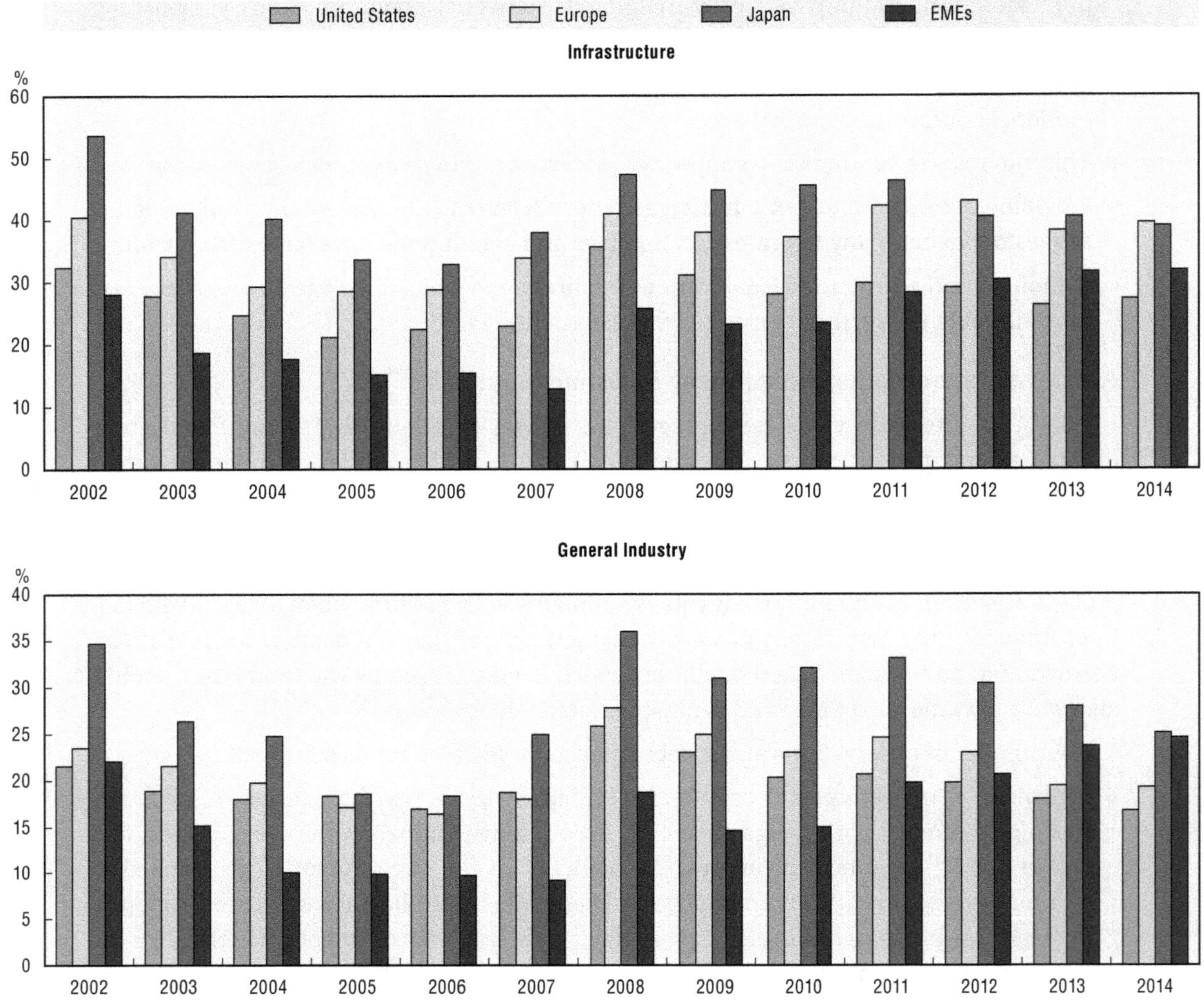

Note: Europe refers to the European Union and Switzerland.

Source: Bloomberg, OECD calculations.

StatLink http://dx.doi.org/10.1787/888933209355

Encouraging sustainable long-term investment requires retained earnings to be put to work and more initial public offerings (IPOs) to be made for new companies to ensure less reliance on debt. The global patterns are uneven, but it seems that the speed of acceleration of borrowing in emerging markets is much greater than elsewhere and reminiscent of 1990s Asia crisis trends. Rising debt-to-enterprise value levels at a time when ROEs are declining is a serious concern. In both infrastructure companies and general industrial companies the value creation proposition in EMEs on average appears negative (ROE minus the cost of equity shown in Figure 2.9). This situation has emerged just as monetary normalisation in the US is supposed to begin, and while Europe and Japan are moving the other way in favour of QE policies—all with implications for a dollar rally risk in the future. This is not a good situation for some countries with dollar-debt-servicing liabilities—many emerging markets issue in dollars, and do in the US capital market. If fundamental selling begins due to the economics of emerging market debt, the problems of liquidity in these markets could become a much larger problem, including for dollar funding of banks from abroad.

A number of structured investment vehicles reference these securities and both are held in institutional investor portfolios in advanced countries. In the event of a major selling cycle liquidity problems could be reinforced by a credit rating downgrades forcing institutional investors to sell (due to benchmark and regulatory restrictions). In the event of extreme volatility broker-dealers could have trouble matching their books in repo and derivatives markets. It is feasible that, if not handled well, this could become a difficult aspect of the monetary policy normalisation in the future. Uncertainty caused by such events, in the risk-case scenario, could undermine further the investment outlook in the global economy. These liquidity issues are taken up in Chapter 3.

Notes

1. It makes little sense to analyse national accounts investment as though this were the result of a domestic company taking decisions for activities within national borders. Nor do the national accounts data permit analysis of investment decisions of private companies—such data does not generally distinguish infrastructure from other forms of investment, nor the split of this between government and private capital expenditure. Infrastructure tends to have a more domestic economy focus, whereas MNEs in general industry operate more within global value chains where national borders are not meaningful. Nor do national accounts data match up with the 'financials' that the companies that invest actually face.
2. Financial repression is not a negative term. It refers to a development strategy to bottle up domestic saving, and to intermediate it via state-owned banks to mainly SOE companies for investment in a catch-up phase. This investment is mainly replicative in nature—using known technology and applying it to labour (often as a part of an urbanisation process). These measures include the capping of interest rates, high bank reserve requirements, prescriptive policies for bank holding of government debt, credit controls, government ownership of domestic banks, non-convertibility of currencies and cross-border capital controls.
3. The individual company data are aggregated in US dollars, for countries and regions.
4. The basic data source is the Bloomberg Index, because it enables a doubling of the number of companies compared to those in the MSCI index. The Bloomberg sectors and how they are divided between infrastructure and non-infrastructure are set out in the data appendix. These take as close a match as possible to the MSCI sectors included in each of: Telecommunications Infrastructure, Utilities, Energy Infrastructure, Transportation Infrastructure and Social Infrastructure. The main difference is the inclusion of the capital-intensive "Oil Exploration and Production" and "Oil and Gas Drilling" sectors of Bloomberg. The Bloomberg "Clean Energy" index is used for that category, noting that it includes some businesses only part of which are dedicated to clean energy production. As a robustness check the two oil and gas sectors were excluded. None of the basic conclusions of this chapter were affected (magnitudes, cycles and model results).
5. Real investment in the digital economy is difficult to analyse and interpret; i.e. with hedonic price indexes falling sharply—computer bytes that filled 3 buildings decades ago can now be done on a hand held device in the living room. This makes the study of total factor productivity and the size of the capital stock very problematic and difficult to interpret.
6. Non-infrastructure sales are, on average, more than 6- to 7-times that of infrastructure in the 10 000 companies considered here.
7. This may exclude some sub-contracting company employment, but the broad definition of infrastructure used here captures a lot of this by including, for example, sectors such as "Oil Field Services". Where temporary labour agencies are used (e.g. to build a pipeline), this is usually of a short duration and not sustainable employment in any case.
8. The cost of equity (COE) is the earnings yield (sometimes the dividend yield) plus the expected trend growth rate of earnings in the future. If the current dividend yield is high, investors demand immediate high returns, so the cost of attracting investors is high. If growth is high, investors demand strong growth and the cost of attracting them is high. A low share price raises the yield implying investors are wary of variations in returns and demand high ('costly' returns). The equity charge is essentially the book value of equity multiplied by the COE. The ROE is the net income divided by the book value of equity. If the ROE is less than the COE, then net income minus the equity charge is negative. In a constant growth model, the discounted present value will require

the share price to fall. Mangers will be incentivised to raise returns by reducing the number of shares, or carry out other reallocations of capital.

9. The Solow-Swan growth model predicts that if productivity is to be the same across countries, then countries with less capital per worker have a higher marginal product of capital (return on equity). Hence in an open world economy investment flows from rich countries to poor countries until these returns are equalised. These types of mechanisms appear to be at work here but in the modern context of internet based global value chains.

10. From 2002 to 2014 the ratio of borrowing to capital expenditure in advanced countries was around 11% for infrastructure and 16% for general industry, whereas operating cash flow was about 141% for infrastructure and 172% for general industry. For emerging markets infrastructure these numbers are 31% and 120% respectively, and 31% and 99% for general industry. The funding sources are greater than investment because firms also engage in other financial activities such as mergers and acquisitions, cash hoarding, and dividends and buybacks.

11. A panel regression study of global companies shows that capital control restrictions, measured by the conditional variance of deviations from covered interest parity, have a significantly negative impact on company investment. See Blundell-Wignall and Roulet (2015).

12. An IMF study purporting to show that through the crisis countries with capital controls had less output loss than others was shown not to be valid on further investigation. See Blundell-Wignall, A. and C. Roulet (2013), "Capital Controls on Inflows, the Global Financial Crisis and Economic Growth: Evidence for Emerging Economies", *OECD Journal: Financial Market Trends*, Vol. 2013/21.

13. For example, Mohamed El Erian at a recent OECD lunch spoke to the fear of activist investor in the board room and the support they muster for resisting grand plans for investment.

14. And helped by the gains form intellectual property rights transfers and global value chain participation noted earlier.

15. To follow this analysis it is useful to keep in mind the accounting identity: *Operating Cash Flow + Net Borrowing = Capital Expenditure + Dividends & Buybacks + Net Asset Purchases + Net Cash Accumulation.*

16. The tax reform of 2009-10 has had a big impact on the observed behaviour of multinational companies. In 2009 most of the dividends received by parent companies were exempted from tax if the ownership in the foreign company is at least 25 percent. Foreign subsidiaries as a result began to remit more dividends to Japanese parents.

17. For example, LCRs for solar panels have adverse effects by raising upstream and downstream costs.

18. See for example: Lee et al., (2012).

19. To capture the influence of reduced openness of economies via their banking systems, a measure based on covered interest parity (CIP) is used. A CIP concept is chosen as it excludes currency risk and focuses on return differentials between currencies which (apart from low transactions cost and white noise) should not be persistently present in a competitive and open banking system. Movements towards greater openness should see covered differentials diminish and their variance decline over time as arbitrage channels are allowed to operate. The 1-year (average) conditional variance of CIP is used, (the technical details of which are set out in Blundell-Wignall and Roulet (2014), *ibid*. The extent of deviations from CIP and the speed with which they can be arbitraged away for the domestic banking system versus open-economy dollar prices can be modelled as an autoregressive structure in both the mean and the variance, and the estimated conditional variance can be used as a measure of openness of the banking system (3-month interbank interest rates and the matching foreign exchange forward and spot rates are used).

20. This is set out quite well in the study by Huang, Y. and X. Wang (2010). "Does Financial Repression Inhibit Economic Growth? Empirical Examination of China's Reform Experience", *China Centre for Economic Research, Peking University*, China. They show an index of financial repression based on principal components analysis of measures of all the above factors. In 1978 their measure was the maximum of 1.0 for highest repression and this fell to the 0.5 to 0.6 range by 2008.

21. This CIP measure pertains only to banking restrictions, and is an approximation for the purposes here. Countries have differing degrees of controls on banks, portfolio flows and foreign direct investment. Some countries to the right hand side of the emerging country group will have greater controls on these other aspects (which are not shown here) and less on banking.

22. FDI by components consists of equity capital, re-invested earnings, and intercompany debt.

23. FDI uses the source of the financing transaction as the methodology for FDI flows, and not the ultimate owner. So a US company buying a Japanese company financed from the US is US FDI into Japan, but financed out of London would be UK FDI into Japan, and financed out of Japan would be no FDI, even though the ultimate owner is a US company. M&A is based on the acquiring company, not the financing transaction.

24. FDI investment is associated with aggressive tax planning by companies and this results in the double counting of some FDI flows. The quality of FDI data is poor and the OECD is currently engaged in a benchmark revision exercise.

25. The results in Table 2.4 are for the long-run model. In fact the dynamic error-correction model following the Engle 2-step procedure is used to generate the projections dynamically.

26. However, for general industry in countries that have NDF markets (where restrictions are particularly strong), the restrictiveness measure has a very negative impact on investment.

27. QE policies should have been restricted to supporting banks during the crisis and accompanied by genuine bank reform separating derivatives from deposit banking that would have reduced the need for huge central bank balance sheets to be maintained to support collateral and margin calls in the derivatives and related markets.

28. For example favouring professional versus retail holders, and amongst all shareholders, depending on capital gains and income tax rates where dividend imputation is available.

29. China for example is the largest global investor in clean energy (mainly solar and wind). The 2005 Renewable Energy Law focused on lower income taxes, and other tax incentives for the sector.

References

Blundell-Wignall and Roulet (2015), "Infrastructure versus other investments in the global economy and stagnation hypotheses: What do company data tell us?", *OECD Journal: Financial Market Trends*. DOI: *http://dx.doi.org/10.1787/fmt-2014-5js4sbd025d6*

Christiansen, H. and Y. Kim (2014), "State-Invested Enterprises in the Global Marketplace: Implications for a Level Playing Field", *OECD Corporate Governance Working Papers*, No. 14, OECD Publishing, Paris. DOI: *http://dx.doi.org/10.1787/5jz0xvfvl6nw-en*

Lazonick, W. (2014), "Profits Without Prosperity", Harvard Business Review, September. *https://hbr.org/2014/09/profits-without-prosperity*

Lee, I.H., M. Syed and L. Xueyan (2012), "*Is China Over-Investing and Does it Matter?*", IMF, WP/12/277. *www.imf.org/external/pubs/ft/wp/2012/wp12277.pdf*

OECD (2013), G20/OECD High-Level Principles of Long-term Investment Financing by Institutional Investors, September. *www.oecd.org/finance/private-pensions/G20-OECD-Principles-LTI-Financing.pdf*

OECD (2014), *OECD Science, Technology and Industry Outlook 2014*, OECD Publishing, Paris. DOI: *http://dx.doi.org/10.1787/sti_outlook-2014-en*

OECD (2015), *Policy Guidance for Investment in Clean Energy Infrastructure: Expanding Access to Clean Energy for Green Growth and Development*, OECD Publishing, Paris. DOI: *http://dx.doi.org/10.1787/9789264212664-en*

OECD, WTO, (2011), "Trade in Value-added: Concepts, Methodologies and Challenges", *www.oecd.org/sti/ind/49894138.pdf, Paris.*

ANNEX 2.A1

Company data and sample description

Company data are based on the Bloomberg World Equity Index including 10130 listed companies in 76 countries operating in infrastructure, general industry and clean energy sectors over the period 2002-2014. 1327 (i.e., 847 in advanced economies and 480 in emerging economies) companies are operating in infrastructure sector, 8033 in general industry sector (i.e., 5 078 in advanced economies and 2 955 in emerging economies) and 770 in clean energy sector (i.e., 478 in advanced economies and 292 in emerging economies). Tables 2.A1.1 and 2.A1.2 present the number of companies by sector and by country.

The infrastructure sector definition is based on the MSCI Infrastructure Index sector classification; i.e., telecommunication infrastructure (3 sectors), utilities (4 sectors), energy infrastructure (1 sector), transportation infrastructure (3 sectors), and social infrastructure (2 sectors). Bloomberg sectors that match these are used because the number of companies covered is nearly double. A decision was made to add oil exploration and production and oil drilling, which are heavily capital intensive and not included in the MSCI definition. A few minor sectors (such as recycling and waste disposal) were also added.

Table 2.A1.1. **Distribution of companies by sector and country**

Advanced Economies	Infrastructure sector	General Industry sector (excl. Financials)	Clean Energy Sector	Emerging Economies	Infrastructure sector	General Industry sector (excl. Financials)	Clean Energy Sector
Australia	33	152	13	Argentina	2	13	0
Austria	4	31	3	Bahrain	1	1	0
Belgium	8	35	2	Bosnia and Herzegovina	2	27	0
United Kingdom	65	354	28	Brazil	32	129	12
Canada	59	224	28	Bulgaria	1	5	0
Cyprus*	3	4	0	Chile	14	38	3
Czech-Republic	3	5	0	China (People's Republic of)	142	1222	182
Denmark	10	35	4	Colombia	7	11	1
Estonia	1	1	0	Croatia	2	19	0
Finland	4	54	6	Egypt	5	48	0
France	35	173	11	Gabon	1	0	0
Germany	25	176	23	Hungary	1	3	0
Greece	13	41	2	India	47	209	29
Hong Kong, China	37	210	25	Indonesia	7	59	0
Ireland	2	30	1	Israel	7	71	1
Italy	22	82	9	Jordan	5	8	0
Japan	59	889	69	Kenya	1	2	1
Jersey	2	4	0	Kuwait	3	30	0
Lithuania	1	0	0	Laos	0	0	1
Luxembourg	2	12	1	FYR of Macedonia	2	6	0
Monaco	1	1	0	Malaysia	22	59	6
Netherlands	13	71	4	Mexico	12	59	0
New Zealand	12	13	6	Montenegro	1	1	0
Norway	23	31	4	Morocco	2	10	0
Portugal	6	14	0	Oman	1	4	0
Singapore	19	83	8	Pakistan	3	19	0
Slovenia	2	12	0	Peru	3	24	1
Spain	18	79	12	Philippines	12	31	4
Sweden	8	99	6	Poland	9	34	1
Switzerland	9	111	6	Qatar	6	10	0
Chinese Taipei	15	211	55	Romania	4	63	0
United States	333	1841	152	Russia	51	192	5
				Saudi Arabia	3	55	0
				Senegal	1	0	0
				Serbia	3	67	0
				South Africa	5	73	0
				Korea	19	160	30
				Sudan	1	0	0
				Thailand	18	71	8
				Turkey	5	51	5
				United Arab Emirates	5	18	1
				Ukraine	8	38	0
				Venezuela	1	1	0
				Viet Nam	3	14	1
TOTAL	**847**	**5078**	**478**	**TOTAL**	**480**	**2955**	**292**

1. Note by Turkey: The information in this document with reference to « Cyprus » relates to the southern part of the Island. There is no single authority representing both Turkish and Greek Cypriot people on the Island. Turkey recognises the Turkish Republic of Northern Cyprus (TRNC). Until a lasting and equitable solution is found within the context of the United Nations, Turkey shall preserve its position concerning the "Cyprus issue".

2. Note by all the European Union Member States of the OECD and the European Union: The Republic of Cyprus is recognised by all members of the United Nations with the exception of Turkey. The information in this document relates to the area under the effective control of the Government of the Republic of Cyprus.

Source: Bloomberg, OECD calculations.

StatLink http://dx.doi.org/10.1787/888933210333

Table 2.A1.2. **Distribution of companies by sub-sectors**

Infrastructure sector	Number of firms	General Industry sector (excl. Financials)	Number of firms	Clean Energy sector	Number of firms
Airport Development/Maintenance	26	Advertising	28	Aerospace/Defense	4
Cable/Satellite TV	28	Aerospace/Defense	55	Agriculture	15
Data Processing	16	Agriculture	58	Apparel	2
Electric-Distribution	28	Airlines	60	Auto Manufacturers	12
Electric-Generation	60	Apparel	145	Auto Parts&Equipment	16
Electric-Transmission	19	Auto Manufacturers	66	Building Materials	29
Energy-Alternate Sources	83	Auto Parts/Equipment	189	Chemicals	39
Environ Monitoring	2	Beverages	93	Coal	1
Gas-Distribution	59	Biotechnology	94	Commercial Services	10
Gas-Transportation	2	Building Materials	334	Computers	8
Hazardous Waste Disposal	10	Chemicals	339	Cosmetics/Personal Care	1
Independent Power Producer	14	Coal	79	Distribution/Wholesale	6
Internet Infrastructure Software	5	Commercial Services	327	Electric	102
Marine Services	7	Computers	128	Electrical Compo&Equip	104
Medical-Hospitals	29	Cosmetics/Personal Care	23	Electronics	47
Medical-Nursing Homes	6	Distribution/Wholesale	177	Energy-Alternate Sources	98
Non-Hazardous Waste Disposals	17	Electric	165	Engineering&Construction	32
Oil Exploration/Production	138	Electrical Components/ Equipements	194	Entertainment	1
Oil Refining/Marketing	49	Electronics	379	Environmental Control	20
Oil-Gas Drilling	15	Engineering/Construction	299	Food	13
Oil-Field Services	66	Entertainment	142	Forest Products&Paper	3
Pipelines	13	Environmental Control	30	Gas	3
Public Thoroughfares	50	Food	283	Hand/Machine Tools	6
Recycling	14	Food Service	18	Healthcare-Products	1
Research/Development	8	Forest Products/Paper	91	Home Builders	3
Retirement/Aged Care	3	Hand/Machine Tools	38	Home Furnishings	4
Satellite Telecom	3	Healthcare-Products	118	Household Products/Wares	1
Schools	30	Healthcare-Services	50	Machinery-Constr&Mining	1
Schools-Day Care	2	Holding Companies-Divers	40	Machinery-Diversified	37
Seismic Data Collection	5	Home Builders	74	Media	2
Stevedoring	1	Home Furnishings	99	Metal Fabricate/Hardware	12
Telecom Services	71	Household Products/Wares	27	Mining	13
Telecommunication Equip	33	Housewares	17	Miscellaneous Manufactur	23
Telephone-Integrated	66	Internet	142	Oil&Gas	4
Television	33	Iron/Steel	180	Packaging&Containers	1
Transport-Equipement/Leasing	7	Leisure Time	97	Pharmaceuticals	1
Transport-Marine	97	Lodging	97	Real Estate	2
Transport-Rail	42	Machinery-Construction/Mining	26	Retail	1
Transport-Services	62	Machinery-Diversified	269	Semiconductors	80
Water	30	Media	107	Shipbuilding	1
Water Treatment Systems	30	Metal Fabricate/Hardware	197	Software	3
Web Portals/ISP	17	Mining	263	Telecommunications	6
Whsing-Harbor Transport Services	31	Miscellaneous Manufacturing	117	Textiles	1
		Office Furnishings	12	Transportation	1
		Office/Business Equipement	11		
		Oil&Gas	88		
		Packaging/Containers	82		
		Pharmaceuticals	184		
		Real Estate	632		
		REITS	238		
		Retail	455		
		Semiconductors	121		

Table 2.A1.2. **Distribution of companies by sub-sectors** *(cont.)*

Infrastructure sector	Number of firms	General Industry sector (excl. Financials)	Number of firms	Clean Energy sector	Number of firms
		Shipbuilding	20		
		Software	132		
		Storage/Warehousing	24		
		Telecommunications	94		
		Textiles	155		
		Toys/Games/Hobbies	9		
		Transportation	22		
TOTAL	**1327**	**TOTAL**	**8033**	**TOTAL**	**770**

Source: Bloomberg, OECD calculations.

StatLink http://dx.doi.org/10.1787/888933210348

ANNEX 2.A2

Study of the determinants of corporate capital spending

Table 2.A2.1. **Modelling**

Cointegration equation
Dependent variable: Capital expenditures (% Net sales)

	Infrastructure	General Industry	Clean Energy
ROE	0.09 ***	0.02 *	0.10 **
	(3.71)	(1.69)	(2.12)
COE	0.04	-0.02 *	-0.09 **
	(1.57)	(-1.57)	(-2.21)
COD	-0.17 **	0.02	-0.15 **
	(-2.15)	(0.57)	(-2.31)
MCAP	0.01 ***	0.03 ***	0.02 ***
	(3.84)	(19.86)	(8.97)
VCIP	-0.04 ***	-0.002	-0.04 ***
	(-4.93)	(-0.41)	(-4.90)
CITR	-0.12 ***	-0.06 ***	-0.13 ***
	(-2.88)	(-4.98)	(-4.82)
TAX	0.04 ***	0.05 ***	0.19 ***
	(3.15)	(6.60)	(15.95)
C	0.12 ***	0.05 ***	0.03 **
	(6.22)	(9.30)	(2.01)
R^2	0.67	0.79	0.70
F-Stat	103.21	192.52	38.12
Prob(F)	0.00	0.00	0.00
Durbin-Watson stat	1.34	1.05	0.91
Total Obs.	462	472	327

Source: OECD calculations.

The variables are:

ROE (return on equity); COE (cost of equity); COD (the spread of AAA over the risk-free short rate which capture credit rating pressures); MCAP (market cap to GDP as an equity bullishness expected earnings variable); VCIP (measuring the openness of the banking sector, reported in Figure 2.17,and described in endnote 19);TAX (based on Figure 2.18, the % of countries in the region that offer tax holidays & exemptions); and CITR (the corporate tax rate of the host country). The error-correction model based on the Engle 2-step process establishes co-integration, and this dynamic model is used in the projections.

The regressions are run on a global panel of 50 countries for the years 2002 to 2013. Individual company data for the main variables in millions of US dollars are aggregated by country for some 10 000 non-financial companies (Blundell-Wignall, A. and

C. Roulet (2014)). The model postulates that capital spending grows in line with sales (the accelerator type mechanism) but will be shifted from this trajectory by variations in the explanatory variables.

ROE, COE, COD & MCAP

These market-based returns and cost of funding variables suggest a powerful influence of returns in infrastructure and clean energy—if more investment in infrastructure is required bankable return need to be there. For general industry ROE matters too but with a lower elasticity, while the market valuation measure is 3-times more important than is the case for infrastructure and clean energy. The cost of equity matters more for general industry and much more for clean energy, while the debt variable is more important for infrastructure. For the clean energy sector the COE and the ROE are of equal and opposite sign suggesting a very powerful influence of both factors.

International openness restrictions

This appears to be extremely important for infrastructure and clean energy. For general industry the restrictions term is not supported by the data, reflecting the greater involvement of these companies in global value chains and not only in their country of origin.

The tax effect

Global multinational companies appear to be very motivated by taxation. The 2 variables are highly significant. The size of the effect for tax holidays and exemptions for infrastructure and clean energy is virtually double that for general industry. Encouraging infrastructure would appear very much to be a tax issue. The tax rate variables too are very significant in all sectors. However, for clean energy, tax rates are around 4-times more powerful than in infrastructure and general industry sectors.

ANNEXE 2.A3

Statistical tables and supplementary data

Table 2.A3.1. **Investment statement indicators (advanced economies)**

	USD billion												
	2002	2003	2004	2005	2006	2007	2008	2009	2010	2011	2012	2013	2014
General Industry													
Capital Expenditure	834	919	1064	1200	1359	1555	1633	1295	1364	1605	1699	1760	1736
Operating Cash Flow	1392	1676	1922	2038	2236	2471	2357	2652	2693	2675	2688	2952	3005
Dividend & Buybacks	269	290	423	602	750	929	858	422	660	862	841	1066	1301
Net Borrowing	-35	-104	-63	172	458	905	832	-67	-82	297	500	316	502
Net Asset Purchase	-203	-165	-227	-296	-597	-874	-704	-502	-581	-825	-782	-257	-397
Other assets (incl. Cash)	51	199	144	112	-12	18	-6	367	5	-320	-135	186	73
ROE (%)	5.5	9.0	12.6	14.3	14.7	13.7	6.9	8.8	12.2	12.0	10.5	11.6	12.7
COE (%)	10.2	9.7	10.2	10.7	10.8	11.3	12.7	9.9	10.7	11.6	11.2	11.4	12.1
Infrastructure													
Capital Expenditure	250	283	319	377	469	554	625	512	543	618	626	634	673
Operating Cash Flow	344	460	536	587	641	729	793	731	767	820	791	829	832
Dividend & Buybacks	28	55	85	104	156	179	188	108	133	197	180	205	202
Net Borrowing	-42	-76	-30	23	204	161	183	70	31	116	155	133	112
Net Asset Purchase	9	-28	-17	-28	-56	-38	-43	-82	-65	-71	-28	-57	-98
Other assets (incl. Cash)	31	18	85	101	164	119	121	99	56	49	113	67	-29
ROE (%)	1.3	7.8	10.0	13.2	13.0	14.0	9.4	8.5	11.8	10.5	9.6	11.4	10.2
COE (%)	9.4	9.8	10.3	10.5	11.1	11.1	13.3	10.5	10.8	12.4	11.8	11.5	11.5
Clean Energy													
Capital Expenditure	67	77	93	103	116	127	164	137	138	157	154	139	139
Operating Cash Flow	99	102	125	124	138	179	171	209	201	198	199	221	210
Dividend & Buybacks	8	6	13	21	31	32	59	22	16	43	35	42	74
Net Borrowing	-11	-12	-2	15	56	48	80	-3	27	33	67	14	33
Net Asset Purchase	4	5	-3	8	-45	-49	-10	-11	-33	-34	-72	-23	-21
Other assets (incl. Cash)	16	13	14	23	3	18	19	36	41	-3	5	31	9
ROE (%)	3.3	8.3	11.9	12.3	13.8	13.1	7.5	5.7	10.5	6.3	4.3	6.5	9.6
COE (%)	9.6	8.7	9.3	9.7	10.1	9.8	13.0	9.6	9.1	11.0	10.4	10.3	12.0

Source: Bloomberg, OECD calculations.

StatLink http://dx.doi.org/10.1787/888933210352

Table 2.A3.2. **Investment statement indicators (emerging economies)**

	USD billion												
	2002	2003	2004	2005	2006	2007	2008	2009	2010	2011	2012	2013	2014
	General Industry												
Capital Expenditure	164	214	283	383	501	679	850	757	896	1146	1129	1226	1087
Operating Cash Flow	182	257	354	428	529	680	682	736	825	871	956	1387	1312
Dividend & Buybacks	29	44	97	99	154	227	171	84	152	303	301	265	272
Net Borrowing	4	16	88	107	179	378	361	222	207	459	384	503	325
Net Asset Purchase	-31	-42	-99	-152	-172	-332	-195	-167	-150	-211	-206	-316	-160
Other assets (incl. Cash)	-38	-28	-36	-98	-120	-180	-173	-51	-166	-329	-297	84	119
ROE (%)	8.7	13.6	15.8	17.6	18.5	17.1	15.1	12.3	14.5	15.1	12.5	11.2	10.2
COE (%)	15.3	14.9	15.1	14.7	15.1	15.2	16.2	14.0	14.6	16.5	16.3	16.0	16.1
	Infrastructure												
Capital Expenditure	39	64	81	109	141	172	216	194	209	223	220	247	230
Operating Cash Flow	69	94	122	137	161	175	194	184	234	232	249	289	274
Dividend & Buybacks	8	12	12	17	17	-4	36	33	38	51	41	53	48
Net Borrowing	-7	12	18	32	52	71	131	90	81	96	66	50	41
Net Asset Purchase	-2	-15	-27	-34	-41	-55	-54	-19	-45	-49	-54	-46	-41
Other assets (incl. Cash)	13	16	19	8	14	23	19	29	23	6	0	-7	-3
ROE (%)	9.2	13.9	16.9	16.2	16.2	15.8	11.7	9.5	12.0	11.7	9.5	9.0	7.9
COE (%)	15.8	15.0	14.6	14.6	14.3	13.0	16.1	15.1	15.1	16.2	15.6	16.3	16.0
	Clean Energy												
Capital Expenditure	4	8	13	16	23	33	49	49	64	71	61	58	52
Operating Cash Flow	8	10	11	11	17	21	28	36	36	24	36	46	38
Dividend & Buybacks	1	-1	-2	-1	-1	-4	-1	-3	0	5	6	4	3
Net Borrowing	0	0	5	6	11	19	29	24	33	54	34	23	23
Net Asset Purchase	0	-1	-1	-1	4	-1	0	4	1	-3	-4	-4	1
Other assets (incl. Cash)	2	3	3	1	9	10	8	18	7	0	-2	4	7
ROE (%)	4.8	5.2	6.7	6.4	7.9	7.0	10.0	8.5	10.3	8.3	3.1	2.2	4.7
COE (%)	15.4	11.8	11.6	12.6	12.8	12.3	12.9	12.5	13.1	14.3	14.9	14.1	13.9

Source: Bloomberg, OECD calculations.

StatLink http://dx.doi.org/10.1787/888933210367

Table 2.A3.3. **Non-financial companies productivity concepts**

	Ratios												
	2002	2003	2004	2005	2006	2007	2008	2009	2010	2011	2012	2013	2014
	General Industry												
Net Sales p/capita													
Advanced Economies	0.26	0.28	0.30	0.31	0.33	0.35	0.38	0.34	0.36	0.37	0.37	0.37	0.36
EMEs	0.12	0.11	0.14	0.17	0.20	0.23	0.28	0.24	0.30	0.35	0.36	0.39	0.37
Value-Added p/capita													
Advanced Economies	0.11	0.11	0.12	0.11	0.11	0.12	0.12	0.12	0.13	0.13	0.13	0.12	0.12
EMEs	0.03	0.03	0.04	0.05	0.06	0.06	0.07	0.06	0.07	0.08	0.08	0.08	0.08
	Infrastructure												
Net Sales p/capita													
Advanced Economies	0.28	0.31	0.34	0.37	0.39	0.45	0.49	0.42	0.46	0.49	0.51	0.47	0.46
EMEs	0.19	0.18	0.20	0.25	0.28	0.32	0.35	0.34	0.40	0.46	0.47	0.54	0.53
Value-Added p/capita													
Advanced Economies	0.16	0.17	0.18	0.18	0.18	0.20	0.21	0.20	0.22	0.22	0.23	0.21	0.21
EMEs	0.06	0.06	0.06	0.07	0.08	0.09	0.09	0.09	0.10	0.11	0.11	0.12	0.12

Source: Bloomberg, OECD calculations.

StatLink http://dx.doi.org/10.1787/888933210371

OECD Business and Finance Outlook 2015

Chapter 3

Shifting risks and the search for yield in financial markets

Policies and regulatory responses to crises tend to roll financial excesses into other sectors or regions. This chapter argues that the response to the 2008 crisis has rolled the risk into the shadow banking and corporate bond sectors. Shadow banks intermediate credit between cash-rich and cash-poor investors in their bid to reuse securities and to gain access directly or synthetically to higher-yield and lower-risk alternative products in a world of low interest rates and rising longevity risk. At the root of the problem are a number of implicit promises that have been made to investors that are unlikely to be met in the absence of structural change and better regulation.

Main findings

- The global financial system is evolving in a way that means certain 'promises' about long-term value creation, pension replacement rates and the safety of the financial system may not in fact be met.
- The rising size of the emerging market 'dollar bloc' and its integration into global supply chains is contributing to low inflation and low interest rates. There are signs that restrictions on cross-border flows are rising again. Over-investment and inefficiencies in parts of the global value chains are at the same time undermining the fundamental longer-term value in equities and bonds.
- Over the next five years pension funds are expected to grow 26% from an estimated USD 28.4 trillion in 2014 to USD 35.8 trillion in 2019; insurance companies 33% from an estimated USD 28.2 trillion in 2014 to USD 37.7 trillion in 2019; and mutual funds 38% from an estimated USD 33.4 trillion in 2014 to USD 46.1 trillion in 2019. These funds are naturally cash-short and securities-long—but the need for new products that improve yields has incentivised them to try to 'unlock' liquidity to obtain cash to manage margins and collateral needs associated with complex products and to reuse their securities by lending them.
- This occurs at a time when banks are being more constrained via regulation and higher costs are associated with counterparty transactions. The balance of financial system risk is shifting away from regular insured deposit banking towards shadow banking (the intermediation of credit for cash poor institutional investors via broker dealers and custody banks).
- At the same time, company borrowing is shifting away from banks towards non-bank bond issuance in the capital markets. The competition amongst lenders is so strong in the high-yield segment that less covenant protection is being traded for higher yields. This is a form of liquidity illusion (more yield now while illiquidity issues will be apparent only later).
- The competition amongst institutional investors for yield products is so strong that the shadow banking system is also facilitating new complex products that promise: higher yield with lower volatility; or synthetic exposure to underlying illiquid securities but with daily liquidity—another form of liquidity illusion.

Introduction

A long sequence of manias resulting in crises has characterised the history of financial policies, both in advanced countries and in emerging markets. Each time the monetary policy, fiscal and/or regulatory responses deemed necessary to soften the impact on society have revitalised financial sector confidence and served to 'roll' the bubble into some new sector or region later on. Some of these 'rolling bubbles' are set out in brief in Box 3.1. This chapter considers the outlook in terms of the risks associated with where the rolling bubble has been pushed since the 2008 financial crisis.

The global financial crisis has resulted in historically unprecedented low short-term interest rates and deflation pressure emanating from the emerging market economy global supply shock. This, together with unconventional quantitative easing (QE), at first was used to support banks when liquidity dried up during the crisis. QE policies have now rotated from the United States (where rates will remain historically low) to Europe and Japan, and emerging market economies (EMEs) are also cutting interest rates and are using exchange rate intervention policy to help keep exchange rates low. Low interest rates can persist for a very long time following a global crisis (see Figure 3.1). Pension funds often aim for a real return of 4% per annum which, for a 2% inflation target, would imply the need to obtain yields of 6% or higher in order to meet future liabilities. In fact United States bond yields above 4% in real terms have occurred on average in only 25 of the past 114 years. From 1933 (when the United States went off gold) real bond yields were below 4% in all but one of the next 42 years and rose above it only temporarily in the Volcker-disinflation 1980s. Low real yields at present may also last for a very long time.

Figure 3.1. **Low interest rates could persist for a long time**

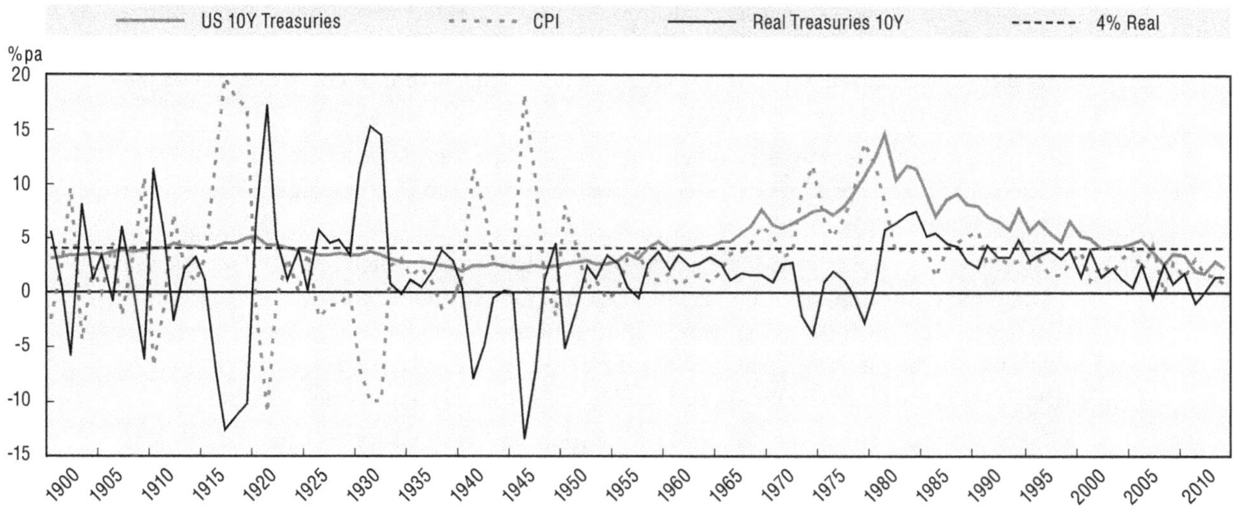

Source: Datastream, Shiller, OECD calculations.

StatLink http://dx.doi.org/10.1787/888933209362

These policy responses and low interest rates in the face of the current global supply shock have resulted in a strange situation: financial investors see very little risk and are buying into the post-crisis equity recovery and are moving into higher-yield corporate bonds and alternative products; the company sector on the other hand appears to see much more risk and is not investing in innovations, social infrastructure and growth on a scale that will justify the market optimism in the long run. Investment and productivity growth in the private sector is stagnating (see Chapter 2).

Promises to meet future liabilities risk being broken

In many ways, the current building up of risk in financial markets may be traced to three interrelated promises that may be inconsistent with each other:

1. *Corporate borrowing and investment associated with the inclusion of EMEs into global supply chains on an unprecedented scale*: the promise here is that corporate bonds and equities will be underpinned by investment that pays off as a better balance between investment- and consumption-led growth emerges between EMEs and advanced countries.

2. *Pension fund and insurance company liabilities*: the promise here is that pension fund replacement rates and insurance company annuity products will meet client expectations for future income in the face of rising longevity risk and very low interest rates.
3. *Insured deposit bank versus shadow bank risk*: here the promise is that regulatory reform has solved financial system risk and taxpayers will not again have to face the socialisation of losses on a major scale.

Box 3.1. **The rolling bubbles and busts from the mid-1990s**

Most crises occur because excessive exuberance leads to over-investment of some form that is incentivised by regulatory, governance and tax distortions that are accommodated for too long by easy monetary policy. The assumptions built into asset prices become unrealistic. Belated attempts to rein in the market excesses (or some extraneous shock) trigger a collapse that leads to an easing of policy to prevent financial contagion and the story repeats itself, often rolling the problem into some other market.

- The Asian 'tigers' were an economic miracle that justified investment and lending without a proper understanding of the governance of the whole process and the distorting policies upon which it was based. Policy in the advanced countries was eased to allay liquidity concerns.
- This easing coincided with technological leaps associated with telecommunications and the internet and talk of a 'new economy'. The tech boom and bust was again followed by easy monetary policy.
- At the same time, policy in EMEs to stimulate development through financial repression and exchange rate management created strong (though inefficient) state-investment-driven growth. The term 'BRIC' was coined and asset allocations to these countries increased. Stock markets soared and resource producing countries and commodity prices were drawn into the boom. Terms like 'the resource super-cycle' were coined.
- The global supply shock resulted in low inflation and easy policy to stem the job loss in advanced countries due to the shifting of gravity of world economic activity to EMEs (see Chapter 2). Financial deregulation and easy policy contributed to the banking, derivatives and structured products boom. Leverage rose (aided by the new fee-for-sale approach to mortgage loans), lending volumes soared and housing in various parts of the world became a new phase of over-investment. Counterparty risk rose and the failure to meet collateral calls for derivatives and structured products was the very essence of the banking crisis that followed. Central banks had little choice but to lower rates and provide the missing liquidity through quantitative easing (QE).
- Europe too was an integral part of the tech boom and bust and the financial sector expansion that followed—but superimposed on this was the euro crisis. The one-size-fits all monetary policy over a group of countries whose structures are very different and affected asymmetrically by the pressures of globalisation is economically problematic.

Japan is the classic case of a country that over-invested and borrowed too much in its boom years. The country's problems were amplified by poor corporate governance structures and it did not deal with bad debt problems in its banking system from the outset. Japan has been in stagnation for a couple of decades.

This chapter analyses the financial market outlook in the context of the consistency or otherwise of these three 'promises'.

Problems in the international monetary system

There are a number of views as to why the international financial system swings from crisis to crisis. One held by the former chairman of the Federal Reserve Ben Bernanke is that EMEs have excess savings (a 'glut' in China, other Asian countries, and OPEC when oil prices are high) which flow to the United States. Their accumulation of foreign exchange reserves also flows into United States Treasury securities given the reserve currency status of the dollar. These inflows were managed poorly by investors, the financial sector and the authorities, resulting in unwise financial product innovation to meet the demand (Bernanke et al., 2009). A related view is that emerging markets don't produce enough safe assets and they seek to accumulate reserve currency assets (mainly United States Treasury securities), which drives down yields. Since safe asset prices can't rise enough (due to the zero rate bound), the flows lead to the manufacture of new alternative assets, the risks of which are under-priced (Caballero and Krishnamurthy, 2009). Still another view is that perceptions of risk in markets are loosely anchored to fundamentals and policy: they are pro-cyclical, and are associated with excessive capital flows and overshooting (White, 2012; Borio, 2014; among others).

While there is truth in all of these views, the OECD Secretariat has focused on the growth of global value chains (supported by tax exemptions in EMEs and labour cost considerations) which, when combined with financial repression policies in EMEs, generated a global supply shock characterised by weakening returns (Chapter 2). Advanced-country profits benefitted, but operational cash flow is often kept offshore and/or given back to shareholders in dividends and buybacks. The problem is less of a savings glut in a traditional balance of payments sense, and more of an issue of over-investment in EMEs: which may occur just as easily in balance of surplus countries like China as in deficit countries like India.[1] 'Over-investment' instead refers to declining value creation possibilities (return-on-equity versus the cost-of-equity). Savings and investment are highly correlated in countries that inhibit cross-border flows and which manage their exchange rates. Less efficient EME investment is drawn into global value chains, while at the same time advanced country investment in operational change in the global economy does not substitute for productivity-enhancing investment. Globally, the underlying 'fundamental' for bonds and equities is being undermined.

Global value chains result in two-way flow between advanced and emerging countries—foreign direct investment and merger and acquisition flows from each to the other (see Chapter 6)—and the impact of inflows on the exchange rate is resisted in many EMEs by foreign exchange intervention, the proceeds of which are re-invested in safe reserve currency assets (mainly United States Treasury securities). Problems in international finance arise not because of flexible exchange rates but, on the contrary, they are caused in part by the inflexibility of a large bloc of currencies versus the dollar in the face of global structural change. This pushes flows and pressures onto exchange rates that do float more freely and onto other asset prices, both of which will evolve very differently to what would occur in a more consistent global financial system. Two very different approaches to economic management are 'butting up' against each other.

The size of the changing shape of the world's top-fifty countries is illustrated in Figure 3.2. In 1980 the economies in the OECD group were around 58% of the world and the BRICS and other EMEs were 42%. By 2014 these shares were almost exactly reversed. These diverging trends are projected to continue. At the same time the expansion of global supply chains discussed in Chapter 2 has shifted the centre of gravity for investment towards EMEs and resulted in more contestable traded goods markets in advanced countries and downward pressure on wages in the affected sectors. Development in EMEs has been facilitated by harnessing national saving and investment, often with a prominent role for state-owned banks, controls on cross-border flows, interest rate ceilings, statutory reserve requirements, ownership restrictions, and the like. This permits governments to bottle up savings, which are often intermediated through state-owned banks, to achieve high levels of investment (see for example the case of China versus the United States in Figure 3.3). This heavy investment in emerging markets more generally contributes to driving down the returns on equity and inhibiting growth (see Huang and Wang, 2010) as illustrated in Chapter 2.[2]

Figure 3.2. **Emerging economies versus Europe, Japan, United States, Canada and Australia**

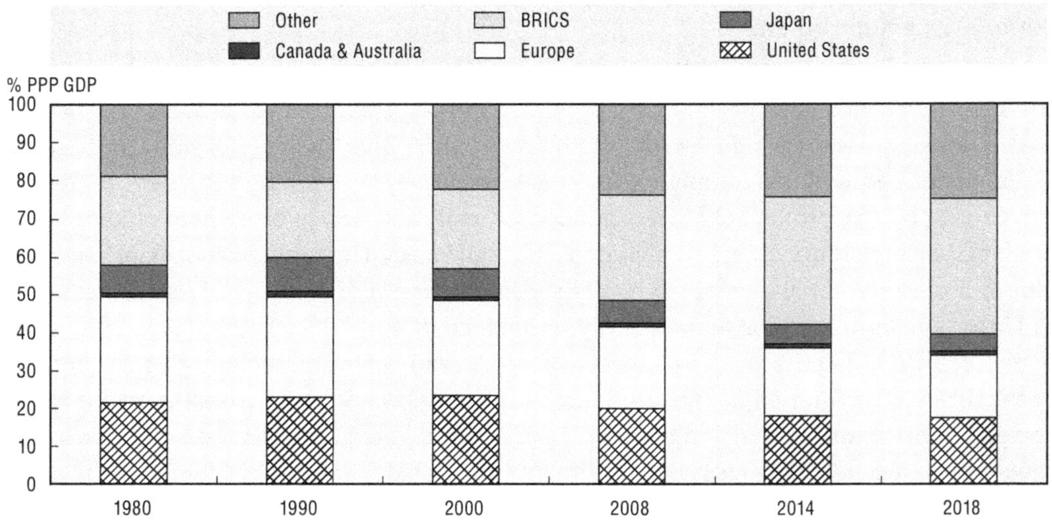

Note: 'Other' includes the following countries: Algeria; Argentina; Chile; Colombia; Egypt; Hong Kong, China; Indonesia; Iraq; Islamic Republic of Iran; Israel; Kazakhstan; Korea; Malaysia; Mexico; Nigeria; Pakistan; Philippines; Saudi Arabia; Singapore; Sweden; Chinese Taipei; Thailand; Turkey; United Arab Emirates and Venezuela. 'Europe' is European Union 15 and Switzerland. Data for Russia in 1980 and 1990 is taken from Angus Maddison.

Source: IMF World Economic Outlook Database, *http://www.imf.org/external/pubs/ft/weo/2015/01/weodata/index.aspx%20 www.imf.org/external/pubs/ft/weo/2015/01/weodata/index.aspx* OECD calculations.

StatLink http://dx.doi.org/10.1787/888933209374

Exchange rate management distorts exchange rates and interest rates

The extent of exchange market intervention versus the dollar is illustrated in Figure 3.4. This shows the vast holdings of US Treasury securities by non-US countries (mainly governments) which greatly exceed the Federal Reserve's own holdings bought as a part of its QE program (also shown). These holdings in large part reflect the selling of dollar bloc currencies to achieve a weaker exchange rate than that to which a free market would give rise, supported by a variety of controls on cross-border flows.

Figure 3.3. **Financial repression: China versus United States national savings and investment**

Source: OECD Quarterly National Accounts Database, *www.oecd-ilibrary.org/economics/data/oecd-national-accounts-statistics_na-data-en.*

StatLink http://dx.doi.org/10.1787/888933209380

Figure 3.4. **Foreign holdings of United States Treasury securities compared to the United States Federal Reserve holdings**

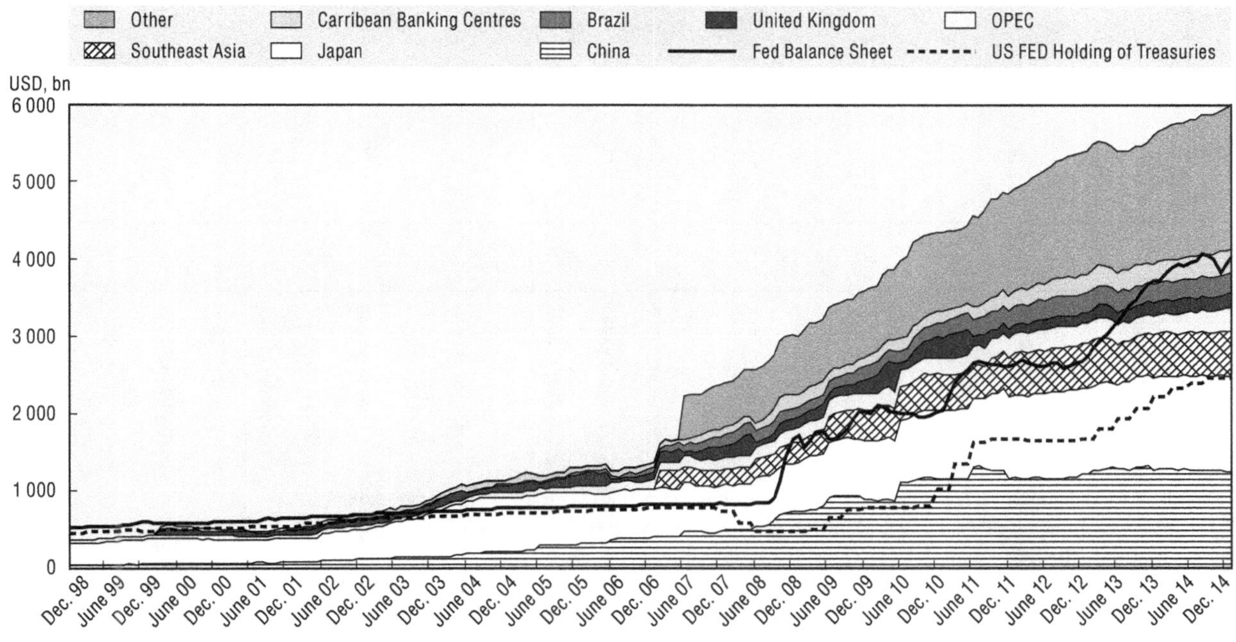

Source: Datastream, OECD calculations.

StatLink http://dx.doi.org/10.1787/888933209390

The foreign buying of United States Treasury securities has forced down Treasury yields and encouraged growth in the non-traded goods sector, and notably in finance and housing sectors. These developments began to interact with financial innovations in ways that became dangerous for the financial system in the lead up to the crisis. Foreign buying of United States Treasury securities, along with the Federal Reserve's QE operations, is estimated to have reduced the 10-year Treasury yield by some 350 basis points compared to what otherwise would have been the case given low short rates (Blundell-Wignall and Roulet, 2014; references therein). Since the crisis this downward pressure on interest rates around the world has pressured institutional investors to buy higher-yielding corporate bonds of lower quality—a topic taken up below.

Signs that controls on cross-border flows are rising again

A high correlation between national saving and investment (S-I) is a measure of openness: just as the saving in a state or province of a country is not expected to finance the investment in that state, so it should also be the case between countries with open capital markets (Feldstein and Horioka, 1980; Feldstein and Bacchetta, 1991; Helliwell and McKitrick, 1999).

These S-I correlations are shown in Figure 3.5 for four groups of countries classified according to their openness and also the liquidity of their markets.

Figure 3.5. **Five-year rolling savings-investment correlations**

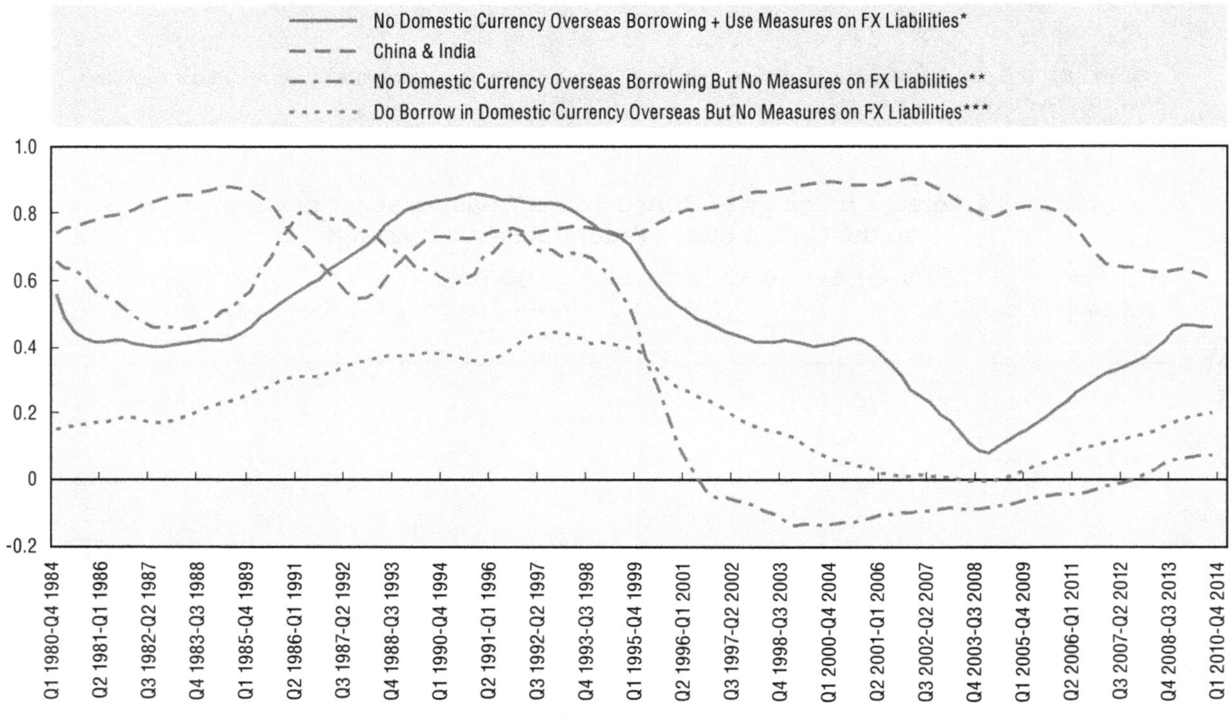

* Korea, Argentina, Russia, Chile, Mexico, Brazil, Iceland, Thailand, Columbia, Peru.

** Estonia, Poland, Hungary, Israel, Denmark, Sweden Norway, Czech R., Australia, Philippines, Malaysia.

*** United States, Japan, Canada, United Kingdom, most of Europe, South Africa, Saudi Arabia.

Source: OECD calculations.

StatLink http://dx.doi.org/10.1787/888933209406

The interface between financial policies in emerging and advanced economies since the crisis has led to new sets of issues and risks for financial markets. Not only are countries managing their exchange rates to improve their net export position versus other countries (which cannot work for everyone since net exports globally sum to zero), but the use of restrictions on cross-border flows is picking up in emerging countries that had previously moved in the direction of more openness—just as China has actually been moving steadily towards introducing a sequencing of flexibility measures[3]. These policies risk a re-emergence of external imbalance problems, and contrast with the need for more widespread domestic-demand-driven growth in the global economy and deeper and more liquid financial systems.

Post-crisis regulatory change: safer banks or enormous policy support?

The aggregate assets of banks in OECD countries are shown in the left column of Table 3.1. A large sample of listed banks monitored by the OECD Secretariat is shown along with their asset composition in the middle section of the table. In contrast to the stable growth in pension and insurance company's assets prior to the crisis, bank assets accelerated sharply, driven mainly by trading assets, derivatives and loans. As the crisis hit, counterparty risk and margin-call pressures became the primary catalyst and promulgator of the crisis globally:

- Repo trading extended into less liquid mortgage and asset-backed securities, and during the crisis the haircuts to these transactions rose sharply, leading to a vast shortage of cash collateral.
- Lenders were forced to recall cash from all global locations, forcing counterparties to sell assets. A sort of global ring-fencing followed as affiliates abroad were forced to provide funding to parents.
- The general rise in price volatility led to huge cash margin calls on derivative positions.

These were the main reasons why the United States and the United Kingdom central banks, in the first instance, had to pump so much cash liquidity into the system—to prevent a collapse of the financial system via the drying up of liquidity.

The decline in banks assets (loans, trading assets and derivatives) since the crisis is due both to security losses and to deleveraging related to Basel III and new trading book rules (see below).

Table 3.1. **Banks and broker-dealer total assets (USD billion)**

Year	Banks*	*Of which*						Broker Dealers
		OECD Listed Banks	*Of which*					
			Cash & Interbank Assets	*Trading Assets & Derivatives*	*Loans*	*Other*		
2002	47,702	-	-	-	-	-		3,239
2003	56,682	-	-	-	-	-		3,898
2004	64,495	-	-	-	-	-		4,678
2005	63,746	42,797	4,404	18,486	17,261	2,646		5,154
2006	75,149	51,965	4,997	22,983	20,770	3,215		5,861
2007	91,779	64,967	6,473	27,379	25,892	5,224		6,746
2008	94,212	72,318	5,815	30,074	27,481	8,947		9,201
2009	96,793	70,787	6,240	28,455	28,426	7,666		7,934
2010	98,235	71,884	6,583	28,448	28,813	8,040		8,669
2011	100,915	75,564	7,270	30,037	29,320	8,937		9,130
2012	100,857	74,788	8,010	29,170	29,346	8,262		9,450
2013	97,463	70,919	8,457	26,304	29,520	6,639		9,299
2014	90,875	69,438	8,249	26,266	27,981	6,943		9,040**

* Including the following countries: United States, Turkey, Switzerland, Sweden, Spain, Korea, Slovakia, Portugal, Poland, Norway, Netherlands, Mexico, Luxembourg, Japan, Italy, Israel, Ireland, Hungary, Greece, Germany, France, Finland, Denmark, Czech Republic, Chile, Canada, United Kingdom, Belgium, Austria, and Australia.
** OECD estimate.

Source: National central banks, Bloomberg; Financial Stability Board, OECD calculations.

StatLink http://dx.doi.org/10.1787/888933210381

Banks have become measurably safer

Large Global banks appear to have become safer in the last year. The OECD Secretariat uses the distance-to-default calculation to monitor the safety of banks in the global economy.[4] Figure 3.6 shows listed banks in Bloomberg large regional banking competitive peer indices from the United States, Europe, Asia and Latin America, each identified by a number for confidentiality reasons. The bars show the most recent position. The pale grey bars show the globally systemically important banks (GSIB) as defined by the Financial Stability Board (FSB, 2014). The black-filled triangles show the average position in the 2008 crisis year, and the empty triangles show the position one year ago in 2013. Numbers above 3-standard deviation are a minimum level of safety.[5]

Figure 3.6. **Bank distance-to-default: United States, Europe, Latin America and Asia**

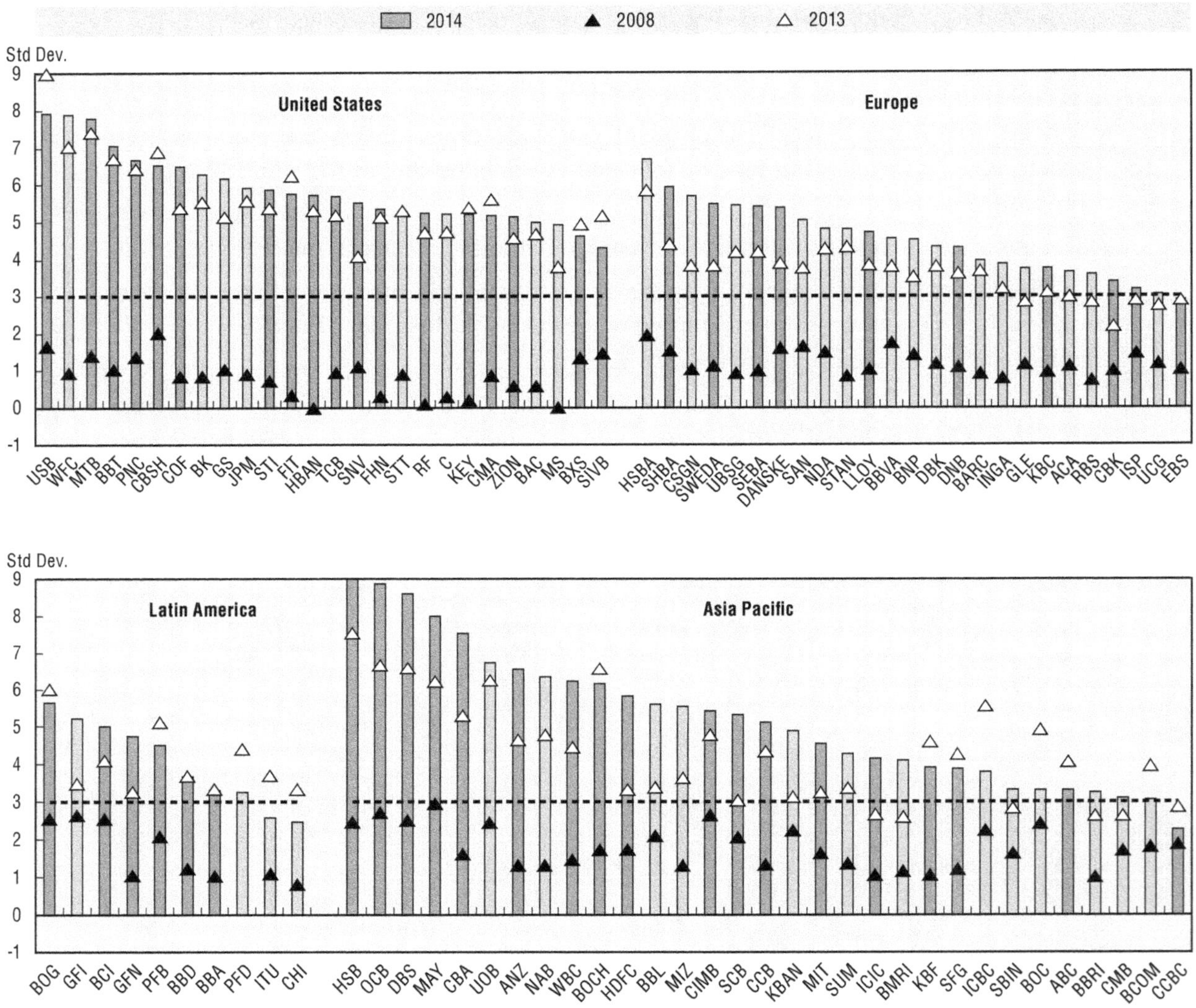

Note: This figure include all listed banks in Bloomberg large regional banking competitive peers indices from the United States, Europe, Asia and Latin America. GSIBs defined by the FSB (2014) are highlighted in grey.

The distance-to-default indicator is the number of standard deviations away from the default point. To derive the measure, it is assumed that a bank defaults (or is bankrupt) when the market value of assets equals (or is lower) than the book value of debt. The formula to calculate the distance-to-default is derived from the option pricing model of Black and Scholes (1973).

Source: Bloomberg, OECD calculations.

StatLink http://dx.doi.org/10.1787/888933209419

But banks remain very interdependent suggesting reform has not gone far enough

There is little doubt that the very strong recovery in bank safety is based on the historically unprecedented policies that have been undertaken, and it is unknowable how the distance-to-default would respond to a full monetary policy normalisation in all countries today.

Figure 3.7 shows the OECD Secretariat tool to monitor the progress of reform as it concerns reducing counterparty interdependence risk. It consists of the asset-weighted correlation of each GSIB's stock price to the regional MSCI.[6] A correlation less than 1.0 would be associated with safer less connected banks in the face of the asset price cycle. The Betas rose in an extreme and correlated way during the first phase of the crisis and did so just as easily again in the 2011-12 euro crisis. In 2014 they are not very different to what they were just prior to the crisis. This suggests that the way banks are evolving in response to regulatory reform is not to exit counterparty risk but to shift it into shadow banking affiliates with whom they are linked. Shadow banking system refers simply to credit intermediation involving entities and activities (fully or partially) outside the regular banking system.

Figure 3.7. **Measuring bank interconnectedness (The Global Bank Beta)**

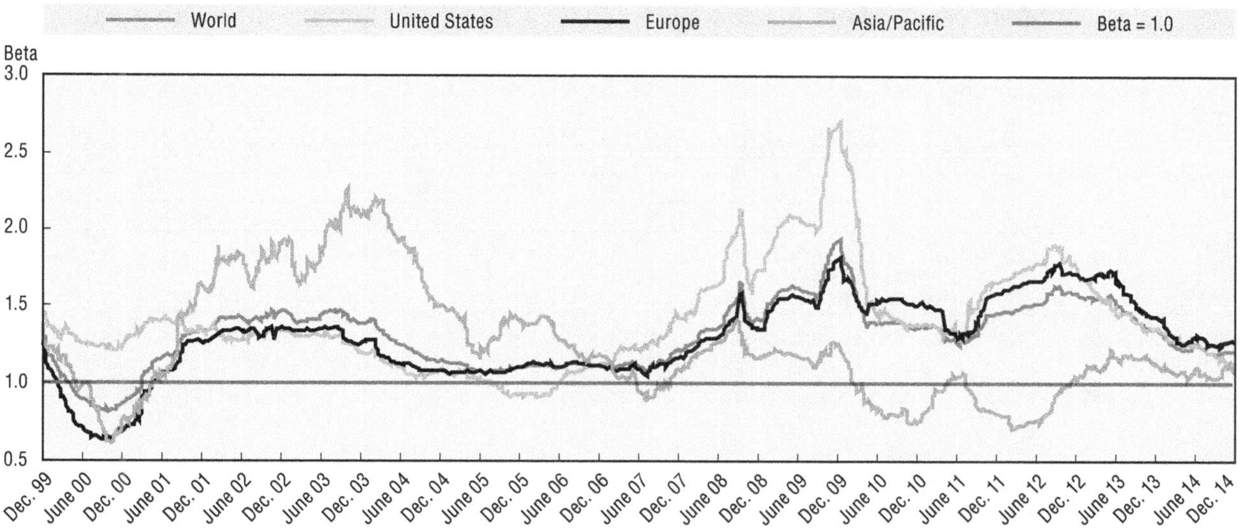

Global Bank Beta is a measure of the correlation of volatility, or systematic risk, of the GSIB's stock in comparison to the market as a whole (the regional index). Beta is used in the capital asset pricing model (CAPM), a model that calculates the expected return of an asset based on its beta and expected market returns.

StatLink http://dx.doi.org/10.1787/888933209428

Post-crisis regulatory change: shadow banking to the fore

The intermediation of credit outside of regular banking really involves the interplay between institutions that are naturally short of cash and need to borrow it to achieve their objectives and those that are long cash and require greater exposure to securities. Between these sit the broker-dealers (which carry out prime brokerage activities) and custody banks (which provide custody and collateral management services). These are not a part of regular banking, but carry out credit intermediation.

Prime Broking: securities borrowing/lending acting as principal; synthetic lending (products based on derivatives including exchange-traded funds that synthetically create equivalent exposures to underlying securities performance); and derivatives clearing. These activities are intermediated with repo transaction funding activities.

Custody and collateral management: which includes lending agent activities for securities held in custody and derivatives collateral management activities.

The following sections look first at institutional investors which are typically cash short in the new regulatory environment. It then examines the products these investors seek in the low interest rate and changed regulatory environment. Subsequently, the way in which these trends interact with shadow banking to shift the location of financial system risk is explored.

Asset owner growth and portfolio allocations

The size of the pension fund and insurance industry as measured by the OECD is shown in Table 3.2. Pension and insurance fund growth was strong prior to the crisis, dropped in 2008, and subsequently recovered as equity and bond markets both rallied together. By 2014 the pension and insurance fund totals were similar, at just over USD 28 trillion. The investment fund industry shown on the right of the table is over USD 43 trillion, made up of USD 33 trillion mutual funds, USD 3.7 trillion private equity, USD 2.8 trillion exchange traded funds (ETFs), USD 2.5 trillion hedge funds, USD 0.5 trillion in the (declining) fund-of-funds industry and a smaller amount in Commodity Trading Advisor funds (CTAs)[7]. It is not possible to add pension fund, insurance company and investment funds together, however, since the main clients of the latter are the institutional investors, and this would involve significant double counting.

Table 3.2. **The size of the institutional investor universe: asset owners (USD billion)**

Year	Pension Funds	Insurance Companies	Investment Funds										
				Of which				Mainly Private Funds					
			Mutual Funds (Regulated)	*Equity*	*Bond & Money Market*	*Loans*	*Other*	Private Equity Funds	ETF's & ETP's	Hedge Funds	Fund of Funds	CTA	TOTAL
2000	12,096	10,846	10,856	4,828	4,151	1,466	411	716	79	237	109	38	12,034
2001	12,233	10,498	10,600	4,322	4,636	1,268	375	751	109	322	155	41	11,978
2002	12,551	11,768	10,775	3,604	5,178	1,562	431	767	146	505	204	51	12,449
2003	14,523	15,354	13,137	5,174	5,557	1,859	547	866	218	826	358	87	15,491
2004	16,276	17,416	15,120	6,339	6,022	2,046	713	958	319	1,229	629	132	18,387
2005	17,334	17,426	16,731	7,493	6,165	2,206	867	1,234	426	1,361	754	131	20,636
2006	19,389	20,222	20,181	9,399	7,381	2,339	1,062	1,694	603	1,713	948	170	25,309
2007	20,947	22,129	23,400	10,662	8,843	2,662	1,232	2,264	857	2,137	1,192	207	30,056
2008	18,580	20,200	20,595	6,448	10,163	2,515	1,469	2,270	774	1,458	747	206	26,050
2009	21,080	22,165	23,961	9,117	10,835	2,429	1,580	2,470	1,158	1,554	556	214	29,913
2010	23,392	23,333	25,661	10,514	10,847	2,481	1,820	2,737	1,478	1,694	562	268	32,399
2011	24,116	23,797	25,257	9,635	11,118	2,615	1,889	3,031	1,526	1,710	532	314	32,371
2012	25,975	25,251	28,148	11,173	12,306	2,654	2,015	3,272	1,949	1,799	501	330	35,998
2013	27,599	25,493	31,676	14,172	12,783	2,708	2,013	3,620	2,398	2,157	474	331	40,656
2014	28,398	28,192	33,384	14,487	13,684	2,854	2,358	3,788	2,785	2,479	448	317	43,200
Projection													
2015	29,190	29,214	34,144	14,840	13,860	2,919	2,525	-	-	-	-	-	-
2016	30,422	30,780	35,999	15,659	14,536	3,078	2,727	-	-	-	-	-	-
2017	32,135	32,956	39,138	17,024	15,803	3,346	2,965	-	-	-	-	-	-
2018	33,917	35,249	42,496	18,484	17,159	3,633	3,219	-	-	-	-	-	-
2019	35,784	37,683	46,115	20,059	18,620	3,943	3,493	-	-	-	-	-	-

Source: OECD Institutional Investor's Assets Database, *www.oecd-ilibrary.org/finance-and-investment/data/oecd-institutional-investors-statistics_instinv-data-en*, 2014 Preqin Global Private Equity Report, ETFGI monthly newsletter (February 2015), BarclayHedge.

StatLink http://dx.doi.org/10.1787/888933210395

Regulated institutional funds

Pension fund projections and asset allocations are shown in Figure 3.8 as a share of world GDP[8]. Over the next five years pension funds are expected to grow 26% from an estimated USD 28.4 trillion in 2014 to USD 35.8 trillion in 2019. Prior to the tech bust pension funds were rising quickly as a share of world GDP, and apparently well on the way to dealing with the problem of longevity risk—assets need to do better than world GDP if the dependency rates are rising due to longevity. This was due to policies which changed saving behaviour as well as to solid pre-crisis returns. Subsequently, however, this asset growth versus GDP has stalled, and is expected to be around 35% of world GDP in 2019.

Figure 3.8. **Asset allocation of pension funds**

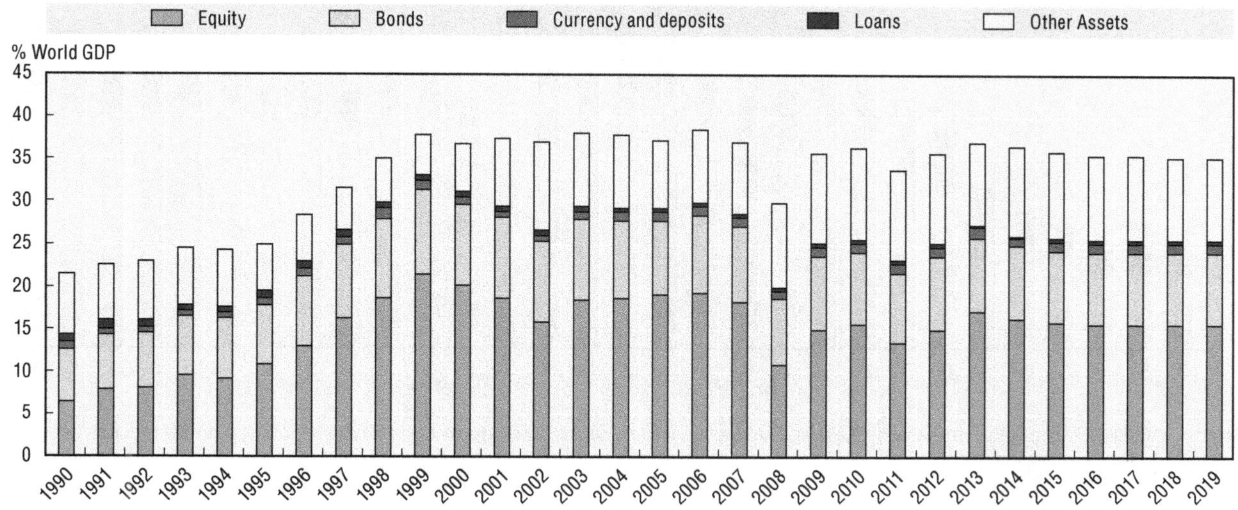

Source: OECD Institutional Investor's Assets Database, *www.oecd-ilibrary.org/finance-and-investment/data/oecd-institutional-investors-statistics_instinv-data-en.*

StatLink http://dx.doi.org/10.1787/888933209434

Prospects for insurance companies are shown in Figure 3.9. Over the next five years insurance companies are expected to grow 33% from an estimated USD 28.2 trillion in 2014 to USD 37.7 trillion in 2019. As a share of world GDP a slight recovery to 37% is expected in 2019—it was over 40% in the mid-2000s.

Prospects for mutual funds (which include a lot of the investments for pension funds and insurance companies) are also set out in Table 3.2. Over the next five years mutual funds are expected to grow 38% from an estimated USD 33.4 trillion in 2014 to USD 46.1trillion in 2019 (45% of world GDP).

Pension funds and insurance companies face a problem

There is a fundamental problem emerging for asset owners with liabilities to meet in a low interest rate world where people are living longer and where companies are not investing in an efficient and productive way.

- If companies do not invest, and prefer to give money back to shareholders via buybacks, or for tax and labour cost reasons allow investment in supply chains to be carried out by EME partners, or engage in merger and acquisition activity which only changes ownership, then innovative investment and the productivity growth needed to underpin the valuation of bonds and equities in the future will be diminished (Chapter 2).

- As older higher-yielding bonds drop out of institutional investor portfolios and are replaced by very low-yielding bonds solvency issues may arise for pension funds and insurance companies, as the valuation of their liabilities rises (Chapter 4).
- The risk becomes that cash from contributions and from dividends and buybacks will be less invested in real assets, and more into leverage and riskier higher-yield and complex products with poor liquidity.

Figure 3.9. **Asset allocation of insurance companies**

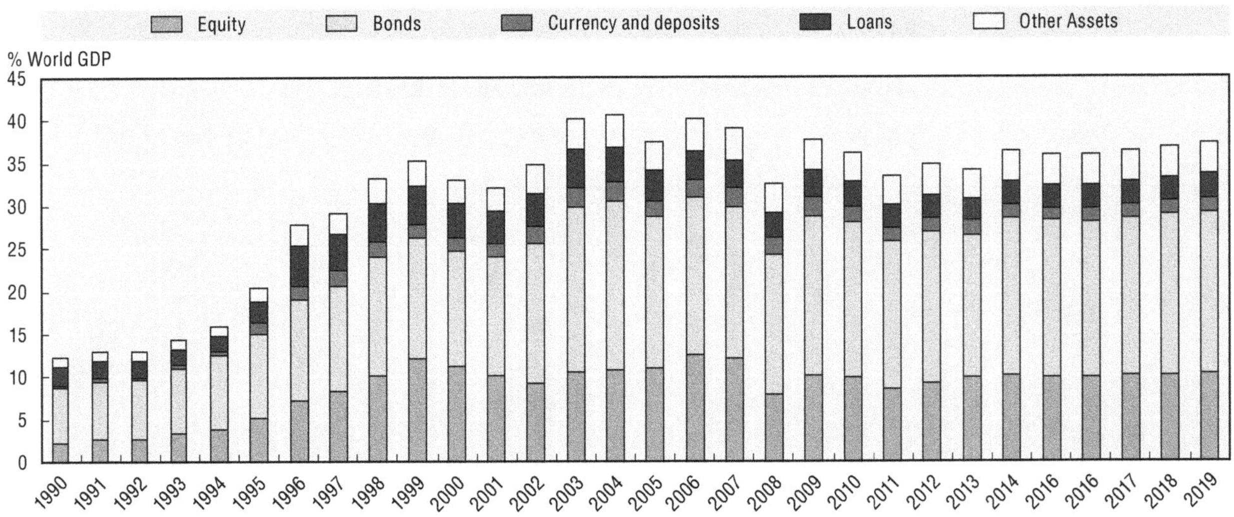

Source: OECD Institutional Investor's Assets Database, *www.oecd-ilibrary.org/finance-and-investment/data/oecd-institutional-investors-statistics_instinv-data-en.*

StatLink http://dx.doi.org/10.1787/888933209447

Asset allocations of regulated funds to broad securities classes

The asset allocations consistent with Table 3.2 and Figures 3.8 and 3.9 for pension funds, insurance companies and mutual funds are shown in Figure 3.10. A number of features stand out:

- Pension funds invest most in equities (on average in the range of 30-60%), and less in bonds, which appear to have declined steadily from around 30% of total assets in 2002 to 26% in 2014. Major asset allocation shifts (either due to market price shifts—not rebalanced—or deliberate portfolio decisions) appear to be between equities and alternative assets (see below).
- Insurance companies hold more in bonds (on average a 40-55% range) and less in equities (a 18-34% range) and a 10% allocation to alternative assets. Assets allocation shifts are mainly between bonds and equities.
- Insurance companies and mutual funds began to participate in the syndicated loan market (including leveraged loans) in the mid-1990s[9], but soon allowed their allocation to decline as securitised products became more popular (wrongly thought to be more liquid).
- Mutual funds (after the early 1990s) have tended to switch between equity and bonds with no structural bias to either, with a small allocation to alternative assets.

These broad asset strategies have not succeeded in raising the size of funds under management relative to GDP since the mid-2000s, and Chapter 4 demonstrates the liability risks that are posed to pension and insurance companies. This has meant that asset owners have been increasing their investments in new products that promise better yield and lower risk. To see what is happening it is important to drill down into more granularity as to the products that institutional investors are moving towards inside these broad asset classes.

Institutional investor moves into alternative assets

To augment returns and diversify the risk after the tech bust in the early 2000s institutional investors began to adopt a 'barbell' strategy[10] of long-only funds at one end and hedge funds and real estate as alternative assets at the other. This was a distinguishing feature of pension funds in particular (Figure 3.10) with such assets in the 12-33% range since 1990 and insurance companies at 10%. The sharp drawdown of equity in the early 2000s and during the more recent crisis were temporary (due to the policy responses), and equity and bond market performances since 2009 have been very strong. Pension funds reduced equity and bond weightings, when in fact both of these asset classes outperformed traditional real estate and fund-of-fund sectors. As it turned out, this held back pension fund performance prior to the crisis.

Figure 3.11 shows the pension and insurance company assets on the right scale versus some of the alternative assets from Table 3.2 on the left scale. One strategy since well before the crisis has been for asset owners to move towards passive (index) funds in their long-only holdings (and away from higher-fee funds that promise but for the most part don't deliver 'alpha' versus a benchmarks)[11]. The almost parabolic growth of ETFs shown in Table 3.2 is a good example of the strength of this trend, with a vast amount also invested with large passive funds provided by Vanguard, Blackrock and others (the impact of the trend to passive on price discovery is discussed in Chapter 7).

Fund-of-funds fall out of favour

Since the crisis it is clear that institutional investors have shifted away from general fund-of-fund hedge funds, due to high fees and because performance has been disappointing[12] as illustrated by the reversal of funds under management since the crisis (Figure 3.11). However, total hedge fund investments have been recovering more recently, suggesting that more specific styles have become popular. They are a part of a stream of new forms of investment by institutional investors that are becoming more 'mainstream' alongside traditional bonds and equities. For the hedge fund community the volatile environment during and since the crisis has resulted in the stronger growth of new product styles (shown on the left side of Figure 3.12) and a flattening-out of some less successful ones (on the right side of Figure 3.12).

New funds that promise better yields with less risk

Hedge funds and private equity are innovating once more with the help of the shadow banking sector (interactions between broker-dealers and prime broking and lending functions; lending agents and custodians; and asset owners themselves). As regulations and rules begin more strongly to tie up liquid assets and increase the costs associated with derivatives (margins, the quality of collateral, segregated accounts, clearing) the sources and uses of funding have had to adjust—with most changes outside of regular insured deposit banking functions.

Figure 3.10. **Asset allocation patterns of mutual funds, pension funds and insurance companies**

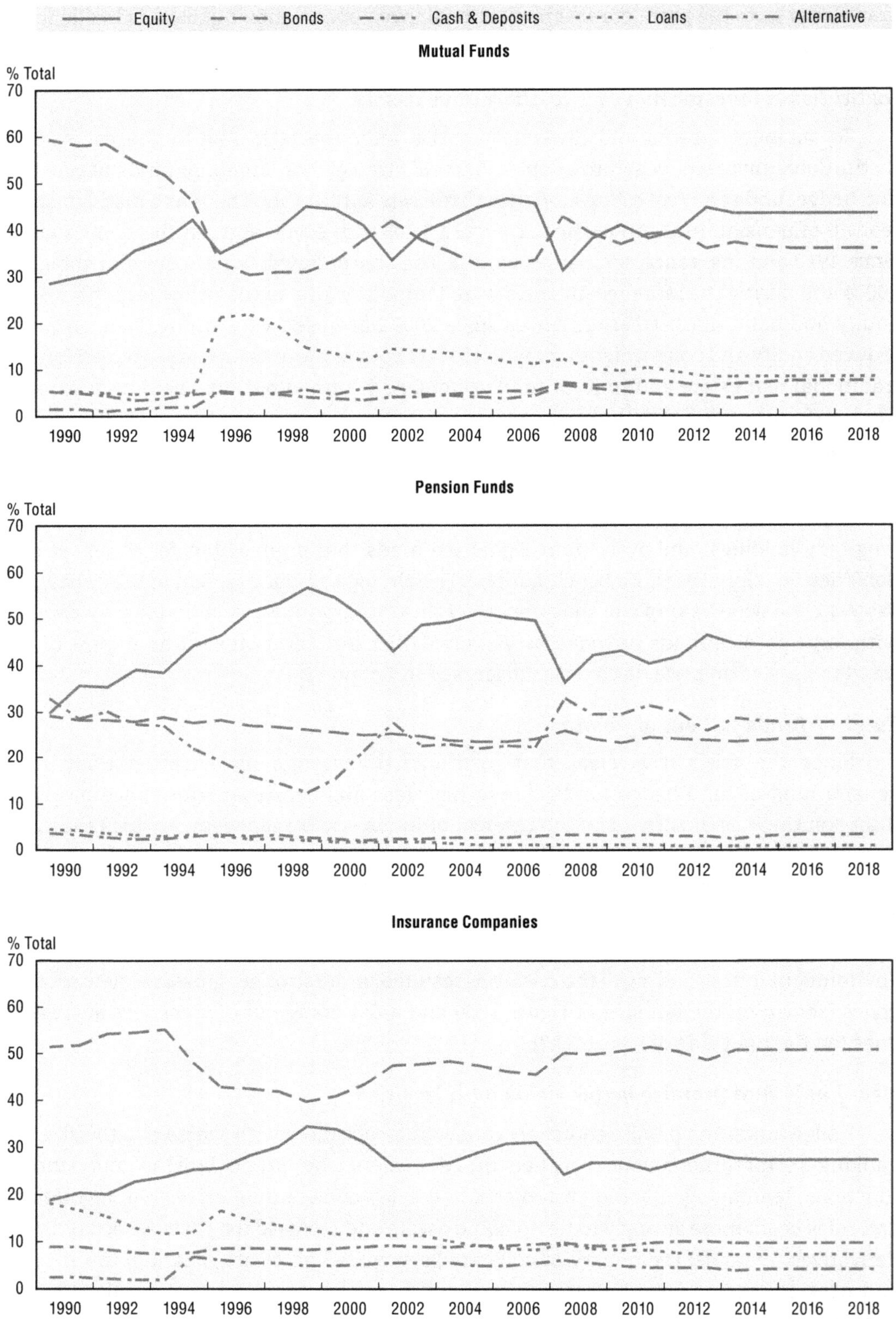

Source: OECD Institutional Investor's Assets Database, *www.oecd-ilibrary.org/finance-and-investment/data/oecd-institutional-investors-statistics_instinv-data-en.*

StatLink *http://dx.doi.org/10.1787/888933209453*

Figure 3.11. **Private funds versus regulated funds**

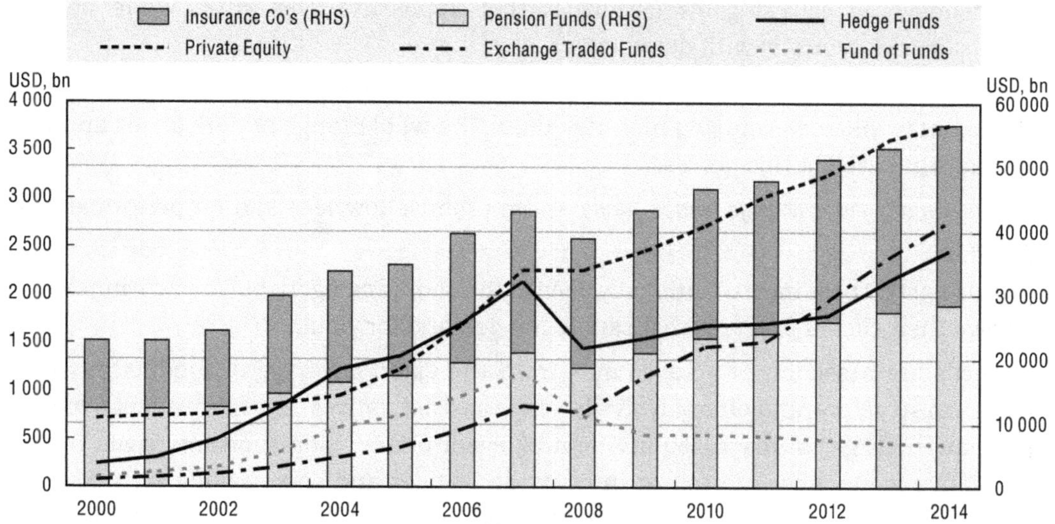

Source: BarclayHedge, 2014 Preqin Global Private Equity Report, ETFGI monthly newsletter (February 2015), OECD calculations.

StatLink http://dx.doi.org/10.1787/888933209465

Figure 3.12. **Growing hedge fund styles versus slowing ones**

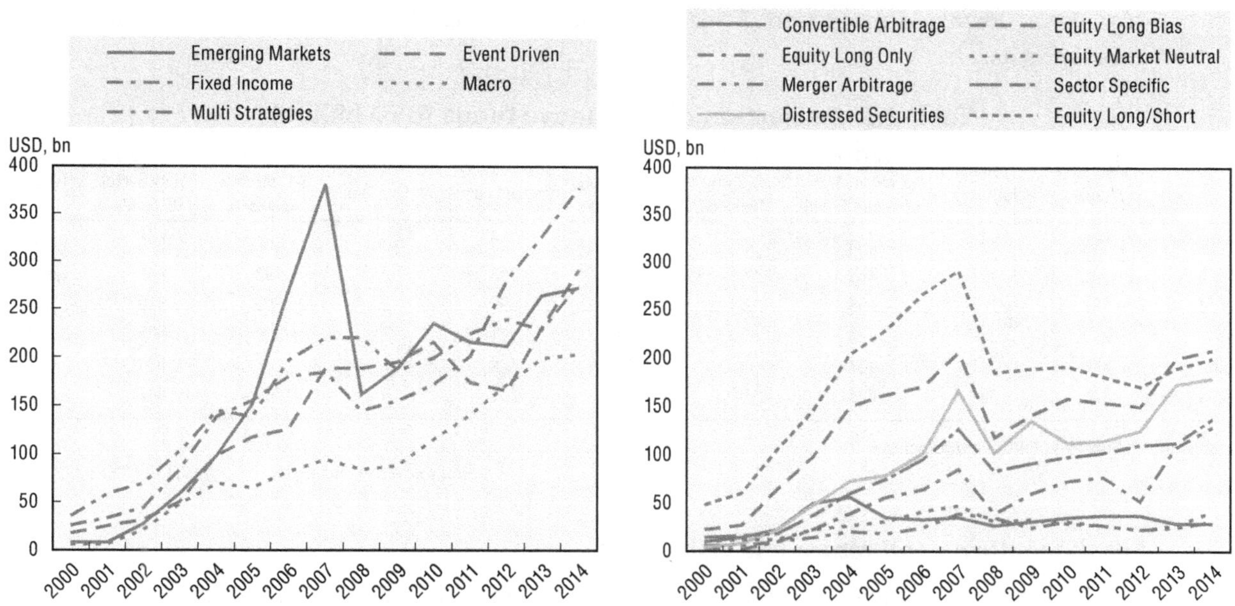

Source: Barclays, OECD calculations.

StatLink http://dx.doi.org/10.1787/888933209479

One way to look at this is the descriptions of styles offered by Barclays in Figure 3.12. Another selection of 'alternative funds' provided by investment managers is shown in Table 3.3. This selection of funds has increased by over USD 1 trillion in only 5 years, from USD 1.6 trillion in 2009 to almost USD 2.7 trillion in 2014. The funds in Figure 3.12 (style) and in Table 3.3 (products) of course overlap. More generally these funds (which often promise better yield with less risk) fall into five generic categories:

- *Absolute return funds*: These promise positive returns in both rising and falling markets. They use a wide number of assets and are not tied to traditional benchmarks. They use derivatives and a variety of methods to short securities.

- *Total return funds:* These promise to maximise gains from both income (interest and dividends) and capital gains (securities that appreciate over time), while hedging downside risk typically with derivatives.
- *Risk parity funds:* These focus on the allocation of risk and do so by leveraging up low-risk assets while deleveraging high-risk ones. The whole range of derivatives and repo markets are used in this process.
- *Actively managed exchange traded funds:* these promise low fees and outperformance of indexes.
- *Private equity:* These have traditionally been in the illiquid category, but are now innovating to give their clients products that satisfy the demand for yield.

These are a section of actual funds from the Eikon coverage of products that are complex in structure, and often involve leverage and derivatives. Alternative funds include credit, currency, global macro, equity neutral, event-driven, long-short, managed futures and relative value. Absolute return involves derivatives and short selling techniques to achieve absolute as opposed to relative returns. Hedge funds here include a multitude of complex strategies. Currency-hedged funds involve forwards, swaps and options. Commodity blended funds involve a risk managed basket of currencies instead of a single commodity like gold. Frontier markets are highly-illiquid securities in the MSCI frontier index. Guaranteed funds usually trade off the upside in market performance for varying degrees of downside protection. Real estate funds promise liquidity for highly illiquid underlying assets.

Table 3.3. **A selection of alternative funds (USD billion)**

Date	Alternative Funds	Absolute Return Funds	Hedge Funds & Money Mkt Leverage Funds	Global IG Bond Currency Hedged	High-Yield Bond Currency Hedged	Commodity Blended Funds	Equity Frontier Markets Funds	Guaranteed & Protected Funds	Real Estate & Equity Sector RE Funds	TOTAL
2009	138	125	409	35	201	123	0	186	389	1,606
2010	191	167	465	54	253	183	2	193	449	1,957
2011	223	183	498	64	287	190	1	208	469	2,122
2012	270	234	525	88	383	211	2	224	535	2,473
2013	377	341	468	98	427	124	5	237	595	2,672
2014	376	389	425	92	411	101	6	208	647	2,657

Source: Eikon/Reuters, OECD calculations.

StatLink http://dx.doi.org/10.1787/888933210408

Absolute return, total return and risk parity

This group of funds feature significantly in Figure 3.12 and Table 3.3. They include strategies that are often called 'hedge strategies' in Table 3.3. These might focus on liquid equities and bonds, but seek to outperform by what might be called 'leveraged beta'. For example a manager might invest in a market or index (beta) and then seek to outperform not by skill and analysis of fundamentals, but simply by writing derivatives to earn income and selling the performance as 'alpha'. Alternatively, this may involve investments in illiquid equity and credit products offering good yields, while promising to protect against the downside with derivatives. Multi strategies include actively managed futures. Finally, long-short strategies can cover liquid markets, emerging countries, or focus on opportunities that arise out of economic and geopolitical events (macro, multi-strategy, etc.). All of these funds offer structures which promise better yield with less volatility.

Exchange traded funds

Exchange traded funds offer daily liquidity (trade on exchanges) while offering exposure to markets the underlying securities of which may not be as liquid: small cap stocks, high-yield credit, and emerging market equity and credit. They have continued to show strong growth in funds under management, because they too have evolved to meet demands in the new environment—and in particular low fees in a lower yield environment. To augment returns these securities may be loaned out, so that the interest earned allows them to outperform while still charging low fees[13]. This activity brings in other players, including: lending agents from a custody bank carry out the loan (and this may involve indemnification); and swap counterparties for synthetic exchange traded funds (which are mainly offered in markets outside the United States). The latter may reference high yield securities and use collateral (that do not necessarily match the reference portfolio), while using swap contracts and options to give returns based on less liquid credit and equity securities (illustrated in Figure 3.13).

Products that offer daily liquidity while referencing illiquid underlying securities may face severe problems were there to be a run of redemptions on this asset class.

Figure 3.13. **Synthetic exchange traded fund (ETF) example**

SYNTHETIC ETF, The Risk Is Even Higher

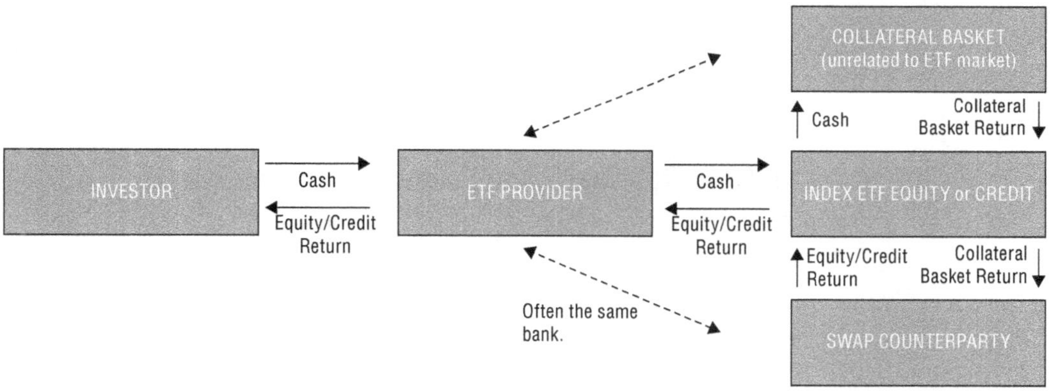

StatLink http://dx.doi.org/10.1787/888933209483

Private equity

Private equity holdings have increased most spectacularly, from USD 963 billion in 2004 to USD 3.5 trillion in 2013—an increase of some 260% over that period (see Figure 3.11). These funds based on limited partnerships, are private and illiquid. Private equity deals have been particularly strong in the low interest rate environment since the crisis as debt is cheap and the demand for alternatives assets is strong. Often the main point of these deals is to transfer risk to lenders and enhance the return on equity for the investors. An under-levered, underperforming company is typically targeted (Blundell-Wignall, 2007)[14]. Debt service tends to rise sharply in the deal phase, profit before tax falls, but due to the tax deductibility of interest after-tax profit falls less and the return for the private equity investors can be very strong.

The business model in recent years has evolved into a broader offering of services for asset owners in the low interest rate environment. For example, private equity deal making with companies and debt enables them to offer credit products with stable 'cash-plus' returns. A private equity fund might buy gas storage facilities at various ports around the world, the value of which might rise as global value chains spread, but some of the cash streams can be channelled back to the underlying investors in giving them access to better yield income. So as not to constrain future restructuring options, 'covenant-lite' bond contracts are most attractive, and investors competing for yield may be happy to accept this ('covenant-lite' trends are discussed below). Investors are attracted to private equity precisely because the offerings allow them to meet both diversification and yield objectives at the same time. The trade-off is that the weight of illiquid products in asset owner portfolios is rising.

The nature of corporate bonds being absorbed by institutional investors is changing

The OECD Secretariat has constructed a comprehensive data set for corporate bond issuance (Çelik et al., 2015)[15] and outstanding amounts (which requires call data to be matched with each individual bond)[16]. The strong demand for corporate bonds (which have better yields than the very low or negative rates on sovereign debt) to feed directly or via alternative products into institutional investor portfolios has led to new trends in this sector. A greater proportion of high-yield and emerging market debt is being issued in the United States dollar market, and the covenant structure of the bonds is changing.

Figure 3.14 shows the issuance of the financial versus non-financial companies. For the former issuance was strong prior to the crisis and subsequently flattened out. The gap in the market left by the banks has led to a greater use of corporate bond markets by the non-financial sector, which picks up more strongly after 2008. In the period from 2008 to 2014 the net outstanding of the non-financial sector bonds rose by USD 4.6 trillion versus USD 1.5 trillion for the financial sector.

Figure 3.14. **Financial versus non-financial corporate bonds**

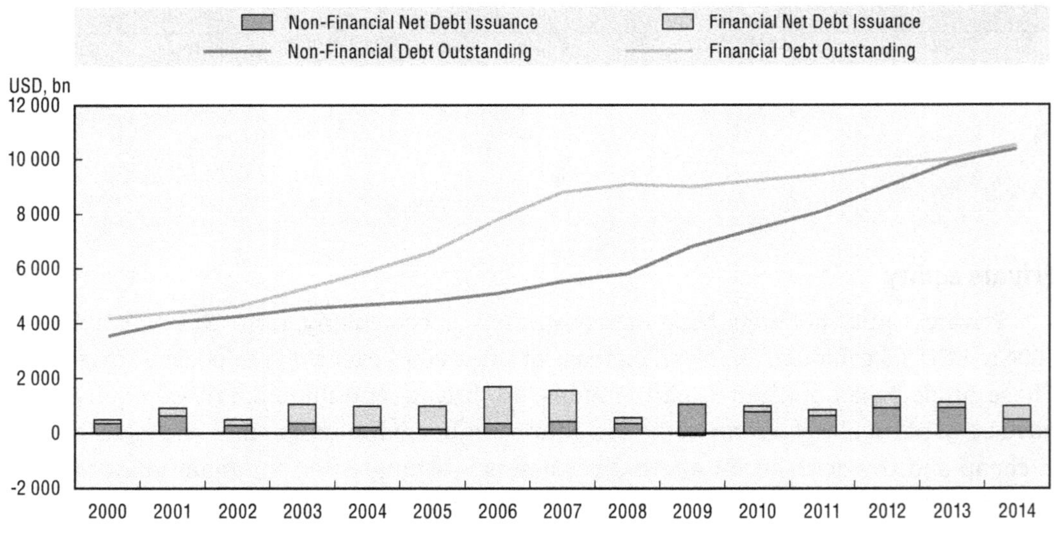

Source: Thomson Reuters, Bloomberg, OECD calculations.

StatLink http://dx.doi.org/10.1787/888933209496

The issuance data in United States dollar bonds are shown in Figure 3.15. United States issuance of high-grade corporate bonds is relatively stable over the period shown, in the USD 500 billion- USD 800 billion per annum range. However, high-yield debt issuance is moving up rapidly: since its low in the crisis of USD 39 billion it is now in the USD 250 billion to USD 300 billion per annum range. Emerging market issuance in both investment grade and high-yield has increased in the dollar market to around USD 220 billion per annum. The emerging market share of issuance in the dollar market has risen to around 20% in recent years (the broken line in Figure 3.15). As the United States dollar rises some of this debt held in advanced country institutional portfolios may see a rise in defaults, particularly if the dollar overshoots.

Figure 3.15. **US dollar net debt issuance: United States versus emerging and high yield versus investment grade**

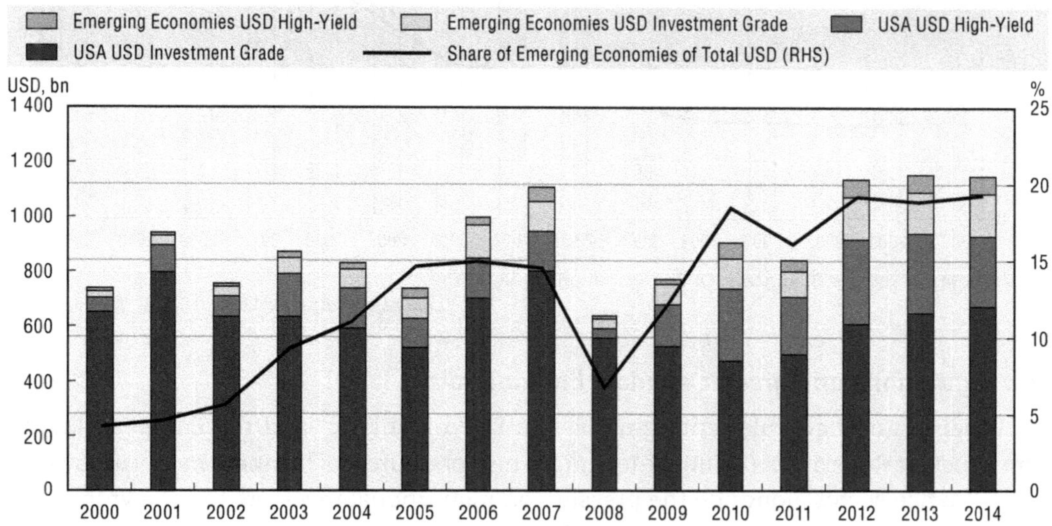

Source: Thomson Reuters, OECD calculations.

StatLink http://dx.doi.org/10.1787/888933209500

The outstanding amounts split between advanced and emerging bonds (all currencies) are shown in Figure 3.16. Advanced-country bonds stand at around USD 17.8 trillion in the most recent year, compared to USD 3.1 trillion in emerging market bonds, which are around 15% of the total[17].

Competition amongst lenders for yield products may give rise to issuers having more scope to reduce covenant protection in bonds with lenders less concerned to resist them. The top panel of Figure 3.17 shows a covenant protection index between 0 (no protection) and 1.0 (high protection) for bonds being issued. The index for high-yield bonds has plunged from around 0.6 to 0.3. The bottom panel shows some of the categories used in the index for high-yield bonds. The reasons behind this appear to be:

- Competition amongst lenders in a low interest rate environment[18].
- A form of short-termism whereby performance pressure leads to investment manager incentives to sacrifice covenant protection for higher yields because the returns are immediately apparent, whereas 'covenant-lite risk' will manifest itself much later (Choi and Triantis, 2012).
- The proliferation of new products that involve securities lending may be facilitating these trends as risk is being continually shifted around and/or is hedged.
- Activist hedge fund actions prior to the crisis (on the basis of the late filing covenants) have led issuers to rephrase provisions in order to avoid such disputes in the future.

'Covenant-lite' bonds are less liquid and would require larger price movements in order to find buyers in a stressed environment.

Figure 3.16. **Outstanding amounts of bonds: advanced versus emerging economies**

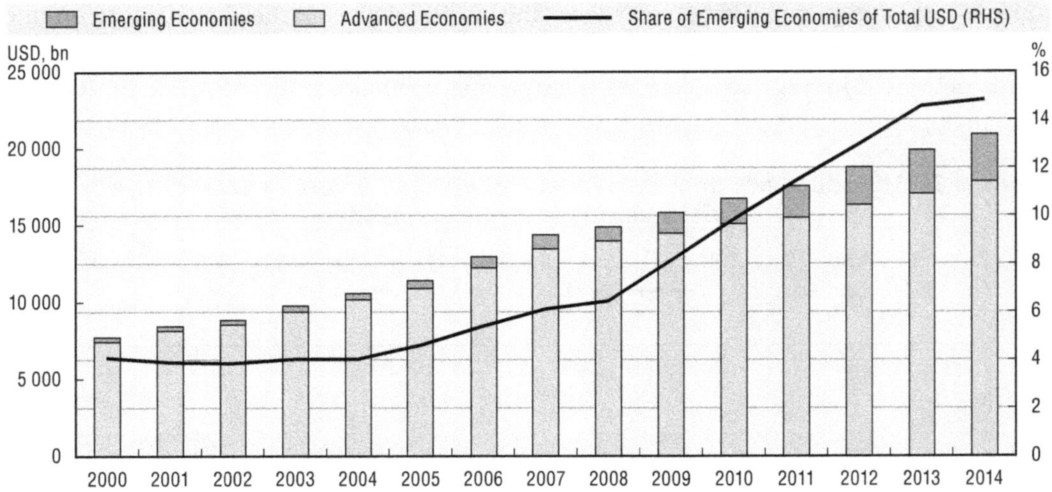

Source: Thomson Reuters, Bloomberg, OECD calculations.

StatLink http://dx.doi.org/10.1787/888933209513

New regulations and greater shadow banking role

Basel III and new rule writing under the Dodd-Frank Act and the European Market Infrastructure Reform Act (EMIR) are leading to new pressures for business model innovation in the finance sector alongside the pressure on institutional investors to cope with a very low interest rate environment by seeking higher yield and lower volatility. Some of the key regulatory changes include:

- Raising the Basel risk-weighted capital requirements (and a leverage ratio 'back-up') by focusing on (a) the quality of capital, and by (b) adding capital buffers for large banks.
- Adding charges for counterparty credit risk (Basel III) and credit limits (Dodd Frank Rule 165(e)) to unaffiliated companies (> USD 50 billion) of 25% of their capital (plus loan loss reserves) and 10% for companies (> USD 500 billion), which are GSIBs. The credit exposure includes repos, reverse repos, securities borrowing and lending, guarantees (including indemnifications to asset owners from lending agents in the custody business), debt sales and counterparty credit exposure for derivatives.
- Use of centralised clearing counterparties (CCPs) and the increased transparency of swap transactions via swap execution facilities required by Dodd Frank and EMIR rules. EMIR also requires: pre-determined minimums for initial and variation margins on uncleared derivative transactions; higher quality collateral; and more thorough reporting of trades to a repository.
- Adding a liquidity coverage ratio (LCR) which requires high-quality liquid assets (HQLA) equal to 100% of the amount of liquidity needed to cover a stressed environment for 30 days.
- A proposal for a net stable funding ratio (NSFR): essentially 'available' stable funding (e.g. customer deposits) to 'required' stable funding of risk-weighted assets.
- A requirement to separate regular insured deposit banking from aspects of prime broking such as under the Volcker and Vickers rules and a set of policies attempting similar reforms in Europe.

Figure 3.17. **Covenant Protection Index and selected covenant frequency**

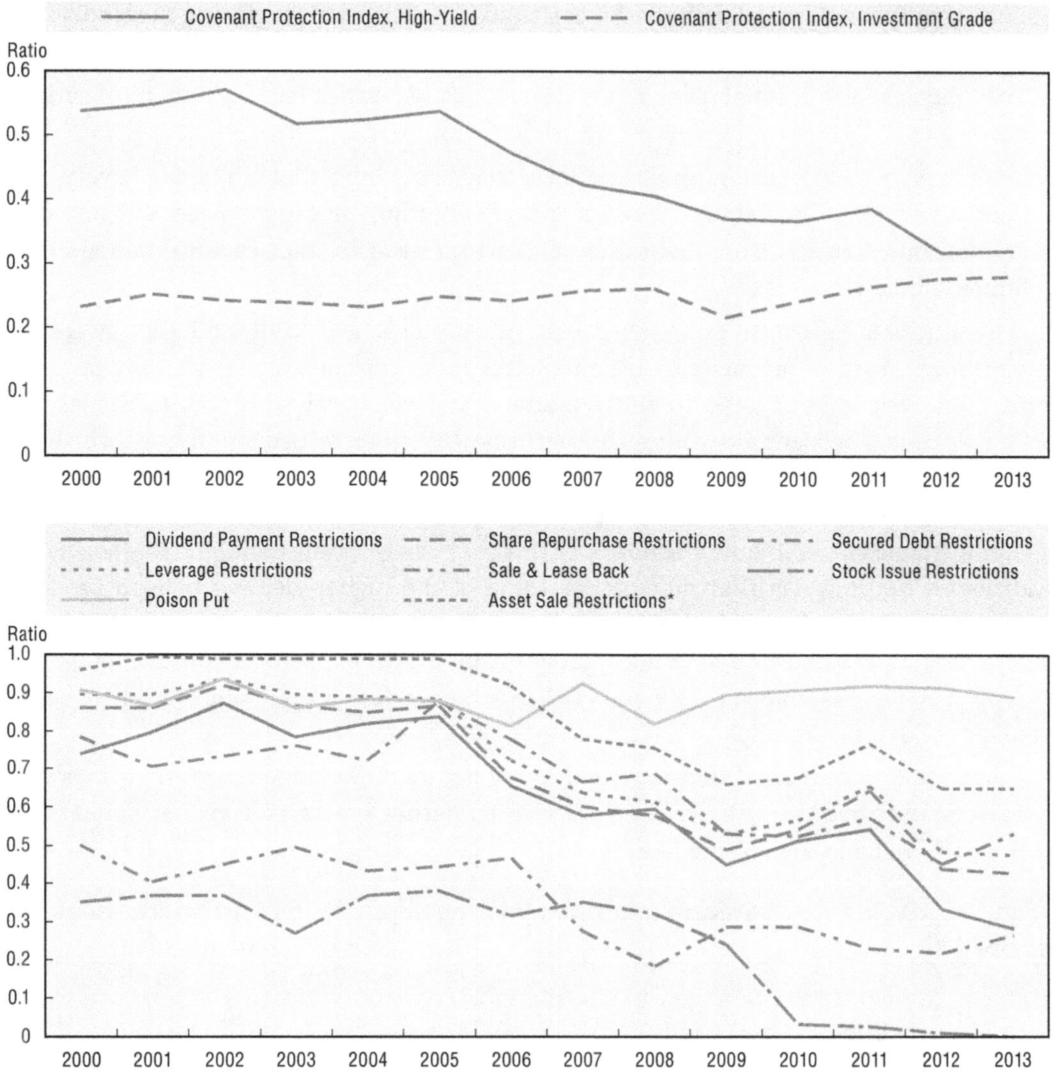

Note: The 34 covenant variables in the dataset are matched to the 15 covenant groups. If a bond had at least one covenant that belongs to a certain covenant group, it was considered to have that covenant type. For each covenant type, a binary variable was generated, which is equal to 1 if the covenant type is available in the bond indenture. The binary variables are then summed, divided by 15 to create an index that ranges from 0 to 1, with the ratio 1 denoting the highest possible protection for bondholders. Data from the binary variables frequency in selected sub-categories are shown in the bottom panel.

* Asset sale restrictions are very highly correlated with cross-default provisions and merger restrictions, the latter two of which are not shown.

Source: Çelik et al., 2015.

StatLink http://dx.doi.org/10.1787/888933209526

- The Dodd Frank Act and the EMIR Act have mandated changes in the way in which over the counter derivatives are cleared including also the use of HQLA. In Europe cash cannot be used for Undertakings for Collective Investment in Transferable Securities (UCITS) margins, which differs from rules for other institutional products.
- The requirement for money market funds to float their net asset value (NAV) so that 'the buck' can be broken and reported transparently for investors and regulators.
- Greater monitoring, disclosure and dispute settlement procedures with supervisors which raises cost.

These rules do the following:

- They greatly increase the demand for cash and HQLA to post margin and meet collateral requirements for banks and asset owners.
- They increase the costs of using repos, derivatives, securities lending, indemnifications, etc.
- They apply also to pension funds and insurance companies that are typically very cash poor. While broker-dealers can take advantage of netting rules under Basel III[19] (Blundell-Wignall and Roulet, 2014), institutional investors need to find ways to manage their limited liquid resources.

Institutional investors confronted both with these new rules and the low-return environment need to reconcile their demand for more complex higher-yielding products with their concomitant need to settle margins and collateral with counterparties and broker-dealers. For example, to improve returns they need to become more involved in higher-yielding products (and hence more leverage and risk) and lending programs to reuse their assets. Frequently the most valuable lending activities concern less liquid assets with higher intrinsic value. To take advantage of this they can repo out their lendable securities, and obtain funding (via that market) for some of the higher-yielding hedged products discussed earlier and cash for collateral management. In a sense institutional investors unlock illiquid assets through lending programs and gain exposure to swaps, long-short products, actively managed future and exchange traded funds, etc.—but they also need to manage collateral carefully.

A simplified version of this activity (leaving out all of the complex cross-arrows with futures clearing members, CCPs, lending agents tri-partite agents, and custody banks listed at the bottom) looks something like Figure 3.18.

Figure 3.18. **Shadow banking example: leveraged portfolios and broker-dealers**

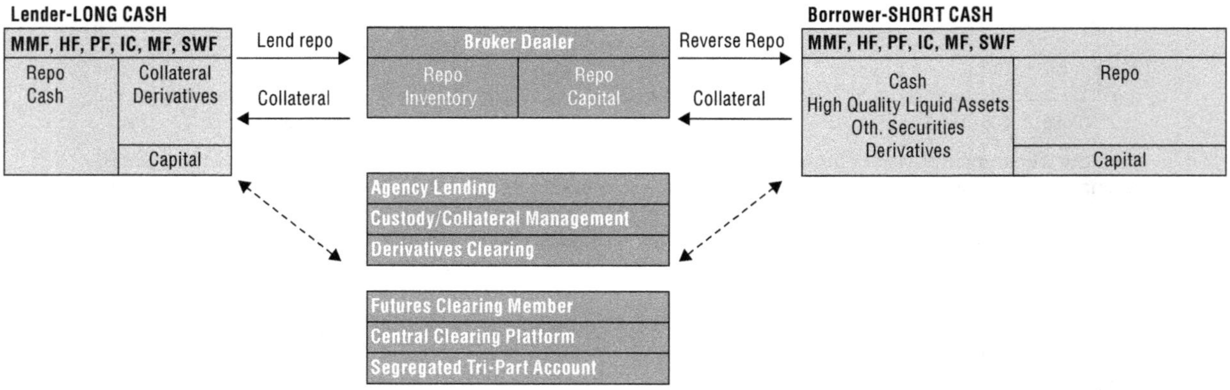

Note: 'MMF': money market funds, 'HF': hedge funds, 'PF': pension funds, 'IC': insurance companies, 'MF': mutual funds, 'SWF': sovereign wealth funds.

StatLink http://dx.doi.org/10.1787/888933209530

The process requires 'long-cash' market participants to deal with 'cash-short' (less liquid) asset owners that are cash short to achieve better-yield goals.

- A short cash fund on the right side of Figure 3.18 carries out a reverse repo with its securities, lending them out and getting access to liquidity. If these are low-yielding HQLA they may do this to get access to cash for exposure to derivatives—the new products noted above—which will require them to post initial margin and pay or receive variation margins to boost returns. Alternatively they may lend out illiquid securities and get access to term repos with a higher yield.

- The long cash fund, such as a money market or sovereign wealth fund, is the other side of the repo, while the broker-dealer runs a matched book and minimises regulatory charges via netting etc.

Risks associated with the shadow banking sector

- *Counterparty credit risk:* the asset owner takes on the credit risk that the broker-dealer doesn't return the lent securities. Typically this risk has been indemnified by the securities lending agent (but may be dispensed with if the cost is too high due to Basel). The risk to the lending agent is the failure of the broker-dealer, in which case the lending agent would liquidate the collateral and buy the loaned securities on the market to return them to the securities lender. If the collateral is not sufficient then the lending agent would take a hit on its capital. The collateral valuation risk also applies to the broker-dealer vis-a-vis the failure of the cash borrower (security lender) in the transaction.
- *Reinvestment risk:* the cash received via the lending agent on behalf of the cash borrower (securities lender) is invested either in pooled funds (products) or a separately managed account. In the absence of indemnification, the securities lender bears the 'interest rate', 'spread', 'credit' and 'liquidity'[20] risk.
- *Re-hypothecation risk*: when invested in separate accounts the cash can be re-hypothecated in repo transactions with other broker-dealers usually involving a tri-partite lending agent. The securities lender is then also subject to the risk of default by the broker-dealer (or the lending agent if indemnified).
- *Maturity transformation risk:* in all the above examples the financing repo may be shorter than the open position being funded, requiring the repo to be rolled a number of times. However, in a period of stressed market conditions the rolling may not be possible.
- *Clearing and CCP credit risks:* here there is a chain of default risk in the same manner as just discussed, i.e. if the collateral is not sufficient to cover the exposure of the defaulting party (to the clearer in the event of a default by customers; or to customer in the event that the clearer fails and the collateral was not held in a segregated account). The CCP and the exchange based clearer are similarly exposed to each other according to the sufficiency of the collateral held.

Potential financial stability risks

More global financial stability risks may result from the above shadow banking funding mechanisms that create leverage and counterparty exposures with the possibility of the above risk outcomes.

- *Pro-cyclicality*: the asset price leverage process works via haircuts on collateral—as asset prices rise there is more room for leverage and more funding helps asset prices rise further.
- *Loss of confidence in counterparties*: in a period of stress may lead to 'cliff effects' of funding being pulled and fire sales of assets following.
- *Contagion risk:* given the strong interconnectedness in the reuse of collateral the failure of any counterparty would spread quickly through the system. Alternatively, a period of market stress may cause the lending market to dry up and mismatches may cause the failure of some intermediaries to meet their commitments.

The market risk outlook

The performance of United States equities, global equities, the United States 10-year Treasury bond, emerging market bonds, hedge funds, private equity, and United States real estate are shown in Figure 3.19. Since 2000 the differences in performance are quite extraordinary. Bonds have benefitted from the move to low interest rates and cross-border private sector and official flows discussed earlier. Fixed income and private equity all outperformed the S&P500 and the MSCI over the past 15 years. The United States and global equity markets sold off more in the crisis because stocks are tradable (liquid). The more liquid equity market is something of a benchmark for measuring the extent that the other sectors may exhibit unrealistic valuations. The fixed income returns will presumably become subject to mean-reversion in a world where monetary policy is being normalised and countries like China gradually allow more exchange rate flexibility.

Figure 3.19. **Total return indexes on various asset classes**

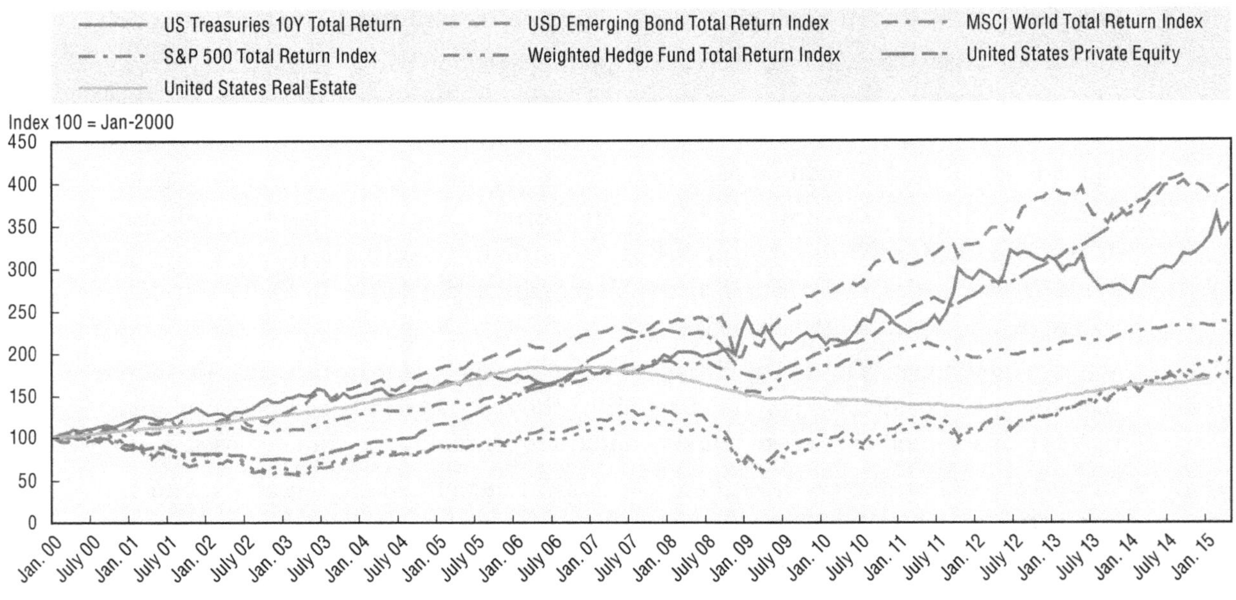

Source: Bloomberg, OECD calculations.

StatLink http://dx.doi.org/10.1787/888933209541

Figure 3.20 shows the 'Buffet model' of equity valuation (Market-cap-to-GDP), but applies it to the entire world, in order to allow for the development of global value chains and the shifting of gravity towards emerging countries and tax havens. Companies don't have to invest in and receive revenue from their own countries, whereas including them all gets around that issue. The global equity market does not appear to be extremely overvalued, though it is approaching levels where corrections back to the mean do become more likely. What this means for other illiquid sectors that have been the focus of asset owners seeking yield in a zero rate and QE world is unclear—but there would seem to be room for some concern. The equity markets have had the best performance since the worst point in the crisis (late 2008) because they declined the most, and the other asset classes were thought of as more defensive. The S&P total return index has moved up over 150% and the MSCI 119% since 2008. But emerging market bonds, United States Treasuries and private equity appear largely to have matched these returns (with increases over the same period of 102%, 71% and 118%, respectively) notwithstanding their relative strength prior to the crisis.

Figure 3.20. **World equity market capitalisation versus world GDP**

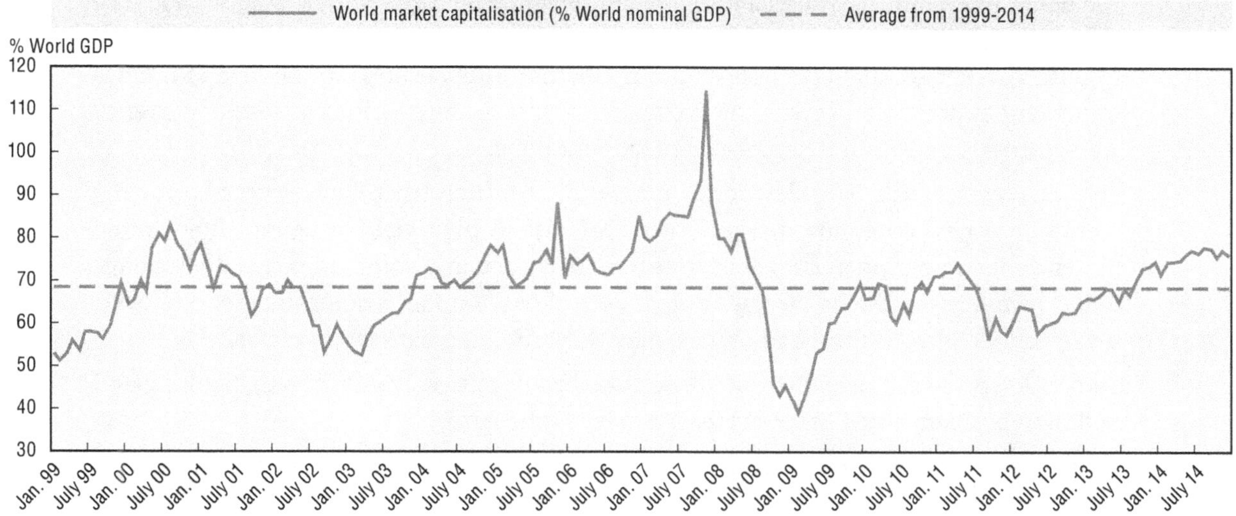

Source: World Federation of Stock Exchanges, OECD calculations.

StatLink http://dx.doi.org/10.1787/888933209558

Liquidity illusion

There appears to be some liquidity illusion in these trends. There has been a veritable 'super-highway' of inflows into these 'illiquidity premium' products: corporate and emerging corporate credit, private equity and alternative assets. The 'super-highway' into these products is not a dual carriageway—and when investors want to sell in a stressed environment they may find that there will be 'accidents' in the reversal of the flows. While pension and insurance funds would aim to hold assets like corporate bonds to maturity, any major and unexpected price falls would at some point cause them to attempt to sell/redeem (perhaps encouraged by prudential rules). High-yield bonds, as noted earlier, have reduced liquidity due to declining covenant protection, making them harder to sell in a stressed event. Holding to maturity is less of an option for alternative products that require counterparty relationships: they may be forced to redeem via collateral management mechanisms. Private equity and hedge funds have built-in gates that prevent investors from divesting. Exchange traded funds and alternative products that offer daily liquidity through trading in secondary markets when referencing illiquid underlying securities could be severely tested by redemptions in a sell off even where shores must be redeemed for in kind securities rather than cash.

There are a number of triggers for a liquidity crisis in credit creation via shadow banking:

- *Monetary policy normalisation:* One candidate is a rate tightening cycle in the United States—the selloff in the 1994 cycle came out of very less exceptional circumstances than those which present now. Zero rates, QE, and forward guidance gave the markets a one-way bet for years, and now the talk of taking this away puts two-way risk back on the table, and markets don't seem to have factored this in (given term premia and market performance).
- *Dollar overshooting:* The United States and the United Kingdom were the most pre-emptive in introducing QE, but now Japan and most recently the European Central Bank have moved to do the same. Currencies have begun to move, and the appreciation of

the dollar has been rapid and fairly extreme by historical comparisons. This means that the dollar bloc countries in Asia (other things given) would rise with the dollar and lose competitiveness versus Japan and Europe. If these countries ease rates and intervene to push currencies down (as opposed to the earlier interventions in the face of inflows to prevent appreciation versus the dollar), leading to a more serious advent of currency wars, capital controls and beggar-thy-neighbour policies.

- *Emerging market crisis:* The slowdown in growth, over-investment and excess borrowing results in a new emerging market crisis: Defaults in high-yield 'covenant-lite' United States dollar emerging market corporate bonds (particularly companies that do not have dollar revenues) as the dollar rises and growth slows. Similarly, domestic credit to over-invested (declining return) companies, may result in financial system crises.
- *Europe*: A worst-case risk whereby QE does not manage to solve its growth, banking and deflation problems, and Greece is forced to leave the euro.
- *A falling oil price surprise* that undermines the oil-related and fracking business investment in the United States, and hits the commodity-exporting countries in Australia, Canada, OPEC, Latin America and Africa. The combination of these negative terms-of-trade factors outweighs the relative price and household income gains in net oil-importing countries.
- *Major geopolitical risks* in the Middle East and Central and Eastern Europe eventuating.

Conclusions

Any of these events would likely trigger asset price volatility, margin and collateral calls within the shadow banking system. Attempts by institutional investors to redeem illiquid corporate bonds and alternative assets in crisis circumstances would amplify volatility. Credit, spread, maturity transformation mismatch, and collateral valuation risks would rise for asset owners, broker-dealers and lending agents. Dollar funding would risk drying up, with basis spreads widening and thereby risking the promulgation of the crisis not only between financial system players but also regions, requiring standing central bank swap arrangements to be triggered alongside a general sliding back into other crisis measures. These sorts of scenarios need to be avoided at all costs. This will require both structural reform in the international financial system and a completion of the financial reform agenda between banks, shadow banks and institutional investors.

Structural reform of the international financial system

At the most basic level many of the problems that asset owners are trying to deal with would not have become issues if structural reform of the global economy had advanced enough to make the achievement of implicit promises more feasible.

- One promise is that the globalisation of supply chains benefits all countries in an equitable way. However, Chapter 2 noted that corporate success in cash flow terms from global re-organisation does not translate into investment in R&D, productivity and innovation, and that the ways in which emerging economies have been drawn into supply chains has led to over-investment, inefficiency and reduced value creation possibilities. The strength of businesses that underpins valuations in bonds and equities will not rise to meet the future needs of asset owners in the absence of reform. To address this situation there is a need for more open competition and responsiveness to market mechanisms. A sensible and gradual sequencing of liberalisation and more exchange rate flexibility consistent with a better balance between investment- and consumption-led-growth in the global economy is essential.

- Countries must be able to use macro-prudential emergency measures which affect cross-border flows on a temporary basis, as and when the economic situation demands it. But such measures should not contribute to a drift towards permanent new cross-border controls aimed at supporting exchange rate management policies at the expense of other countries' trade and growth. This would raise the risk of a currency war outcome. Macro-prudential measures should not become a substitute for taking required monetary policy decisions and structural reforms to promote more competitiveness and dynamic industries[21].

Pension and insurance reform in the face of longevity risk

Another promise is that pension funds and insurance companies will be able to meet their future liabilities in a low interest rate environment in the face of ageing populations and the very real issue of longevity risk. This requires policies such as those discussed in Chapter 4. On the structural side a re-negotiation of unrealistic promises including a matching of the retirement age with longevity risk may be important. Facilitating socially-useful financial instruments such as longevity bonds and swaps is important, as is the need for government support for the framework within which the pricing of such products occurs: official longevity indexes on the basis of which private product offerings can be evaluated; standardisation and transparency built around such indexes; and government issuance of longevity bonds to help build liquidity in these markets.

Financial system interdependence and counterparty risk

The OECD Secretariat has long argued that the greatest risk to financial stability is interdependence and counterparty risk the costs of which outweigh the alleged benefit of a lower cost of financial intermediation. This latter assertion is strange to say the least:

- The financial sector of the S&P500 in the United States was a sizeable 9.4% of all listed-company earnings in 1990 and rose to 18.3% by 2007. Following the post-crisis recovery this has become 21.7% in 2014.
- In Europe the financial sector of the STOXX was a costly 20.8% of all listed company earnings in 1990 and rose to 33.1% by 2007. With post-crisis recovery it has reached 28.7% in 2014.

These large shares reflect costs that are borne by the non-financial sector. The financial sector earnings share seems largely impervious to regulatory change, while interdependence risk remains (Figure 3.7). The policy that will best address this risk is a clear separation of regular retail banking, prime broking and custody and collateral management services so that losses in any one business in the group do not risk the capital of another. In this respect the Volcker rule, Vickers and European legislation did not go far enough. Indeed banks are pushing back on regulation of their business models and are promoting a unified bank services model, arguing that they are best placed to manage collateral for institutional investors since it is too costly for them to buy the teams to do it themselves[22].

The Dodd-Frank Act required insured banks to trade risky swaps in separate swap execution facilities to which federal assistance would be forbidden. Banks succeeded in lobbying for a large number of exceptions and, most recently, succeeded in removing all but one type of swap transaction from the required list. In Europe the lobbying against the sensible 'Barnier' separation proposals is quite intense.

Other measures that could reduce counterparty risk without directly separating businesses include:

- *Improve transparency*: via more granular mark-to-market data reporting by shadow banking activities—notably derivatives, collateral and pricing. This would help financial market participants and supervisors to deal with collateral valuation risk.
- *Establish minimum percentages of cash*: to be held in short-term deposits in high-quality institutions or in Treasury securities or overnight repos for all broker dealer and custody/lending activities (a sort of LCR for shadow banking). This would help address maturity transformation risks. Such a rule could be accompanied by weighted-average maturity and concentration limits. Regular stress testing might also help.
- *Limit the reuse of cash in repo markets*: this addresses re-hypothecation risk. One option to consider is limiting re-hypothecation to uses purely for a client's own financing of long positions and the covering of their shorts. It should not be used for the broker-dealer's own account.
- *Set minimum capital requirements for CCP risk*: this would address counterpart credit risk. Designing the rule to prevent competition between clearers on the basis of margin requirements (which would reduce safety) would support this approach.
- *Establish dealer-of-last-resort facilities*: as recently announced by the Bank of England (Bank of England, 2014). This goes in the opposite direction of the swap push-out rule, but has increased merit if full business model separation is excluded. This addresses liquidity crises amongst counterparties and related failures. The conditions under which this would be used as a backstop would need to be narrow (and possibly carry penalties) to avoid the mispricing of risk.

Notes

1. Large surpluses and deficits are mixed between advanced and emerging countries. Germany for example has a large surplus. Many EMEs have deficits.
2. See the discussion of efficiency also in Chapter 2. Huang and Wang show that financial repression inhibited growth by 3-3.6% in 1978 and by 1.7-2.1% in 2008. They argue that growth was hurt by the inhibition of financial development.
3. China has actually been making some steady progress - See Huang, Y. and X. Wang (2010). They show an index of financial repression based on principal components analysis of measures of all the above factors. In 1978 their measure was the maximum of 1.0 for highest repression and this fell to the 0.5 to 0.6 range by 2008.
4. The distance to default is a measure that uses a combination of bank reported data, and market information to calculate the number of standard deviations a bank is from the default point, where the market values of assets equals the book value of liabilities. See Blundell-Wignall and Roulet, C. (2014).
5. Banks above 3-standard deviations prior to the crisis managed to remain just above the default point of zero during the crisis.
6. Each bank's individual beta to the regional MSCI for a rolling 1-year window is calculated. These are aggregated with the 1-year rolling asset weights of that bank in total bank assets.
7. CTAs operate like a hedge fund using managed futures.
8. The estimates are based on forecasts of world GDP by the OECD, the return assumptions in Chapter 2, and the VIX index which is assumed to return to its historical average from the current low levels.

9. As a consequence of two events: (a) Moody's and S&P began to issue loan ratings in 1995, and in 1994 the Fed Funds rate rise and related bond sell-off began. Since loans outperform bonds in a rate rising environment there was a marked shift towards the latter and out of bonds.
10. Holding long-only products at one end, and private alternative funds at the other with the analogy to a weight lifter's barbell.
11. Traditional funds management establishes a benchmark, e.g. the Morgan Stanley Capital Index (MSCI), and have a process that tries to outperform the market (benchmark)—the market "beta" of their fund is the correlation to the benchmark (the return they would have got anyway) and the alpha is the outperformance over and above the return they got due to beta.
12. In fact these funds have an extra layer of fees, after which the blending of styles leads to little more that balanced-fund-like returns.
13. Market estimates that 21% of lendable securities were utilised in this way in early 2014.
14. For a discussion of traditional pre-crisis deals see Blundell-Wignall (2007).
15. This study focuses on the issuance data.
16. Essential as bonds are often called before their maturity date and the gross issuance data cannot be simply cumulated.
17. This rising share of emerging markets is entirely consistent with the analysis of flow borrowing based on income statements of individual companies in Chapter 2.
18. The Bank of England has recently noted this in a British context: see Bank of England (2014), Trends in Lending, October.
19. Banks have a huge opportunity to optimise under Basel Regulatory Framework, as cross-product netting is permitted within netting pools—building an incentive for even more concentrated derivatives trading banks. See Antolin et al. (2011), Office of Financial Research (2014), and Pozsar (2015).
20. This arises where the callable cash loan is invested in longer-term assets.
21. In the 1950s-1970s what is now called macro-prudential was then the status quo of a sector-based approach to monetary policy: capital flow controls, managed exchange rates, shifts in required bank reserves and liquid government security minimums, interest rates and credit ceilings for particular sectors, and the like. This approach did not work for the collective whole, and had to be abandoned in favour of deregulation.
22. See, for example, Citi Investor Services (2014).

References

Antolin, P., Sebastian Schich and Juan Yermo (2011), "The Economic Impact of Protracted Low Interest Rates on Pension Funds and Insurance Companies", *OECD Journal: Financial Market Trends*, Vol. 2011/1. DOI: *http://dx.doi.org/10.1787/fmt-2011-5kg55qw0m56l*

Bank of England (2014), *The Bank of England's Sterling Monetary Framework*, November.

Bernanke, B., C. Bertaut, L. P. DeMarco, and S. Kamin (2009), "Financial Reform to Address Systemic Risk", Council of Foreign Relations speech, March, and related references.

Blundell-Wignall, A. (2007), "The Private Equity Boom: Causes and Policy Issues", *Financial Market Trends*, Vol. 2007/1. DOI: *http://dx.doi.org/10.1787/fmt-v2007-art4-en*

Blundell-Wignall, A. and Caroline Roulet (2014), "Problems in the international financial system", *OECD Journal: Financial Market Trends*, Vol. 2014/1. DOI: *http://dx.doi.org/10.1787/fmt-2014-5jxzmkg91s0t*

Blundell-Wignall, A., Paul Atkinson and Caroline Roulet (2014), "Bank business models and the Basel system: Complexity and interconnectedness", *OECD Journal: Financial Market Trends*, Vol. 2013/2. DOI: *http://dx.doi.org/10.1787/fmt-2013-5jzb2rhkd65b*

Borio, C. (2014), "The International Monetary and Financial System: Its Achilles Heel and What to do About It", BIS Working Paper, No. 456.

Caballero, R. and A. Krishnamurthy (2009), "Global Imbalances and Financial Fragility", *NBER Working Paper*, No. 14688.

Çelik, S., G. Demirtaş and M. Isaksson (2015), "Corporate Bonds, Bondholders and Corporate Governance", *OECD Corporate Governance Working Papers*, No. 16, OECD Publishing, Paris. DOI: *http://dx.doi.org/10.1787/5js69lj4hvnw-en*

Choi, A.H. and G.G. Triantis (2012), "The Effect of Bargaining Power on Contract Design", *Virginia Law Review*, 98:8.

Citi Investor Services (2014), *Enhanced Uses of Supply through Asset & Collateral Optimisation & the Impact on the Securities Lending Markets*, October, pages 45 and 57.

Feldstein, M. and P. Bacchetta (1991), "National Saving and International Investment", in *National Saving and Economic Performance*, Bernheim and Shoven (eds), University of Chicago Press.

Feldstein, M. and C. Horioka (1980), "Domestic Savings and International Capital Flows", The Economic Journal,Vol. 90 (June).

Helliwell, J. and R. McKitrick (1999), "Comparing Capital Mobility Across Provincial and National Borders", *Canadian Journal of Economics*, Canadian Economics Association, Vol. 32(5).

Huang, Y. and X. Wang (2010), "Does Financial Repression Inhibit Economic Growth? Empirical Examination of China's Reform Experience", *China Centre for Economic Research, Peking University*, China.

OECD (2015) Institutional Investor's Assets Database, *www.oecd-ilibrary.org/finance-and-investment/data/oecd-institutional-investors-statistics_instinv-data-en.*

OECD Quarterly National Accounts Database, *www.oecd-ilibrary.org/economics/data/oecd-national-accounts-statistics_na-data-en.*

Office of Financial Research (2014), "Securities Lending Collateral Flow Map", January. *http://financialresearch.gov/frac/files/FRAC_FSRM_Collateral_Map_Recommendation.pdf*

Pozsar, Z. (2015), "A Macro View of Shadow Banking: Leveraged Betas and Wholesale Funding in the Context of Secular Stagnation". *http://ssrn.com/abstract=2558945*

White, W. (2012), "Ultra Easy Monetary Policy and the Law of Unintended Consequences", Working Paper No. 126, Federal Reserve Bank of Dallas, Globalization and Monetary Policy Institute.

World Economic Outlook Database (2015) *www.imf.org/external/pubs/ft/weo/2015/01/weodata/index.aspx.*

ANNEX 3.A1

Statistical tables and supplementary data

Table 3. A1.1. **Outstanding corporate bonds**

	USD billion														
	2000	2001	2002	2003	2004	2005	2006	2007	2008	2009	2010	2011	2012	2013	2014
World	**7,734**	**8,468**	**8,881**	**9,749**	**10,579**	**11,445**	**12,935**	**14,353**	**14,892**	**15,795**	**16,704**	**17,515**	**18,806**	**19,915**	**20,936**
Non-financial	3,549	4,028	4,251	4,525	4,689	4,813	5,132	5,511	5,820	6,790	7,491	8,067	8,992	9,880	10,408
Financial	4,185	4,440	4,630	5,225	5,889	6,633	7,804	8,842	9,072	9,005	9,213	9,448	9,814	10,036	10,528
Investment grade	6,974	7,665	8,055	8,831	9,560	10,350	11,704	13,038	13,671	14,478	15,134	15,790	16,799	17,594	18,375
High yield	760	803	826	918	1,019	1,095	1,231	1,315	1,221	1,316	1,570	1,725	2,007	2,322	2,561
Advanced economies	**7,417**	**8,136**	**8,537**	**9,355**	**10,149**	**10,916**	**12,236**	**13,470**	**13,927**	**14,505**	**15,060**	**15,503**	**16,365**	**17,011**	**17,832**
Non-financial	3,387	3,851	4,059	4,311	4,457	4,529	4,788	5,086	5,315	6,064	6,559	6,943	7,683	8,279	8,779
Financial	4,030	4,284	4,478	5,045	5,692	6,387	7,448	8,384	8,613	8,441	8,501	8,560	8,683	8,732	9,053
Investment grade	6,741	7,416	7,793	8,528	9,223	9,938	11,140	12,322	12,866	13,351	13,690	14,010	14,634	15,011	15,629
High yield	675	720	745	827	926	979	1,095	1,148	1,061	1,154	1,370	1,494	1,732	2,000	2,203
Emerging markets	**317**	**332**	**343**	**394**	**430**	**529**	**700**	**883**	**965**	**1,289**	**1,644**	**2,012**	**2,441**	**2,904**	**3,104**
Non-financial	162	177	191	214	232	283	344	425	505	726	932	1,124	1,309	1,601	1,629
Financial	155	155	152	180	198	245	356	458	460	564	711	888	1,132	1,303	1,475
Investment grade	232	249	262	304	337	412	564	717	805	1,127	1,444	1,781	2,166	2,583	2,746
High yield	85	83	81	91	93	117	136	166	160	162	200	231	275	322	358
United States	**3,299**	**3,685**	**3,898**	**4,152**	**4,388**	**4,545**	**4,957**	**5,470**	**5,519**	**5,548**	**5,690**	**5,748**	**6,036**	**6,427**	**6,844**
Non-financial	1,974	2,248	2,381	2,519	2,593	2,603	2,717	2,874	2,945	3,152	3,417	3,570	3,914	4,245	4,566
Financial	1,325	1,437	1,517	1,633	1,795	1,941	2,239	2,596	2,574	2,396	2,273	2,178	2,123	2,182	2,278
Investment grade	2,724	3,071	3,262	3,451	3,624	3,743	4,081	4,553	4,681	4,666	4,644	4,628	4,748	5,016	5,364
High yield	575	614	636	701	764	801	875	917	838	882	1,046	1,120	1,288	1,410	1,480
Europe	**2,978**	**3,220**	**3,358**	**3,818**	**4,308**	**4,811**	**5,572**	**6,161**	**6,441**	**6,788**	**6,970**	**7,172**	**7,470**	**7,497**	**7,704**
Non-financial	679	831	904	1,019	1,095	1,148	1,280	1,388	1,511	1,928	2,053	2,179	2,447	2,604	2,731
Financial	2,299	2,389	2,454	2,799	3,213	3,663	4,292	4,773	4,930	4,859	4,917	4,993	5,023	4,893	4,973
Investment grade	2,929	3,167	3,302	3,747	4,211	4,701	5,430	6,012	6,294	6,597	6,742	6,903	7,146	7,051	7,134
High yield	48	53	56	71	97	110	142	149	146	190	228	269	324	445	570
OECD Total	**7,429**	**8,139**	**8,537**	**9,331**	**10,115**	**10,879**	**12,199**	**13,434**	**13,892**	**14,473**	**15,028**	**15,485**	**16,320**	**16,981**	**17,780**
Non-financial	3,391	3,848	4,058	4,307	4,460	4,539	4,799	5,100	5,328	6,084	6,588	6,993	7,726	8,341	8,847
Financial	4,038	4,291	4,478	5,024	5,656	6,340	7,400	8,334	8,563	8,389	8,440	8,493	8,594	8,640	8,933
Investment grade	6,727	7,396	7,769	8,486	9,178	9,893	11,099	12,287	12,835	13,322	13,656	13,986	14,575	14,970	15,561
High yield	702	743	768	845	937	986	1,100	1,148	1,057	1,151	1,372	1,500	1,745	2,011	2,219

Note: Corporate bonds issuance data obtained from Thomson Reuters New Issues Database and call date data obtained from Bloomberg. Outstanding amounts are calculated based on annual net issuance amounts and actual call data matched with individual bond. Data exclude convertible bonds, preferred shares, sukuk bonds and bonds with an original maturity less than 1 year or an issue size less than USD 1 million. The country breakdown was carried out based on the domicile country of the issuer.

Source: Thomson Reuters, Bloomberg, OECD calculations.

StatLink http://dx.doi.org/10.1787/888933210416

Table 3. A1.2. **Banks Distance-to-Default**

	Number of standard deviations away from the default point														
	2000	2001	2002	2003	2004	2005	2006	2007	2008	2009	2010	2011	2012	2013	2014
All Banks	**2.91**	**2.78**	**2.50**	**3.52**	**5.25**	**6.20**	**5.38**	**3.96**	**1.26**	**1.33**	**2.88**	**2.64**	**3.50**	**4.16**	**5.05**
United States	2.47	3.00	2.78	4.49	6.74	7.50	7.23	4.04	0.79	0.56	3.08	2.36	3.54	5.26	6.15
Europe	3.07	2.87	2.46	3.50	5.25	6.23	4.97	4.18	1.26	1.07	2.32	1.85	2.34	3.62	4.57
Asia/Pacific	3.15	2.27	2.32	2.41	3.40	4.53	4.47	3.24	1.71	2.44	3.84	4.03	5.02	4.27	5.13
Latin America	2.40	1.94	1.82	2.84	3.00	3.22	2.59	3.04	1.25	2.26	3.33	2.94	3.47	3.66	3.46
GSIBs	**2.92**	**2.65**	**2.32**	**3.37**	**5.30**	**6.33**	**5.43**	**4.01**	**1.20**	**1.16**	**2.74**	**2.33**	**3.02**	**4.03**	**4.96**
United States	2.43	2.80	2.61	4.32	6.75	7.62	7.11	4.01	0.75	0.56	3.10	2.29	3.35	5.09	6.04
Europe	3.16	2.82	2.46	3.52	5.33	6.38	5.10	4.18	1.26	1.13	2.32	1.87	2.35	3.67	4.60
Asia/Pacific	2.89	1.74	1.53	1.41	2.63	3.75	3.80	3.12	1.65	2.15	3.80	3.88	4.54	3.72	4.59
Other Large Banks	**2.90**	**3.18**	**3.11**	**4.03**	**5.07**	**5.69**	**5.20**	**3.78**	**1.46**	**1.76**	**3.22**	**3.27**	**4.38**	**4.37**	**5.22**
United States	2.63	3.83	3.48	5.25	6.65	6.93	7.86	4.20	1.01	0.57	2.98	2.71	4.50	6.13	6.71
Europe	2.78	3.04	2.43	3.42	4.92	5.43	4.35	4.19	1.28	0.85	2.31	1.73	2.27	3.39	4.46
Asia/Pacific	3.35	3.17	4.14	4.27	4.65	5.73	5.29	3.35	1.76	2.70	3.88	4.13	5.33	4.57	5.40
Latin America	2.40	1.94	1.82	2.84	3.00	3.22	2.59	3.04	1.25	2.26	3.33	2.94	3.47	3.66	3.46

Notes: This table includes all listed banks in Bloomberg large regional banking competitive peers indices from the USA, Europe, Asia and Latin America. GSIBs, as defined by the FSB (2014), are highlighted in grey.

The distance-to-default is a measure that uses a combination of bank reported data, and market information to calculate the number of standard deviations a bank is from the default point, where the market values of assets equals the book value of liabilities.

Source: Bloomberg, OECD calculations.

StatLink http://dx.doi.org/10.1787/888933210422

Chapter 4

Can pension funds and life insurance companies keep their promises?

This chapter examines the potential impact of an environment of protracted low interest rates on pension systems and life insurance companies. It describes the mechanisms through which prolonged low interest rates can affect the solvency position of these institutions and uses available data to assess potential impacts. The outlook for the solvency position of pension funds and life insurance companies is of concern. Insofar as their promises are linked to evolving parameters or can be adjusted to the new environment of low interest rates, low inflation and low growth, these institutions may be able to weather the situation. However, there is a very serious concern for the financial outlook should these institutions become heavily involved in an excessive 'search for yield' in order to fulfil any fixed guarantee promises they may have made when interest rates were higher. Regulators and policy makers should remain vigilant.

Main findings

- An environment of prolonged low interest rates linked to ongoing low growth and falling inflation rates poses serious challenges to insurance and pension systems and in particular to defined benefit pension funds and life insurance companies offering long-term financial promises.
- The outlook depends foremost on the nature of the promises made by pension funds and life insurance companies and the potential for their adjustment or reversibility. The adverse effect of low interest rates is higher where the liabilities of these institutions consist of a fixed investment return or fixed benefit or pay-out promises.
- For pension funds and life insurance companies in particular, the outlook is troubling as their solvency positions will deteriorate unless they have actively adopted risk management strategies. Given problems being experienced by these institutions, some countries are already adjusting their regulatory framework on an exceptional basis, or otherwise maintaining measures adopted during the financial crisis to relax regulation while increasing monitoring.
- Potential solutions include increasing the duration of assets to be in line with that of liabilities, renegotiating promises and adjusting existing contracts, increasing contributions (for DB pension plans), and regulatory forbearance.
- The main concern is whether pension funds and life insurance companies have, or might, become involved in an excessive 'search for yield' in an attempt to match the level of returns promised earlier to beneficiaries or policyholders when financial markets were delivering higher returns. This might heighten insolvency risks.

Introduction

The financial crisis and ensuing environment of low growth and falling inflation have led to an environment of protracted low interest rates, amplified further by quantitative easing in several major economies that has spurred interest rate declines, with real yields turning negative in a number of countries. This environment of low interest rates, which is expected to prevail for the foreseeable future, poses serious challenges to insurance and pension systems, and in particular, to defined benefit pension funds and life insurance companies. Given the importance that these institutions play in mobilising large amounts of long-term capital, this could have serious implications for their role in successfully acting as long-term investors and potential stabilising forces within the global financial system.

The key concern is the extent to which the low interest rate environment has the potential to lead to a serious deterioration in the solvency position of pension funds and insurance companies that make long-term financial promises.

The outlook for pension systems, including defined benefits (DB) pension funds, and for life insurance companies is troubling since their solvency positions – the degree to which their current assets exceed current liabilities – will deteriorate in an environment of protracted low interest rates unless they have actively adopted risk management strategies.

In the first instance, this should have included immunisation of their investment portfolios against interest rate changes. The overall effect of protracted low interest rates depends on the nature of the promises made by pension funds and life insurance companies, the matching of duration of their liabilities with that of the assets backing these liabilities, the composition of their portfolio investments, and the extent to which these institutions have aggressively increased asset risk exposures in a 'search for yield'.[1]

The outlook depends foremost on the nature of the long-term promise made by pension funds and life insurance companies and the potential for adjustment or reversibility of the said promise. The adverse effect of low interest rates is higher where the liabilities of life insurance companies and pension funds consist of promised fixed investment returns, or fixed benefit or pay-out promises. Pension promises for current retirees and guaranteed promises in insurance contracts are fixed by nature. However, pension promises are parameter-dependent for members currently saving for retirement. These pension promises will depend on future wages; insofar as low interest rates are the result of macroeconomic conditions that lead to lower future wages, the pension promise will also adjust downwards.

The potential for fixed pension and guaranteed promises to undermine the solvency position of pension funds and insurance companies in an environment of protracted low interest rates can be partially offset by changing the terms of the promises. However, this solution is far from being simple or equitable. In the case of pension funds, the plan sponsor (e.g. corporation, public sector entity) is typically called upon to fund any shortfall, but instead efforts may be made to amend the structure of private pension plans to curtail benefits. Pension promises have been made more flexible in the last decade in many countries (e.g. the Netherlands), but not in all (e.g. the United Kingdom). Renegotiating the terms of insurance contracts has proven to be more difficult. Nonetheless, bankruptcy or its threat has led to a renegotiation of the terms of insurance contracts with high guarantees in some countries (e.g. Japan), while in other countries the structure of some of these contracts (group policies) appears to have made renegotiation easier (e.g. France).

Any significant mismatch between the duration of liabilities and assets is a cause for concern. Pension funds and life insurance companies typically hold long-dated bonds in order to meet future liabilities. However, their liabilities may have a longer duration due to the time horizon of their promises (e.g. life expectancy at age 65 can exceed 20 years). Therefore, life insurance companies and pension funds may face reinvestment risk unless they have developed asset-liability management (ALM) strategies to manage this risk. ALM strategies may require good quality debt instruments with long maturities; however, these instruments may not be available in sufficient quantities. Also, derivative instruments such as long-term interest rate swaps may need to be purchased in order to extend asset duration and ensure better ALM matching.[2]

The main concern for the outlook is whether pension funds and insurance companies have, or might become, involved in an excessive 'search for yield' in an attempt to match the level of returns promised to beneficiaries or policyholders when financial markets were delivering higher returns. Such a strategy might heighten insolvency risks. Insofar as the regulatory framework requires institutions which increase the risk profile of their investment portfolio to augment the reserves set aside to cover their promises or otherwise ensure adequate capital, the 'search for yield' should only be a moderate cause for concern as increasing capital reserves increases the costs of searching for yield, thus acting as a deterrent. Regulators should remain vigilant. While there is at present a lack of detailed data on investment portfolios which might indicate an enhanced 'search for yield', such a shift may loom on the horizon.

Interest rates have had a long-term downward trend

Interest rates have been trending downwards over the past four decades. Figure 4.1 shows nominal yields on long-term (10-year) government bonds in a few OECD countries. They have fallen from two-digit rates in the late 1970s to 1980s to below 2% recently. Other interest rate measures confirm the downward trend in long-term interest rates (Figure 4.2).

Figure 4.1. **Nominal yields on 10-year government bonds in selected OECD countries, 1970-2014**

Percentage

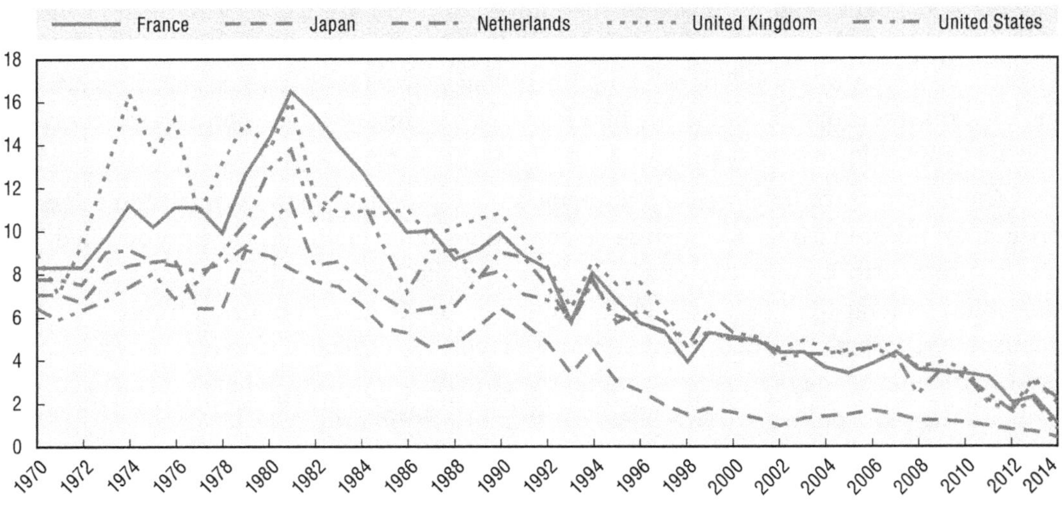

Source: Datastream.

StatLink http://dx.doi.org/10.1787/888933209569

Figure 4.2. **Other measures of long-term interest rates, 2000-2014**

Percentage

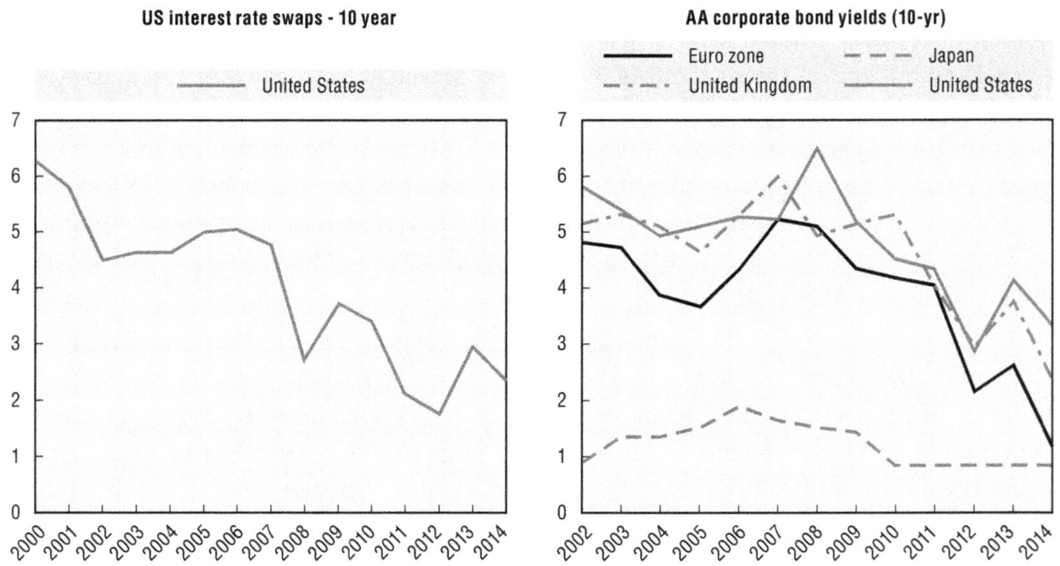

Source: Datastream.

StatLink http://dx.doi.org/10.1787/888933209573

Protracted low interest rates appear to reflect economic conditions characterised by low inflation (in both prices and salaries) and low returns on investment. The fall in interest rates has occurred in conjunction with declining inflation rates (Figure 4.3). The correlation between 10-year government bond yields and inflation confirms this observation. For the period 1970-2014, this correlation ranges from 0.63 for the United States to 0.83 for France, with 0.69 for Japan and 0.79 for the United Kingdom (Figure 4.4).[3] Real yields on 10-year government bonds have also been trending downwards (Figure 4.5). While real yields do not affect pension liabilities, which are typically nominal promises, they do have an impact on assets as lower real yields entail lower potential accumulation of assets to back future liabilities.

Figure 4.3. **Annual variation of prices, Consumer Price Index, 1970-2014**

Percentage

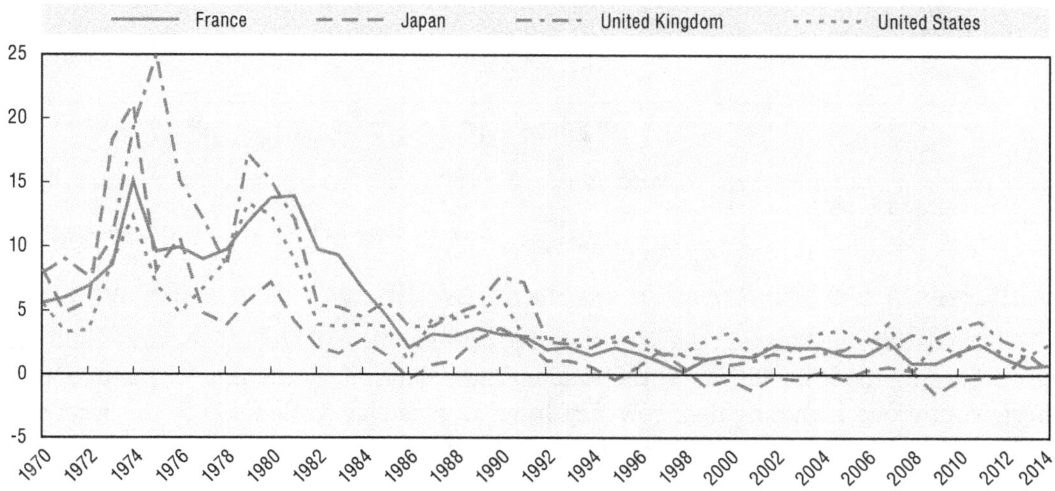

Source: IMF International Financial Statistics and OECD Main Economic Indicators databases, OECD (2015), *http://dx.doi.org/10.1787/data-00052-en.*

StatLink http://dx.doi.org/10.1787/888933209585

Figure 4.4. **Yields on 10-year government bonds and Consumer Price Index in selected OECD countries, 1970-2014**

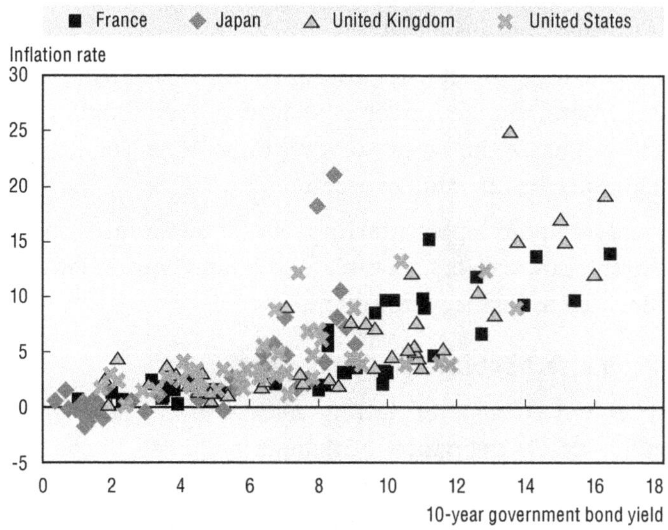

Source: Datastream; IMF International Financial Statistics and OECD Main Economic Indicators databases, *http://dx.doi.org/10.1787/data-00052-en.*

StatLink http://dx.doi.org/10.1787/888933209596

Figure 4.5. **Real yields on 10-year government bonds, 1970-2014**
Percentage

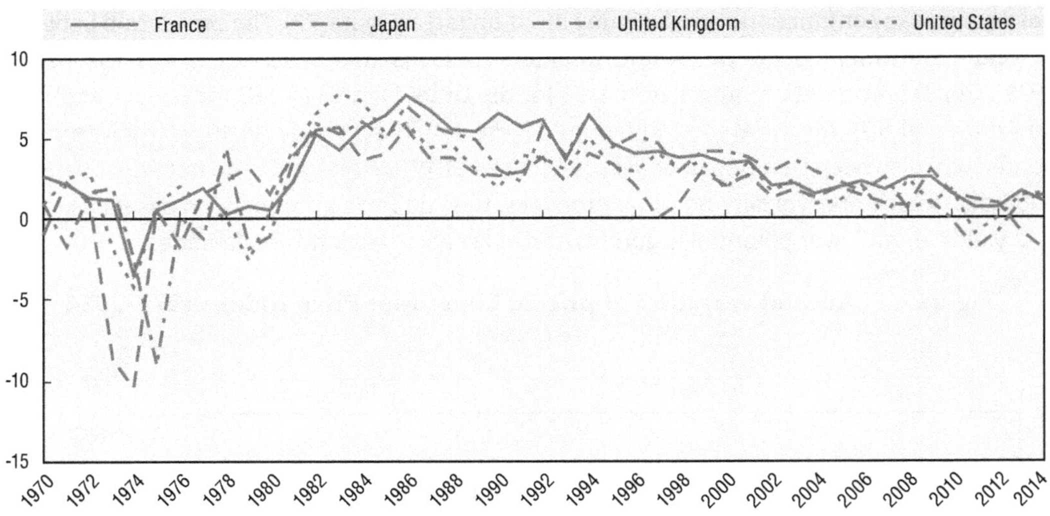

Source: Datastream; IMF International Financial Statistics and OECD Main Economic Indicators databases, *http://dx.doi.org/10.1787/data-00052-en*.

StatLink http://dx.doi.org/10.1787/888933209601

The low interest rate affects both the asset and liability side of pension systems

The relationship between the liabilities of pension funds and annuity providers and the assets backing those liabilities (i.e. the funding ratio) determines the financial situation of these institutions, including their solvency. Interest rates play a role for both the asset and the liability side of the balance sheet of these institutions and understanding how interest rates affect both is essential to understanding the potential impact of low interest rates.

Low interest rates affect the liabilities of pension funds and annuity providers because the liabilities depend on the discount rate used to calculate the present value of future promises. The discount rate used to calculate the net present value is generally assumed to be the risk-free rate, usually the long-term government bond yield (e.g. the 10-year government bond yield). Other things equal, when government bond yields decline, the estimated value of future liabilities increases.

Low interest rates also affect the future value of savings, which is the assets accumulated at retirement, as fixed-income securities, including long-term government bonds, are often a large part of the investment portfolio. However, low interest rates going forward do not affect the current value of assets.

Therefore, to understand the potential impact of interest rates on pension systems, it is necessary to examine how assets accumulate to finance retirement in old age and how those assets are allocated to finance retirement.

Interest rates directly affect savings for retirement

Saving for retirement consists of putting aside a proportion of one's income while working to accumulate assets to finance retirement in old age. Those savings are invested and earn a return, thus leading to asset accumulation. The amount of assets accumulated (the future value of savings, Box 4.1) is a function of the contribution rate, the growth of wages (taking into account inflation and productivity growth) and the return earned on the portfolio. The return earned on the portfolio is a positive function of the returns earned on the different assets held within the portfolio.

Box 4.1. The future value of savings (FVS) - assets accumulated at retirement

The future value of saving accumulated during the individual's working life span is:

$$FVS = FVS(S,r,N) = \sum_{i=1}^{N} S_i (1+r_i)^{N-i+1} \quad [1]$$

FVS is valued at the age of retirement, which is accumulated over N periods. N is the working life span or the period of accumulation, which is calculated as the difference between the retirement age (RA) and the age at which the individual began accumulating savings (EA). S_i is the amount saved in each period and r_i is the annual rate of return on investment (assume $r_i = r \forall i$ for simplicity). Assuming that the amount saved is a fixed share of current wages (i.e. a contribution rate, c), and wages grow from an initial wage W_0 according to inflation (p) and productivity (pr):

$$S_i = cW_i = c \cdot (1+p)^{i-1} \cdot (1+pr)^{i-1} \cdot W_0 \quad [2]$$

Contributions in the first year are paid from the initial wage W_0, in the second year they are paid from the new wage (W_1) that has grown according to inflation and productivity gains, i.e. they are paid from (1+p)*(1+pr) W_0. Contributions paid at year j are paid from wage $W_j = (1+p)^{i-1} \cdot (1+pr)^{i-1} W_0$, where i=j-EA.

$$FVS = FVS(S,r,N) = \sum_{i=1}^{N} c \cdot (1+p)^{i-1} \cdot (1+pr)^{i-1} \cdot W_0 \cdot (1+r)^{N-i+1} \quad [3]$$

Therefore, at retirement, the individual has accumulated assets A_N = FVS. At this point, given the amount of assets accumulated, A_N, and the length of the period expected to receive pension payments, the amount of retirement income the individual receives can be calculated, which determines how much s/he can consume.

The growth of wages depends, in equilibrium, on inflation and productivity growth. However, outside equilibrium, wages could grow above or below inflation and productivity growth if there are changes in the bargaining power of workers (unions) and/or employers, which may lead to changes in the wage share of the economy. The future value of saving (assets accumulated at retirement) is a positive function of wage growth, w, and the return on investment, r.

$$FVS = FVS(S,r,N) = \sum_{i=1}^{N} c \cdot (1+w)^{i-1} \cdot W_0 \cdot (1+r)^{N-i+1} \quad [4]$$

Lower interest rates lead to lower accumulated assets for retirement because of lower government bond yields

One of the key asset classes in any retirement portfolio is fixed-income securities, which include long-term government bonds. Lower interest rates (i.e. lower long-term government bonds yields) will therefore lead to lower accumulated assets to finance retirement. How much lower depends on the proportion of assets in the portfolio in the fixed-income category and in long-term government bonds.

Pension funds and life insurance companies have a large proportion of assets invested in fixed income securities. Indeed, Figure 4.6 shows that pension funds in many countries invest around 40% of their assets in fixed-income securities; that share implies that the impact of low interest rates on asset accumulation should be weighted by the proportion of assets invested in fixed-income securities.

Figure 4.6. **Pension funds asset allocation in selected investment categories, 2013**

Percentage of total assets

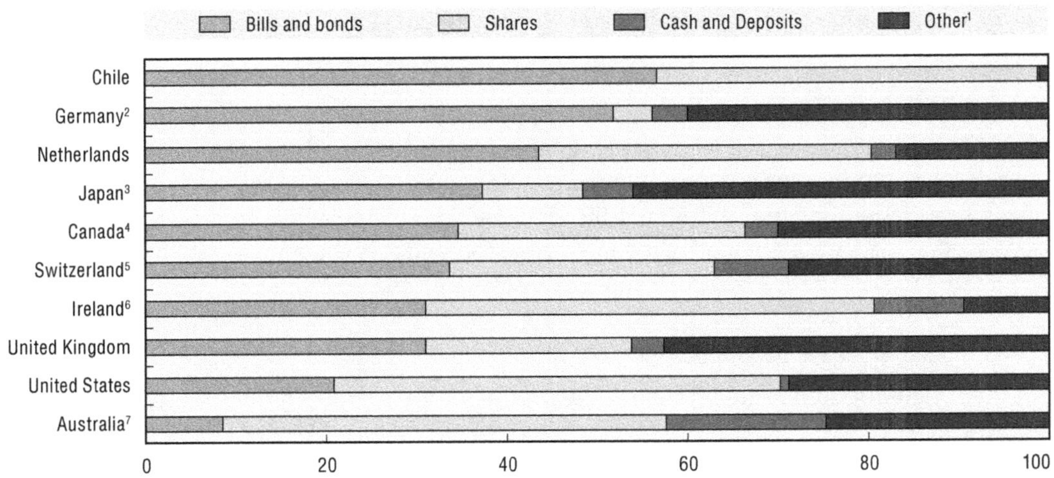

Notes: More detailed information on the data can be found in the descriptions provided in the GPS database, *www.oecd.org/pensions/globalpensionstatistics.htm*. Pension funds' asset allocation for other OECD countries can be found in the *OECD Pension Markets in Focus 2014*, *www.oecd.org/pensions/pensionmarketsinfocus.htm*. (1) The 'Other' category includes loans, land and buildings, unallocated insurance contracts, hedge funds, private equity funds, structured products, other mutual funds (i.e. not invested in cash, bills and bonds, or shares) and other investments. (2) The high value for the 'Other' category is driven mainly by loans (16% of total investment) and other investments of collective investment schemes (16% of total investment). (3) Source: Bank of Japan. The high value for the 'Other' category is driven mainly by outward investments in securities (21% of total investment) and accounts payable and receivable (19% of total investment). (4) The high value for the 'Other' category is driven mainly by other investments of collective investment schemes (17% of total investment). (5) The high value for the 'Other' category is driven mainly by land and buildings (direct and indirect investment in this category accounts for 17% of total investment). (6) Source: Based on data from the IAPF Pension Investment Survey. (7) Source: Australian Bureau of Statistics (ABS). Data refer to the end of June 2013. The high value for the 'Other' category is driven mainly by net equity of pension funds in life office reserves (14% of total investment).

Source: OECD Global Pension Statistics, *www.oecd.org/pensions/globalpensionstatistics.htm*.

StatLink http://dx.doi.org/10.1787/888933209614

Figure 4.7 shows that life insurance companies have an even larger share of their portfolio invested in fixed income securities than pension funds, which means, other things equal, that the impact of low interest rates will be higher than for pension funds given the higher share of interest sensitive assets.[4]

The impact of a reduction in interest rates on the value of the assets backing the liabilities of these investors depends not only on the proportion of the portfolio invested in fixed income securities, but also on the valuation methods, and the maturity of those securities. A drop in interest rates may have an immediate impact on the current value of assets when mark-to-market valuations are applied. However, this drop could translate into an increase in the current value of assets as a drop in yields would be reflected in an increase in prices and therefore returns. However, the actual or face value of current assets might not change at all when pension funds and insurance companies hold their fixed-income securities to maturity. To the extent that interest rates remain low into the future and the fixed-income securities in the portfolio reach maturity, reinvestments into new fixed-income securities carrying lower yields would reduce the future value of assets, in proportion with the share of the portfolio invested in fixed-income securities. As a result of this lower future value of assets, pension funds' and insurance companies' assets might not be sufficient to back up their promises, unless the pension or payment promise is adjusted to the new environment of low interest rates, low inflation and low growth.

Figure 4.7. **Life insurers' asset allocation in selected investment categories, 2013**

Percentage of total assets

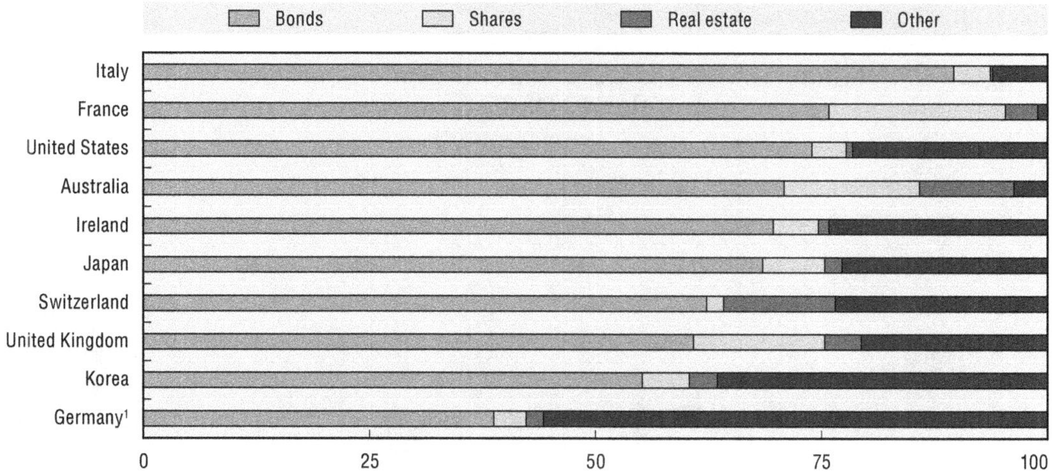

Notes: Data only refer to domestic direct insurers, and exclude assets linked to unit-linked products where risk is fully borne by policyholders. Life insurers' asset allocation in other OECD countries can be found in the report *Global Insurance Market Trends 2014*, *www.oecd.org/finance/insurance/globalinsurancemarkettrends.htm*. (1) The 'Other' category mainly comprises loans and mutual fund investments for which no look-through was available.

Source: Based on OECD *Global Insurance Market Trends 2014*, *www.oecd.org/finance/insurance/globalinsurancemarkettrends.htm*.

StatLink http://dx.doi.org/10.1787/888933209626

Figure 4.8. **Variation in pension funds' asset allocation between 2003 and 2013 in selected OECD countries**

In percentage points

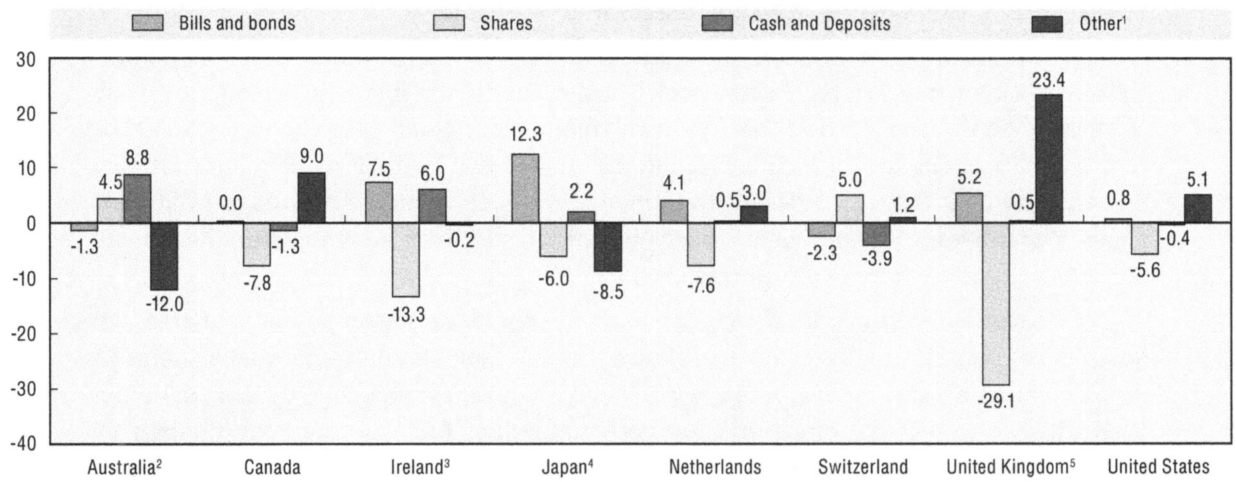

Notes: (1) The 'Other' category includes loans, land and buildings, unallocated insurance contracts, hedge funds, private equity funds, structured products, other mutual funds (i.e. not invested in cash, bills and bonds, or shares) and other investments. (2) Source: Australian Bureau of Statistics (ABS). Data refer to the variation between end of June 2003 and end of June 2013. The 'Other' category includes net equity of pension funds in life office reserves. (3) Source: Based on data from the IAPF Pension Investment Survey. (4) Source: Bank of Japan. The 'Other' category includes outward investments in securities and accounts payable and receivable. (5) Data only refer to occupational pension schemes.

Source: OECD Global Pension Statistics, *www.oecd.org/daf/fin/private-pensions/globalpensionstatistics.htm*.

StatLink http://dx.doi.org/10.1787/888933209631

The share of fixed-income securities in the investment portfolio of pension funds in the main economies has not changed much in the past decade (Figure 4.8) while that for life insurers have increased (Figure 4.9).

Figure 4.9. **Variation in life insurers' asset allocation between 2006 and 2013 in selected OECD countries**

In percentage points

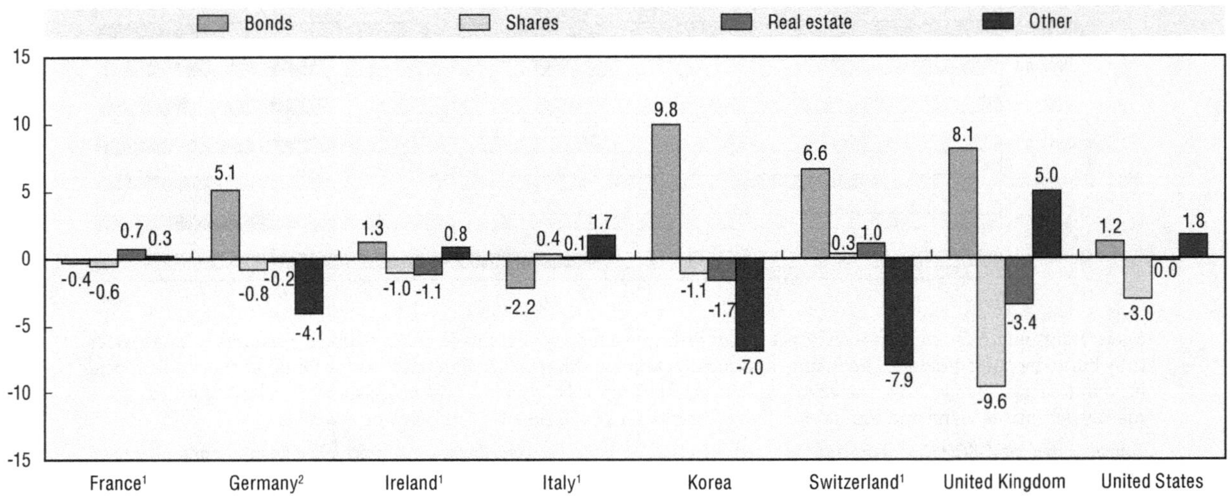

Notes: Data only refer to domestic direct insurers. (1) The shift is shown between 2009 and 2013. (2) The 'Other' category mainly comprises loans and mutual fund investments for which no look-through was available.

Source: OECD Global Insurance Statistics, *www.oecd.org/daf/fin/insurance/oecdinsurancestatistics.htm.*

StatLink *http://dx.doi.org/10.1787/888933209643*

Some concern for investing in riskier assets in a 'search for yield'

The extent to which pension funds and insurance companies engage in a 'search for yield' is the main concern for their outlook. Pension funds (and insurance companies) may shift their portfolio allocation towards investments that could potentially fetch higher returns but in exchange for an increased overall risk profile for their investment portfolio. As pension funds move into riskier investments in search of higher returns to fulfil their pension promises, they may be seriously compromising their solvency situation in the event of a negative shock (e.g. liquidity freeze).

The observed shift in portfolio composition to 'other assets' may be a sign of a 'search for yield' by pension funds. Figure 4.10 shows that the dollar amount invested by pension funds in 'other assets' has increased steadily over the past decade, thereby increasing the potential risk to pension funds and the potential risk to financial markets (Chapter 3). However, this may be just the result of a larger total investment portfolio. The category 'other assets' as a share of total portfolio investment has increased but much less so than the dollar amount would have suggested. Although the 'search for yield' remains one of the main worries for the outlook, available data do not show that it is happening on a large scale yet, except perhaps in the United Kingdom.

The data available for the United Kingdom show that pension funds may already be engaging in a 'search for yield' (Figure 4.11). There is a clear upward trend in the current value of investment in 'other assets', which include private equity, derivatives and structured products, as well as in the proportion of the total investment portfolio invested in those assets classes.[5]

Figure 4.10. **Total investment by pension funds in 'other assets', OECD countries**

Current values and as percentage of total investment

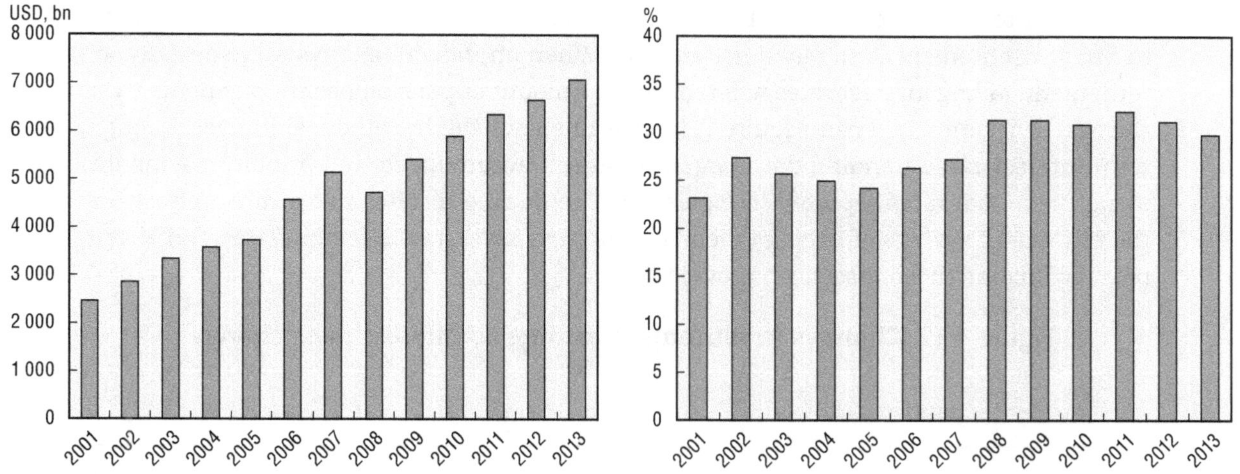

Source: OECD Global Pension Statistics, *www.oecd.org/daf/fin/private-pensions/globalpensionstatistics.htm.*

StatLink http://dx.doi.org/10.1787/888933209655

Figure 4.11. **Total investment by pension funds in 'other assets', United Kingdom**

Current values and as percentage of total investment

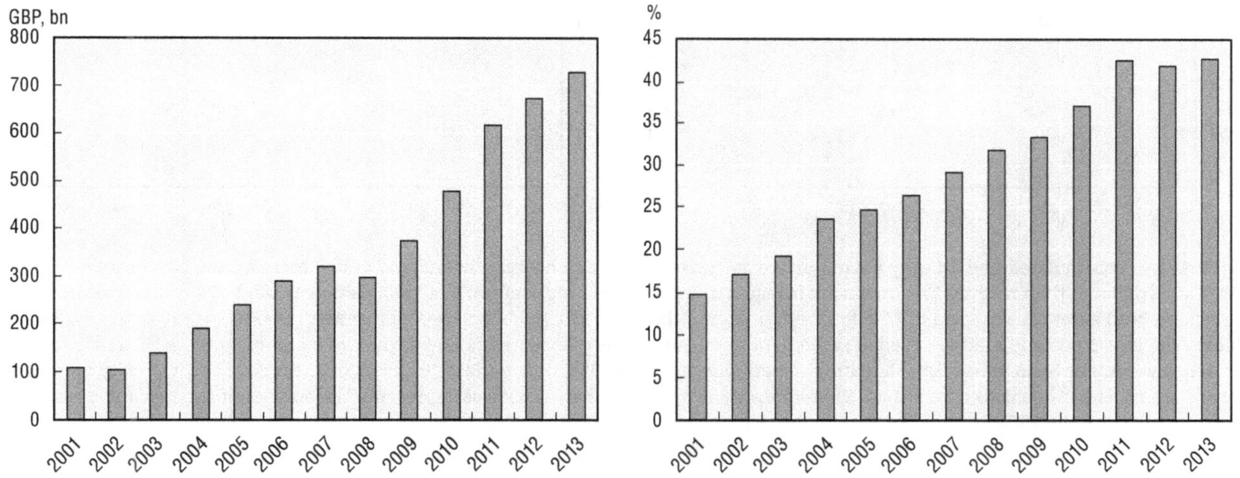

Source: OECD Global Pension Statistics, *www.oecd.org/daf/fin/private-pensions/globalpensionstatistics.htm.*

StatLink http://dx.doi.org/10.1787/888933209661

Low interest rates have a different impact on defined contribution (DC) and defined benefit (DB) pension plans[6]

Who bears the impact of low interest rates on assets depends on whether a plan is of the DB or DC type. In DB pension plans, pension funds take contributions, manage the assets, and in exchange promise a certain level of income at retirement. The impact of low interest rates on the people saving for retirement in DB pension plans is, in principle, negligible, as they are promised a certain level of income irrespective of the amount of assets accumulated. It is the DB pension fund which bears the risk of the assets accumulated being lower than needed to fulfill the income promise.

The impact of low interest rates on people saving in DC pension plans is a reduction in the amount of assets accumulated to finance retirement and an increase in annuity prices, which can affect the adequacy of their retirement income. In DC pension plans, pension funds take in contributions and manage the assets, but they are not involved in providing retirement income. Individuals need to allocate the assets accumulated at retirement to finance old age in DC pension plans. One common way to allocate assets to finance retirement is to buy a life annuity. When an individual buys a life annuity at retirement, falling interest rates will reduce the amount of pension benefit payments that the assets accumulated can acquire.[7] Figure 4.12 shows the hypothetical impact of long-term interest rates trending downwards on assets accumulated and annuity payments using the actual rates reported in Figure 4.1. The decline in rates has a direct effect on the retirement savings of DC plan members through lower assets accumulated and lower pension income those assets can provide.

Figure 4.12. **Changes in retirement income as interest rates change**

1970 = 100

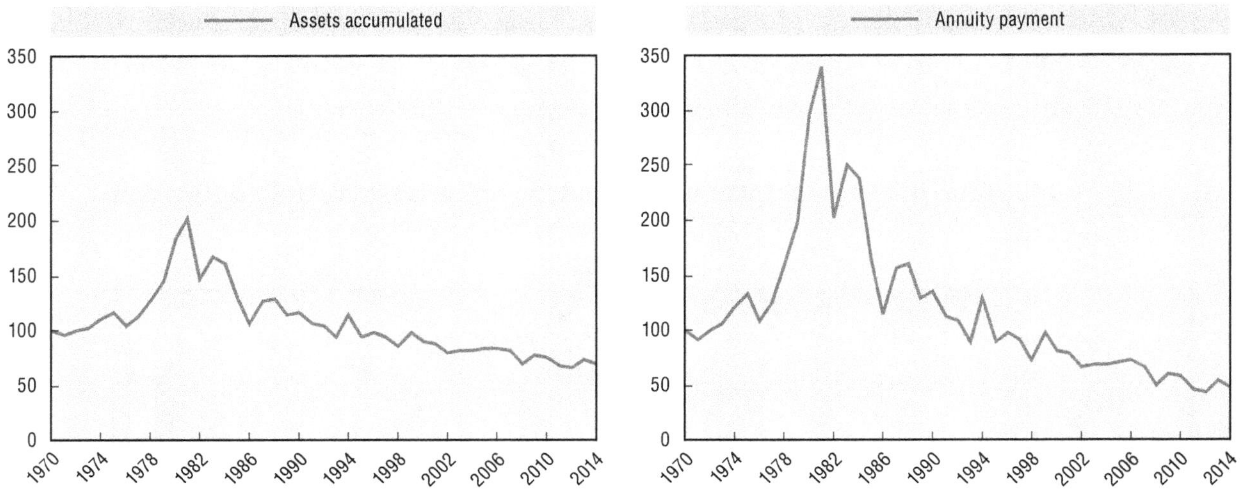

Note: Assets accumulated and annuity payments are calculated for the same hypothetical individual contributing 10% of wages over a 40 year period and then retiring. The assets are invested in a portfolio comprising 60% of variable income and 40% of fixed income. The return on both asset classes used is 4.5% for the former and the historical yields for 10-yr government bonds, kept to maturity, for the latter. The assets accumulated are used at retirement to buy an annuity 20 years making payments for starting at age 65 and using the actual government bond yields for calculating the annuity premium. The only variable evolving over time is the yield on government bonds which is set equal to actual data. Therefore, the evolution of both variables represents the impact of interest rates trending downwards since the 1970.

Source: OECD calculations.

StatLink http://dx.doi.org/10.1787/888933209673

On the other side of the transaction is the annuity provider, usually an insurance company, which takes the assets in exchange for a promise of regular, periodic payments during the retirement period. Once the annuity contract is in place and the promise made, the insurance company bears the risk of lower than expected interest rates, given annuity premiums and expected annuity payments (see Box 4.2).

This section has shown the impact low interest rates have on the future value of current assets and savings depends on the weight that fixed-income assets, and in particular long-term government bonds, have in the portfolio of pension funds. The section has also shown that low interest rates affect the asset side of the balance sheet of both DB and DC pension plans. In DC pension plans, individuals are negatively affected by low interest rates in their retirement as they receive lower retirement income for a given amount of assets when buying an annuity because the price references for annuities are based on long-term interest rates. In DB pension plans individuals are not affected because DB plans involve a promise. Employers and plan sponsors may have to come up with more resources. The main concern for the outlook from the asset side of balance sheets is the degree to which pension funds and annuity providers attempt to meet their payment promises by shifting their portfolio composition towards investments with a higher return potential, a shift that results in an increased average risk profile for their portfolio. This 'search for yield' does not yet appear in the data except, perhaps, in the United Kingdom. The United Kingdom is a country with large defined benefit pension plans, most of them already closed, which may have already moved into riskier assets or investments to achieve higher returns and thus able to keep their pension promises. This may be the direction in which pension funds will move.

Box 4.2. **Annuity payments**

Consider a simple, immediate individual life annuity, for which the insurer pays a stream of regular, periodic payments to an individual for his lifetime in exchange for an upfront, lump sum premium payment. The price of this product for an individual should be the net present value of expected future cash flows. The insurer must take into account the discount rate, the expected survival of the individual and any expenses incurred by the insurer for offering the promised regular payment. The insurer must define appropriate assumptions for each of these variables to calculate a price which is expected to cover the future payments owed in order to avoid making a loss on the product.

A discount rate is assumed in order to account for the time value of money. Generally, the risk-free rate is the discount rate assumed, because, in financial markets, products with the same expected cash flows should be sold at the same price. The insurer could take a risk-free investment strategy for the term of the bond and invest the premium received in government bonds, which would pay coupons which could be matched to the payments owed to the annuitant.

If the discount rate used to price the annuity is higher than the risk-free rate, the insurer is obliged to invest in higher risk assets offering a higher return in order to meet the future payments. This investment strategy would then no longer be risk-free, as there is a chance that actual investment returns will be below the expected return and that the insurer will have to default on its future payments, exposing the annuitant to credit risk.

The expected survival of the individual must also be accounted for, since the annuity payments will be made for his/her remaining life. Thus when calculating the present value of expected future cash flows, the probability that the individual will survive to receive each cash flow has to be taken into account. These mortality assumptions generally vary by gender (unless regulation expressly forbids pricing by gender) and attained age. Improvements in mortality should also be assumed to account for the fact that mortality is expected to decrease over time (i.e. life expectancy is expected to increase).

The annuity factor will take into account the survival probabilities in each period. In this context, annuity factor = $1+p_{65}v + {}_2p_{65}v^2 + \dots + {}_np_{65}v^n$, where ${}_np_{65}$ is the probability of surviving n periods at age 65, $v = 1/(1+d)$, and d is the discount rate.

The impact of low interest rates depends on the nature of the promise of DB pension plans and annuities

The next step in the analysis is to assess the impact of interest rates on the liability side of the balance sheet. The focus is on pension funds that have some type of promises linked to retirement income (e.g. final salary DB plans) and insurance companies that take assets in exchange for a promised return (e.g. annuity products involving regular annuity payments).[8]

Current liabilities depend on the nature of the promise and the discount rate used to calculate the present value of those promises. The discount rate used to calculate the present value is generally a risk-free rate, usually the nominal long-term government bond yield. Lower discount rates translate directly into higher present value of liabilities for a given amount, all else equal.

The impact of interest rates also depends on whether the promise is fixed or not. The promise can be fixed or can be parameter dependent, whereby the promise is linked to certain parameters such as wages or inflation (e.g. DB pension funds). The nature of the promise would also depend on whether the pension or annuity payment promised is already incurred or is embedded in a new contract. In the case of DB pension funds with current retirees and insurance companies already engaged in a contract with the annuitant, low interest rates (lower than the interest rates assumed in their actuarial and pricing calculations) mean that the current assets backing those promises may not grow as much as was expected at the time the promise was made, thereby compromising their solvency position.

The impact of low interest rates will be highest when the promise is fixed in nature. As interest rates fall, resulting in a decline in the discount rate applied to calculate the present value of future pay-outs, the present value of a fixed promise or cash flow becomes bigger in the future. Figure 4.13 shows the evolution over the period 1970-2014 of the present value of a cash flow of 100 currency units payable for 20 years to approximate life expectancy at 65, using as discount rates the actual United States long-term government yield (Figure 4.1). The fall in interest rates over the period from 6.24% to 2.21% results in an increase of 69% in the present value of the liabilities.

Figure 4.13. **Evolution of the present value of an hypothetical fixed cash flow promise payable over 20 years when interest rates fall**

(First year present value = 100)

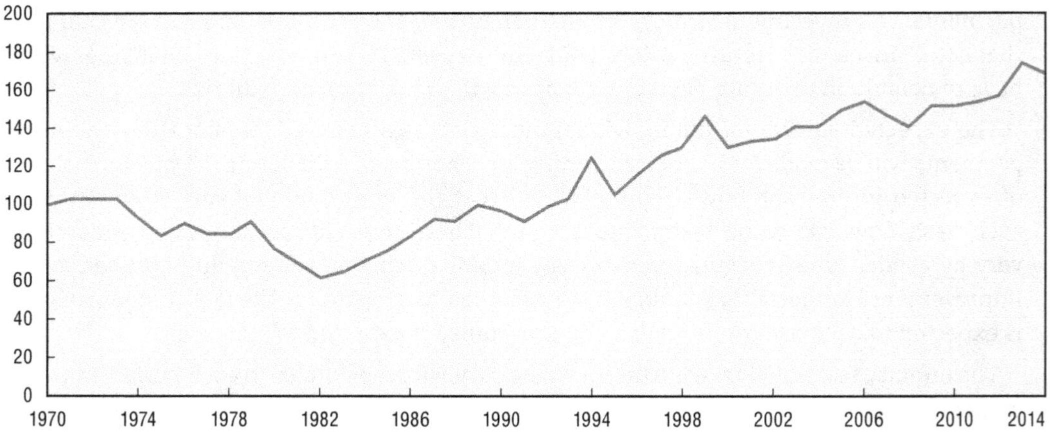

Note: The historical long-term US government bond yield is used to discount the cash flows. The yield in 1970 is used for the present value of the first year. The yield for 2014 is used for calculating the present value of the last year.

Source: OECD calculations.

StatLink http://dx.doi.org/10.1787/888933209684

The promise for people still saving for retirement depends on the evolution of various parameters. To the extent that protracted low interest rates accurately anticipate future economic conditions characterised by low growth, low inflation (in both prices and salaries) and low returns on investment, future pension benefits may also be lower. In the case of insurance companies offering life annuities, the low interest rates should be reflected in the new pricing.[9] Only when interest rates turn out to be lower than the rate used in pricing life annuities might problems arise for insurance companies offering life annuities. Additionally, the low interest rates lead to annuity contracts that provide lower annuity income to the annuitant for a given amount of assets. This is similar to the problem discussed above for individuals in DC pension plans, whose retirement income adequacy will be negatively affected by low interest rates (Figure 4.12).

Consequently, the liabilities of DB pension funds should gradually adjust to reflect the new environment of lower interest rates. If low interest rates mean that for the foreseeable future inflation and wage growth will be lower, then the future promise will also be lower (the typical promise of a DB pension plan is the result of applying an accrual rate to a reference salary, e.g. final salary, and multiplying it by the years of service or contribution).

In short, the impact of low interest rates going forward for DB pension plans will depend on the relationship between the growth of the promise, which is determined by the future growth of wages (w in equation [4] in box 4.1), and the discounting of future liabilities. When both the value of the promise and the discount factor fall, the solvency position will deteriorate if the change in the growth of the promise, Δ(1+w), relative to the factor used to discount the future liabilities, $\Delta \Sigma_{j=1,n} (1+i)^j$, is greater than one. However, the worsening of the solvency position is less than if the promise were to remain constant and only the discount rate declined. Figure 4.14 shows that discount rates (given by 10-year government yields) have fallen a bit more than growth rates of nominal wages.

Figure 4.14. **Nominal wage growth and interest rates, 1991-2013**

Percentage

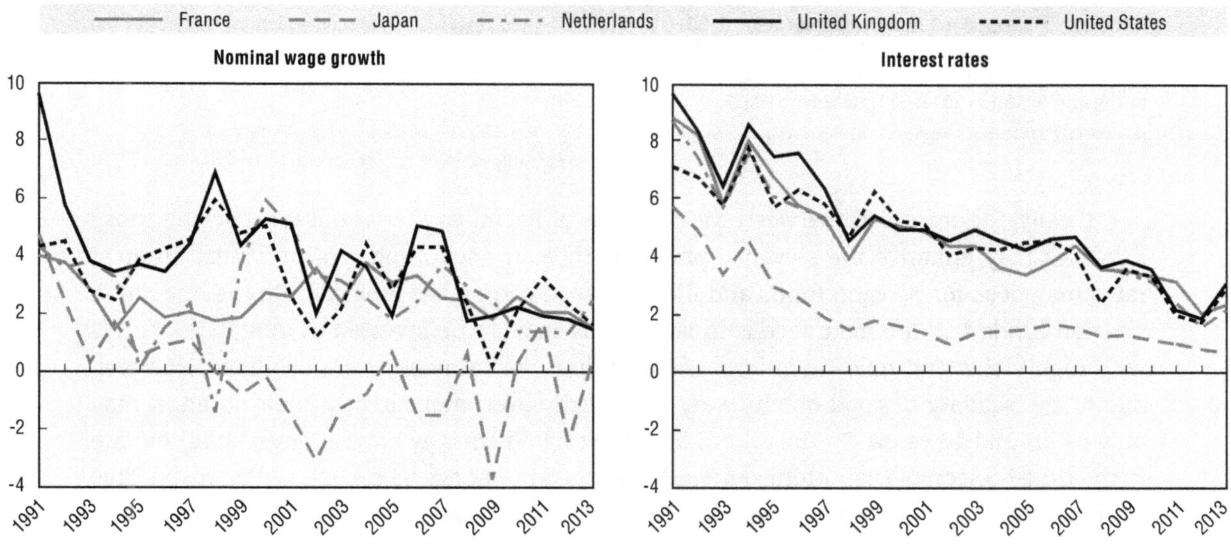

Note: The chart on the left-hand side shows the variation of economy wide nominal average annual wages growth for a full-time, full-year equivalent employee in the total economy. They are obtained by dividing the national-accounts-based total wage bill by the average number of employees in the total economy, which is then multiplied by the ratio of average usual weekly hours per full-time employee to average usual weekly hours for all employees.

Source: «Average annual wages», OECD Employment and Labour Market Statistics (database); Datastream.

StatLink http://dx.doi.org/10.1787/888933209693

The percentage of members already retired relative to active members serves as a proxy for the potential magnitude of the problem, as the promise is fixed for those already retired and parameter dependent for those still active.[10] The higher the proportion of retired people in the membership of pension funds the larger is the part of the promise that is fixed relative to the promise that is parameter-dependent. The figure below clearly shows that for countries like Canada and the United Kingdom, where the percentage of members of pension funds who are retired is close to 50% and 40% respectively, the problem is larger than for countries like Germany and the Netherlands where the percentage of retired people is only around 15%.

Figure 4.15. **Share of active and retired members of DB pension funds in selected OECD countries, 2013**

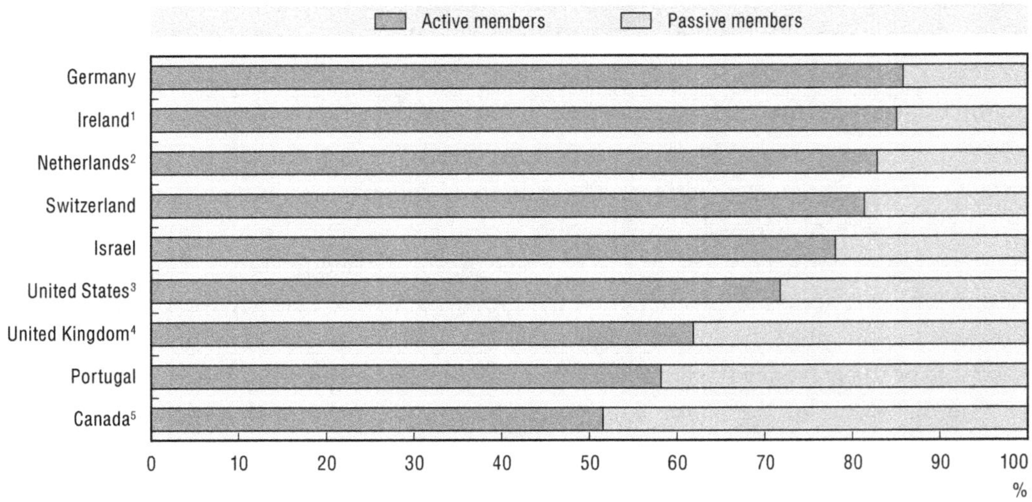

Notes: Active members are defined as persons at present accumulating benefits or who have accrued benefits in the past and are not yet retired. Passive members are members who are receiving benefits from the plan.

(1) Source: the Pensions Authority. Data refer to 2014, and to active and frozen DB schemes which are subject to the funding standard and which submitted an Annual Actuarial Data Return to the Pensions Authority at the end of 2014. (2) Data include members of occupational DC plans. (3) Data refer to 2011. (4) Source: The Purple Book 2014. Data refer to the end of March 2014. (5) Data refer to 2012.

Source: OECD Global Pension Statistics, *www.oecd.org/daf/fin/private-pensions/globalpensionstatistics.htm*.

StatLink http://dx.doi.org/10.1787/888933209706

Finally, the mismatch between the duration of liabilities and the assets backing those liabilities may enhance the solvency problems that an environment of prolonged interest rates may pose for pension funds and life insurance companies (Box 4.3). On the one hand, pension funds and life insurance companies may have to be invested in long dated bonds with high yields and hold them until maturity in order to meet future liabilities. However, due to the scarcity of good quality, very long-term government bonds, their duration may only be around 10 years. On the other hand, their liabilities may have a longer duration due to the time horizon of their promises (e.g. life expectancy at age 65 can exceed 20 years). This mismatch will cause insurance companies and pension funds to be exposed to re-investment risk. Their future long dated bonds may yield much less, reducing their capacity for meeting their payment obligations.

Box 4.3. **How changes in interest rates affect pension funds and insurers: the duration match between assets and liabilities**

In general, when calculating liabilities, defined pension funds and insurance companies discount future cash flows by using a discount rate linked to long-term interest rates. A reduction in long-term interest rates means that the liabilities, or the discounted value of future cash flows of a pension plan or an insurance company, would increase. At the same time, the value of pension fund and insurer asset portfolios would rise given the increased value of future cash flows.

Box 4.3. **How changes in interest rates affect pension funds and insurers: the duration match between assets and liabilities** *(cont.)*

The net effect depends on the duration of assets and liabilities. It can be expected that defined benefit pension funds and life companies with long-dated, interest-rate-sensitive liabilities will, unless they are hedged, have a negative duration gap, i.e. the weighted duration of liabilities exceeds the weighted duration of assets. Where there is a negative duration gap, an increase in interest rates will have positive effect. Thus, defined benefit pension funds and life insurers will be negatively affected by a reduction in long-term interest rates.

Where the duration gap is negative, a period of low interest rates poses challenges for asset-liability management in that current lower-yielding assets are expected to meet the return assumptions made in the past. Interest income falls as coupon payments from fixed-income instruments and the principal from maturing debt must be rolled over into lower-yielding debt. The extent of this reinvestment risk depends on the extent of the mismatch between the duration of the insurer's liabilities (its effective investment horizon) and the duration of the insurer's assets.

Further, when interest rates fall, insurance policyholders tend to stick to their (generous) contracts, unless insurers can convince them to do otherwise by encouraging them to switch to new contracts, which raises potential consumer protection issues.

The regulatory framework and valuation methods play a role in solvency

The regulatory framework also plays a role in the solvency position of pension funds and insurance companies as it sets the valuation approach for assets and liabilities. Moreover, the regulatory framework also establishes requirements for pension funds and insurance companies to fulfil in order to ensure a high likelihood that their promises are covered. For example, the regulatory framework requires pension funds and insurance companies to maintain a minimum funding or solvency ratio – that is a relationship between assets and liabilities – so that the likelihood of fulfilling their promises is adequately high. The regulatory framework also requires these institutions to manage the assets and associated risks affecting their ability to fulfill their promises.

The actual impact of low interest rates on reported DB funding ratios also depends on the regulatory framework and in particular on the required valuation method for liabilities and assets. Defined benefit plans can have several different funding levels depending on the purpose of the calculation: for financial reporting purposes; for regulation (to be used by supervisors in determining minimum required contributions, the regulatory solvency funding level); for tax reporting; and for termination purposes (to be used upon plan closing or the buy-out of accrued benefits by an insurance company). For example, the discount rate and other assumptions, the actuarial method for valuing liabilities, or the asset evaluation method could be different for each of these distinct purposes.

In some countries, the level of liabilities used to determine minimum required contributions (the regulatory solvency level) is calculated as if the pension fund were to be terminated as of the valuation date. In such cases, the cash flows promised would be fixed, based on salaries and indexation as of the valuation date; hence, the impact of protracted lower interest rates would be quite large (as there would be no downward adjustment to future expected cash flows due to lower wage growth and inflation expectations).

Some countries (e.g. plans for public sector employees in the United States and United Kingdom) set regulatory solvency levels for liabilities and minimum required contributions based on a fixed discount rate not explicitly linked to actual bond yields; as such, the effect of a drop in bond yields would not be immediately felt. Certain other countries, such Japan and the United States, also apply smoothing mechanisms to market rates when calculating the discount rate to be used in pension valuations. Canada also revised its measure for determining funding ratios in 2011. The solvency ratio for federally regulated plans is being calculated using a three-year average. In general, such smoothing measures would tend to limit or at least delay the effects of a low interest rate environment on reported funding values.

For accounting purposes, methodologies are much more consistent across countries than is the case for regulatory solvency purposes. For accounting, discount rates tend to reflect actual bond yields, while future salary growth is included in benefit estimations. The assumptions used for inflation and future salary growth are, however, usually adjusted only gradually. A lower discount rate would increase liabilities and charges to plan sponsors' profit-loss statements, but to the extent that inflation and salary growth expectations are adjusted downward over time, the impact of protracted lower interest rates would be reduced due to lower expected future benefits. In practice, the anticipated inflation and salary levels used by pension funds are not adjusted often. Small pension funds and annuity providers, for instance, may not have the resources to have a full actuarial model and to change the cash flows assumptions regularly. Instead, they would use their central bank's long-term inflation target to calculate liability levels (for example, the recent European Central Bank inflation target of 2%) and adjust their assumptions only when the central bank revises inflation expectations.

The OECD has argued that the regulatory framework should be flexible in times of distress (Antolin and Stewart, 2009). In this context, funding and solvency rules for DB pension plans should be counter-cyclical and regulatory and supervisory bodies should grant pension funds flexibility in meeting funding requirements. In permitting flexibility, they avoid 'pro-cyclical policies' and allow pension funds to act as long-term investors and thereby serve as potential stabilising forces within the global financial system. However, in allowing for this flexibility in meeting funding requirements it is important to distinguish between temporary impacts of the economic cycle on sponsor cash flows and long-term structural changes to strengthen the scheme sponsor. It is also important that solvency rules aim at increasing funding levels in good times, well above one hundred percent, to act as a buffer in bad times when they could be allowed to temporarily fall below one hundred percent. However, this may present consistency problems as flexibility in funding during difficult market conditions must be matched by a consensus to increase contributions during better economic times, which may be perceived later on as a drag on economic recovery or as depressing wage improvements.

In response to the financial and economic crisis, several countries have increased flexibility. Policy responses include the extension of the time required to submit recovery plans (e.g. the Netherlands, Ireland) and the lengthening of recovery period for pensions funds (e.g. Canada, the Netherlands, Ireland, the United States).

Additionally, the crisis has reopened the debate over accounting rules, in particular mark-to-market valuation rules versus book value. There is also an ongoing discussion about appropriate discount rates to be used (corporate triple-A bonds, government bonds or the swap curve). This discussion has been strong in countries such as the Netherlands, Sweden and the United Kingdom.

Funding ratios are affected by the low interest rate to some extent

The previous sections have discussed how an environment of protracted low interest rates may affect the liabilities and assets backing those liabilities of pension funds and annuity providers. They have also used actual data to highlight the different mechanisms through which this impact could evolve. The relationship between both the liabilities and the assets backing those liabilities provides a measure of the potential solvency problems that those institutions may have and face in a protracted low interest rate environment.

This relationship is generally accounted for by the regulatory framework by requiring pension funds to maintain certain funding ratios, which measure how much of the liabilities current assets would cover.[11] However, the way in which liabilities and assets are measured to calculate funding ratios differ across valuation methods and sometimes across countries.

The level of funding ratios permitted for pension funds also varies across countries. For example, in the Netherlands pension funds are advised to have a funding ratio above 115% and when it is below 105% pension funds have to provide a plan to bring funding ratios up again. The Pension Protection Act in the United States recommends pension funds to have funding ratios of at least 90%.

Funding ratios fell with the crisis and although they have recovered they remain slightly below pre-crisis levels in most countries (Figure 4.16), with the value of their assets failing to cover their pension liabilities. For example, funding levels in the United States remain below pre-crisis levels and well below the Pension Protection Act recommendation of bringing them to at least 90%. The Dutch regulator (DNB) and the Dutch Association of Industry-Wide Pension Funds (VB) reported that the coverage ratio in most pensions funds in the Netherlands dropped below 100% in 2008 (Figure 4.16). Funding levels in the United Kingdom dropped from around 94% to 85% in 2009. The same pattern can be observed in Canada and Switzerland.

Figures 4.16 and 4.17 also show the joint evolution of funding ratios with interest rates, and returns on pension funds' investments in selected OECD countries. Funding ratios seem to be more responsive to interest rates than to rates of return. The correlation of funding ratios and long-term interest rates, measured by the 10-year government bond yield, is relatively high in the six countries examined, ranging from 0.8 in the United States to 0.2 in the United Kingdom, with 0.8 for Canada and 0.6 for the Netherlands and Switzerland for the period 2006 to 2013. This is much higher than the correlation of funding ratios to returns. The relative improvement in funding ratios is nonetheless in part due to the improvement in pension funds' rates of returns (Figure 4.17).

Exposure to longevity risk is exacerbated in an environment of low interest rates

The present value of future liabilities of pension funds and annuity providers is also affected by the assumptions on mortality taken into account when calculating pensions' liabilities and annuity premiums. OECD work on Mortality Assumptions and Longevity Risk[12] highlights the potential longevity risk to which those institutions may be exposed, given the assumptions on mortality improvements used.

Low interest rates, when discounting future liabilities, increase the weight of future payments. Therefore, future deviations in mortality improvements from those assumed (longevity risk) become more problematic.

The exposure to longevity risk coming from different mortality assumptions used by pension funds and annuity providers is exacerbated in an environment of low interest rates. The graph below (Figure 4.18) shows the sensitivity to interest rates of the exposure to longevity risk based on the different mortality assumptions used in different countries for pension funds and annuity providers. The grey bar shows the increase in this exposure associated with a fall in interest rates from 4.5% nominal assumed in the original calculation of the OECD work to 2%.

Figure 4.16. **Funding ratio of defined benefit (DB) pension plans and 10-year government bond yields in selected OECD countries, 2006-2013**

Percentage

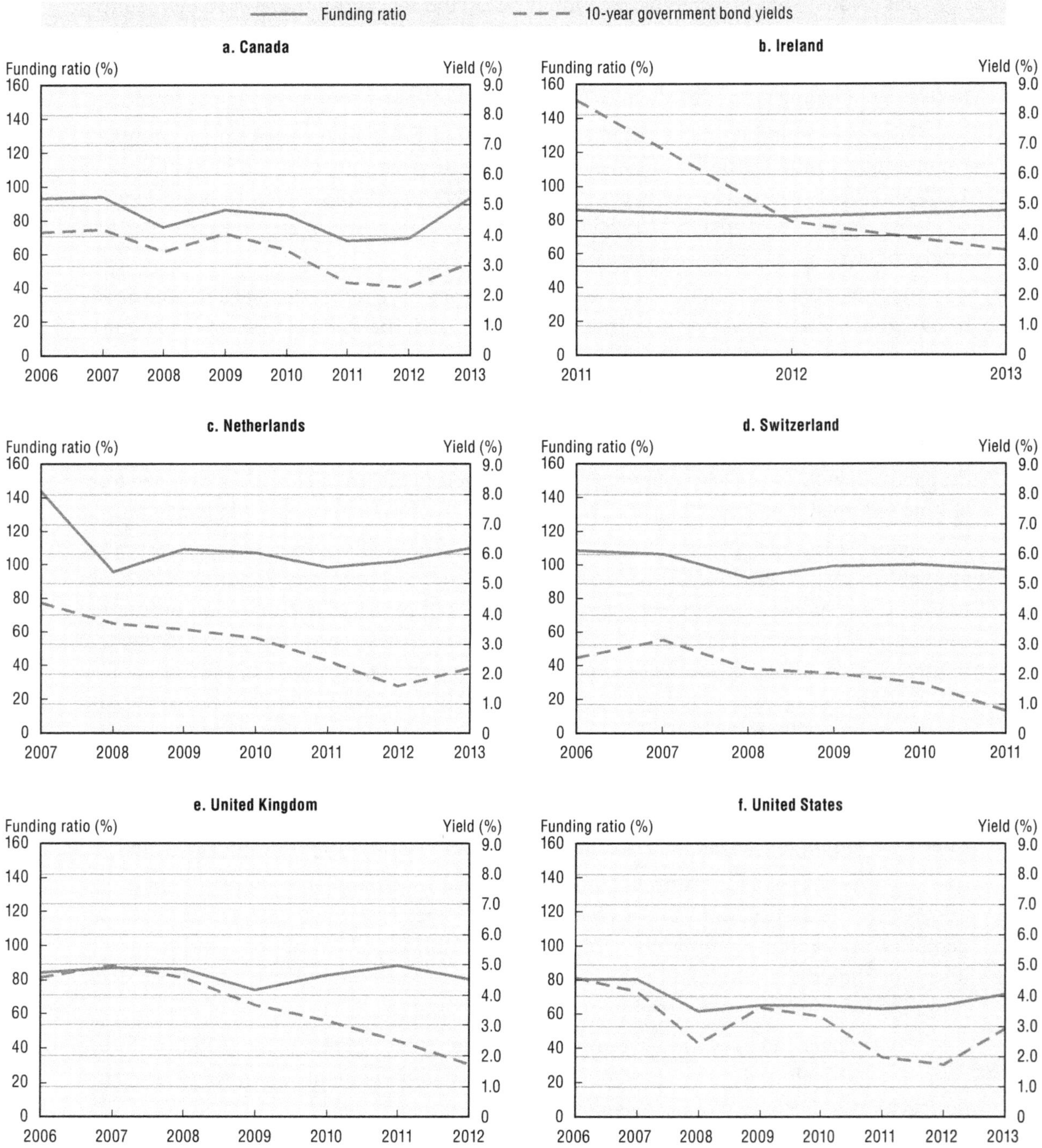

Source: OECD calculations based on data from AON Hewitt; LCP Ireland, Pensions Accounting Briefing series; De Nederlandsche Bank (DNB); Swisscanto Pensionkassen-Monitor; The Pensions Regulator; Federal Reserve Board; Datastream.

StatLink http://dx.doi.org/10.1787/888933209711

Figure 4.17. **Funding ratio of DB pension funds and pension funds' nominal average annual rate of return for all pension funds, 2006-2013**

Percentage

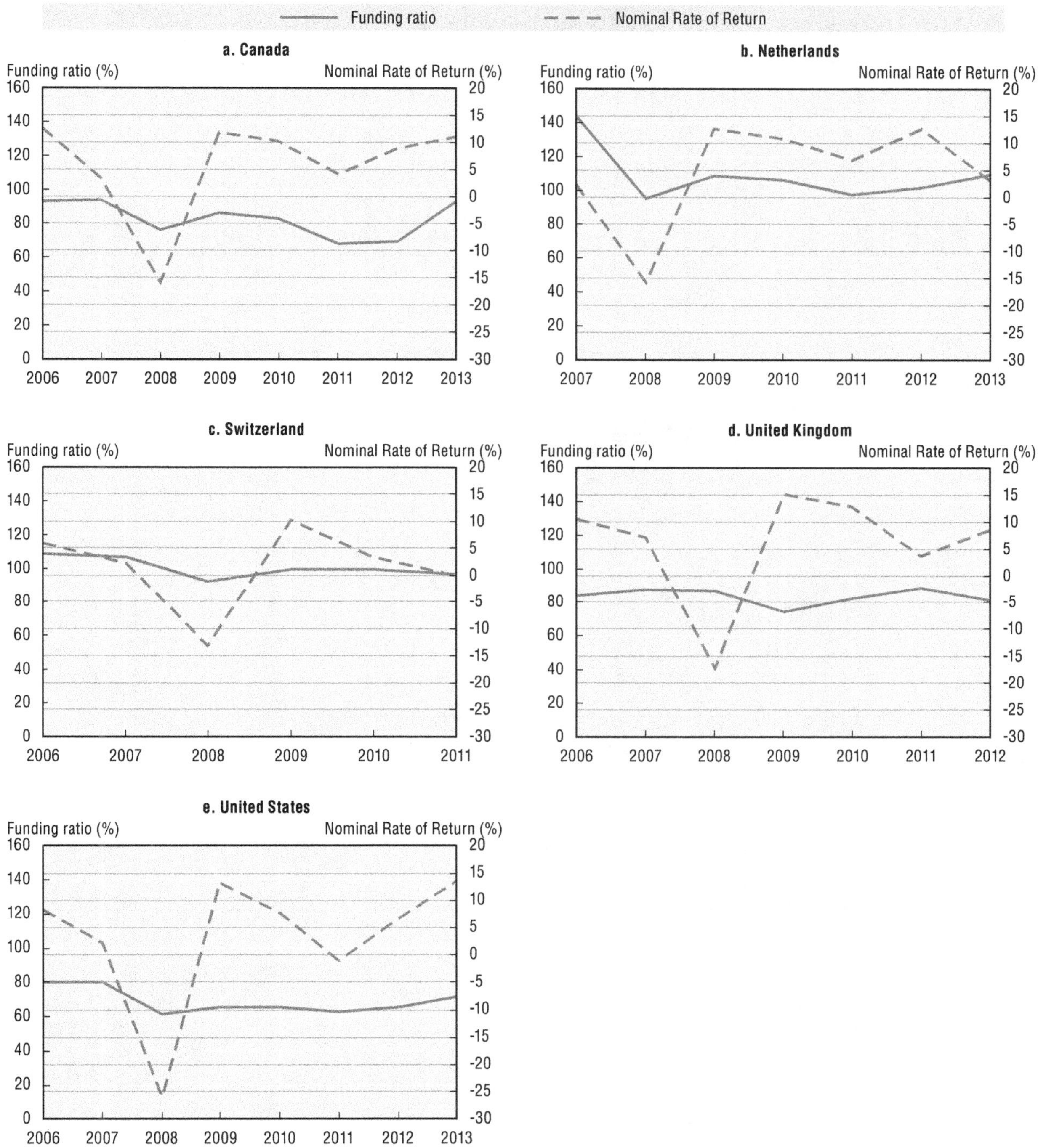

Source: OECD calculations based on data from AON Hewitt; De Nederlandsche Bank (DNB); Swisscanto Pensionkassen-Monitor; The Pensions Regulator; UBS Pension Fund Indicators 2014; and Federal Reserve Board; OECD Global Pension Statistics, *www.oecd.org/daf/fin/private-pensions/globalpensionstatistics.htm*.

StatLink http://dx.doi.org/10.1787/888933209729

Figure 4.18. **Drop in interest rates increases exposure to longevity risk of mortality tables across countries, by gender**

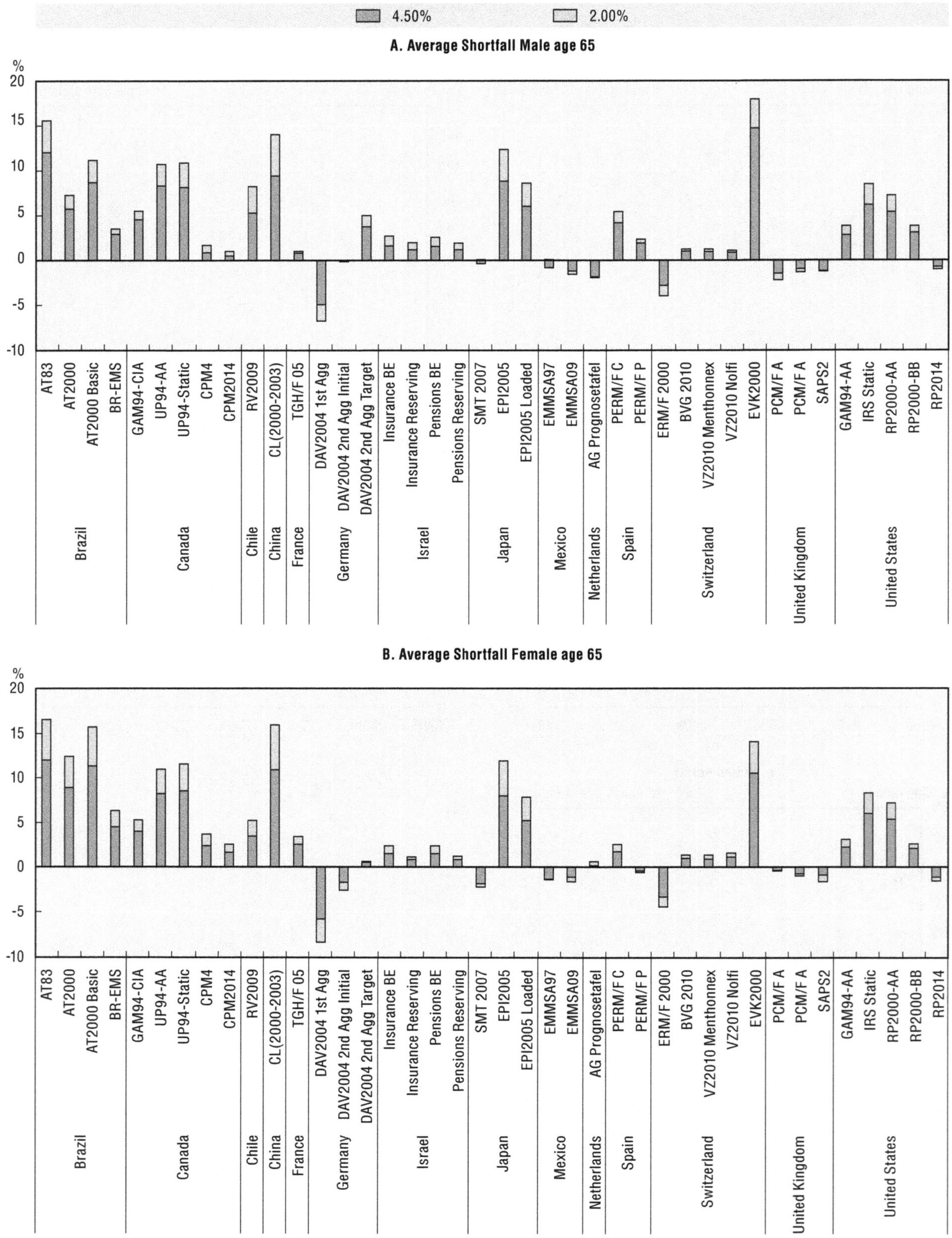

Source: OECD calculations using OECD work on Mortality Assumptions and Longevity Risk *http://dx.doi.org/10.1787/9789264222748-en.*

StatLink *http://dx.doi.org/10.1787/888933209738*

The low interest rate environment could impact life insurers through both their asset and liability sides

This section focuses specifically on the impact of prolonged low interest rates on life insurers. Previous sections have shown that this impact on pension funds and life insurance companies depends on the nature of the promise, the composition of the portfolio and the duration mismatch between assets and liabilities. The nature of the promise of life insurers is generally a fixed promise or guarantee related to interest rates, much more so than in pension systems. Previous sections have also stressed that the main risk for the outlook is the extent to which pension funds and insurance companies may be engaging in a 'search for yield' in an attempt to back their promises, but at a cost of increasing the risk profile of their portfolio. The search for yield may lead insurers and pension funds to enter new business activities, which could take the form of non-bank financial intermediation. Non-bank financial intermediation takes place when non-banks, such as insurers and pension funds, provide financing to areas which have traditionally been financed by banks. This could include, for example, SME financing. Insurers and pension funds may also seek higher returns by investing more in alternative investments, such as foreign assets, longer-term investments, and emerging market assets. As the yield curve of fixed-income securities shifts down, insurers and pension funds may invest in longer-dated instruments to gain greater yield. Returns on equities and possible revenue generation from non-bank financial intermediation would also affect the extent to which the shift into equities may influence the profitability of insurers and pension funds.

The nature of a life insurance promise will change how the promise can be addressed

Life insurance products with a minimum interest rate guarantee promise an *ex ante* level of guarantee to the policyholder, and in some cases an additional share in profits. Such contracts in Germany, for example, can have a savings accumulation period of over 40 years, although about half of the contracts are cancelled before maturity (Schmeiser and Wagner, 2014). In the United States, some policies and guarantees can last for more than 50 years. The guarantees are part of embedded options, which may include choosing between a single payment on expiry or a series of payments. In German-speaking countries, life insurance contracts with minimum guarantees have a participation in the annual return of the insurer's asset portfolio with the minimum guarantee provided on a year-by-year basis, cliquet style,[13] for the whole duration of the contract. On the liability side of insurers' balance sheets, these are accompanied by a bonus account, where an investment surplus is set aside in years with good investment return to be used to cover the annual guarantee in years when the investment return is lower than the guarantee.

Also, they may take the form of a participating policy (Italy) or a universal life insurance product (United States), which have a saving component with a guaranteed return, premiums that could be offset with investment returns, the possibility of borrowing against the cash value, and usually include a death benefit. Interest to participating policies is credited to the policy periodically. When the projected guaranteed returns cannot be achieved, the insurer has the possibility of reducing the cash value of the savings component to offset this in a universal life product. For a universal product, premiums are paid periodically.

The minimum guarantee established for guaranteed saving products with guaranteed interest-rate returns or guaranteed minimum income (annuity) streams cannot be changed during the lifetime of the contract in most cases. The natural implication of this product feature is the simultaneous existence in the insurer's portfolio of products with different minimum investment returns. The low interest rate environment renders the provision of explicit or implicit yield guarantees on long-term savings products more costly. In addition, products with minimum guarantees in the existing stock of liabilities will become increasingly expensive to fund, as assets that come due are reinvested at a lower rate of return (Holsboer, 2000).

The surrender option embedded in many life insurance contracts can be a major challenge for insurers that provide products featuring such an option as policyholders, in times of volatile financial markets, may opt for more attractive investments, and giving incentive to life insurers to offer higher guaranteed returns, with a consequent increase in their interest rate risk exposure (Albizzati and Geman, 1994). When interest rates begin to rise, there is also a risk that policyholders will surrender their contracts, to migrate to contracts with higher guarantees. Uncertain market conditions may also discourage policyholders from lapsing, as there may be disadvantages in losing a pre-existing contract. Early death of or early surrender by policyholders – in terms of surrender and mortality risk – are significant drivers of insurers' default risk (Gerstner et al., 2008). However, in reality, longevity risk has exceeded forecasts which may give some relief to life insurers, although not for annuity products.

Life insurance products are subject to low yield ...

The impact of the low interest rate environment has been discussed in the context of life insurers in terms of how it may affect the balance sheet of life insurers (Bergin and Grundl, 2014) and how they may react when interest rates begin to rise (Bruning, 2014). Other relevant research in this area has addressed investment sensitivity to lower interest rates (Sharpe and Suarez, 2013) and risks relevant to the low interest rates (Turner, 2014; Cooke and Gavin, 2014; van den End and Hoeberichts, 2014). The impact on annuities has been mentioned above, but otherwise products most at risk are those that have a promise that the insurer bears the interest rate or market risk.

In terms of the relation between interest rate guarantees, solvency requirements, and asset allocation for life insurers, although the risk-free interest rate (i.e. government bonds) has approached the guaranteed interest rate, some insurers' are investing less in equity (Schmeiser and Wagner, 2012). This may explain why a number of countries tend to have a majority of bond holdings in their investment portfolio (Figure 4.7). The proportion of shares has decreased in all four countries, and has been substantial in the Netherlands and the United Kingdom. Some countries, such as the Netherlands and Germany, show a clear shift to other investments which includes any investments that do not fall in the other categories. The investment allocations of United States' life insurers remain similar to those levels in 2006 (Figure 4.9).

...and guarantees that may no longer be sustainable

In Germany, life insurers typically offer products with minimum investment return guarantees and minimum profit participation ratios. The average duration of life insurance contract in Germany is 28 years. Regulators decide on the maximum of the allowed minimum return according to the presently achievable interest rates. The minimum return set at contract inception cannot be changed during the lifetime of the contract. As a result, the estimated average weighted guaranteed return of life insurance contracts was 3.12% in 2013, and products with a guaranteed return of 4% account for approximately 24% of the extant contracts (Figure 4.19). The Bundesbank estimates that if the current environment continues, 17% of life insurers by market share would not be able to fulfil their own funds' requirements by 2023 (Bundesbank, 2014).

Figure 4.19. **Proportion of the life insurance contracts with guaranteed returns in Germany**

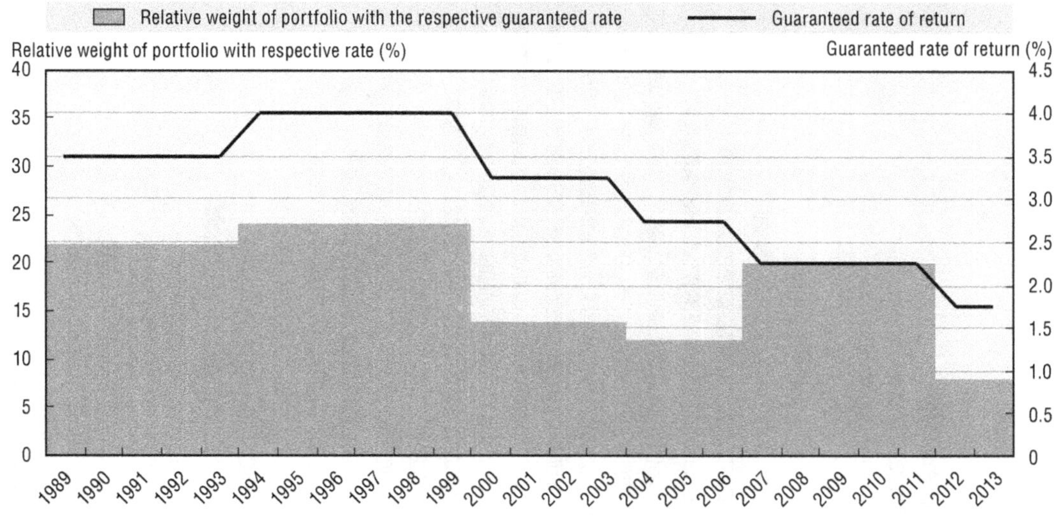

Source: Based on estimates from Berdin and Gründl (2014).

StatLink http://dx.doi.org/10.1787/888933209744

Low interest rates may be becoming a particular issue for life insurers in countries such as Germany, Italy, and the United States, where saving products with high guaranteed returns sold in the past represent a prominent share of the total portfolio of life insurers.[14]

In the Netherlands, 60% of life insurers' portfolios are individual life contracts with guarantees and group life with guarantees, with the risk-free interest rate lower than the average level of guarantees since 2009. The average guaranteed rate is a little below 4% which is higher than many countries, with conditional profit-sharing (De Nederlandsche Bank, 2013).

To shed light on how legacy policies may be impacting life insurers it is useful to examine the proportion of policies which have a high guarantee promise. Using contract data for Japan and the United Kingdom (Figures 4.20 and 4.21), the amount of such contracts peaks in 1996 and 2007 respectively, and as for new business, the 1995-1996 period in Japan and 2007 in the United Kingdom witnessed the largest amount of new business. In Japan, contracts exchanged in the 1990s have a guaranteed interest rate of approximately 6%.

Further, as indicated earlier (Figure 4.19), the proportion of German life insurers' portfolio which has a relatively high guaranteed rate remains significant. For contracts issued between 1995 and 2000, the 4.00% guaranteed rate is applicable to 24% of the portfolio, a 3.50% guarantee to 22%, and a 3.25% guarantee on 14% of the portfolio. When looking at data on new business and business in force, the level of contracts for life insurance policies has remained remarkably the same (Figure 4.22) compared to the declining trend of Japan and the United Kingdom.

In France and the United Kingdom, similar guaranteed policies have been sold with interest rate guarantees between 0 and 1% (De Nederlandsche Bank, 2013).

Figure 4.20. **Business in force and new business of the life insurance sector of Japan, 1980-2013**

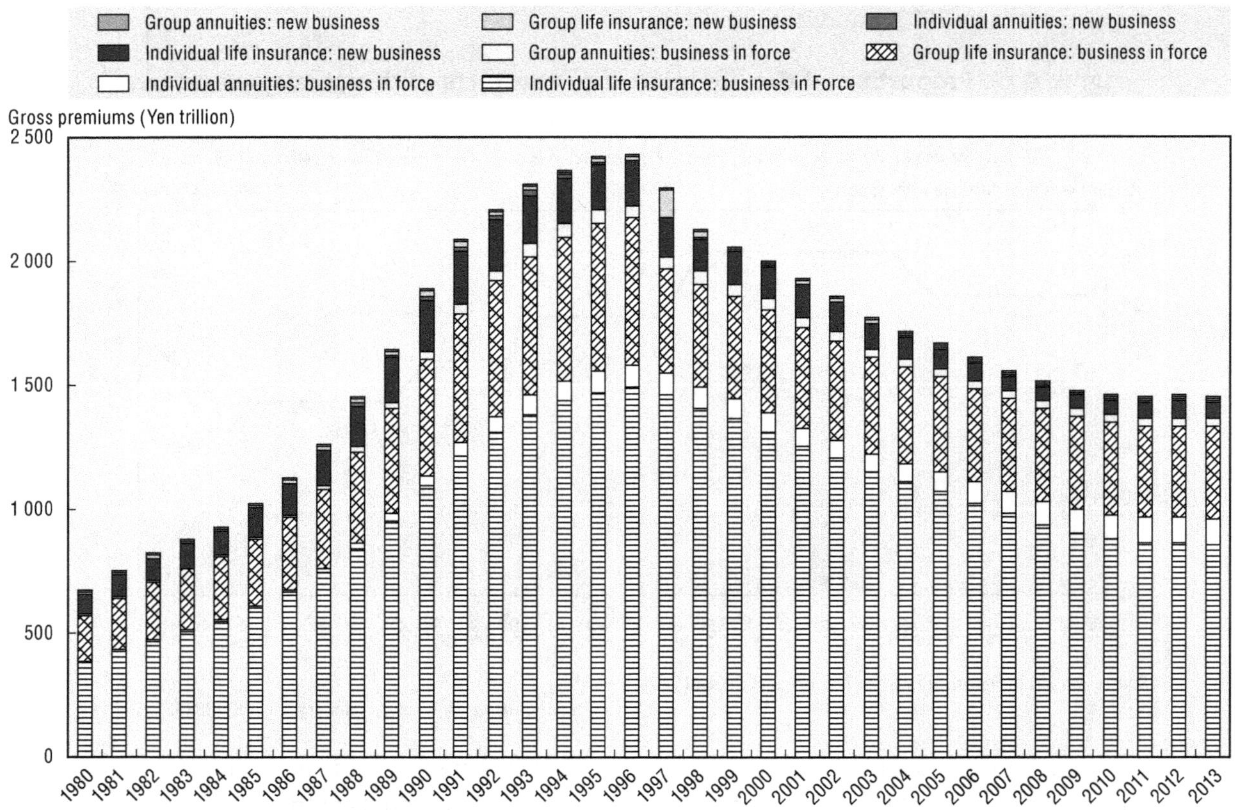

Source: Japanese Life Insurance Association database.

StatLink http://dx.doi.org/10.1787/888933209751

Figure 4.21. **New business in life insurance, United Kingdom, 2005-2013**

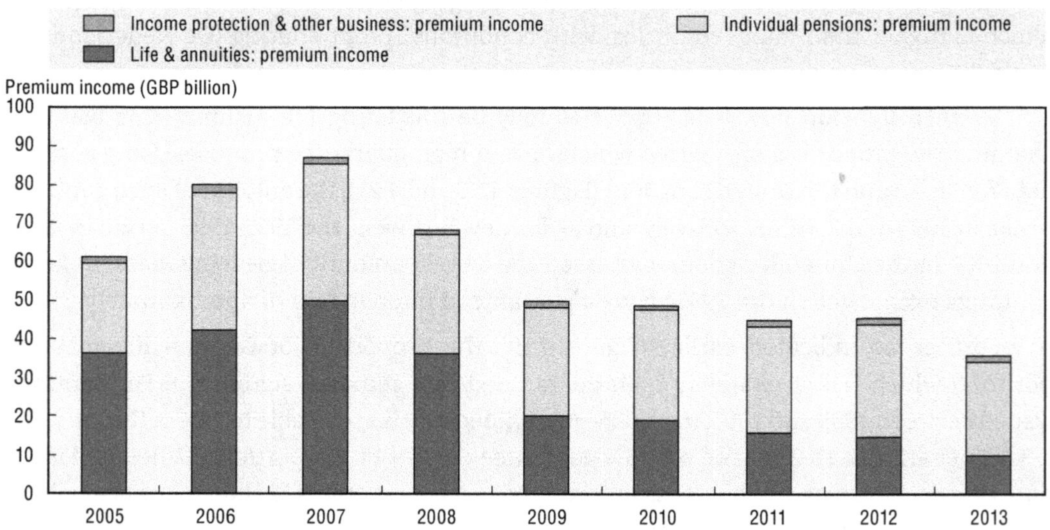

Source: Association of British Insurers, Annual long-term insurance for 2013: overview statistics.

StatLink http://dx.doi.org/10.1787/888933209760

There is some concern that, given the competitive pressures on insurers, life insurers may continue to offer high interest rate guarantees, from which the premium income gained could cover their fixed cost base. This may be at the detriment of capital buffers of life insurers, and increases their susceptibility to further falls in the short-term interest rate.

Figure 4.22. **Business in force and new business of the life insurance sector of Germany, 2007-2013**

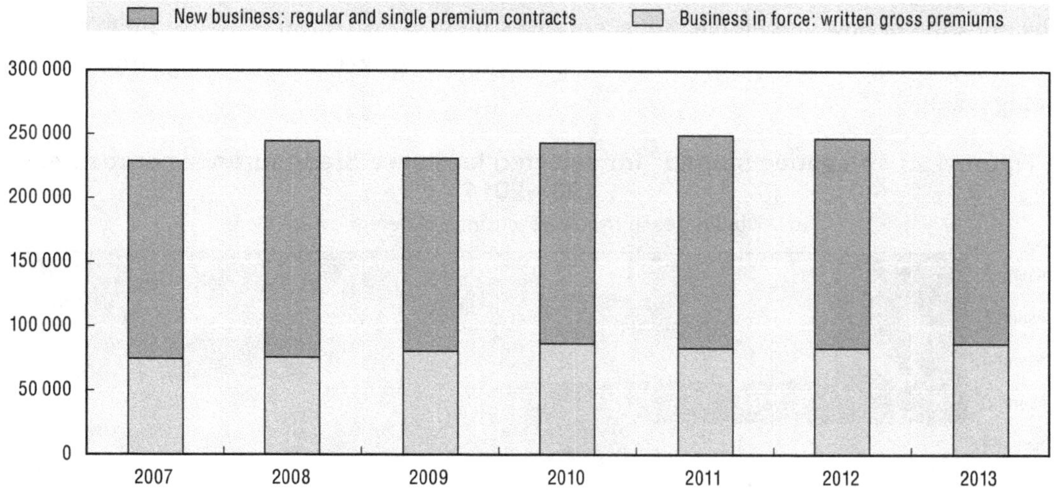

Source: GDV, Statistical Yearbook of German Insurance, 2013 and 2012.

StatLink http://dx.doi.org/10.1787/888933209775

The performance of life insurers remains relatively stable

The return on equity of life insurers as a measure of profitability, as well as the investment return of their portfolio, has not evolved in line with interest rates. Despite the real yield on long-term government bonds being lower than 2% for nearly a decade and despite the drop in 2008, the annual net investment return has not experienced a general downturn, and returns on equity appear to be more volatile but without a clear trend (Table 4.A1.2).

Japanese life insurers have been confronted with low interest rates

Japanese life insurance companies have been confronted with a situation of low domestic fixed income yields for some time now. Against the backdrop of guaranteed return promises to their policyholders, several small and also some mid-sized life insurers failed during the late 1990s and early 2000s as a result of declining interest rates and unfavourable equity and real estate price developments. Many surviving life insurance companies were able to rely on higher premium income from core business and cost-cutting to compensate for the effects of the so-called 'negative spread' on their overall profitability. Limits to further cost-cutting seem to have been reached at the beginning of this decade, however. As well, looking forward, premium income from new life insurance core business is unlikely to grow substantially given that the conditions for new policies effectively imply a form of cross-subsidisation from new to existing policyholders that benefit from more generous return guarantees.

A notable development during recent years has been that the 'negative spread' turned positive for many life insurance companies despite continuously low domestic bond yields (Figure 4.23). Japanese life insurance companies achieved higher yields on their portfolio investments over recent years in part through their allocations to foreign securities, mainly bonds, as opposed for example to domestic bonds.[15] In fact, the share of foreign securities as part of the overall Japanese life insurance industry portfolio has varied over time and currently stands at close to 18%, which is fairly high by historical standards.[16] The change in that share from one year to another seems to be significantly determined by the yield differential between domestic bonds and those on foreign securities. Looking ahead, the current fairly substantial exposure of the life insurance sector to foreign securities raises the question of how vulnerable the recent investment return improvements are to sudden and rapid foreign exchange deteriorations, although it is likely that hedging strategies are being taken.

Figure 4.23. **"Negative spread" for selected Japanese life insurance companies, 2006-2014**

in JPY billion, each row representing a different company

	Mar. 06	Mar. 07	Mar. 08	Mar. 09	Mar. 10	Mar. 11	Mar. 12	Mar. 13	Mar. 14
Insurer A	150	30	-30	40	60	-	-32	-32	-115
Insurer B	122	43	-1	65	83	90	91	61	-28
Insurer C	107	83	57	69	59	1	-19	-43	-119
Insurer D	171	131	110	103	91	75	67	51	16
Insurer E	33	39	39	155	59	56	56	53	49
Insurer F	39	25	18	20	13	7	7	-2	-12
Insurer G	33	17	3	12	15	8	7	0	-11
Insurer H	86	87	82	88	84	83	84	80	71
Insurer I	29	-8	-22	130	42	19	11	-2	-24

Note: Numbers indicate the absolute amount of actual (negative) investment yield in JPY billion of the respective in given year (each row corresponds to one company; companies ordered starting from top row by size in terms of total assets). Positive numbers indicate a «negative spread», with guaranteed returns to policyholders exceeding actual portfolio return investments.

Colour-shading added for convenience.

indicates a positive spread;
indicates a negative spread between 0 and 10 billion yen;
indicates a negative spread between 11 and 50 billion yen
indicates a negative spread between 51 and 100 billion yen.
indicates a negative spread over 101 billion yen

Source: OECD Secretariat estimates based on selected life insurance company annual reports (data reported by Asahi Life, Dai-ichi Life, Daido Life, Fukuoka Life, Meiji Yasuda Life, Mitsui Life, Nippon Life, Sumitomo Life and Taiyo Life).

StatLink http://dx.doi.org/10.1787/888933209787

Another consideration is how Japanese insurers have been able to remain relatively profitable despite the low interest rate environment and high guarantees. As Japanese life insurers provide the breakdown of their profits, and while the negative spread is taken into account, the manner in which mortality risk is accounted for appears to be offsetting any investment return losses (Figure 4.24). Mortality profit is the difference between the actual amount of insurance claims and benefit payments on the one hand and the expected amount of insurance claims and benefit payments calculated using the occurrence rates of insurance events estimated at the time the premium was fixed on the other. It appears that the estimated level of claims on mortality were not realised, allowing the overall profit margin to remain positive. This was confirmed during discussions with the Japanese life insurers (see Box 4.4).

Box 4.4. **OECD Roundtable discussion on the impact of the low interest rate environment on life insurers (December 2014)**

The OECD's Insurance and Private Pensions Committee held a Roundtable with private sector participants on the impact of the low interest rate environment on insurers in December 2014. This box highlights the input provided from the private sector participants during the discussions that took place in the Roundtable. The input is mainly anecdotal, while highlighting the approaches that life insurers have been taking to adapt to this environment.

Given the ongoing low interest rate environment, in terms of profitability and capitalisation, life insurers have fared remarkably well. Life insurers have indicated that although the return on assets has decreased due to the low interest rates, capital gains from equity and bonds have supported profitability to some extent. In the United States, fixed-income investment, in particular in United States' corporate bonds, has allowed United States' life insurers to better cope with the low interest rates. French insurers have also increased their holdings of corporate bonds or reinvested in loans to SMEs. Some insurers have shifted their investment to relatively profitable securitised loans to SMEs and leveraged funds. Also insurance-linked securities, such as catastrophe and earthquake bonds, are being purchased by life insurers, as their returns are decoupled from the macroeconomic environment. In France, guaranteed rates were 3-4% in the 1990s, with the rates slowly decreasing over the years to 0-1% guaranteed rates in recent years.

Some insurers have taken measures to lengthen the duration of their investment (8-9 years), in particular by investing in infrastructure, although regulatory restrictions will limit their exposure to such asset classes in Solvency II. Lengthening duration also limits the reinvestment risks going forward, although it would increase the risk of an interest rate increase. Japanese life insurers have extended the average asset duration to 10.9 years for domestic public and corporate bonds.

Life insurers have remarked upon the intentional shift of policies from guaranteed saving products to protection policies which do not entail interest rate risks. For French insurers, where a significant proportion of the guaranteed saving products were group contracts, some of these contracts have been renegotiated via trade unions to non-guaranteed contracts in exchange for greater profit sharing. In Japan, the single endowment saving policy is being retired, and the stable mortality profit base has assisted life insurers to remain profitable.

There were a number of life insurer insolvencies around the year 2000 in Japan. Eight insurers failed between 1997 and 2008. The insurer resolution system of Japan, while guaranteeing 90% of existing policyholder's interest at the time of the insolvency, adjusts future interest rates to the market rate. This has excused life insurers taking over insolvent insurers from having to take over contracts which are subject to the negative spread (see below for discussion on the negative spread).

However, the risks posed by life insurance saving contracts may continue to pressure the business of some life insurers regardless of the interest rate situation. Aviva France took over another insurer in 2002 which had contracts that policyholders could allocate their moneys in different investment funds offered by the insurer. Prices of the funds were published every Friday, with policyholders able to switch funds at those prices any time before the next price was published. This enabled customers to arbitrage the market, already knowing the movement of the market in the next week. In France, there are a number of ongoing litigations on the validity of these contracts, although the courts have been recognising policyholders' claims so far. If so, with the liability growing at 68% a year, for a contract that was exchanged in 1997, Aviva France may potentially be facing a €9.3 million pay-out in 2015, with the pay-out potentially growing to €234 billion by 2030. Further, as the contract is still valid, policyholders are able to add fresh capital to the savings component.

Source: OECD roundtable discussions with life insurers (4 December 2014). FTAlphaville, "Meet the man who could own Aviva France" (27 February 2015).

Figure 4.24. **Contributions to annual base profit at selected Japanese life insurers**

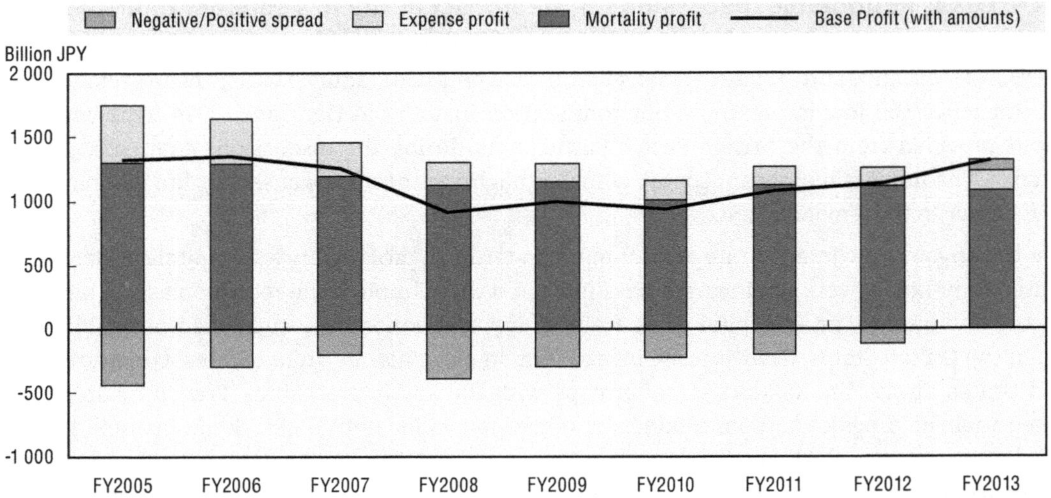

Note: Contribution of different types of business lines/activities to annual base profits in percentages at selected Japanese life insurance companies (average of data reported by of Daiichi, Meiji-Yasuda, Sumitomo and Mitsui Life). Japanese fiscal year starts in April and ends in 31 March the following year; e.g. FY2013 ends in March 2014.

- Base profits (indicated by continuous line) consist of mortality profit, expense profit and negative (positive) spread.
- 'Mortality profit' (dark blue-shaded) is the difference between the actual amount of insurance claims and benefit payments on the one hand and the expected amount of insurance claims and benefit payments calculated using the occurrence rates of insurance events estimated at the time the premium was fixed on the other.
- 'Expense profit' (grey-shaded) is the difference between the actual amount of business expenses and the expected business expenses calculated using the business expense rates estimated at the time the premium was fixed.
- 'Negative/positive spread' (light blue-shaded) is the spread between investment returns and yields guaranteed to policyholders at the time the premium was fixed.

Source: OECD estimates based on annual company reports.

StatLink http://dx.doi.org/10.1787/888933209799

Japan's life insurance market was dominated by long-term insurance products with high guaranteed returns, which led to negative spreads in the mid-1990s, whereby the guaranteed rate is higher than the investment return. The supervisor introduced the Standard Reserve Valuation System in 1996, which requires insurers to accumulate the minimum policy reserve using an interest rate prescribed by the supervisory authority which is based on 10 year Japanese government bonds yield. For new contracts with guarantees that are relatively higher than the prescribed interest rate, insurers are required to have additional reserves.

Valuation standards of life insurers are coming into play

EU countries will be transitioning to the Solvency II regime for implementation in January 2016, and countries such as Mexico, Switzerland and the United States have already transitioned to a risk-based capital regime. This is a period of major regulatory reforms in many countries, with life insurers more likely to be conservative in their asset and liability management to ensure compliance with the new requirements.

Solvency modernisation initiatives will have a large impact on how assets and liabilities are assessed, and this is apparent from countries that are in the transition phase. When countries adopt a risk-based capital regime, valuations for assets and liabilities shift, for the most part, to market-based values. For example, Switzerland's Swiss Solvency Test requires assets and liabilities to be market consistent, with strict requirements for valuation when an asset does not have observable prices. The United States' approach assumes that fixed-income assets will be held at amortised cost for a ten-year holding period at a 95% confidence level. Such market consistent valuation limits the scope for insurers to invest in assets that cannot be mark-to-market, and may have the effect of discouraging investments in certain asset classes.

As accounting standards and regulatory capital standards shift to market-consistent value for liabilities, the low interest rate environment will have the potential to raise the level of liabilities and the need to increase regulatory capital. Solvency II does introduce volatility adjustments to address such interest rate risks, but this is primarily for the purpose of short-term fluctuations and not necessarily for long periods of low interest rates.

EU directives require that interest rate guarantees do not exceed 60% of the rate of return on government debt. In terms of regulatory actions taken to alleviate some of the issues caused by the low interest rate, the Swiss financial supervisor (FINMA), for instance, decided in 2012 to allow such alleviation for the valuation of liabilities for periods of low interest rates for the years 2013 to 2015. This permits an adjusted solvency capital requirement with an increased interest rate used for discounting of liabilities of in force business, which 2/3 of the Swiss life insurers have used. Germany has been requiring an additional premium reserve for life insurers to establish an additional buffer since 2011. In January 2015, the Life Insurance Reform Act was implemented in Germany which limits the sharing of valuation reserves with policyholders upon the expiry of their contract to only when the life insurers have sufficient reserves to meet interest rate guarantees. A new maximum interest rate is being applied as well from January 2015, reducing from 1.75% to 1.25%. In Japan, life insurers are required to accumulate additional policy reserves that correspond to the estimated future effect of negative spreads.

Conclusions

This chapter has discussed the challenges that an environment of prolonged low interest rates poses to life insurance companies and pension systems, in particular defined benefit pension funds. The financial crisis and ensuing environment of low growth and falling inflation have led to an environment of protracted low interest rates, amplified further by quantitative easing in several major economies that has spurred interest rate declines, with yields turning negative in a number of countries. This environment of low interest rates, which is expected to prevail for the foreseeable future, poses serious problems of adequacy of retirement income given current contributions and contribution periods to defined contribution pension arrangements.

It also poses serious problems to the solvency – the degree to which current liabilities are backed up by current assets – of defined benefit pension funds and life insurers.

The outlook for pension funds and insurance companies depends foremost on the nature of the promise made and the potential for its adjustment or reversibility. The adverse effect of low interest rates is higher where the liabilities of these institutions consist of a fixed investment return or fixed benefit or pay-out promises such as constant, annuity-type payments.

The outlook is troubling for pension funds and life insurance companies as their solvency positions will deteriorate unless they have actively adopted risk management strategies. Some countries are already adjusting their regulatory frameworks on an exceptional basis (or otherwise maintaining measures adopted during the financial crisis to relax regulation while increasing monitoring) given problems being experienced by these institutions.

The impact on the solvency position of pension funds and life insurance companies of a prolonged period of low interest rates also depends on the composition of their portfolio, in particular the proportion invested in long-term government bonds, and on the duration mismatch between assets and liabilities, which may bring in problems with re-investment risk, unless these institutions have developed risk management strategies such as ALM. However, the lack of good quality, very long-term financial assets in sufficient quantities poses serious problems to these risk management strategies.

Several options and instruments exist to address the risks posed by an environment of protracted low interest rates. Insurers and pension funds could increase the duration of their assets in order to reduce the duration gap between their assets and liabilities. Insurers could alter the contractual terms of new policies, for example by lowering the guaranteed rates, thereby progressively reducing liabilities, while pension plan sponsors could terminate existing plans and offer less attractive terms to new employees. DB pension plan sponsors, and plan members where relevant, could increase contributions to pension funds. Insurers and pension funds could also consider renegotiating or adjusting existing promises where this is feasible. Finally, proactive regulatory initiatives could be implemented. For example, policymakers should avoid putting excessive pressure on institutions to quickly correct solvency and funding deficits at a time of market weakness (regulatory forbearance).

Finally, the main concern for the outlook is the extent to which pension funds and insurance companies have, or might become, involved in an excessive 'search for yield' in an attempt to match the level of returns promised to beneficiaries or policyholders when financial markets were delivering higher returns, which might heighten insolvency risks. The regulatory framework and policy makers have an important role to play in this regard and need to remain vigilant to prevent excessive 'search for yield', especially on pension funds as life insurance companies make be deterred by higher capital reserves required by solvency regulations when increasing the risks profile of their portfolios.

Notes

1. Previous OECD work on this subject (Antolin et al., 2011) highlighted some of these factors.
2. Large volumes may lead to higher counter party risk.
3. Correlation is not necessarily causation.
4. Both figures report information on the major OECD countries in terms of pension funds' and life insurers' assets, respectively.
5. Office of National Statistics (ONS) data show that the rise of derivatives used by pension funds has been quite substantial in the last decade.
6. Pension systems involve defined benefit, DB, and defined contribution, DC, pension plans. In DB pension plans pension funds manage both the accumulation or saving phase, and the decumulation or pay-out phase. In DC pension plans, pension funds only manage the saving or accumulation phase, and the individual is left with an amount of assets accumulated when retiring that they need to allocate to finance retirement. They can buy a life annuity and shift the investment and longevity risk to the annuity providers, generally an insurance company. Therefore, when talking about the impact of interest rates on pension systems, the chapter looks at both.
7. Going instead for a phased withdrawal may not be much better because the individual retains the risk of outliving his/her resources (i.e. longevity risk), the investment risk, and is also exposed to the impact of low interest rates through the investment risk. The *OECD Roadmap for the Good Design of DC Pension Plans* argues that partial annuitisation of the assets accumulated at retirement is essential to have protection from longevity risk, *www.oecd.org/pensions/designingfundedpensionplans.htm*.

8. The analysis focuses on a few selected OECD countries, those with large amounts of assets in pension funds (in dollar terms and as a percentage of GDP) and with a large share of DB pension plans. See Figures 3, 4 and 7 in *OECD Pension Markets in Focus 2014*, *www.oecd.org/pensions/pensionmarketsinfocus.htm*.
9. However, competition pressures may push insurance companies to offer annuity prices that have been calculated using discount rates higher than the risk-free interest rate. This practice will increase their risk exposures and how they manage the risk that returns on their investments turn out to be lower than the interest rate promised or guaranteed in their pricing of annuity products.
10. Adjustment by age would be necessary to have a more accurate picture.
11. Annuity providers, insurance companies, are regulated differently. Solvency frameworks require them to keep certain levels of capital to make sure that they can fulfil the promises contracted, weighted by the level of risk.
12. See *www.oecd.org/pensions/mortality-assumptions-and-longevity-risk-9789264222748-en.htm*. OECD (2014).
13. Cliquet style means that the guaranteed return must be credited to the policyholder's account each year.
14. According to Swiss Re (2012), based on their product characteristics, Germany, Italy and the United States have the highest exposure to interest rate risk among major insurance markets around the world.
15. Investment yields realised by Japanese life insurance companies on domestic stocks have been fairly volatile; they have exceeded those on foreign (and domestic) bonds during fiscal year 2013, but were inferior to those on foreign bonds during the five preceding fiscal years (see *The Life Insurance Association of Japan*, 2014).
16. The proportion of the industry portfolio allocated to foreign securities was only 0.1% in 1975 and never exceeded 2.5% in any year during the 1970s. The ratio increased thereafter, reaching its historical peak of more than 19% in 2004. The proportion of the industry portfolio allocated to foreign securities seems to be a positive function of the difference between the yields on foreign securities (taking into account foreign-exchange effects) and domestic bonds. For example, a simple regression (using time series data from 1977 to 2013 available from the *The Life Insurance Association of Japan*, 2014) of that proportion (or, alternatively, the change in it) on a first-order autoregressive term plus the annual foreign-domestic return yield spread (which takes into account the effect of exchange rate variation) suggests that the spread is positively significant at the 5% level and that its addition to the regression greatly enhances the explanatory power of the regression.

References

Albizzati, M.-O., and Geman, H. (1994), Interest rate risk management and valuation of the surrender option in life insurance policies, *The Journal of Risk and Insurance, 61* (2), 616–637.

Antolin, P., Sebastian Schich and Juan Yermo (2011), "The Economic Impact of Protracted Low Interest Rates on Pension Funds and Insurance Companies", *OECD Journal: Financial Market Trends*, Vol. 2011/1. DOI: *http://dx.doi.org/10.1787/fmt-2011-5kg55qw0m56l*

Antolin, P. and Fiona Stewart (2009), "Private pensions and policy responses to the financial economic crisis", *OECD Journal: Financial Market Trends*, Vol. 2009/1. DOI: *http://dx.doi.org/10.1787/fmt-v2009-art5-en*

Bergin, E. and Grundl, H. (2014): *The Effects of a Low Interest Rate Environment on Life Insurers* (July, ICIR Working Paper Series No. 15/14).

Bruning, L. (2014), *Life insurers to benefit from rising interest rate*. January, CIPR Newsletter

Bundesbank (2013), *Financial Stability Review*.

Bundesbank (2014), *Monthly Report* (July).

Cooke and Gavin (2014), *Three scenarios for Interest Rates in the Transition to Normalcy* (October, Federal Reserve Bank of St Louis Working Paper Series 2014-027A)

De Nederlandsche Bank (2013), *Overview of the Financial Stability in the Netherlands* (Spring) (17).

Gerstner, T., Griebel, M., Goschnick, R., and Haep, M. (2008), A general asset-liability management model for the efficient simulation of portfolios of life insurance policies. *Insurance: Mathematics and Economics,* 42 (2), 704–716

Holsboer, J. H. (2000): The impact of low interest rates on insurers. *Geneva Papers on Risk and Insurance—Issues and Practice*, 25 (1), 38–58.

OECD (2015), Main Economic Indicators - database, DOI: *http://dx.doi.org/10.1787/data-00052-en*

OECD (2015), Global Pension Statistics, *www.oecd.org/pensions/globalpensionstatistics.htm.*

OECD (2014), *Mortality Assumptions and Longevity Risk: Implications for pension funds and annuity providers*, December 2014.

Schmeiser, H., and Wagner, J. (2012): The influence of interest rate guarantees and solvency requirements on the asset allocation of life insurers, *Working Papers on Risk Management and Insurance* No. 111.

Sharpe and Suarez (2013): *The insensitivity of investment to interest rates: Evidence from a survey of CFOs* (December, Federal Reserve Board finance and economics discussion series, 2014-2).

Swiss Re (2012): *Sigma: Facing the interest rate challenge.*

The Life Insurance Association of Japan (2014) Summary of Life Insurance in Fiscal 2013 (CD-ROM),

Turner, P. (2014): *The global long-term interest rate, financial risks and policy choices in EMEs* (February, BIS Working Papers No. 441).

van den End and Hoeberichts (2014): *Low real rates as drivers of secular stagnation: empirical assessment* (October, DNB Working Paper No. 444).

ANNEX 4.A1

Statistical tables and supplementary data

Table 4.A1.1. **Pension funds' real average net annual rate of investment returns in selected OECD countries**

In per cent

	2003	2004	2005	2006	2007	2008	2009	2010	2011	2012	2013
Australia	-2.02	8.61	10.08	8.88	12.93	-11.49	-10.21	5.63	5.22	0.63	10.25
Austria	5.75	3.58	8.97	3.79	-1.77	-14.45	7.29	3.67	-5.98	5.47	2.94
Belgium	5.99	5.99	10.31	10.34	7.70	-22.27	13.43	4.43	-4.62	9.26	5.80
Canada	11.28	9.01	10.70	10.76	0.99	-16.89	10.29	7.58	1.82	7.88	9.76
Chile	10.13	8.13	4.98	14.38	4.40	-24.07	23.48	8.29	-5.98	5.07	3.55
Czech Republic	2.16	0.74	2.73	1.26	-2.11	-1.51	-0.62	0.69	0.53	0.21	0.19
Denmark	6.30	11.51	14.76	1.34	-3.28	5.08	1.22	7.12	12.13	5.40	-4.57
Estonia	2.88	3.66	7.24	2.18	-5.36	-32.43	14.85	2.13	-8.00	5.24	0.90
Finland (1)	-	-	-	-	-	-	-	-	-	5.23	5.96
Germany	3.42	2.66	3.61	3.34	1.08	0.52	4.02	3.76	1.07	2.73	2.81
Greece	-	-	-	-	-	2.34	0.27	-7.85	-5.57	5.01	7.37
Hungary (2)	-2.57	9.49	7.57	1.18	-3.88	-21.66	12.80	4.17	-	7.85	7.00
Iceland	10.35	9.56	11.84	8.75	0.36	-23.14	0.94	1.32	2.33	7.08	4.85
Ireland	-	-	-	-	-7.35	-35.74	-	-	-	-	-
Israel (3)	-	-	7.14	5.70	3.51	-16.29	20.09	6.95	-4.29	7.84	8.41
Italy	2.54	3.72	6.09	2.08	0.28	-5.33	5.34	1.21	-2.78	4.02	3.85
Japan	11.12	-7.46	9.15	-7.63	-4.09	-13.44	12.79	-5.09	-3.66	7.25	8.92
Korea	1.79	1.23	0.59	5.97	0.56	-2.71	-2.22	2.06	0.02	3.31	2.63
Luxembourg	-	-	-	4.89	-2.48	-11.35	6.51	0.68	-2.26	6.00	1.73
Mexico (4)	-	-	4.85	5.57	-0.13	-7.79	7.52	6.55	1.16	9.69	-1.45
Netherlands	8.74	8.45	10.92	6.77	0.57	-17.29	11.52	8.85	4.31	9.47	1.61
New Zealand	-3.86	8.65	4.31	8.78	5.02	-5.48	-9.50	10.54	3.09	1.61	9.52
Norway	11.45	7.45	9.22	7.36	3.14	-10.58	9.75	5.53	-0.12	6.06	7.91
Poland (5)	8.77	8.56	12.93	13.36	1.50	-17.33	8.93	7.16	-9.09	1.64	2.67
Portugal	7.31	6.62	7.06	7.12	5.50	-13.20	11.59	-2.98	-7.26	5.80	4.92
Slovak Republic	-	-	-	-	-0.11	-8.93	0.96	-0.01	-3.77	0.42	1.07
Slovenia	-	-	-	-	-1.01	-5.37	4.21	1.79	-1.79	4.51	2.47
Spain	-	-	-	-	-	-9.91	6.87	-2.22	-2.27	3.65	7.90
Sweden	-	-	-	-	-	-	-	-	-0.97	7.86	6.65
Switzerland	4.91	2.77	9.18	5.30	0.24	-13.81	9.88	2.78	0.62	7.53	5.89
Turkey (4)	-	-	22.08	1.44	13.24	0.94	17.58	1.89	-	9.61	-
United States (6)	13.24	2.52	1.63	5.76	-1.88	-26.07	10.25	6.26	-3.80	4.78	11.73

Note: Data have been calculated using a common formula for the average nominal net investment return (ratio between the net investment income at the end of the year and the average level of assets during the year).

Average real net investment returns have been calculated using the nominal investment rates of return (using the formula described above; for more information about this formula, see the *OECD Pension Markets in Focus 2014*) and the variation of the end-of-period consumer price index between 2012 and 2013 for all countries, except for Austria (2011,2012), Israel (all years), for which values have been provided by the countries.

The 2012-Q2 and 2013-Q2 consumer price index per year have been used for Australia, while 2012-Q1 and 2013-Q1 index have been used for New Zealand.

1. There is a break in series in 2011 is due to the exclusion of public buffer funds which were included before.
2. The break in series in 2011 corresponds to the pension reform leading to a decrease in the assets of mandatory pension funds in 2011.
3. Data refer to new pension funds only.
4. Data refer to personal pension plans only.
5. The financial result (i.e. the sum of result on investment and the realized and unrealized profits/losses on investment/valuation of investment and the income from the coverage of the deficit) is used as a proxy for net investment income. Since 2007, the financial result of occupational pension plans has been included (1% of pension funds total assets).
6. The revaluation of assets is taken as a proxy for net investment income. Only equity and mutual fund holdings have revaluations for the state and local and federal plans while the private plans revaluations also include gains on real estate and unallocated insurance contracts. There is no correction in the data for interest or dividend income, or capital gains on bonds or other securities.

Source: OECD Global Pension Statistics and other national sources.

StatLink http://dx.doi.org/10.1787/888933210432

Table 4.A1.2. **Average real net investment return of life insurers in selected OECD countries**

	In per cent				
	2009	2010	2011	2012	2013
Australia	4.87	3.28	-2.59	12.20	13.00
Belgium	4.08	-5.15	-6.47	2.33	3.57
Canada	5.34	-2.30	1.37	-	-
Chile	7.00	6.71	3.33	5.43	4.76
Czech Republic	0.40	4.78	0.16	-0.61	-0.04
Estonia	8.73	-1.59	-2.56	1.19	0.52
Finland	10.31	-	-	-	-
Germany	4.42	-1.24	1.49	3.00	4.02
Hungary	0.43	3.88	5.89	1.68	5.55
Iceland	8.18	6.87	3.46	-3.98	1.53
Ireland	7.55	-0.23	-	5.28	-1.44
Israel	-	-	-	-	-0.22
Italy	3.62	0.91	-2.07	3.23	3.26
Japan	3.52	2.12	1.41	3.29	0.77
Korea	2.22	-2.90	0.65	2.79	2.97
Luxembourg	2.84	1.64	0.01	-2.23	1.93
Netherlands	7.11	-	-	5.81	4.65
Norway	3.71	3.92	-	4.44	3.23
Poland	2.94	4.55	0.50	3.98	4.49
Portugal	2.90	0.35	-1.63	1.04	2.30
Spain	-	-	1.45	2.19	3.96
Switzerland	2.61	2.53	4.07	3.96	3.09
Turkey	-1.13	-1.98	-4.46	0.25	-0.68

Note: Average real net investment return calculations are based on nominal net investment return reported by countries and CPI figures.
1. The rates of return are nominal.

Source: OECD Global Insurance Statistics.

StatLink http://dx.doi.org/10.1787/888933210448

OECD Business and Finance Outlook 2015

Chapter 5

Bank and capital market financing of small and medium-sized enterprises

Small and medium-sized enterprises (SMEs) play a significant role in their economies as key generators of employment and income, and as drivers of innovation and growth. They are essential for the economic recovery from the current economic and financial crisis, which has reduced bank lending and affected SMEs in particular because credit sources tend to dry up more rapidly for small firms than for large companies during economic downturns. This chapter identifies bank lending gaps that have opened up since the crisis and that are especially pertinent outside the United States. Therefore, a two-pronged approach to fostering SME financing (in as far as it is a supply problem) is proposed: first, restoring banks' health to improve bank lending; and second, supporting the development of a broad range of non-bank financing for SMEs in debt and equity markets, the latter being especially well-suited for small dynamic, innovation-oriented SMEs. The chapter concludes that, owing to their diversity, the financing of SMEs remains complex and requires a variety of instruments and approaches. Policy makers can help by providing regulatory support and assist in the improvement of data transparency, standardisation, and raising awareness about available financing options.

Main findings

- The crisis has had a negative effect on bank lending. Current bank lending is still below its long-term trend in major OECD economies and this bank lending gap is estimated to be especially pertinent outside the United States. Small- and medium-sized enterprises (SMEs) have been more vulnerable and affected than larger corporations.
- A two-pronged approach to foster SME finance – in so far as it is a supply problem – is needed: restoring banks' health to improve bank lending, and supporting the development of a broad range of non-bank financing for SMEs, in particular in debt and equity markets, with the latter being especially well-suited for small dynamic, innovation-oriented SMEs.
- SMEs access to bank finance during the crisis was especially difficult, against a background of a sharp decline in bank profitability and an erosion of bank capital that negatively affected lending. Restoring the health of banks' balance sheets and undertaking structural bank reforms can help to restart bank lending to the real economy.
- Among non-bank debt financing instruments, securitisation, private placements and bonds can play an important role. Securitisation was tarnished by the crisis and has experienced decline, but could help to fill the lending gap if placed on the right footing. For mid-sized companies, bond issuance and private placements provide useful alternatives.
- Equity finance takes place across a wide spectrum of instruments, in line with the various stages in a typical life-cycle of an SME. There are potential benefits for policy support targeting the development of SME equity financing platforms and instruments. Fostering SME equity financing, which would support riskier, but more dynamic and innovative SMEs, can be especially helpful in facilitating growth of the real economy.

Introduction

The economic importance of SMEs warrants closing financing gaps

Small- and medium-sized enterprises (SMEs[1]) play a significant role in their economies as key generators of employment and income, and as drivers of innovation and growth. SMEs employ more than half of the private sector labour force in OECD economies. Given their importance in all economies, they are essential for recovery from the current economic and financial crisis. But the crisis has had a negative effect on bank lending. When bank lending is reduced, SMEs – which rely largely on bank finance – tend to be more vulnerable and affected than larger corporations.

While credit sources tend to dry up more rapidly for small firms than for large companies during economic downturns – a cyclical lending shortage – SMEs can also experience difficulties in obtaining financing during 'normal' times. Such a 'structural' financing gap can arise from more general credit constraints in an economy through which SMEs are disproportionately more affected.[2] These constraints can stem from several sources, such as the lack of an appropriate range of financial products and services and gaps in the legal framework. They also stem from monitoring problems inherent in SMEs that put them at a disadvantage relative to larger and more established firms (for which credit ratings may exist). This asymmetric information between borrower and lender may lead lower credit provision to SMEs than would be the case be under full information (the so-called 'credit rationing' phenomenon).[3] Such structural problems in access to financing may be compounded by an unfavourable business environment (lack of transparency, weak legal framework and enforcement, presence of monopolies, etc.).

Specific problems exist for start-ups and very young firms, which tend to be higher risk and typically lack sufficient collateral, or for small ventures whose activities are innovative but of specifically higher risk. Such venture capital firms tend to be equity financed, with forms ranging from, e.g., seed finance by angel investors at their initial stages to public shares traded on specialised exchanges at later stages.

A two-pronged approach is needed to foster SME finance

The chapter attempts to set out how SME financing might be enhanced, without creating increased risk in the financial system. A two-pronged approach to foster SME finance – in so far as it is a supply problem – is proposed: restoring banks' health to improve bank lending, and supporting the development of a broad range of non-bank financing for SMEs, in particular on debt and equity markets.[4] Bank lending, the traditional and still predominant source of financing for SMEs, remains below its long-term trend in many major OECD economies, with the exception of the United States. Governments have been adopting various direct or indirect measures to support bank lending to SMEs as part of their policy response to the crisis; however, as the banking sectors remain weak and banks are adjusting to a new, stricter regulatory environment, bank lending is more constrained.

As reduced bank lending may become the 'new normal' in a post-crisis (and perhaps 'secular stagnation') environment, the development of capital markets – especially in those OECD economies that are still largely bank-financed – becomes ever more important in providing financing alternatives for SMEs. SME financing via capital markets also opens the possibility to draw on the large amounts of capital available from institutional investors and other non-banks. This will require appropriate regulatory frameworks, financing infrastructures and instruments. A key policy issue is whether market-based financing can provide a sustained, viable channel of funding for SMEs.

While the OECD has been studying a large gamut of financing alternatives,[5] this chapter will focus on recent developments in non-bank debt financing as well as later-stage equity finance with a view to tapping the vast financing potential of institutional investors. Before doing so, it provides an outlook for bank lending based on long-term trends. It reviews the difficulties related to SMEs' access to finance during the crisis against a background of a sharp decline in bank profitability and erosion of bank capital that negatively affected lending. With a view to guiding policy makers in the current environment of financial deleveraging, it highlights the importance of the health of banks' balance sheets and structural bank reforms to restore bank lending to the real economy.

As for capital market financing of SMEs, debt financing in the form of securitisation, private placements and bonds can play a role, albeit with caveats. Securitisation could play an important role in filling the lending gap, although it needs to be revitalised since it was tarnished by the crisis and volumes have dropped. It could rebound as 'Securitisation 2.0' by making it safer, simpler and more transparent. Offering some (initial) government and regulatory support could also help. But our analysis also points to the difficulties of SME securitisation becoming economically viable. Similarly, covered bonds can be attractive instruments for SME finance, although their use is limited by asset encumbrance. For mid-sized companies, bond issuance and private placements may also provide useful alternatives. All these instruments can and should be tailored to fit the investors' needs.

Regarding equity finance, options for seed and early stage finance for SMEs and possible policies to support innovation financing are briefly explored. Special focus in this chapter is given to equity finance beyond private equity. For SMEs, admission cost and listing requirements in main markets may be discouragingly high, and a perceived reluctance of institutional investors to invest and the absence of a level playing field between equity and debt financing may be impeding SME public equity financing. Furthermore, a lack of liquidity of SME stocks is one of the key challenges in publicly traded SME equity, hindering investors from realising their investment. Some policy support may be required for developing SME equity financing platforms and instruments. Fostering SME equity financing, which would support the riskier, but more dynamic and innovative SMEs, can be especially helpful in facilitating growth of the real economy.

In concluding, we stress the fact that, owing to their diversity, the financing of SMEs remains complex and requires a variety of instruments and approaches. Policy makers can help by providing regulatory support and assist in the improvement of data transparency, standardisation, and raising awareness about available financing options.

Prospects for bank financing for the whole private sector

The crisis has resulted in bank lending gaps...

There are signs that banks are far safer than they were in the first years after the crisis (Chapter 3). However, lending outside of the United States has not picked up to the extent needed to fill the gap in financing since 2009. The recent increased safety of banks follows a period of substantial deleveraging and the subsequent implementation of regulations that will limit to some degree the risk they will be able to take onto their balance sheets in the future. This increase in safety is a conscious trade-off by policy makers *vis-à-vis* the extent to which banks can play a role in supporting the economic recovery.

...which will close in the United States...

Bank lending projections for the United States, euro area, the United Kingdom and Japan until Q4 2016 are shown in Figure 5.1, based on OECD economic projections for GDP and interest rates, but with unchanged regulatory rules.[6]

United States lending picked up earlier than elsewhere, and is unique amongst the economies shown and beginning to approach lending growth more reminiscent of the pre-crisis period. There are two basic reasons for this: *(i)* the more pre-emptive policies followed during and after the crisis; and *(ii)* the fact that the government-sponsored enterprises (GSEs) Fannie Mae and Freddie Mac absorbed a large amount of problematic mortgage loans that were pushed off banks' balance sheets. Consequently, with nominal

GDP set to grow by 4¾% in 2015 and 2016, lending is projected to accelerate further and is set to peak at over 10% in late 2015 before beginning to slow somewhat through 2016. When actual credit is compared to that which would restore a 'normalised' relationship with trend nominal GDP, the US lending gap is relatively small and is virtually closed towards the end of the projection period at the end of 2016 (see Figure 5.2).[7]

Figure 5.1. **Lending in major economies outside the United States is projected to pick up less strongly**

Bank lending to the non-financial private sector,[a] year-on-year percentage changes, projections until Q4 2016

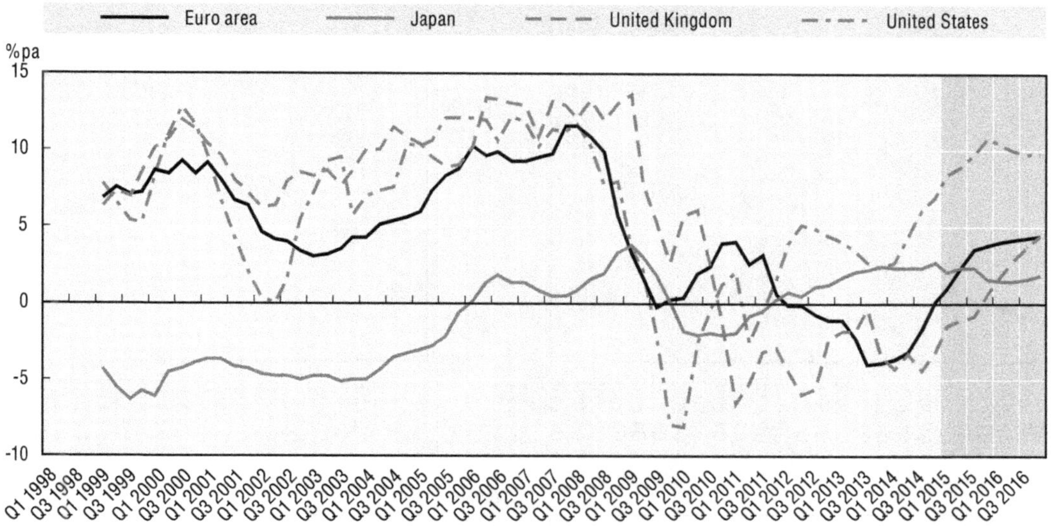

a) Commercial Bank loans and leases for the United States; M4 sterling lending for the United Kingdom; MFI & Eurosystem loans to euro area residents for the euro area; aggregate bank lending (excluding Shinkin Banks) for Japan.

Source: OECD calculations, Thomson Reuters Datastream.

StatLink http://dx.doi.org/10.1787/888933209805

...but not in most other advanced economies

The absence of large GSEs in the United Kingdom and the euro area to absorb mortgage loans has meant in practice the presence of much more 'forbearance' on the part of banks, i.e. the keeping non-performing loans alive on banks' balance sheets via restructuring.[8] This makes it difficult for them to lend to new and potentially more dynamic companies while at the same time provisioning for bad loans and raising regulatory capital. The loan loss and capital requirement term in the lending model is strong for the euro area (see Box 5.1), and has been and remains an important factor holding back loans in the projection period alongside weak economic growth and disinflation pressures (the OECD projections for nominal GDP growth for the euro area are 3.5% and 4% in 2015 and 2016, respectively). After a long period of deleveraging, euro area lending growth is likely to pick up during the projection period to around 4% per annum by 2016. This recovery is sub-par compared to the pre-crisis period and is lagging the projected recovery in economic activity and inflation. The 'gap' of actual projected credit compared to that based on a 'normal' relationship with trend nominal GDP is around 9.5% of trend loans by the end of 2016 (see Figure 5.2).

United Kingdom lending growth also accelerates moderately over the projection period compared to past cycles, reaching a moderate 4% rate of growth only by 2016. The 'gap' to the lending relationship based on trend nominal GDP is a much larger 25% of trend loans (Figure 5.2). The size of this estimated 'gap' reflects the sheer size of the credit boom in the United Kingdom prior to the crisis: M4 sterling lending reached close to 170% of GDP in 2009-10, compared to 50% in the United States (due in part to the presence of GSEs) and 125% in the bank-based euro area economy.

Figure 5.2. **Actual versus trend lending levels indicate bank lending gaps**

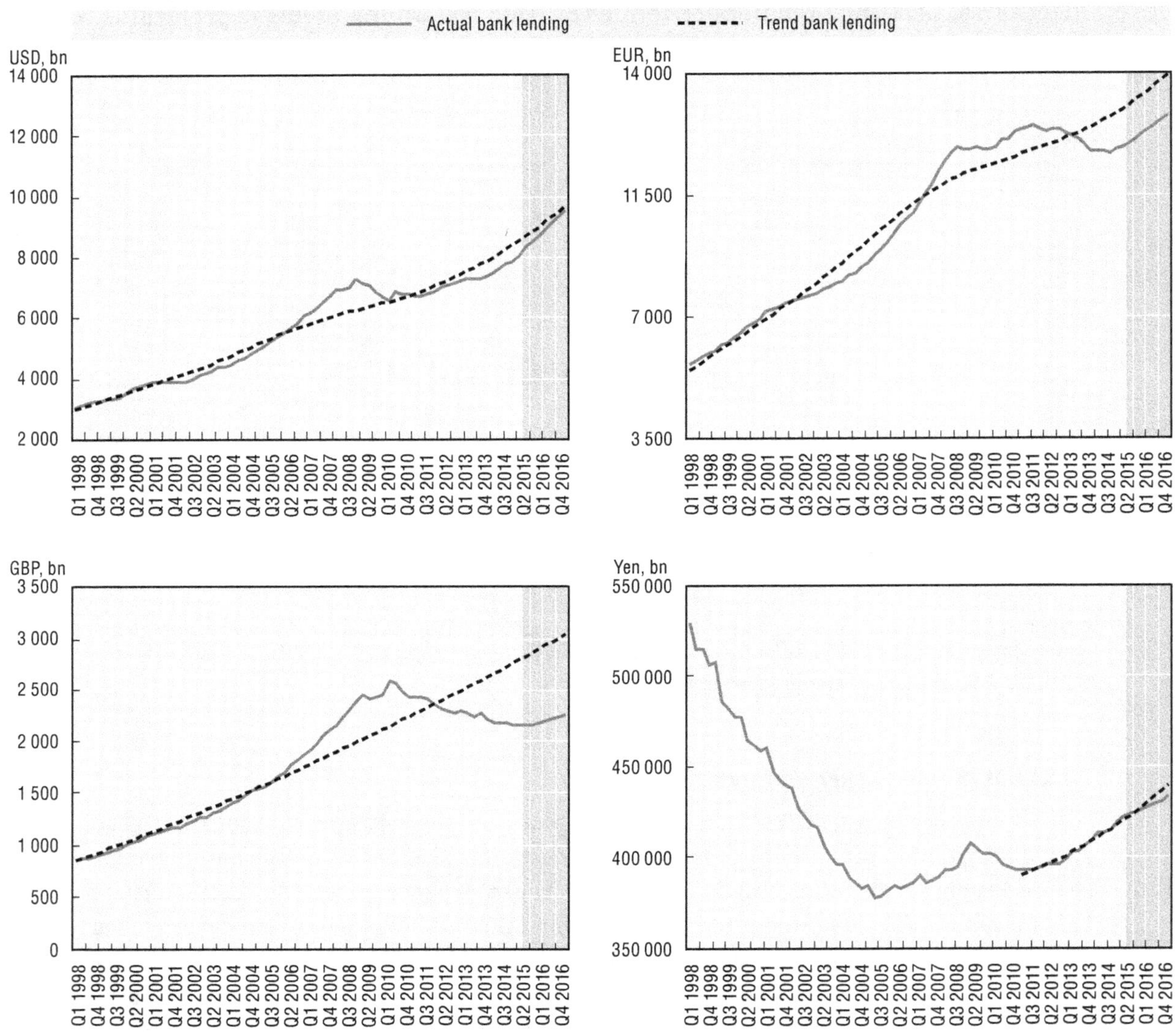

Source: OECD calculations, Thomson Reuters Datastream.

StatLink http://dx.doi.org/10.1787/888933209813

Japan had its banking crisis sometime earlier, and decades of deflation pressure and very slow GDP growth have seen the level of lending fall from very high levels to bottom at around 75% of GDP just prior to the crisis. The subsequent recovery towards weak lending growth in the 1-3% range extends well into the projection period. While the 'gap' to loans matched to trend GDP is not large, it tends to follow rather than lead nominal economic activity. The issue in Japan is less about finding ways to fill the gap as to finding better financial channels to support a better long-run growth process.

Box 5.1. **Study of the determinants of aggregate bank lending**

The model

Previous research has modelled bank lending in a panel study based on micro or individual bank data that focuses on the portfolio allocation decision of banks – the share of loans in their total assets portfolio.[9] That model focused on regulatory capital constructs, loan loss provisioning, relative interest rates, the asset price cycle and the riskiness of the individual bank (the distance-to-default). For the purposes of the Business and Finance Outlook, this approach from the supply side of lending was combined into a reduced-form model with similar supply side effects, but introducing nominal GDP to capture the demand side while leaving open the question of whether the interest rate terms would reflect either demand or supply-side influences (the sign is essentially ambiguous in this simplified model).

Table 5.1. **Co-integration model, log of bank lending**

	United States	Euro Area	Japan	United Kingdom
LN_GDP	1.55 ***	1.56 ***	1.00	1.56 ***
	(13.40)	(7.53)	(-)	(6.97)
BLR_CB	1.88 ***	0.04 ***	-1.54	-6.10
	(2.68)	(5.87)	(-0.43)	(-1.42)
BLR_GBY	2.58 ***	0.001	3.88	0.05
	(3.14)	(0.15)	(0.71)	(0.03)
LN_HPI	0.03	0.09	0.55 **	0.04
	(0.36)	(0.78)	(2.17)	(0.31)
LLP_K(-1)	-1.71 ***	-2.43 ***	-1.38 **	-1.64 **
	(-2.78)	(-5.18)	(-2.37)	(-2.33)
C	-10.14 ***	-9.02 ***	-2.65 **	-7.60 ***
	(-6.83)	(-3.27)	(-2.32)	(-3.13)
R^2	0.98	0.99	0.19	0.99
DW Stat	0.31	0.59	0.17	0.70
Total Obs.	67	67	67	67

Notes: ** and *** indicate statistical significance at the 5% and 1% levels, respectively.

The error-correction model based on the above long-run relationship, using the Engle 2-step method is well supported by the data. The speed of adjustment coefficients for the United States, European Union and United Kingdom are significant and their values broadly consistent with expectations at 0.19, 0.21 and 0.20, respectively, implying a mean lag of around 5 quarters for adjustment to the above long-run relationship (if the variables in the latter were to be held constant). Japan on the other hand has a speed of adjustment of 0.08, which is significant at the 1% level, but implies a much slower mean lag of closer to 3 years. The deflation deleveraging cycle in Japan has been extreme and to help deal with technical problems related to this, the model estimates the long-run relationship as the ratio of loans to GDP (effectively implying a unit coefficient on GDP).

StatLink http://dx.doi.org/10.1787/888933210457

The variables

The dependent variable consists of commercial bank loans and leases for the United States; M4 sterling lending for the United Kingdom; MFI & euro-system loans to euro area residents for the euro area; and aggregate bank lending (excluding Shinkin Banks) for Japan. The explanatory variables are: Ln_GDP (natural logarithm of nominal gross domestic product), BLR_CB (bank prime lending rate minus central bank policy rate), BLR_GBY (bank prime lending rate minus 10 year government bond yield), Ln_HPI (natural logarithm of house price index), LLP_K (logarithm of the one-year lagged value of the ratio of the banks' loan loss provisions plus total equity versus total loans estimated from bank data).

Estimation methods

Time series regressions are run using aggregate quarterly data for the United States, the euro area, Japan and the United Kingdom over the period Q1 1998–Q4 2014. The error-correction model based on the Engle 2-step process establishes co-integration, and this dynamic model is used in the projections over the period Q1 2015-Q4 2019. The long-run co-integration equation is used to calculate the trend of aggregate bank lending by region. Nominal trend GDP is estimated using the Hodrick-Prescott filter.

The above 'gap' calculations are only suggestive, and as noted for Japan they do not factor in structural policies and inflation scenarios that could help to push nominal GDP growth higher. The past dependence on bank finance in the case of the euro area, the United Kingdom and Japan is a potential constraint of economic performance, and policies to encourage greater capital market funding through pooling and securitisation could be useful – provided that the new funding structures do not introduce new forms of risk within the financial system. These risks typically include:

- Loan provision dependent on excessive use of short-term wholesale funding.
- Capital market products that are excessively dependent on guarantees that facilitate the credit creation process, such as the role played by monoline insurers and affiliates of insurance companies during the crisis, often via the writing of credit default swaps (CDS), which can lead to a meaningful under-pricing of risk.[10]
- Securitisations such as asset-backed commercial paper (ABCP) provided by banks and non-bank financial institutions (NBFIs) which invest in very illiquid assets (including those with bank liquidity facilities attached).

Bank lending for SME financing

Current lending conditions for SME finance: some light on the horizon?

Banks are an essential source of financing for SMEs and households.[11] In fact, bank lending still makes up for the majority of SME finance in OECD countries.[12] While the crisis has had a negative effect on bank lending overall as discussed above, lending to SME was particularly affected and, despite a recovery, has remained below pre-crisis peaks in major OECD economies.[13] There are, however, some positive signs of improving lending conditions for SMEs. In the United States, the movement to more normalised bank lending conditions is borne out in lending surveys, where there are signs of lending conditions easing for smaller firms (Figure 5.3). In Japan, financing conditions for small as compared to larger enterprises remain more difficult, even though they have been easing to above pre-crisis levels (Figure 5.4).

Figure 5.3. **Bank lending conditions in the United States have eased**

Net percentage of domestic respondents tightening standards for commercial and industrial loans

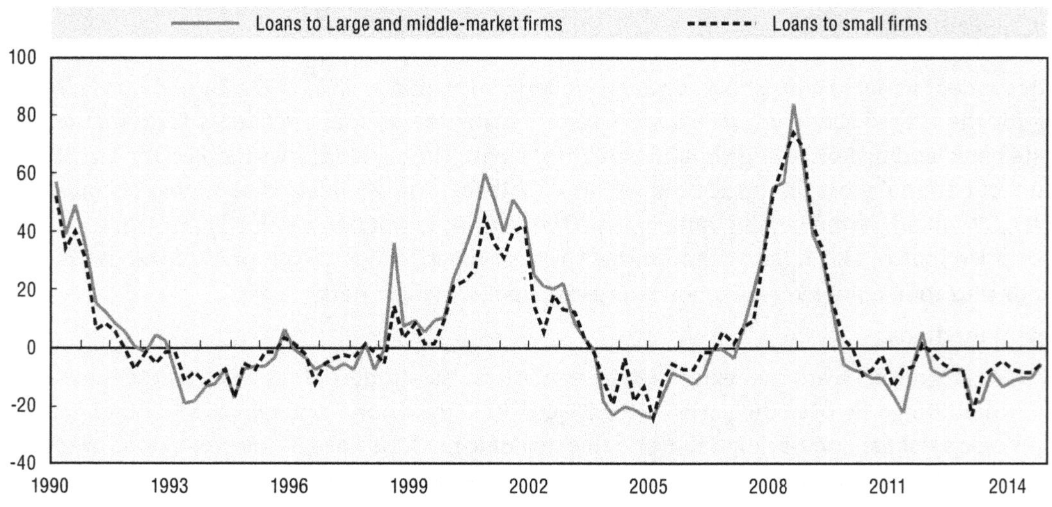

Source: Senior Loan Officer Opinion Survey on Bank Lending Practices, January 2015.

StatLink http://dx.doi.org/10.1787/888933209822

Figure 5.4. **Financing conditions of Japanese enterprises have eased less for SMEs**

Financing conditions of large versus medium-sized and small enterprises, in percentage points (ppt)

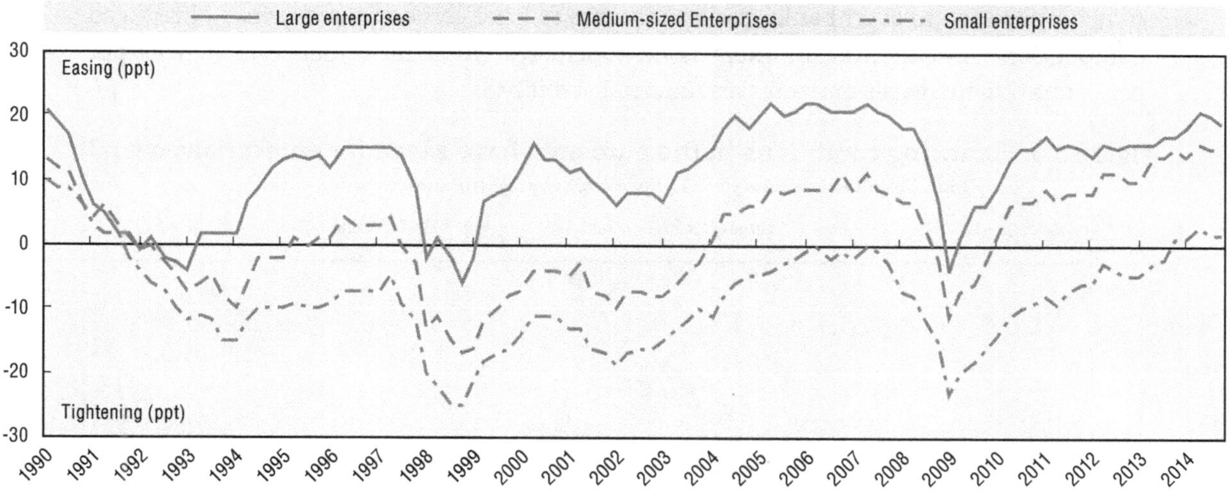

Source: Bank of Japan, Short-term Economic Survey of Enterprises in Japan (TANKAN).

StatLink http://dx.doi.org/10.1787/888933209836

In the euro area, while credit conditions have been easing for both large and small enterprises (Figure 5.5), the problem of obtaining financing has been a major problem in some of the weaker economies (Figure 5.6), even though policy support has been helping to overcome many of the financing constraints faced by SMEs. SMEs in these countries are encountering specific difficulties in accessing finance owing to the fragmentation of financial and banking markets. Sovereign spreads and macroeconomic weakness, in addition to borrowers' risk, are likely to influence financing costs in their local home markets.

Credit crunch and financing difficulties for SMEs during the crisis

The economic and financial crisis has had detrimental consequences for borrowers and lenders. The crisis led to a sharp decline in bank profitability and an erosion of bank capital cushions that hit lenders. The disruptions in banks' access to wholesale funding and the impairment of their ability to securitise assets put severe pressure on their liquidity positions. All these developments imposed serious strains on banks' balance sheet positions and consequently impaired their lending capacity as they were forced to readjust their balance sheets.

Several studies have explored the effect of the crisis on the supply of credit and on the real economy.[14] There is large empirical evidence for credit crunch effects during crises, but these effects may vary across firms and, as in the current global financial crisis, also across economies. Especially in the current crisis, strong policy support appears to have attenuated or abated the risk of a true or more severe credit crunch. Several issues are emerging from such analyses: the impairment of the bank-credit channel and its economic effects; factors potentially attenuating the effect of a financial squeeze; and the role of global banking in attenuating but also transmitting financial shocks in an environment of financial deleveraging. .

Given the importance of bank lending for the financing of SMEs, banks should remain a key priority for policy makers when SME financing suffers. Improving bank's health can attenuate the effect of a general financial squeeze: safer banks make for better lending. Furthermore, the type of business activities of banks can have an impact on their lending behaviour, as well as their responsiveness to unconventional monetary policy.[15] While the enhancement of bank financial stability through (forced) M&As during the crisis that may have helped to avert bankruptcies, it seems to have come at the expense of reduced competition.[16] But then again, there is no conclusive empirical evidence as to whether concentration increases or decreases financial stability.[17]

Figure 5.5. **Financing conditions in the euro area have eased for enterprises overall**

Credit Standards, weighted net percentage change (tightened minus eased)

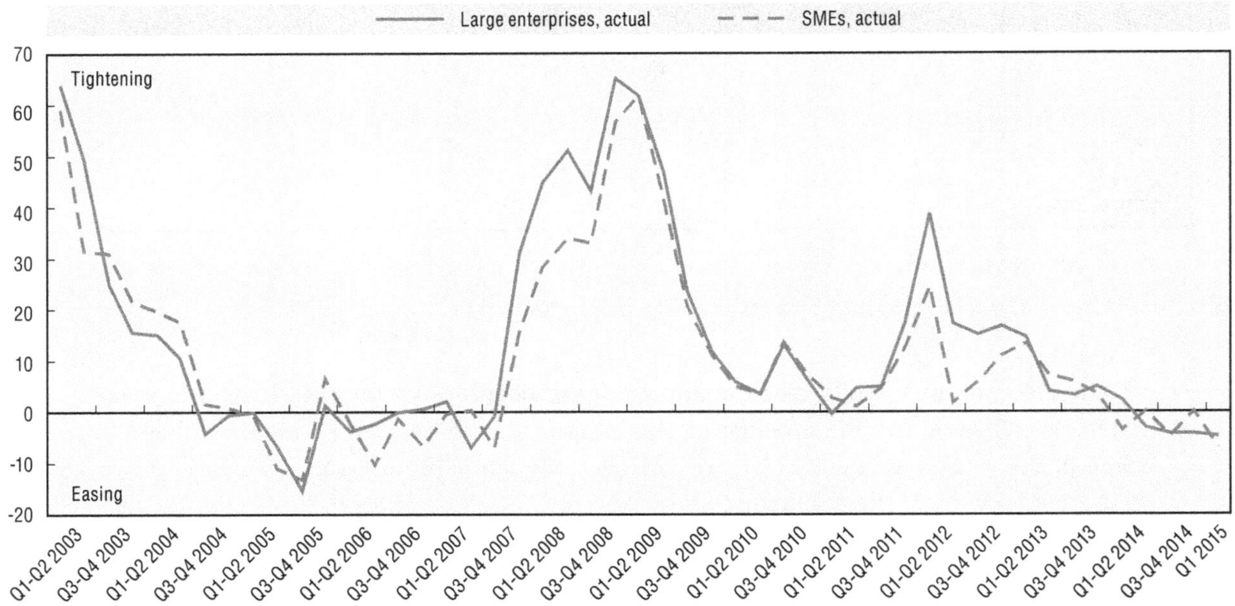

Notes: Net percentages are defined as the difference between the sum of the percentages of banks responding 'tightened considerably' and 'tightened somewhat' and the sum of the percentages of banks responding 'eased somewhat' and 'eased considerably'. Weighted net percentage (tightened minus eased or reverse) based on the share of each country in the total loan outstanding amounts of the area aggregate and of each bank in the total loan outstanding amount of the BLS banks sample

Source: ECB Bank Lending Survey (Q1, Q6 Credit Standards).

StatLink http://dx.doi.org/10.1787/888933209845

...and the role of monetary policy and safer, smaller banks in improving bank lending

The crisis and policy responses have highlighted the role played by monetary policy in assuring the availability of credit to corporations and households. Expansionary monetary policy should not only stimulate investment but also counter a deepening credit crunch. This policy mainly works through the credit channel.[18] Where banks have taken losses as mark-to-market assets have fallen in value, as was the case for many banks during the crisis, monetary policy can serve to reflate these assets without a strong impact on lending. There is evidence that global systemically important banks (G-SIBs) have been least responsive to monetary policy, while non-G-SIBs appear to have responded to the lending rate spread to cash rates, the spread between lending rates and the alternative investment in government bonds, and the distance to default (the banks' solvency). It seems that better lending conditions in the United States during the crisis were the result of safer banks and a supportive spread to government bonds; yields on the latter have been too attractive relative to lending rates in Europe.[19]

Figure 5.6. **Problems of access to financing exists for SMEs in weaker euro area economies**

The most pressing problems faced by euro area SMEs across euro area countries: percentage of respondents

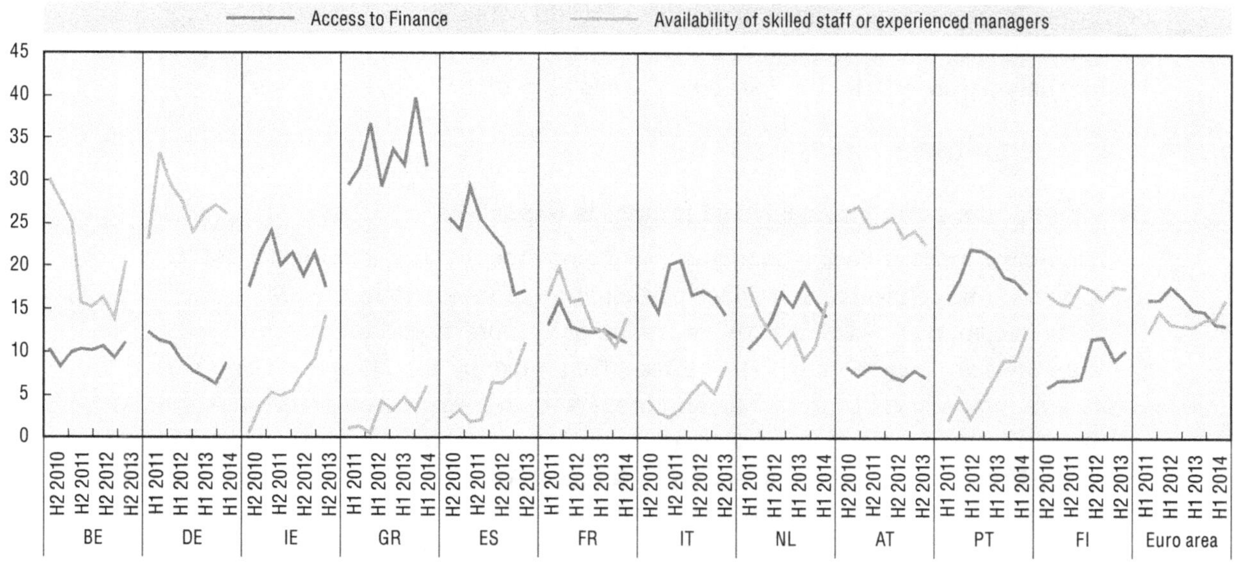

Notes:.Base: all SMEs. Figures refer to rounds four (October 2010-March 2011) to 11 (April-September 2014) of the survey.

Source: ECB, Survey on the access to finance of enterprises (November 2014).

StatLink http://dx.doi.org/10.1787/888933209855

In the context of monetary operations of quantitative easing that involve securitisation (as discussed below), it is also interesting to note that there is empirical evidence that banks that are more involved in securitisation activities relax credit constraints.[20] However, this seems to be true only in normal periods, as such banks increase credit rationing during crisis periods. This would indicate that securitisation generates supply effects which differ in normal and crisis periods. Furthermore, different types of securitisation – covered bonds and mortgage-backed securities (MBS) – have different effects on credit rationing. While both types of securitisation reduce credit rationing in normal periods, the issuance of MBS aggravates credit rationing in crisis periods. This may indicate the role that the ECB may have played since 2007 when offering liquidity in exchange for covered bonds (see below).

There is also evidence for the positive role of small banks in the provision of lending. However, their close ties to local customers ('relationship banking') may also have negative effects in that it leads to 'evergreening' of loans (i.e. providing cheap credit to a risky borrower in order to postpone credit losses from the lender's default) and too much 'patience' in financing 'zombie' companies that are de facto bankrupt.[21] Evergreening is presumably easier for a smaller bank where discretion in lending decisions is higher and the weight of credit scoring is lower than for a larger bank, where lending decisions are based on more automatic procedures. Similar arguments apply to forbearance lending or debt restructuring to help a potentially profitable lender through temporary difficulties and to regain its competitiveness, which is easier for small banks to apply.

Nevertheless, small banks can act as non-myopic lender that do not only have to rely on a firm's (current) balance sheet information and credit scoring but can also take into account more forward-looking measures of a firm's economic prospects and other, 'soft' information, which is particularly important for SME lending as public information on such companies is scarce. Empirical evidence indicates that pressure on bank capital may induce two opposite and simultaneous lending biases: a generalised excessive tightening on the one hand, and on the other some excessive loosening of credit policies towards risky borrowers (evergreening).[22] Overall, the role of relationship lending seems to be a positive one (perhaps also due to more guidance on prudence for the lender), and small banks with healthy balance sheets can improve credit availability for SMEs during crises.

Non-bank debt financing for SMEs

Developing non-bank market-based finance is important

Non-bank market-based financing can complement bank lending to SMEs, while allowing for a more diverse and wider participation of investors in the SME space. In the United States, market-based finance has traditionally more important than in, for example, the euro area or Japan (Figure 5.7). The recent initiative by the European Commission to create a Capital Market Union (CMU) in Europe should remedy this situation.[23] The CMU is intended to reduce the barriers that are impeding cross-border investments within the European Union and businesses' access to finance. A major aim is to unlock non-bank funding to help companies expand. For example, if EU venture capital markets had been as deep as they are in the United States, as much as EUR 90 billion more in funds would have been available to companies between 2008 and 2013, according to the European Commission.

Figure 5.7. **Bank vs. capital market financing: catch-up needed in the euro area**

Loans vs. bond finance in the United States and euro area

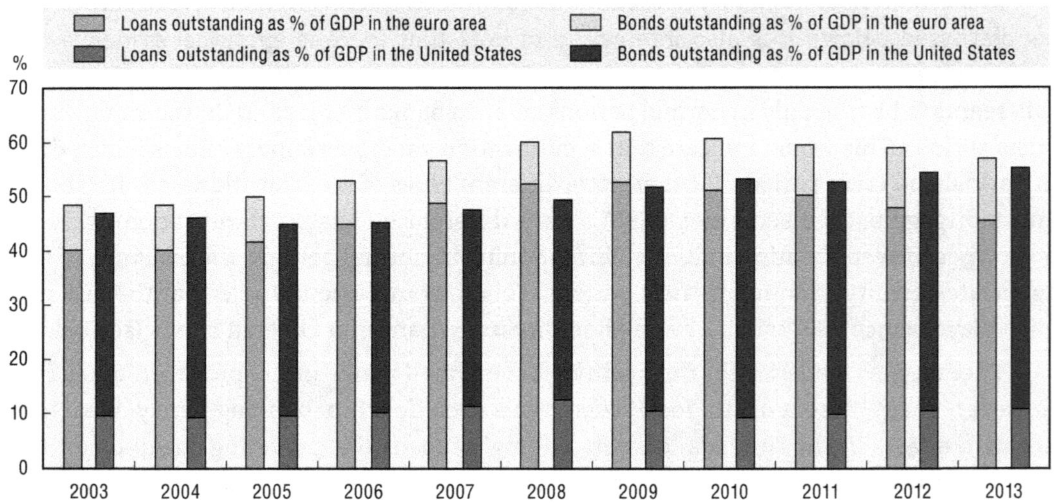

Notes: Loans are loans to non-financial corporations.

Source: OECD calculations, Thomson Reuters Datastream.

StatLink http://dx.doi.org/10.1787/888933209867

In the following, the most pertinent debt financing alternatives to bank loans are discussed: SME securitisation, (covered) bonds and private placements. These instruments could be promoted to fill some of the bank lending gaps. While as such they help to ease SMEs' financing constraints, they also allow for a better distribution of risk amongst investors.[24]

Securitisation has important advantages...

Securitisation can help mitigate credit supply problems by allowing banks to refinance loans, diversify their funding and benefit from regulatory capital relief. Securitised assets can also be particularly attractive to institutional investors because they are more liquid than their underlying assets. As such, they also offer investors opportunities to diversify in asset classes that they would or could normally not invest in. However, in the run-up to the 2007 subprime crisis, complex structuring to 'improve' risk diversification and misalignments of interest between originator and investor (full offloading of risks, 'originate-to-distribute' models) led to under-pricing of risk. Such developments, paired with potentially inadequate regulation for some types of securitisation, led to higher than expected default rates.[25] Such defaults, together with liquidity squeezes, tarnished the image of securitisation instruments more broadly and eventually undermined the securitisation model as a whole. This resulted in a sharp contraction of securitisation issuance overall after the crisis.

This is shown in Figure 5.8 which, interestingly, also illustrates the large differences in the use of such instruments: While in the United States the securitisation market is very large, in Europe such market-based finance instruments have a long way to go to catch up with their US counterpart, and the penetration is smallest in Japan. In all economies, MBS have traditionally been dominating the market, while the share of SME securitisation has been small.

Figure 5.8. **Securitisation issuance in major economies**

Annual issuance levels, in per cent of GDP

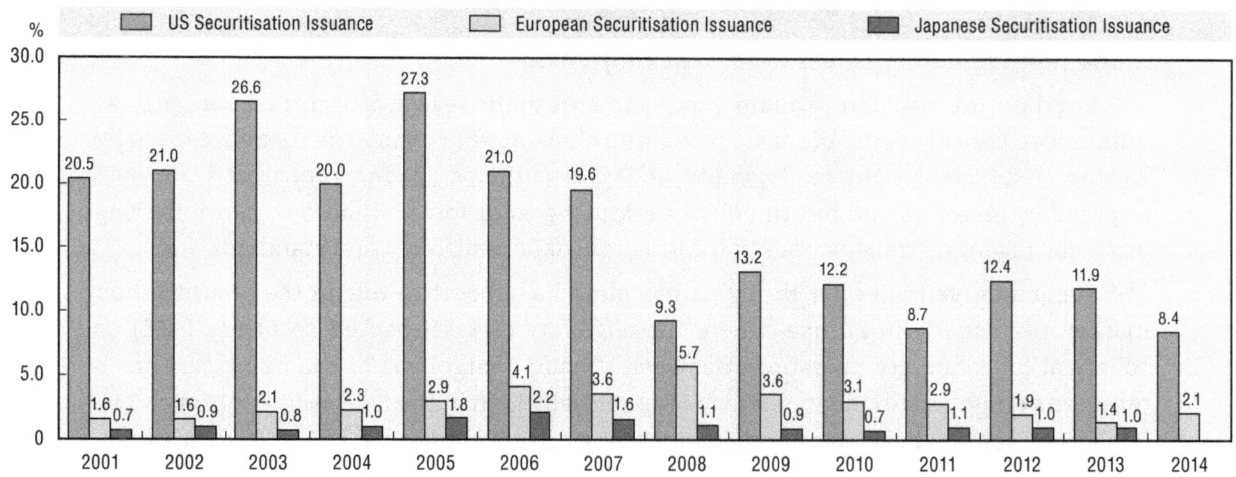

Notes: Based on annual exchange rates and on GDP in current prices. European securitisation issuance for 2013 based on announced annualised Q3 2014 GDP (data available up until Q3 2014).

Sources: OECD calculations, AFME, Thomson Reuters Datastream.

StatLink http://dx.doi.org/10.1787/888933209871

...but designing the regulatory framework well is a challenge...

Policy responses to the crisis have recognised these past problems with securitisation. To avoid pitfalls of the past and to restore investor confidence, post-crisis regulations require risk retention or 'skin in the game' from the issuers' side, removing misalignments of interest and information asymmetries between originators and investors. Such information asymmetries are also mitigated by more stringent due diligence and enhanced transparency. The latter can be achieved by improving the availability of information on loan-level data, asset performance, documentation and other deal structure-related information. There are also various approaches to high-quality securitisation[26] that should help a renaissance of a new, safer and more transparent 'Securitisation 2.0'.

However, some regulatory reforms like Basel III and Solvency II tend to have a curbing impact on the revival of securitisation. Furthermore, different treatment of securitisation across the various types of securitisation instruments may create a non-level playing field which would call for a coordinated regulatory approach at all levels. Regulatory support for a safe and high quality securitisation would be an important step to revive the market. This would generate additional capital market funding for SMEs while providing banks with capital relief. This would generate resources for potential further on-lending to the real economy and allow securitisation to act as a credit risk transfer mechanism, potentially resulting in a deeper and sounder financial system.

While regulatory reforms are required to improve financial stability and avoid pitfalls of the recent past, some of these reforms may also unduly dis-incentivise originators and investors and thus potentially inhibit the revival of a healthy securitisation market. Complex and sometimes conceptually contradictory regulation may have unintended consequences that should be considered when designing new rules. Clarity over ongoing regulatory work streams is also important for originators and investors, especially institutional investors, to fully engage in these markets that could benefit from their search for yield in the current low interest rate environment. Appropriate calibration of ongoing regulatory reforms (e.g. liquidity ratios of Basel III, capital charges in Solvency II, retention rate requirements) are important for unlocking the potential of securitisation.

...and non-regulatory issues need to be confronted

But there are also non-regulatory impediments to the revival of securitisation, such as unintended consequences of public policy and challenges in disintermediation, especially lacking is sufficient economic viability of SME securitised products (mismatch of yield required by investors and return on the underlying asset for the issuer) in part reflecting problems regarding transparency of information, data availability and standardisation.

Public intervention after the crisis has played a supportive role in the securitisation market, particularly in Europe, where the eligibility of asset-backed securities (ABS) as collateral for monetary operations has been driving a large part of the issuance. This is reflected in high retention rates, which are especially high in the SME segment (Figure 5.9). Public intervention has not succeeded in reviving private market-based SME securitisation. Although such intervention is undoubtedly considered as important for banks' funding, it has not fostered further on-lending to the economy. But public intervention is also an important factor in the United States, where SBA loans, partially guaranteed by the US Small Business Administration, are a major driver of SME securitisation (Figure 5.10). Such effects and other potential unintended consequences of public intervention should be taken into account in relevant policy making. Intervention that does not foster further on-lending to the economy and provides no capital relief to benefiting banks should be reconsidered.

Specific problems arise in the context of the quantitative easing (QE) asset purchase programmes undertaken by many central banks. The empirical evidence on whether quantitative easing exercises have a significant effect on bank lending is moot, and the necessity for public intervention can be questioned when it comes to senior tranches of high-quality issuances, as private investor demand for that part of the structure is consistently strong in capital markets. However, including SME ABS in the quantitative easing exercise by the ECB may entail several benefits for the SME securitisation market, like improving secondary market liquidity and, given that the programme also involves

Figure 5.9. **Retention rates are high for European SME securitisation**

Placed vs. retained SME securitisation issuance in Europe, in USD billion (l.h.s.) and retained in percent of total (r.h.s.)

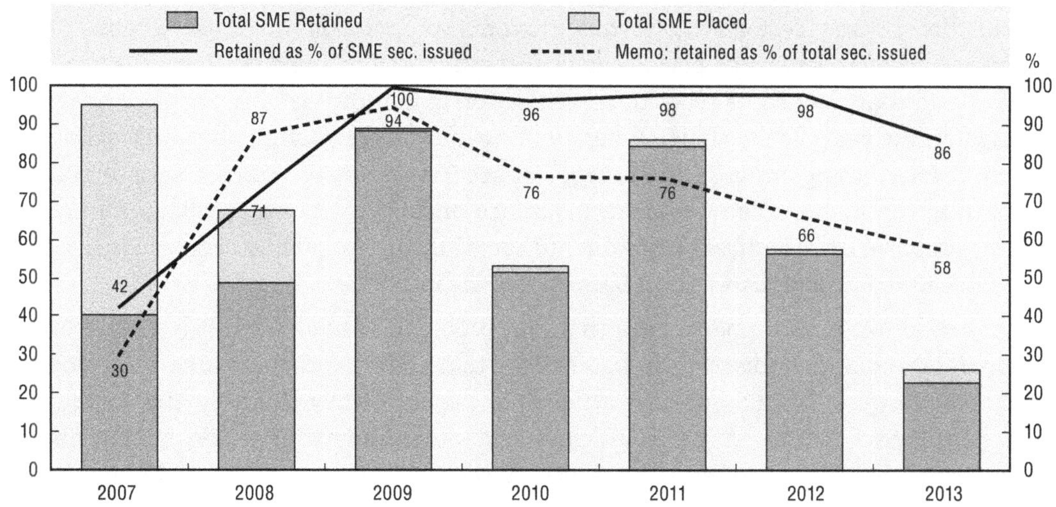

Sources: OECD calculations, AFME, SIFMA, Bloomberg, Dealogic, Thomson Reuters.

StatLink http://dx.doi.org/10.1787/888933209880

Figure 5.10. **Small Business Loan Administration ABS Outstanding**

Annually, 1985-2013, in USD billion

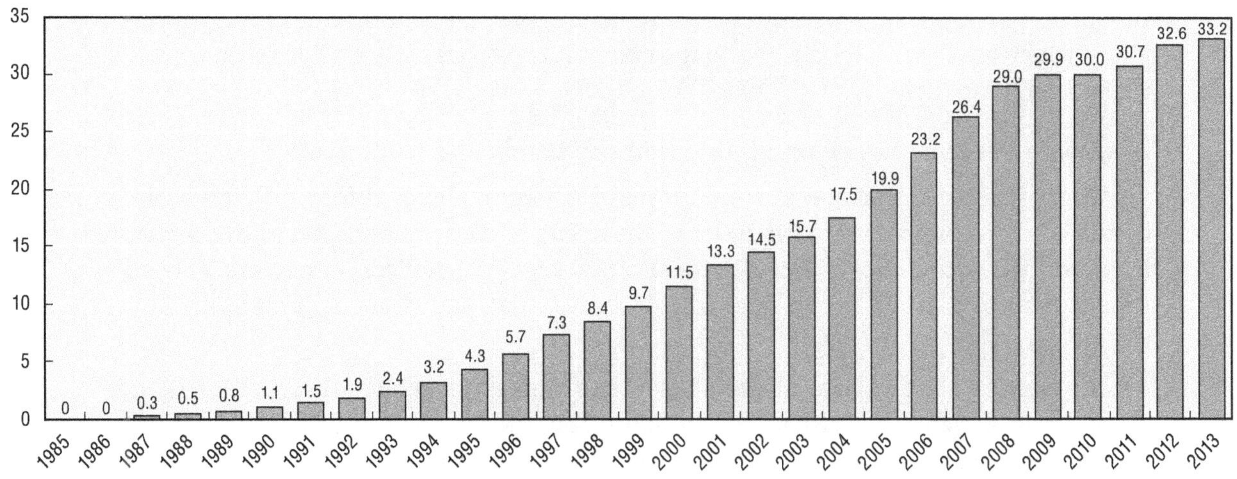

Source: OECD calculations, SIFMA, Bloomberg, Dealogic, Thomson Reuters.

StatLink http://dx.doi.org/10.1787/888933209896

purchases in the primary market, primary origination of SME ABS may be fostered as banks will pursue risk transfer that will assist in delevering their balance sheet. Lowering ABS interest rates across the board would help bring back issuances that were priced out as uneconomical and perhaps also incentivise other players such as institutional investors to enter this market. However, record low levels of interest rates may undermine the funding benefit of participation in such programme.

Due to the heterogeneity of and typically scant credit information for SMEs, market-based SME finance remains challenging and limits the role that capital markets can play in complementing bank lending. Furthermore, there are fixed costs which can make underwriting and monitoring of rather small and mostly local firms relatively expensive.

Such factors hamper disintermediation of banks when it comes to the origination of SME loans. The limited economic viability of SME collateralised loan obligations (CLOs) is one of the potential impediments to the revitalisation of that market, since prevailing underlying spreads do not provide for an attractive economic proposition, not least because of the riskiness and relatively weak performance of the underlying loans. At the same time, the recent performance of some types of securitisation in Europe has been particularly robust throughout the years of the crisis. Understanding the structural strengths and weaknesses of and differentiating among various types of securitisations would be a step forward in revitalising the market. The European Insurance and Occupational Pensions Authority's (EIOPA) proposal on identifying high-quality securitisations could be seen as such a step, as could be the Prime Collateralised Securities (PCS) initiative.

To tackle the asymmetric information problem associated with SME lending, transparent and standardised data warehouses that collect and share credit information on smaller firms with all market participants (as is already done by the Banque de France for French SMEs) can be an effective tool. Such transparency allows institutional investors to make their own assessment as to the creditworthiness of the underlying loans. Standardisation of SME securitisation products can also help to overcome information problems. However, views differ over the desirability of such standardisation. Some argue that the capacity to have various degrees of credit enhancement is consistent with the different characteristics of SMEs, while at the same time aggregating large pools of SME loans allows for the smoothing out of idiosyncrasies. Contrary to other capital market products, standardisation of SME-related issuance could be counter to the very nature of SMEs, which are inherently diverse, to the extent it takes away the flexible terms on which many small firms rely.

Assessing the potential of small- and mid-cap bonds and bond funds

Corporate bond issuance is commonly used by large companies for which it is easier to obtain credit ratings and that can issue bonds in large denominations, typically purchased by financial institutions. For SMEs, however, bond finance is not commonly available, even though several possibilities for midcap companies exist, and financing cost are relatively high (Figure 5.11).

In the past years several markets have been created for retail bonds. In 2010, BondM market was launched in Germany. In the same year, the London Stock Exchange launched the Order Book for Retail Bonds (ORB) retail bond trading platform. In 2012, *Emissions Obligataires par Offre au Public* (IBO) were launched in France. That programme allows listed and unlisted SMEs to issue bonds on NYSE Euronext and Alternext Paris. In 2013, Italy followed by launching ExtraMOT PRO. The emergence of mini-bonds in Italy was in large part driven by regulatory reform and favourable fiscal treatment for SMEs. At the end of 2013, MARF (New Alternative Fixed Income Market) was launched in Spain. A number of similar initiatives are underway (e.g. at Athens Stock Exchange's EN.A STEP alternative market, and at the Irish Stock Exchange) for the development of markets that allow investors to invest in securities generating SME debt.

However, capital markets remain relatively fragmented and cross-border investment remains low for SMEs and mid-caps despite – or because of – such national initiatives. Different securities laws, bankruptcy laws and tax incentives, but also investors' tendency to discriminate between the different types of bonds (depending on the perceived quality

Figure 5.11. **Select mini-bond issuance rates vs. SME loan rates in Italy**

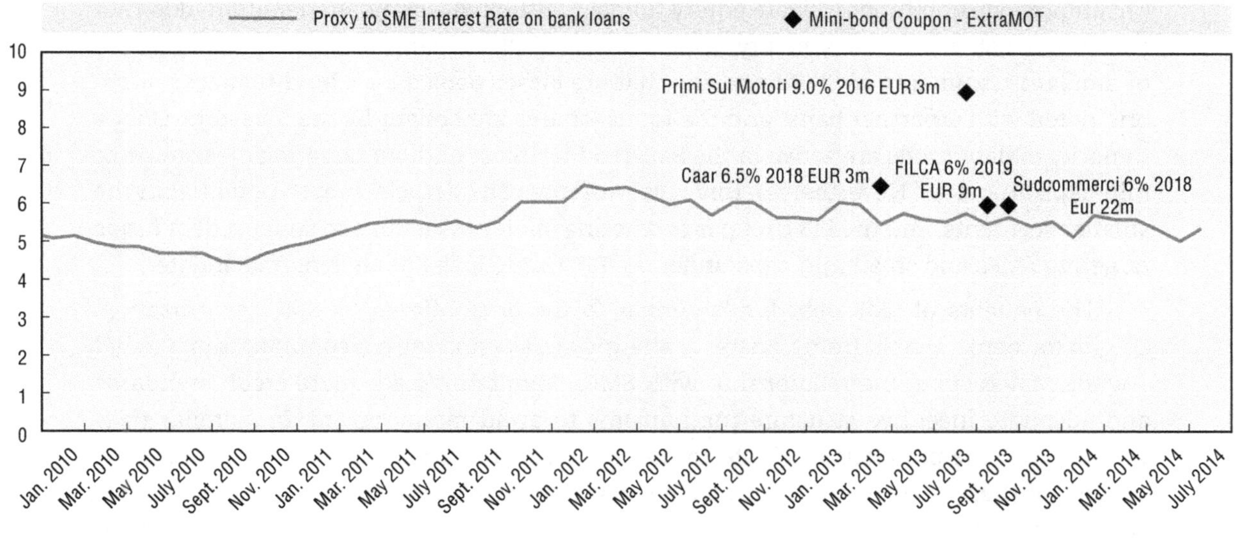

Notes: Interest rates applying to non-financial corporations for new loans of up to EUR 1 million used as a proxy for SME loan rates (for the methodology see OECD, 2015a).

Source: Borsa Italiana, Banca d'Italia.

StatLink http://dx.doi.org/10.1787/888933209904

of the underlying collateral) are the main obstacles for a more vibrant development of such markets and instruments. But another reason may also be some negative experiences with SME bonds, especially in Germany, with many downgrades and high default rates.

Small and mid-cap trading bond platforms have a number of attractive characteristics for issuers and investors alike. Issuers can place bonds in the market with listing requirements that are more relaxed than those for larger blue-chip companies. SMEs can issue bonds on an unrated basis, improve their financial flexibility and access a larger investor base. Investors on the other hand have the opportunity to invest in bonds at yields well above the ones offered by large caps, which makes them particularly attractive in the current low interest rate environment. Smaller trading denominations on certain markets give retail investors the possibility to diversify their investment portfolio beyond traditional bank deposits.

Due to relatively high cost and reporting requirements bond issuance is suited mostly to the upper segment of SMEs and beyond, essentially medium-sized and larger companies. The role of brokers is also important in getting those bonds to institutional investors. Given that most bond investors look into placements in large scale bond issuances, the promotion by brokers of SME asset classes can be instrumental for the fostering of the market. When it comes to retail micro and small company bonds, investors face challenges such as scarce liquidity, relative lack of transparency compared to medium and large corporate bond issuances and incomplete ratings coverage. However, some of these problems may be overcome by the maturing of the market and improved information tools while maintaining adequate credit standards.

Small cap bonds and other SME debt can also be pooled in funds. Such intermediary vehicles offer diversification to investors and help to channel institutional investments to non-bank lending for SMEs. The small cap bond fund Micado in France is an example of such bundling, but such structures, and their success, have been rather limited. There are also specialised institutional debt funds created by non-bank institutional investors (insurance, pension funds, private equity funds).[27] Although a standard definition does not currently exist, such debt funds typically consist of plain loans, SME bonds, mini-bonds or similar instruments of SME financing that are either pooled by a fund manager or co-originated with a partner bank, and the funds' shares are bought by the investors. Only a minority of debt funds are active in the SME lending, most of them targeting mezzanine or mid-cap corporates. Nevertheless, this area presents considerable growth potential in the smaller segments, and the EIB Group is promoting pilot transactions to support debt funds targeting SMEs and small mid-caps under the EIB Group Risk Enhancement Mandate.

The benefits of SME debt funds similar to the ones offered by SME securitisation. Originator-banks benefit from transfer or sharing of risk – and the concomitant capital relief – while still keeping the relationship with SMEs. Maintaining adequate credit standards and adequate incentive structure mechanisms to avoid moral hazard and similar risks witnessed in the pre-crisis originate-to-distribute securitisation models is crucial for the success of these instruments. With such safeguards in place, institutional investors can benefit from attractive returns and secure access to the SME asset class which is difficult to tap. At the same time, SMEs enjoy an additional alternative source of finance and potentially longer maturities than the ones offered by traditional bank lending.

Developing private placement markets to attract institutional investors

Potentially lower-cost alternatives to public corporate bond issuance can be offered by private placements (PP). These instruments can broaden the availability of finance for medium-to-large unlisted companies without the need for a formal credit rating and reporting requirements expected in other capital market debt products. Where regulatory frameworks allow private placements, some markets have already been developed. Besides the US private placement market, which is available to both US and non-US companies, the most well-known PP markets in Europe are the *Schuldschein* market in Germany and the *Euro PP* in France. While private placements have dropped during the crisis, growth in the US market has since resumed and was in recent years strongly driven by non-US issuances (Figure 5.12). Growth of the existing markets, as well as cross-border issuance (mostly tapping the US market) indicate that there is a growing supply and demand for these products. However, lack of standardised documentation and information on the creditworthiness of issuers, lack of liquidity in the secondary market and differences in insolvency laws are all obstacles that hinder stronger growth of these markets on a national and cross-border level. So far, international investor demand is mostly met by US PPs.

While private placements obviate the need for formal credit ratings that are required for publicly traded debt issuance, some assessment of their creditworthiness is required. To that end, credit rating agencies have been active in providing special mid-market evaluation procedures that analyse mid-sized companies' credit profiles and help to inform especially smaller investors without the in-house research capability necessary to assess this complex and relatively opaque market. As there is also no minimum size limit, privately placed bonds can cater to SMEs with smaller funding needs, with issuances in the single digit USD millions being delivered to very small companies.

Private placements require a direct relationship between lenders and borrowers which allows for the development of a closer connection with investors. This is beneficial to smaller companies with limited visibility in the public markets and the wider investor community. The role of institutional investors in promoting the private placement market is

Figure 5.12. **United States private placements**

Annual transaction levels of private debt placements on US markets, 2000-2013; USD billion

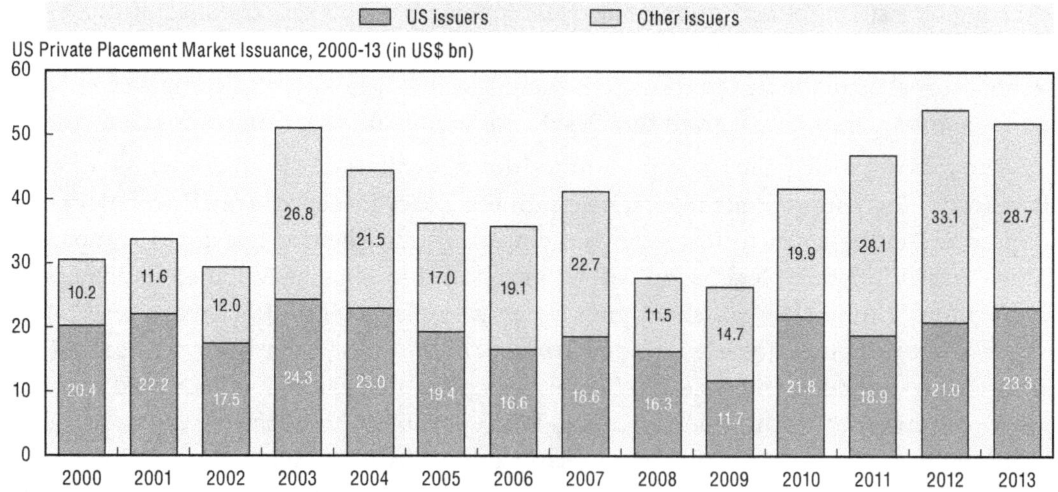

Source: Thomson Reuters.

StatLink http://dx.doi.org/10.1787/888933209914

critical and essential, as they constitute the driving force in the efforts made particularly in Europe. These instruments are especially well-suited for buy-and-hold long-term investors for whom the lack of liquidity and secondary markets is not an obstacle.

Besides an as of yet under-developed investor base, lack of standardisation is one of the key barriers to the development of the nascent PP market in Europe. Lack of standardised documentation increases the issuing cost (advisory, legal fees and other), as individual agreements need to be drafted for each transaction. Documentation standardisation is one of the enabling factors in the US PP market, which benefits from standard loan documentation (Model Note Purchase Agreement) and covenants, rendering it a user-friendly 'off-the-shelf' product which is more straightforward and attractive to both investors and issuers.

Credit scoring mechanisms can be an important enabling factor for the development of private placement markets. Indeed, a large part of the success of the US PP market is attributed to the role of the National Association of Insurance Commissioners (NAIC) in attributing credit scores to US PP issuances and the regulatory guidance on capital weighting investors receive. It is a moot question whether such credit scoring initiatives should be led by the public or the private sector. Arguments for a private sector lead are that this would ensure high quality of service provided and harmonisation of accounting and regulatory discrepancies across markets. For Europe, the establishment of a similar mechanism on a European-wide level would be a way to create the level of uniformity necessary for investors to engage in the European PP market.

European issuers have been actively tapping the US PP market over the years, with a third of the US PP market reported to consist of European companies' placements. Investor demand, especially by institutional investors, helps to push for more harmonisation and standardisation of the European PP markets and support their growth, as evidenced by initiatives to create a pan-European private placement market. Developing a European PP market along the lines of the successful US PP model could hold great potential for medium-sized companies.

Standardisation of documentation to the extent possible, credit scoring, regulatory recognition for capital weighting purposes as well as information sharing and financial reporting by issuers to institutional investors are some of the cornerstones of this effort towards the recognition of PPs as an asset class. Banks can also have an active role in this debate as intermediaries, even though they are less involved in PPs as compared to other capital market instruments, given that PPs do not require underwriting or market making.

The role of public policy is important for the recognition of PPs in Europe as an asset class and for their appropriate regulatory treatment. Policy measures are increasingly being adopted in Europe so as to foster private placement markets for mid-sized companies. In the United Kingdom, legislation will be introduced in Finance Bill 2015 to enable the provision of withholding tax exemption for private placements (HM Treasury, 2014). In France, authorities have fostered the development of the Euro PP market by a reform of the French insurance code and other initiatives, also promoted through a dedicated industry task force supported by the French ministry of the economy. At industry level, an initiative led by the International Capital Markets Association (ICMA) is underway, building on the French initiative, focusing on the investor side and looking at the essential principles and market practices that will attract investors into a PP market with European-wide appeal.

SME equity finance: selected issues

Startup-finance: barriers to seed and early stage capital need to be reduced

Start-ups and very young firms that tend to be higher risk, typically lacking sufficient collateral, or small ventures whose activities are innovative but of higher risk face specific financing problems. Such venture capital firms tend to be equity financed, its forms ranging from, e.g., seed finance by angel investors at their initial stages to public shares traded on specialised exchanges at later stages. Lack of finance in appropriate forms may be a serious barrier to expansion of potential high-growth companies that act as innovators, employ new technology and can play a crucial role in raising employment, productivity and competitiveness. Most commonly, risk capital is provided as equity (rather than debt) and includes investments by business angels, venture capital or other private equity firms in (non-listed) high growth companies, or investment in companies listed on dedicated 'growth' equity markets.

The financial crisis has increased concern by policy makers about the growing financing gap for high growth firms for which traditional financing techniques based mainly upon debt and guarantees are less suited. Indeed, particularly the seed and early stage equity market has faced great difficulties during the crisis.[28] Banks have been unable or unwilling to provide loans to young innovative start-ups, while venture capital firms have become more risk adverse due to pressures on the industry and have focused on later stage investments. Angel investors have engaged in this market through groups, syndicates and networks but also face difficulties.[29] Besides providing capital, angel investors can also play a crucial role in the early stages of a company by filling gaps in specific expertise needed to get a new, innovative idea off the ground and tackle problems that young entrepreneurs may not be well equipped to deal with.

To address perceived market failures and the financing gap that had grown during the crisis, governments in many OECD countries have sought to provide support for the seed and early stage market. Measures taken range from supply side interventions (guarantees, tax incentives, co-investments etc.) to those on the demand side (e.g. training, incubators, matchmaking services) as well as regulatory measures and improving framework conditions for a well-functioning market. Further evidence is needed on the appropriate role of the public versus the private sector in these areas.

Be that as it may, various regulatory and administrative barriers to seed and early stage investment still exist, particularly as they affect institutional investors, venture capital funds, angel investors and high growth firms. Exit markets play a critical role (as discussed below) as well as bankruptcy regulations and other framework conditions. In fact, some analysts argue that these framework conditions are more important for governments to address than trying to 'catalyse' the seed and early stage market through financing instruments.

Mezzanine finance can be strengthened as a source of 'growth capital'

Traditional financing techniques, based mainly upon debt and guarantees, have only limited capability for new, innovative and fast-growing SMEs and companies seeking to effect important transitions in their activities or to deleverage and improve capital structures. A range of non-bank financing instruments available to SMEs and entrepreneurs, in particular mezzanine finance, has proven effective in supplying 'growth capital' and has potential for wider usage, especially in the post-crisis environment of reduced bank lending. 'Mezzanine finance', incorporating elements of debt and equity in a single investment vehicle, is most relevant in a later (expansion) phase of a firm and complements rather than replaces other forms of finance.[30]

A well-developed commercial market in mezzanine finance, restricted to professional and institutional investors that generally hold such positions for relatively long periods, has functioned for more than two decades with minimal public involvement in many OECD economies. With public support via public entities or direct public financing it has become increasingly possible to offer mezzanine products to SMEs with lower credit ratings and smaller funding needs. A beneficial role for the development of this segment has been played by the Mezzanine Facility for Growth of the European Investment Fund, and there are also several direct public mezzanine finance schemes in Austria, Canada, Czech Republic, Estonia, France, Germany, the United Kingdom and the United States. Evidence suggests that officially supported mezzanine credit has helped SMEs weather the crisis and, with a few exceptions, utilisation has been recovering in countries where it was well established and has remained strong in countries where it was introduced during the crisis.

However, many SMEs are not well-suited for this form of finance and most firms using mezzanine finance will continue to need traditional debt and equity finance. Traditional bank credit, based mainly upon debt and official guarantees, is well suited to established low risk companies, but has only limited applicability to firms seeking growth capital. Venture capital is relevant for start-ups, technology-based companies and those with exceptionally high growth prospects, but such companies only constitute a tiny, albeit critical, part of all SMEs. Mezzanine finance can be an important part of the continuum of financing options that together constitute an efficient financial system.[31]

Crowdfunding is increasing but raises consumer protection issues

One of the specific innovations that has emerged as a financing alternative is 'crowdfunding' or peer-to-peer (P2P) lending whereby individuals lend to each other and small businesses, or invest in such business, via internet platforms.[32] Financial crowdfunding can be classified in peer-to-peer lending and crowd investing, to be distinguished from non-financial crowdfunding with a social motivation (charity) or for in-kind benefits (pre-order of a product, or a ticket to a show). While crowdfunding can help to close part of the finance gap for small firms, it also brings non-financial benefits, such as validation of R&D outputs, an estimation of the potential demand for a product, and brings in knowledge, network and expertise from founders.

Crowdfunding as a funding source for projects has been increasing rapidly since 2009 (first year with records of activity), although total amounts still remain small when compared to bank finance or seed and early stage equity funding. Peer-to-peer (P2P) lending has been growing in the United States, China, Germany and the United Kingdom. By avoiding complex structures and procedures of normal banks and thus some overhead costs, as well as regulatory burden, P2P lenders can offer credit at relatively low rates (lower than, *e, g.*, interest on credit card debt) and offer relatively higher returns to their investors to whom the loans are sold in slices. Many of these lending websites are becoming more active in lending to SMEs. While they currently account only for a small share of overall lending, they have been growing strongly and some policy makers see a bigger role for them in replacing bank lending and adding to SMEs' financing options.

One of the specificities to crowdfunding is that it finances projects, not firms. It therefore alleviates only part of SME finance needs, but it is not suitable as the main funding source for firms and entrepreneurs, because it cannot cover working capital or growth needs unrelated to new projects. Furthermore, crowdfunding depends on well-functioning bank instruments. Bank accounts, credit cards, an online payment system and credit records are all necessary for crowdfunding to work. Amounts traded through crowdfunding are relatively small and, so far do not present a systemic risk. Moreover, there is no leveraging of finance, as the amounts lent go directly to project financing. It will be necessary to monitor the evolution of this instrument, in order to assess the appropriate regulatory environment for crowdfunding. To do so, more information is needed, but at present there are no publicly available data on the previous use of crowdfunding of the borrowers, to further assess their characteristics, the evolution of the amounts needed, and the projects financed. This information would be useful in identifying potential measure to support the use of crowdfunding as a finance instrument.

Crowdfunding also presents some risks, notably, risk of failure, fraud, and lack of an exit option. There are concerns that investors who are offered attractive rates (which have risks factored in) may not be aware of the risks involved and that there is no 'money back guarantee'. Should P2P lending grow and become, as some observers expect, an attractive investment for 'well-informed' institutional investors and wealthy individuals, these concerns may be somewhat attenuated as due diligence and credit information may improve. In fact, the 'loan slices' or notes that are marketed to investors could eventually become listed on an exchange and be rated in a similar way to some corporate bonds. At the same time, with the growth of such intermediaries and the creation of new instruments their regulatory oversight could be expected to increase.

Indeed, despite the still small size of the crowdfunding market, the phenomenon has increasingly drawn the attention of regulators and stakeholders. In the United States, the Securities and Exchange Commission has been working on federal crowdfunding rules,[33] and in Europe the European Securities and Markets Authority (ESMA) highlighted risks for investors and warned about incentives for crowdfunding companies to try to avoid regulation. In the United Kingdom, the Financial Conduct Authority introduced rules in 2014 with the aim of making sure the risks were clear and marketing was limited. It also recently performed a crowdfunding review. In France, a new regulatory framework for crowdfunding came into effect in 2014 aiming to increase transparency in the market and help investors screen opportunities. Meanwhile, the industry had, already in 2012, taken steps to develop "A Framework for European Crowdfunding".[34] The Framework claims to present "the overarching principles under which the European Crowdfunding industry will develop and structure in the next few years" and aims at *(i)* creating a professional and globally competitive industry with an established set of rules in the best interest of the European economy; *(ii)* fostering public awareness and understanding of citizens' ability to innovate and help economic development; and *(iii)* maintaining a public and transparent data repository for research purposes in order to understand its social and economic impacts.

Obstacles to initial public offerings and wider use of public equity finance platforms for SMEs need to be reduced

The share of SME financing provided through equity markets is currently very small, despite the fact that public/organised exchanges and other platforms offer an attractive and abundant long-term financing source. Equity capital is critical to growth and infrastructure investment and the development of small markets for initial public offerings (IPOs) and, together with securitisation and other non-bank financing instruments, could encourage appropriate allocation of risk and risk taking, and thus support a quicker, more sustainable rebound of economic growth.

A number of equity markets targeting smaller listings have been established in different parts of the world (e.g. the Alternate Investment Market in London, TSX Venture in Canada, HK GEM in Hong Kong, Mothers in Japan, Alternext/Euronext and Alternativa in Europe, AltX in South Africa). Such markets offer more flexible listing criteria, eased disclosure requirements and comparatively low admission costs so as to cater to SMEs' inherent characteristics. Public listing of SME equity through primary and secondary issuance has the potential to provide funding for a company's growth and can increase the availability of, and improve conditions for, subsequent debt financing. Existing SME owners can realise their capital gains and tap a wide investor universe, including retail investors and sophisticated long-term institutional investors.

Nevertheless, important obstacles to the wider use of public equities for SMEs (by issuers and investors alike) remain to be resolved. Difficulties facing SMEs seeking public equity financing are not limited to the respective cost burden (admission fees, advisors and broker commissions), red tape and reporting requirements. Loss of confidence to go through the offering process, fear of being exposed to share price volatility, aversion to sharing sensitive information but also lack of education around the process of listing and life after an IPO are other reasons explaining the reluctance of SMEs in joining equity capital markets. In addition, entrepreneurs tend to be unwilling to relinquish any share of ownership or control of their business (as is the case with VC investments) or accept potential lock-in periods upon listing.

On the investor side of the market, equity investors seeking to provide equity financing to SMEs are confronted with information asymmetries, leading to potentially high monitoring costs relative to the level of investment, possibly unfavourable or onerous regulatory frameworks (particularly on a relative basis) and investor protection considerations. Low levels of liquidity in SME growth markets (somehow inherent in the SME asset class) act as one of the main deterrents to investment in public SME equities. Promotion of SME listed shares to retail investors might be one of the ways to enhance market liquidity.

Equity (but also bond) capital markets remain fragmented and not highly attractive to SMEs and mid-caps, especially in Europe, with low levels of cross-border investment in such securities. Despite undisputable efficiencies that are to be gained by standardising and unifying regional markets, the existence of separate platforms might have strong merits in terms of financial stability and risk management ('fail-safe mechanisms') – increasingly important in today's interconnected financial system.

While the numbers of IPOs globally has declined after the crisis, some indication for a more difficult post-crisis environment for smaller IPOs may be gathered from the fact that (in terms of numbers of IPOs) the share of smaller IPOs has declined (Figure 5.13).[35] Likewise, while IPO issuance proceeds have not regained pre-crisis peaks, the median for these proceeds has been well above pre-crisis level in an environment that seems to be favouring larger IPOs (Figure 5.14).

Figure 5.13. **The number of small initial public offerings has decreased post-crisis**

Absolute number of IPOs (l.h.s.) and number of small IPOs in % of total (r.h.s.), global, 2000–Q1 2015

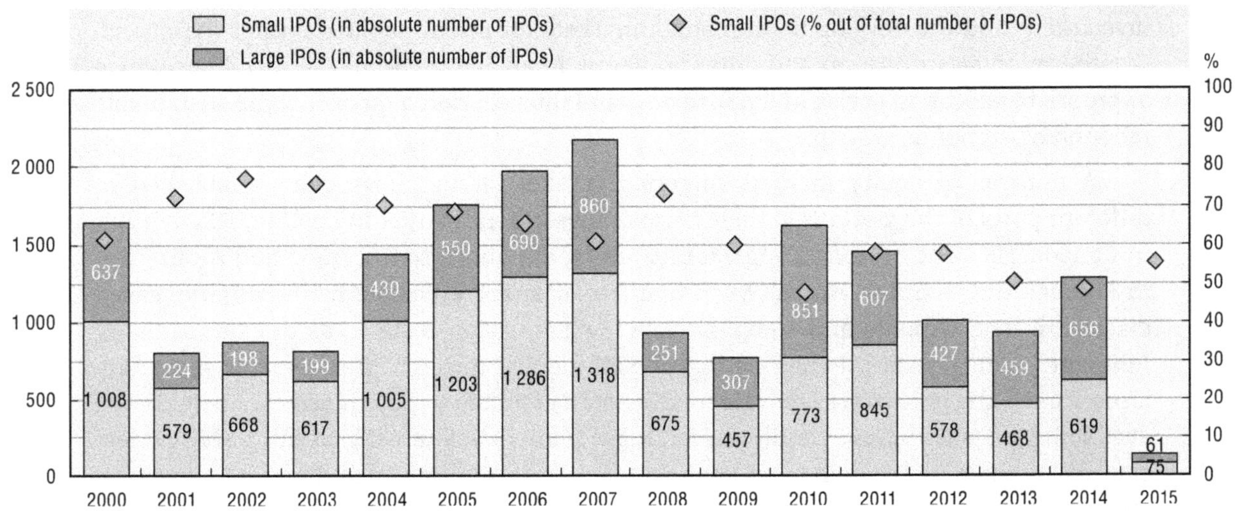

Notes: Assuming a USD 50 million threshold as the cut-off for small IPOs. Excluding real estate investment trusts (REITs) and blank check companies or special purpose acquisition vehicles (SPACs).

Source: OECD calculations, Factset.

StatLink http://dx.doi.org/10.1787/888933209925

There is a role for governments and regulators to make efforts to promote the financing of SMEs through equity markets. Improvements in the economic incentives for equity financing, and in turn in the rate of SME capital formation, could be used to help foster innovation and job creation.[36] The cost of going public needs to be reasonable and tailored to the size of the SME. Policy measures to reduce the bias against equity financing, such as relevant tax treatment of equity and/or incentives for the use of equity financing – both for issuers and for investors – need to be considered by policy makers (see the example of the United Kingdom). Trading (tick size) incentives for smaller cap stocks and the possibility of allowing such companies to choose their tick size might boost liquidity and thus investment in SME equities.[37] Another alternative to help increase liquidity and thus investment in smaller cap stocks would be to have regulators choose or set different tick sizes for SME equities. The creation of an active retail investor market could enhance liquidity of SME listed shares, provided that appropriate mechanisms are in place to defend against sales practice abuses which may occur. Given that SME platforms are inherently different from large cap markets, it might be preferable for their regulation and infrastructure to evolve separately from large cap markets (as is the case under Markets in Financial Instruments Directive).

Figure 5.14. **The size of initial public offering proceeds has increased post-crisis**

IPO issuance proceeds in USD billion (l.h.s.) and median IPO size (r.h.s.), global, 2000–Q1 2015

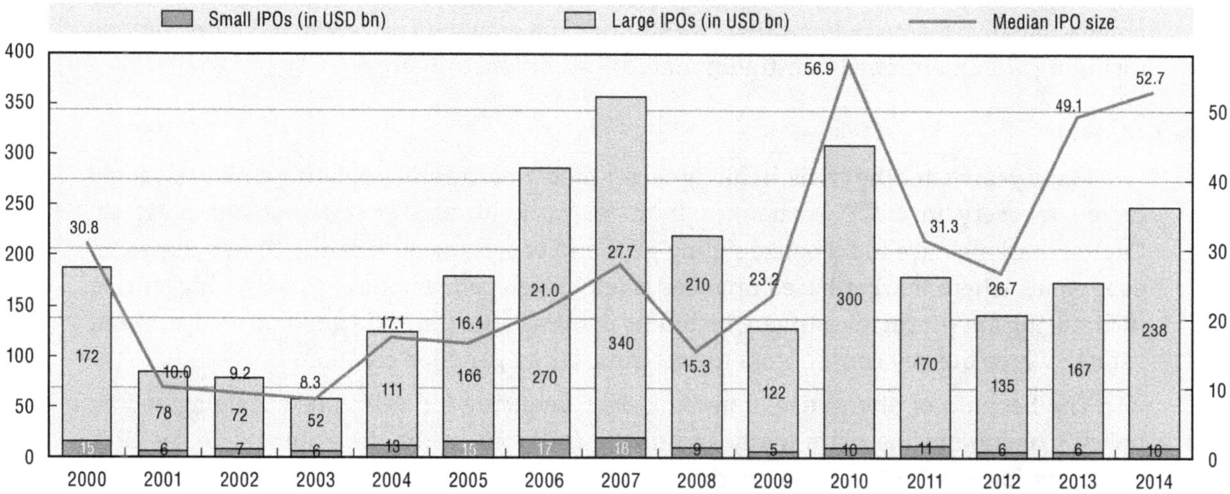

Notes: Assuming a USD 50 million threshold as the cut-off for small IPOs. Excluding real estate investment trusts (REITs) and blank check companies or special purpose acquisition vehicles (SPACs).

Source: OECD calculations, Factset.

StatLink http://dx.doi.org/10.1787/888933209936

Listing in SME growth markets benefits in most cases from more flexible or somehow 'lighter' regulations than main markets require. Nevertheless, there are numerous instances where rules and regulations may obstruct the flow of funding to SMEs. The right balance between administrative and regulatory burden and due diligence needs to be achieved such that the flexibility provided to SMEs does not result in weak investor protection or compromised integrity of market participants (e.g. nominated advisors), weak corporate governance or insufficient transparency. The same holds for recent market practices that may inhibit the development of SME equities, such as high-frequency trading or a focus on low cost trading execution which tend to be incompatible with SME listed shares.

The relative low volume of shares traded on growth markets compared to main markets and the limited free float that small caps regularly offer (retained stakes by management and owners) as well as buy-and-hold strategies limiting day-to-day trading are all problematic, particularly when seeking to attract institutional investors. The existence of well-functioning market-making systems is instrumental to the fostering of SME markets, particularly given their importance for professional and institutional investors.

There is a role for policy makers to ensure that ecosystems comprising market makers, small cap and SME equity research, brokers, sales, ratings and specialised SME banks are in place to foster the development of SME financing through growth markets. It is important for policy makers to incentivise (economically and otherwise) market participants in a way that diverts them from competition based on price of trade execution, which is arguably toxic to SME markets (e.g. tax incentives, higher commissions, higher tick sizes). Pure for-profit models for growth platforms can have perverse incentives (e.g. promotion of highly liquid stocks to electronic order book markets) and cannot ensure sustained capacity to bring SMEs to the market and, equally importantly, support them in the aftermarket.

The existence of such an ecosystem will in turn be useful as a platform for the development of other, non-traditional SME equity instruments such as equity private placements, equity crowdfunding, listed funds (with potential co-funding and risk sharing between the private and public sectors), corporate venturing, which can all, in turn, rely on that same ecosystem. Lack of vibrant SME IPO markets and aftermarkets ultimately creates negative feedback loops that risk stunting the growth of private market innovations including aforementioned non-traditional SME equity instruments.

Conclusions

Many years after the crisis, banking sector problems are still inhibiting a more strongly footed recovery in OECD economies from taking hold, and growth remains sluggish. Capital markets have to fill bank lending gaps and especially outside the United States, in economies where market-based finances is less developed, will have to play a bigger role in financing long-term investment, including in infrastructure, SMEs and knowledge-based capital, which are key contributors to economic growth and job creation.

The benefits of alternative, non-bank debt financing for SMEs are widely agreed by policy makers and there are many arguments in favour of the development of the SME securitisation, covered and other corporate bond and private placement markets. As credit sources tend to dry up more rapidly for SMEs than for large companies during economic downturns, broadening the range of non-bank debt financing instruments for SMEs should help making them more resilient to financial shocks. Given SMEs' importance across economies, this is also essential for economic recovery from the current economic and financial crisis. Given that there are many arguments in favour of the development of SME debt instruments markets, a wide range of policy measures may be warranted.

Regarding regulation, markets for market-based debt financing for SMEs should be carefully designed and overseen and so as to foster the use of alternative financing instruments without putting at stake the overall resilience of the financial system. Sensible and balanced calibration of the existing regulatory frameworks affecting such instruments should be pursued. Regulation should also take a holistic and coordinated approach to avoid regulatory arbitrage with respect to different instruments and stimulate investor appetite. Healthy competition should be secured across similar financing solutions, eliminating any imbalances or disincentives that might direct investor and issuer preferences away from some of these instruments. The creation of solid frameworks for the SME covered bond and private placement asset classes at national or broader international levels should be encouraged.

Regarding market infrastructure, the build-up of loan-level data, performance track records, the encouragement of ongoing reporting and data sharing need be prioritised. Pooling of such information in centralised data platforms, set up and maintained through a certain public initiative, could benefit all participants by increasing the transparency of the SME financing market and allowing an informed decision-making by capital holders. Appropriate balance in the level of disclosure requirements should be nonetheless safeguarded so as to stimulate investor appetite without rendering such issuance/ investment overly costly or cumbersome.

Standardisation plays an important role, too. For example, the development of 'off-the-shelf' versions of non-bank debt financing instruments for SMEs could be supported with a view to lowering the cost of such instruments and increase the efficiency and accessibility of those instruments to SMEs and retail investors. Likewise, the creation of indices could enhance liquidity and investor participation in publicly traded SME debt.

On the demand side, the official sector could provide support for raising awareness – among SME entrepreneurs as well as smaller local financial institutions traditionally serving SMEs – about the availability and attractiveness of such financing alternatives for SMEs and financial intermediaries. The official sector could also cooperate with private sector institutions in improving the visibility of successful transactions and platforms for such instruments.

On the supply side, investors should be assisted and incentivised to set up internal infrastructures that would allow them to participate in the SME-debt market. Furthermore, the potential impact from the provision of incentive schemes particularly to investors but also to SMEs (e.g. tax incentives) targeted to such instruments should be critically evaluated.

With regard to public intervention, the official sector should raise the profile of the public debate required to overcome the barriers identified and encourage the appropriate and safe use of non-bank debt financing instruments for SMEs. Public intervention should be designed in such a way that private sector participation is not crowded out. Specific evaluation and control procedures (beyond a standard impact assessment) would need to be put in place to ensure that the intended (capital, funding) benefit is passed on to the real economy through the provision of additional SME financing.

While the size of the SME securitisation market is insignificant in terms of the wider financial system, careful assessment of the riskiness of inappropriate design and use of such instruments needs to be encouraged in the context of a widely interconnected financial system. The corresponding benefits to the real economy and their materiality to SMEs need to also be accounted for.

Policy makers also need to acknowledge that SME finance is, like SMEs themselves are, exceptionally diverse and complex, and faces unique challenges. As such, there is no 'magic bullet' for SME finance and it is only by pushing different ideas, avenues and instruments that the different constraints and predicaments can be tackled in developing a healthy non-bank debt market for SMEs. To achieve this, a joint effort may be needed, involving all constituents concerned: investors, issuers, intermediaries, regulators and public policy makers. Governments and regulators can provide valuable support for developing the necessary infrastructure for new financing instruments for SME financing and incentivise investment in securitisation and other non-bank debt instruments suitable for SMEs. Such financing, when used properly, can play a significant role in the recovery of the real economy by unlocking resources and capacity for further lending, broadening the SME investor base and diversifying their portfolios, as well as assisting in the creation of a sounder financial system through better risk sharing within the economy.

Notes

1. The OECD defines small and medium-sized enterprises (SMEs) as "non-subsidiary, independent firms which employ fewer than a given number of employees. This number varies across countries. The most frequent upper limit designating an SME is 250 employees, as in the European Union. However, some countries set the limit at 200 employees, while the United States considers SMEs to include firms with fewer than 500 employees. Small firms are generally those with fewer than 50 employees, while micro-enterprises have at most 10, or in some cases 5, workers". See *http://stats.oecd.org/glossary/detail.asp?ID=3123*.

2. For this and the following see OECD (2006) that contains a more detailed definition and discussion of financing gaps in the context of SME financing, as well as further references.

3. Asymmetric information may lead to adverse selection in which normally creditworthy SMEs may cease to seek external financing as lending rates (and thus costs) increase to compensate for banks' perception of heightened risks, leaving higher-risk SMEs in the pool of loan applicants; moreover, there may be increased incentives for those receiving (higher rate) loans to take on increased risk, highlighting a moral hazard issue. These potential effects may lead to (non-price) credit rationing to enhance the quality of the SME loan pool.

4. This chapter draws on work developed under the project "New approaches to SME and entrepreneurship finance". See OECD (2015b) and the satellite studies referenced therein and in this chapter.

5. OECD (2015b).

6. Provisioning and capital adequacy are explicitly taken into account in the lending models. These factors exert a powerful influence on outcomes, strongly supported by data (see Box 5.1).

7. Trend GDP is calculated using the Hodrick-Prescott filter, with *lambda* at 1600. To avoid end point sensitivity, forecasts from a longer-term scenario to 2019 are included in the calculations. The normal relationship regresses credit on trend nominal GDP so calculated.

8. Including repayment restructuring.

9. Blundell-Wignall and Roulet (2013).

10. As pointed out by Schich (2008), excessive reliance on the judgements of rating agencies contributed to the under-pricing of risk prior to the global financial crisis. Because of the complexity of the instruments and the lack of verifiable public information on the specificities of the structure and composition of many of the structured financial products guaranteed by financial guarantee insurers (often just referred to in the press as "bond insurers" or "monolines"), investors relied much more heavily on the ratings assigned by credit rating agencies to the instrument tranches and guarantor backing them than they would in the case of other more traditional, and less complex, securities. Unfortunately, however, the incentive problems faced by rating agencies were not sufficiently acknowledged either by investors in structured products or by the financial guarantee insurance companies that played an important role in making these securities based on sub-prime loans attractive to a wide range of investors: The monolines provided "credit enhancements" by writing CDSs. Traditionally, bond insurers have provided guarantees of payments on municipal bonds, where defaults have been very limited. But since the late 1990s they had become increasingly involved as guarantors of elements of various structured financial products, attracted by the profits from this fast-growing business. It is this trend change in their activity, and the observation that the guarantees were provided in the form of CDSs, that explains the subsequent rapid demise of that sector during the early stages of the global financial crisis. This example is also a reminder that financial firms can make bad decisions even when they do have "skin in the game".

11. Note that for very small businesses it is often difficult to distinguish mortgages and business lending, when housing is used as collateral for a loan.

12. OECD (2015a).

13. See also OECD (2015a) for an overview and current trends of SME financing across the OECD.

14. For more details, see Wehinger (2014).

15. For this and the following see Blundell-Wignall and Roulet (2013).

16. Schoenmaker and Peek (2014).

17. E.g. Anginer and Demirguç-Kunt (2011).

18. Bernanke and Gertler (1995); see Jimenez *et al.* (2011) for empirical evidence of the existence of credit channel and the (changing) relative importance of a distinct bank lending and balance sheet through which the credit channel monetary policy transmission operates.

19. Such findings are also supported by other studies (e.g. Schoenmaker and Peek, 2014).

20. Carbó-Valverde *et al.* (2012).

21. E.g. Albertazzi and Marchetti (2010).

22. As noted by Albertazzi and Marchetti (2010); for the following, see e.g. Carbó-Valverde et al. (2012).

23. On 18 February 2015, the European Commission launched a three-month consultation on a Green Paper, the outcome of which will shape an Action Plan to help establish a Capital Markets Union (CMU); see *http://ec.europa.eu/finance/consultations/2015/capital-markets-union/index_en.htm* and European Commission (2015).
24. More details on the topics of this section can be found in Nassr and Wehinger (2014, 2015).
25. Such defaults affected mainly US securitisations of mortgage loans of certain vintages in the subprime segment.
26. Efforts for "simple, transparent and comparable" securitisations have also been pursued by the Basel Committee on Banking Supervision (BCBS) and the International Organization of Securities Commissions (IOSCO).
27. See Kraemer-Eis, Battazzi *et al.* (2014).
28. For this and the following see Wilson and Silva (2013).
29. On the role of angel investors in start-up finance see OECD (2011).
30. For this and the following see OECD (2014).
31. At present, the ability to assess the full potential of mezzanine finance for SMEs and entrepreneurs, and the effectiveness of public institutions in providing these facilities, is hampered by the lack of data on commercial mezzanine finance, in terms of financing volume, number and type of firms, as well as data on public investment funds in OECD countries and international organisations. More precise statistical data on the size of programmes and beneficiaries and information on existing programmes in a broader range of OECD and non-OECD countries would be desirable.
32. For this and the following, see also Box 2.3 in OECD (2015a).
33. Final rules have not been adopted in the United States to permit securities-based crowd funding.
34. De Buysere *et al.* (2012).
35. The set of global IPOs comprises of listings on: Abu Dhabi Securities Exchange, Aktie Torget, Alberta Stock Exchange, Alternext Paris, Athens, Australian Securities Exchange, Bahrain (Manama), Bangkok, Barcelona Stock Exchange, BATS Exchange, Belgrade Stock Exchange, Berlin, Berne Stock Exchange, BM&F Bovespa SA, Bogota, Bolsa Mexicana de Valores, Bombay, Borsa Istanbul, Borsa Italiana S.P.A., Budapest, Buenos Aires, Cairo, Canadian Securities Exchange, Casablanca, Colombo, Copenhagen, Cyprus Stock Exchange, Dhaka Stock Exchange Ltd, Dubai Financial Market, Dublin, Euronext Amsterdam, Euronext Brussels/Lisbon/Paris, Frankfurt, Gretai Securities Market, Hanoi Stock Exchange, Helsinki, Hong Kong, Indonesian Stock Exchange, JASDAQ, Johannesburg, Jordan (Amman), Korea Stock Exchange, Kuala Lumpur, London Alternative Market, London Stock Exchange, Malta, Moscow, NASDAQ, NSE, NYSE, Oslo Bors, Plus Markets (London), Prague, Qatar Exchange, Reykjavik, Riga, Romania (Bucharest), Santiago, Sapporo (JP), Saudi Stock Exchange, Shanghai, Shenzhen, Singapore, SIX Swiss Exchange, Sofia, Taiwan Stock Exchange, Tel Aviv, Tokyo, Toronto, TSX Venture Exchange, Vietnam Stock Market, Warsaw Stock Exchange, Wellington, Zagreb.

    1. Note by Turkey: The information in this document with reference to « Cyprus » relates to the southern part of the Island. There is no single authority representing both Turkish and Greek Cypriot people on the Island. Turkey recognises the Turkish Republic of Northern Cyprus (TRNC). Until a lasting and equitable solution is found within the context of the United Nations, Turkey shall preserve its position concerning the "Cyprus issue".

    2. Note by all the European Union Member States of the OECD and the European Union: The Republic of Cyprus is recognised by all members of the United Nations with the exception of Turkey. The information in this document relates to the area under the effective control of the Government of the Republic of Cyprus.
36. According to an OECD study (Weild *et al.*, 2013), GDP growth rates only predicts 10% of small IPO activity while economic incentives explain 70% of it.
37. Tick sizes as a percent of share prices for sub $500 million market value companies probably need to exceed 1% of share price to fuel investment (Weild *et al.*, 2013).

References

Albertazzi, U., and D.J. Marchetti (2010), "Credit Supply, Flight to Quality and Evergreening: An Analysis of Bank-firm Relationships after Lehman", *Banca d'Italia Temi di Discussione* (Discussion Papers) 756.

Anginer, Deniz and Asli Demirguç-Kunt, (2011), "Has the Global Banking System Become More Fragile over Time?" *Policy Research Working Paper* 5849, World Bank, Development Research Group; available at *http://www-wds.worldbank.org/servlet/WDSContentServer/WDSP/IB/2011/11/08/000158349_20111108124433/Rendered/PDF/WPS5849.pdf*.

Bank of Japan (2014), *Short-term Economic Survey of Enterprises in Japan (TANKAN)*, February; available at *www.stat-search.boj.or.jp/ssi/mtshtml/q_en.html*.

Bernanke, Ben S., and Mark Gertler (1995), "Inside the Black Box: The Credit Channel of Monetary Policy Transmission", *Journal of Economic Perspectives* 9, pp.27-48.

Blundell-Wignall, Adrian and Caroline Roulet (2013), "Bank lending puzzles: Business models and the responsiveness to policy", *OECD Journal: Financial Market Trends*, Vol. 2013/1. DOI: *http://dx.doi.org/10.1787/fmt-2013-5k40m1nz55wj*.

Carbó-Valverde, S., H. Degryse, and Francisco Rodriguez-Fernandez (2012), *Lending relationships and credit rationing: the impact of securitization*, Paper presented at the Central Bank of Ireland Conference on the SME Lending Market, 2 March 2012.

De Buysere, Kristof, Oliver Gajda, Ronald Kleverlaan and Dan Marom (2012), *A Framework for European Crowdfunding*, European Crowdfunding Network (ECN); available at *www.europecrowdfunding.org/european_crowdfunding_framework*.

ECB (2014), Survey *on the Access to Finance of Small and Medium-Sized Enterprises in the euro area*, Database, European Central Bank; available at *www.ecb.europa.eu/stats/money/surveys/sme/html/index.en.html*.

European Commission (2015), *Green Paper: Building a Capital Markets Union*, COM(2015) 63 final; available at *http://ec.europa.eu/finance/consultations/2015/capital-markets-union/docs/green-paper_en.pdf*.

Federal Reserve Board (2015), *Senior Loan Officer Opinion Survey on Bank Lending Practices*, January; available at *www.federalreserve.gov/boarddocs/snloansurvey*.

HM Treasury (2014), *Overview of Legislation in Draft*, 10 December; available at *https://www.gov.uk/government/uploads/system/uploads/attachment_data/file/385370/OLD_complete_v3.pdf*.

Isaksson, M. and S. Çelik (2013), "Who Cares? Corporate Governance in Today's Equity Markets", *OECD Corporate Governance Working Papers*, No. 8, OECD Publishing. doi: *10.1787/5k47zw5kdnmp-en*.

Jimenez, G, S. Ongena, J. L. Peydro and J. Saurina (2011), "Monetary Policy and the Credit Crunch: Identifying Simultaneously the Bank Lending and Balance Sheet Channels", working paper (mimeo).

Kraemer-Eis, H., with contributions from F. Battazzi, R. Charrier, M. Natoli, and M. Squilloni (2014), *Institutional non-bank lending and the role of Debt Funds, EIF Working Paper* 2014/25; available at *http://www.eif.org/news_centre/publications/eif_wp_25.pdf*.

Nassr, I.K. and G. Wehinger (2014), "Non-bank debt financing for SMEs: The role of securitisation, private placements and bonds", *OECD Journal: Financial Market Trends*, Vol. 2014/1. DOI: *http://dx.doi.org/10.1787/fmt-2014-5jxx05svvw34*

Nassr, I.K. and G. Wehinger (2015), "Unlocking SME finance through market-based debt: Securitisation, private placements and bonds", *OECD Journal: Financial Market Trends*. DOI: *http://dx.doi.org/10.1787/fmt-2014-5js3bg1g53ln*

OECD (2015b), *New approaches to SME and entrepreneurship finance: Broadening the range of instruments*, *www.oecd.org/industry/smes/New-Approaches-SME-full-report.pdf*.

OECD (2015a), *Financing SMEs and Entrepreneurs 2015: An OECD Scoreboard*, OECD Publishing, Paris. DOI: *http://dx.doi.org/10.1787/fin_sme_ent-2015-en*.

OECD (2014), "Alternative financing instruments: The case of mezzanine finance", in OECD, *Financing SMEs and Entrepreneurs 2014: An OECD Scoreboard*, OECD Publishing, Paris. DOI: *http://dx.doi.org/10.1787/fin_sme_ent-2014-6-en*.

OECD (2011), *Financing High-Growth Firms: The Role of Angel Investors*, OECD Publishing, Paris. DOI: *http://dx.doi.org/10.1787/9789264118782-en*.

OECD (2010), *Assessment of Government Support Programmes for SMEs' and Entrepreneurs' Access to Finance during the Crisis*, OECD, Paris; available at *http://www.oecd.org/cfe/smes/Assessment_Government_Support_Programmes.pdf*.

OECD (2009), *The Impact of the Global Crisis on SME and Entrepreneurship Financing and Policy Responses*, OECD Publishing,Paris; available at *www.oecd.org/dataoecd/40/34/43183090.pdf*.

OECD (2006), *The SME Financing Gap (Vol. I): Theory and Evidence*, OECD Publishing, Paris. DOI: *http://dx.doi.org/10.1787/9789264029415-en*.

Schich, S. (2008), "Challenges related to financial guarantee insurance", *OECD Journal: Financial Market Trends*, Vol. 2008/1. DOI: *http://dx.doi.org/10.1787/fmt-v2008-art4-en*.

Schoenmaker, D. and T. Peek (2014), "The State of the Banking Sector in Europe", *OECD Economics Department Working Papers*, No. 1102, OECD Publishing; *http://dx.doi.org/10.1787/5k3ttg7n4r32-en*.

Wehinger, G. (2014), "SMEs and the credit crunch: Current financing difficulties, policy measures and a review of literature", *OECD Journal: Financial Market Trends*, Vol. 2013/2.DOI: *http://dx.doi.org/10.1787/fmt-2013-5jz734p6b8jg*.

Weild, D., E. Kim and L. Newport (2013), "Making Stock Markets Work to Support Economic Growth: Implications for Governments, Regulators, Stock Exchanges, Corporate Issuers and their Investors", *OECD Corporate Governance Working Papers*, No. 10, OECD Publishing, Paris. DOI: *http://dx.doi.org/10.1787/5k43m4p6ccs3-en*.

Wilson, K. E. and F. Silva (2013), "Policies for Seed and Early Stage Finance: Findings from the 2012 OECD Financing Questionnaire", *OECD Science, Technology and Industry Policy Papers*, No. 9, OECD Publishing, Paris.DOI: *http://dx.doi.org/10.1787/5k3xqsf00j33-en*.

ANNEX 5.A1

Statistical tables and supplementary data

Table 5.A1.1. **Global initial public offerings (IPOs): small vs. large IPOs**

	Number of IPOs				Gross proceeds (including over-allotment) in USD million				
	Total IPOs	of which: small IPOs(1)	of which: large IPOs(1)	Small in per cent of total	Total IPOs	of which: small IPOs(1)	of which: large IPOs(1)	Small in per cent of total	Median IPO size
2000	1645	1,008	637	61.3%	1,87,055	14,565	1,72,490	7.8%	30.8
2001	803	579	224	72.1%	84,246	5,883	78,363	7.0%	10.0
2002	868	667	201	76.8%	78,649	7,119	71,530	9.1%	9.2
2003	817	617	200	75.5%	57,911	5,791	52,120	10.0%	8.3
2004	1435	1,004	431	70.0%	1,23,654	12,607	1,11,046	10.2%	17.1
2005	1754	1,203	551	68.6%	1,80,765	15,169	1,65,596	8.4%	16.4
2006	1978	1,285	693	65.0%	2,86,511	16,959	2,69,552	5.9%	21.0
2007	2182	1,314	868	60.2%	3,58,552	18,368	3,40,185	5.1%	27.7
2008	930	675	255	72.6%	2,19,318	8,839	2,10,479	4.0%	15.3
2009	764	457	307	59.8%	1,27,659	5,286	1,22,373	4.1%	23.2
2010	1630	770	860	47.2%	3,10,105	10,410	2,99,695	3.4%	56.9
2011	1452	844	608	58.1%	1,80,638	10,832	1,69,806	6.0%	31.3
2012	1006	578	428	57.5%	1,41,718	6,323	1,35,394	4.5%	26.7
2013	927	467	460	50.4%	1,73,254	6,437	1,66,817	3.7%	49.1
2014	1277	618	659	48.4%	2,48,637	10,320	2,38,317	4.2%	52.7
2015 Q1	136	75	61	55.1%	22,169	1,584	20,584	7.1%	42.8

Notes: Data excluding real estate investment trusts (REITs) and blank check companies or special purpose acquisition vehicles (SPACs). The set of global IPOs comprises of listings on: Abu Dhabi Securities Exchange, Aktie Torget, Alberta Stock Exchange, Alternext Paris, Athens, Australian Securities Exchange, Bahrain (Manama), Bangkok, Barcelona Stock Exchange, BATS Exchange, Belgrade Stock Exchange, Berlin, Berne Stock Exchange, BM&F Bovespa SA, Bogota, Bolsa Mexicana de Valores, Bombay, Borsa Istanbul, Borsa Italiana S.P.A., Budapest, Buenos Aires, Cairo, Canadian Securities Exchange, Casablanca, Colombo, Copenhagen, Cyprus Stock Exchange, Dhaka Stock Exchange Ltd, Dubai Financial Market, Dublin, Euronext Amsterdam, Euronext Brussels/Lisbon/Paris, Frankfurt, Gretai Securities Market, Hanoi Stock Exchange, Helsinki, Hong Kong, Indonesian Stock Exchange, JASDAQ, Johannesburg, Jordan (Amman), Korea Stock Exchange, Kuala Lumpur, London Alternative Market, London Stock Exchange, Malta, Moscow, NASDAQ, NSE, NYSE, Oslo Bors, Plus Markets (London), Prague, Qatar Exchange, Reykjavik, Riga, Romania (Bucharest), Santiago, Sapporo (JP), Saudi Stock Exchange, Shanghai, Shenzhen, Singapore, SIX Swiss Exchange, Sofia, Taiwan Stock Exchange, Tel Aviv, Tokyo, Toronto, TSX Venture Exchange, Vietnam Stock Market, Warsaw Stock Exchange, Wellington, Zagreb.

1. Small IPOs are defined here as those with proceeds below or equal to USD 50 million, large IPOs are those with proceeds above USD 50 million.
2. Note by Turkey: The information in this document with reference to « Cyprus » relates to the southern part of the Island. There is no single authority representing both Turkish and Greek Cypriot people on the Island. Turkey recognises the Turkish Republic of Northern Cyprus (TRNC). Until a lasting and equitable solution is found within the context of the United Nations, Turkey shall preserve its position concerning the "Cyprus issue".
3. Note by all the European Union Member States of the OECD and the European Union: The Republic of Cyprus is recognised by all members of the United Nations with the exception of Turkey. The information in this document relates to the area under the effective control of the Government of the Republic of Cyprus.

Source: Factset and OECD calculations.

StatLink http://dx.doi.org/10.1787/888933210465

OECD Business and Finance Outlook 2015

Chapter 6

Multinational enterprises and the shifting global business landscape

This chapter examines the topic of cross-border financial flows involving multinational enterprises using data on international mergers and acquisitions and foreign direct investment. It begins with a survey of recent trends from a global and regional perspective. It then considers three factors that are shaping the outlook going forward. These are: broader economic trends, the growing involvement of governments in the governance of the global economy, and the sustainability of MNE investment from emerging market economies.

Main findings

- The outlook for international investment by multinational enterprises (MNEs) is mixed. While the current gap between merger and acquisition (M&A) transactions and stock market valuations hints at the possibility of a significant increase of cross-border M&A transactions over the next few years, weakness in the emerging market economies and a sharp rise in international business divestment are factors pushing in the opposite direction.
- Although governments have resisted protectionist pressures and remain generally open to cross-border investment, various forms of government involvement in the governance of the global marketplace, such as support schemes for green energy and the review of cross-border mergers and acquisitions, would seem to be holding MNE investment back in some sectors and markets.
- Cross-border investment has shifted gears from a pre-financial crisis growth trajectory to a post-crisis restructuring trajectory, with record levels of divestments of MNE assets being sold back into domestic ownership.
- An important counter-cyclical source of cross-border investment during the crisis came from emerging market economies. This trend now seems to have changed course, with emerging market shares of inward and outward cross-border M&A declining in recent years. Outward cross-border M&A from the emerging market economies, China in particular, may be unsustainable.

Introduction

This chapter surveys recent trends in cross-border financial flows involving multinational enterprises (MNEs). It then examines some factors that are shaping the outlook for these flows going forward. These flows constitute an important part of the investment activities of MNEs since they finance both new business capital formation and transfers of control of existing assets and enterprises.

Global trends in cross-border investment

International economic integration has risen persistently despite business cycle fluctuations

The rapid integration of the world economy in recent decades has resulted in a powerful upward trend in the stock of global cross-border investment (Figure 6.1). This trend displays little evidence of being affected by global recessions in the early 1990s and during the tech bust of 2001-02. After stopping briefly at the beginning of the recent financial crisis it has resumed its steady rise, if somewhat less rapidly. Since 1990 the value of total foreign direct investment (FDI) outstanding had risen by 2012 from less than USD 2 trillion to nearly USD 23 trillion, i.e. more than tenfold, and it has almost certainly risen further since then. This has greatly outstripped growth of the world economy and inflation.

Figure 6.1. **Global foreign direct investment stocks**
(USD billions)

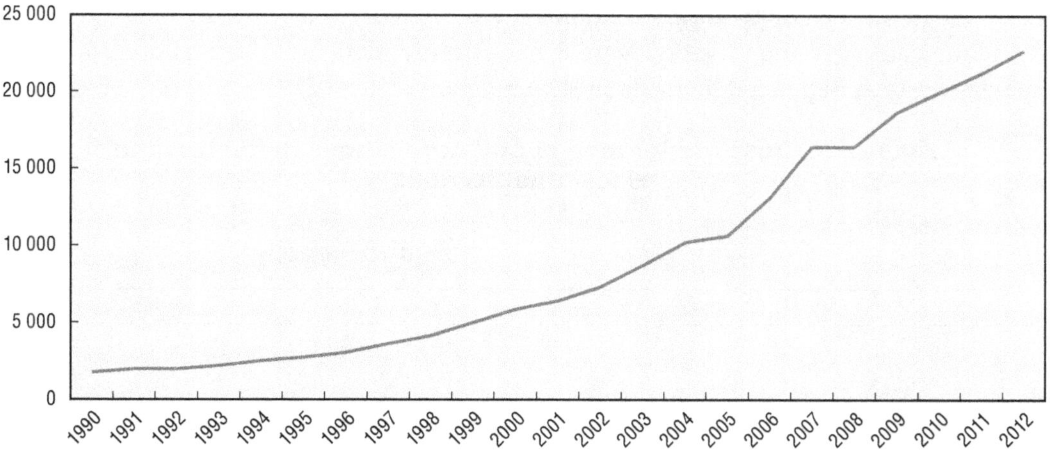

Source: OECD International Investment Statistics database, International Monetary Fund.

StatLink http://dx.doi.org/10.1787/888933209940

In the short term, however, flows of such investment have been volatile, displaying a marked cyclical pattern. Figure 6.2 shows the evolution of two measures of cross-border investment activity: global FDI outflows from 1997 to 2013 and global cross-border mergers and acquisition (M&A) flows from 1997 to 2014.[1] The two recent boom and bust cycles, the first associated with the 'dot.com' bubble and the second linked to the 2008 financial crisis, are clearly evident. Currently, global FDI flows remain around 40% below the record level set in 2007 and the value of cross-border M&A is down almost 50%.

Figure 6.2. **Global cross-border investment since 1997**
(USD billions)

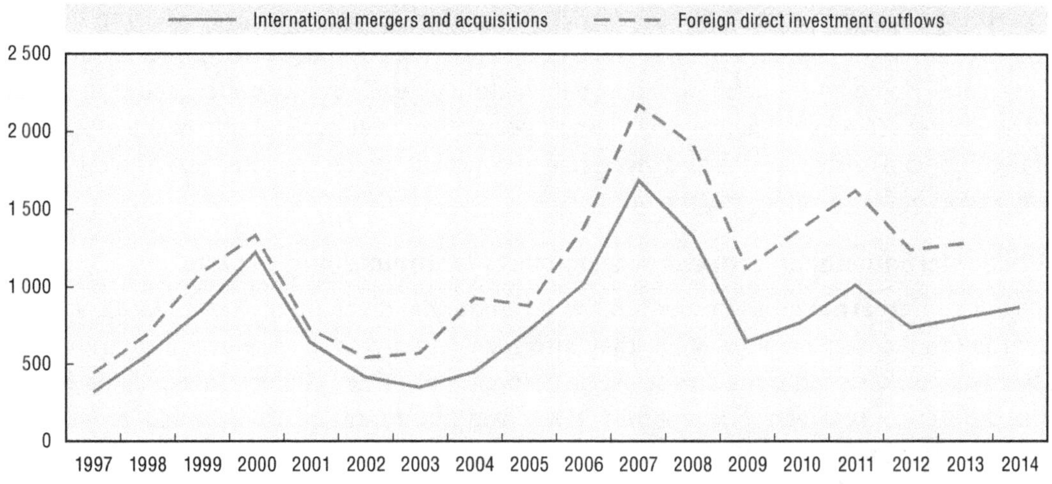

Source: OECD International Investment Statistics database, International Monetary Fund, Dealogic M&A Analytics database, OECD calculations.

StatLink http://dx.doi.org/10.1787/888933209955

Sectoral cross-border flows display no signs of excess

The industry composition of cross-border M&A remains evenly balanced at the global level. The top eight sectors accounted for 66% of total cross-border M&A in 2014, with no sector accounting for more than 11%. Previous M&A cycles have tended to be driven by activity in one or two leading sectors. In the lead-up to the 2000 peak in international investment activity, telecommunications, propelled by a global wave of privatisations, was the driver. In the lead up to the international investment boom of 2007, the financial sector and real estate were the drivers (Figure 6.3). Currently there is no indication of a sector breaking away as happened in previous M&A booms.

Figure 6.3. **Cross-border merger and acquisitions in finance and telecommunications**

(USD billions)

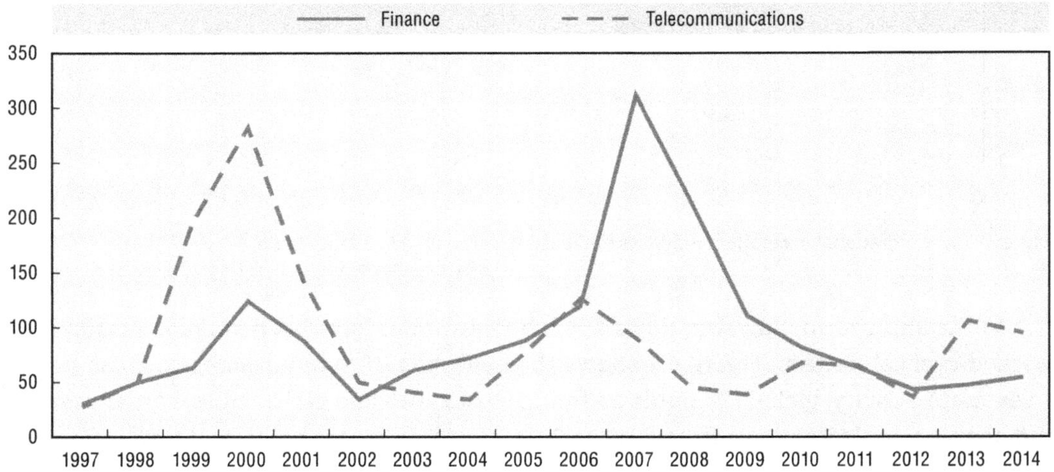

Source: Dealogic M&A Analytics database, OECD calculations.

StatLink http://dx.doi.org/10.1787/888933209964

State-owned enterprises have been increasingly active internationally

One segment that has been booming in the post-financial crisis era is the state-owned enterprise (SOE) segment. Cross-border M&A by SOEs increased sharply starting in 2008 and accounted for over 20% of total cross-border M&A in 2009 (Figure 6.4). SOE activity has since come down but remains well above its historical levels at just under 10% of the total. Cross-border M&A by SOEs has played an important counter-cyclical role in the aftermath of the financial crisis, but has also given rise to concerns which are considered below in the discussion of factors affecting the outlook.

While international divestment now accounts for around half the total

A counterpart to cross-border M&A is international divestment. Just as MNEs acquire international assets through M&A, they also regularly divest themselves of international assets as market conditions and strategic corporate priorities change. In aggregate terms, the difference between cross-border M&A and international divestment provides a measure of how much MNEs are adding to the stock of international investment in the form of net cross-border M&A. It does so by eliminating two types of transaction that do not add new linkages between an economy and international production networks. These are international transactions in which an MNE sells assets to another MNE and those in which an MNE sells assets to a domestic buyer. Net cross-border M&A thereby measures the value of previously domestically-owned assets that become internationally-owned assets. This is useful because:

- It shows by how much and in which sectors cross-border M&A is creating new economic linkages between countries;

- It also shows by how much and in which sectors MNE investment linkages between countries are weakening or even disappearing altogether as when international disinvestment exceeds cross-border M&A; and
- It provides an indication of the degree to which cross-border M&A is being driven more by corporate-level restructuring, as when a high share of transactions is taking the form of MNE-to-MNE deals, versus the possible decline in competitiveness signalled by MNEs exiting an economy and selling assets to domestic buyers.

Figure 6.4. **Cross-border mergers and acquisitions by state-owned enterprises**

(USD billions and percent, right axis)

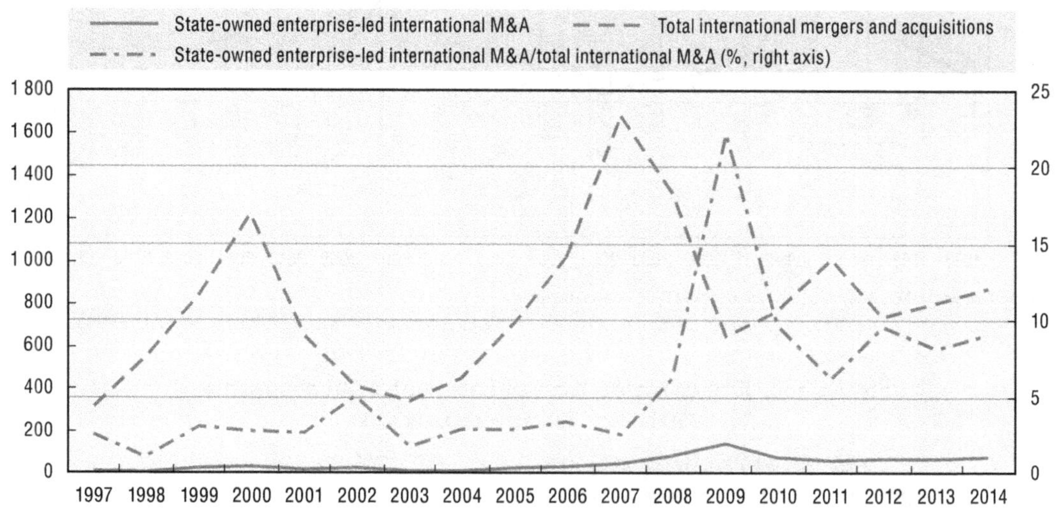

Source: Dealogic M&A Analytics database, OECD calculations.

StatLink http://dx.doi.org/10.1787/888933209976

At the global level, net cross-border M&A declined by 9% in 2014, in contrast with gross cross-border M&A which increased by 8% (Figure 6.5). This was due to a 25% increase in international divestment. In addition, the ratio of international divestment to cross-border M&A reached 57%, its highest levels since 2004 (which itself was an exceptional year due to a number of major international divestments coinciding with record low M&A levels). This suggests that a growth trajectory for MNE investment, characterised by high levels of net cross-border M&A and a low international divestment-to-cross-border M&A ratio, has transitioned to a post-crisis restructuring trajectory with the opposite characteristics. In other words, the increase in cross-border M&A now occurring is more focussed on international corporate restructuring than on creating new economic linkages between countries.

Figure 6.6 presents the breakdown of international divestment over time and the share of divestments in which the acquirer is domestic, transactions that could be described as cases of 'de-globalisation'. This share has risen sharply from 46% in 2011 to 64% in 2014. This shows that around two-thirds of the value of international divestment in 2014 consisted of de-globalising deals. Not counting 2004, this is the highest level going back to 1997.

One possible explanation for the elevated levels of international divestment experienced since 2007 relates to the shift of world economic activity towards the emerging market economies and the resulting need for MNEs to re-shape, significantly,

Figure 6.5. **Global cross-border mergers and acquisitions and international divestment**

(USD billions and percent, right axis)

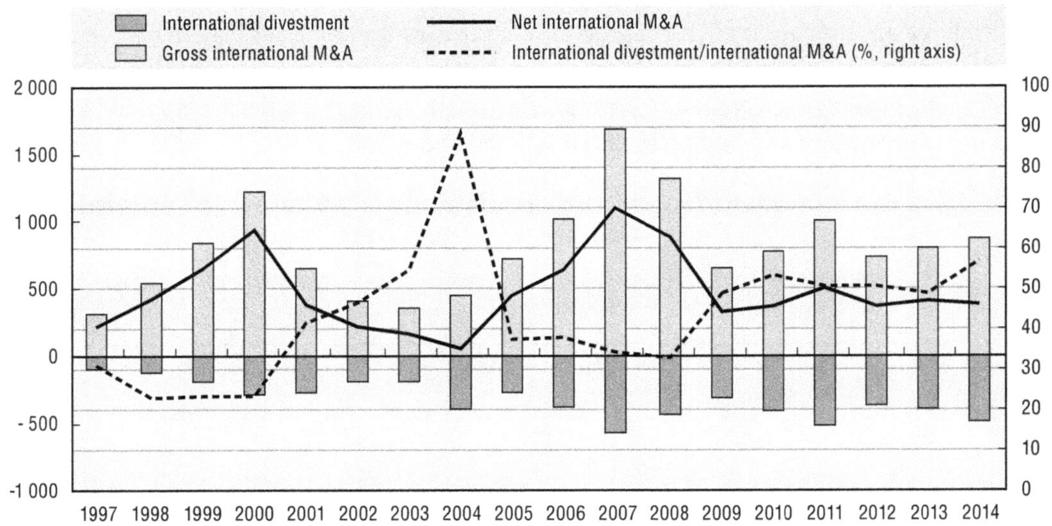

Source: Dealogic M&A Analytics database, OECD calculations.

StatLink http://dx.doi.org/10.1787/888933209989

Figure 6.6. **The composition of international divestment**

(USD billions and percent, right axis)

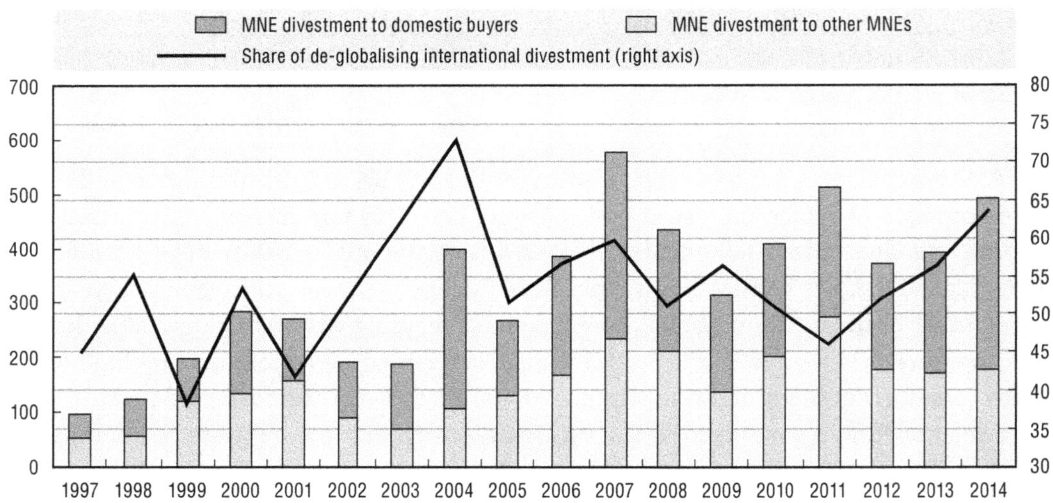

Source: Dealogic M&A Analytics database, OECD calculations.

StatLink http://dx.doi.org/10.1787/888933209999

the way they organise their international operations. The growing share of de-globalising deals in international divestment could be due to the tendency towards more reliance on contractual and other non-equity forms of international business relationships within the context of global value chains. Firms are resorting less to FDI as the main vehicle for building international businesses.

Regional trends

Cross-border divestment by European Union companies has been high

Among the advanced economies, the European Union was the region whose cross-border M&A declined the most in the early years of the financial crisis. In the period 2008-2009 inward cross-border M&A shrank by 70% (Figure 6.7). Since then recovery has been modest but steady with gross inward M&A rising in 2014 to USD 350 billion, 40% of the global total. The top five sources, accounting for over 60% in 2014, are the United States, the United Kingdom, Germany, France and China. International divestment in the European Union has remained relatively low permitting net inward cross-border M&A to reach USD 200 billion in 2014, up from around USD 120 billion in 2010. Intra-European Union cross-border M&A also rose in 2014, accounting for 35% of the global total.

With respect to outward cross-border M&A, European Union companies seem to be undergoing major international restructuring as reflected in high levels of international divestment. This has resulted in near zero levels of net outward cross-border M&A for a third year running. Having sold off around USD 300 billion worth of their international assets in 2014, EU companies accounted for 60% of global international divestment. Much of this was accounted for by UK firms, which sold off USD 155 billion in foreign assets.[2]

While in non-EU advanced economies net outward flows remain substantial

The other advanced economies[3] have also seen increases in their inward cross-border M&A, reaching USD 340 billion in 2014, an increase of 13% over 2013. However, just as with the EU economies, a sharp increase in international divestment sent net inward M&A in the opposite direction, a decline of 40% to USD 230 billion.[4] Net cross-border M&A into the non-EU advanced economies is less than a third of gross inward M&A.

Outward cross-border M&A from this group of economies declined only marginally to USD 400 billion in 2014. This has been relatively strong throughout the post-crisis period, accounting for close to 50% of the global total, up from around 30% in 2007. Unlike the situation for inward M&A, low levels of divestment on the outward side result in a much higher share of outward M&A going into new net cross-border M&A (60%).

And in emerging economies both inward disinvestment and net outward flows have been high

MNE investment to and from the emerging market economies was generally not as badly affected as in the advanced economies during the financial crisis.[5] But more recently it has weakened. In 2014, cross-border M&A both to and from emerging markets declined and the share of these countries in total global flows fell below 20%. As in other regions and consistent with global trends, the emerging economies have experienced rising inward international divestment. Consequently, net inward M&A has been about a third of gross inward M&A.

Outward M&A from the EMEs has behaved differently from other cross-border flows from other groups of economies. Given the 'newness' of international investment from the emerging market economies, the focus of their MNEs has clearly been on building up their presence in international markets, and much less on restructuring international operations. Consequently 80% of outward M&A from emerging market economies is new net cross-border M&A.

Figure 6.7. **Regional trends in cross-border mergers and acquisitions and international divestment**

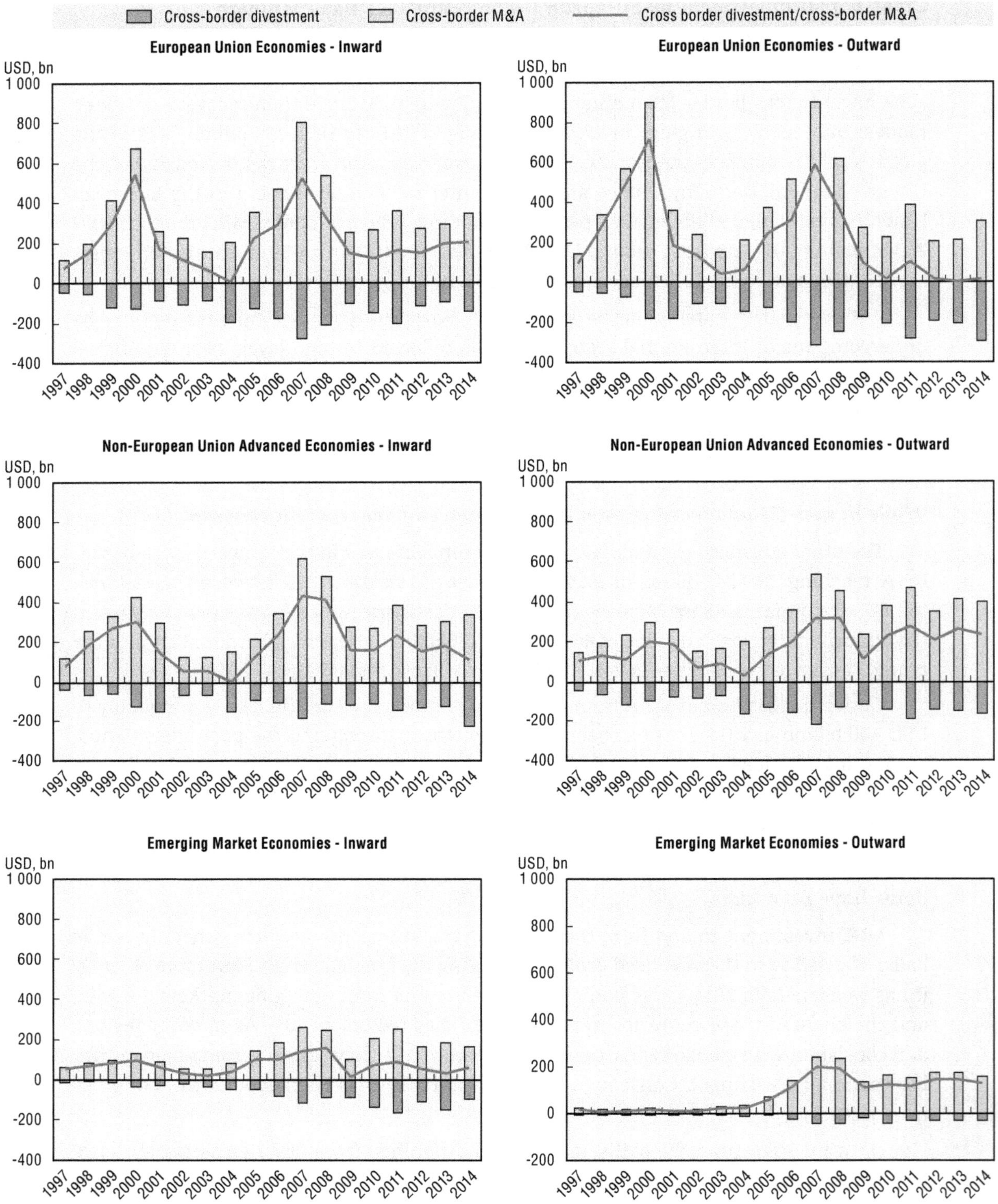

Source: Dealogic M&A Analytics database, OECD calculations.

StatLink http://dx.doi.org/10.1787/888933210004

Factors shaping the outlook for cross-border investment by multinational enterprises

Three broad factors will influence where MNE investment goes from here:

- Broader economic trends;
- Governments and the governance of global markets; and
- The sustainability of MNE investment from emerging market economies.

Broader economic trends are encouraging

Cross-border investment by MNEs is pro-cyclical and tends to move with broader macro-economic variables. For example, FDI tends to move in the same direction as global GDP.[6] On the assumption that this relationship continues to hold, the outlook for MNE investment is for it to improve, although there are several potential sources of uncertainty. The factors that are expected to boost global economic growth include lower oil prices, low interest rates, the implementation of the Juncker Plan to boost private investment in the European Union, and the decision taken by the European Central Bank in January 2015 to begin a quantitative easing programme scheduled to last until at least September 2016. According to the OECD's latest economic projections, growth rates will increase in 2015 to 4.0% (from 3.7% in 2014), and to 4.3% in 2016 (OECD, 2015).

Cross-border investment by MNEs has also tended to follow market valuations closely. For example, cross-border M&A and the MSCI World Index have generally moved in the same direction, sometimes with a one year lag for cross-border M&A (Figure 6.8). When equities started to recover from declines in 2002 and 2008, cross-border M&A started to recover soon afterward. However, since 2011 the two series have diverged, opening up an apparent gap between global equities and cross-border M&A. A similar gap is identified in analysis by Citi Research that focuses on the relationship between market valuations and total M&A volumes (Citi, 2015). According to this analysis, closing this gap would require USD 4 trillion in total M&A deals in 2015, an increase of USD 1 trillion over 2014 levels.

Figure 6.8. **Cross-border mergers and acquisitions and equity valuations**

(Index: 2000=100)

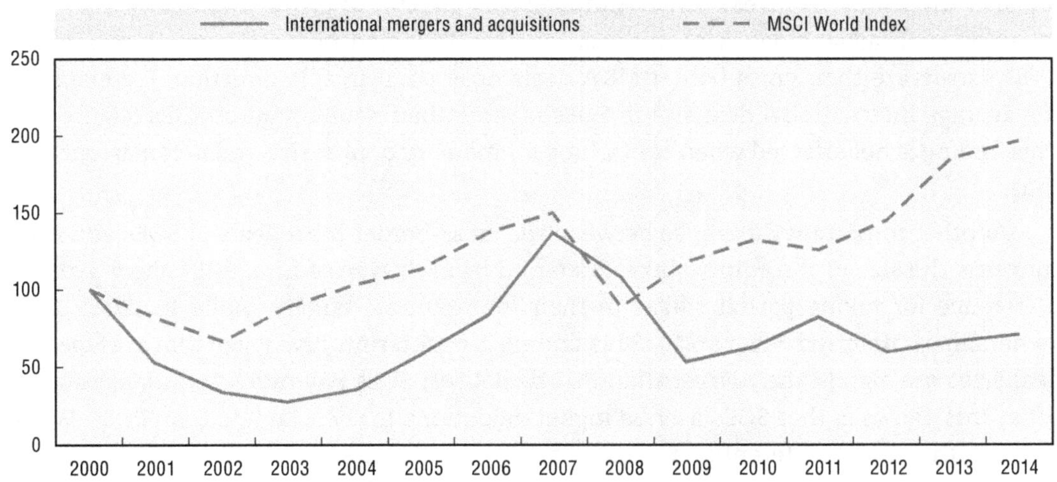

Source: Dealogic M&A Analytics database, MSCI (2015), OECD calculations.

StatLink http://dx.doi.org/10.1787/888933210010

In terms of the outlook for cross-border investment by MNEs, generally positive broader economic trends would seem to bode well. Tailwinds are driving a modest acceleration in economic growth, and equity valuations suggest that a pick-up in cross-border M&A is overdue. However, the valuation gap identified above could also point to structural factors that might be running counter to the pull of broader economic trends. These are considered below.

The governance of global markets may be discouraging international investment

Investment policy makers have traditionally focussed on explicit impediments to international investment, such as limits on foreign ownership, trade-related investment measures, and screening requirements. In recent years, the general trend has been towards more open investment regimes. Even during the financial crisis, regular G20 monitoring has not found any clear evidence of a general trend towards rising investment protectionism.

However, governments play an important role in the governance of the global economy, both directly and indirectly, and in some instances heightened government involvement is generating distortions and inefficiencies that could act as a brake on MNE investment. This section considers three areas of government involvement in global governance issues and how these (and others like them) are shaping the outlook for MNE investment. These are SOEs in the global marketplace, international co-operation in competition law enforcement, and policies aimed at supporting the development of domestic capacity in new sectors (with a focus on investment in green energy).

State ownership appears to be an advantage in arranging acquisitions

As highlighted in the general trends section above, SOEs have become important players in the global marketplace (Figure 6.4), in particular during the global financial crisis that started in 2008, when SOEs played an important counter-cyclical role. However, concerns have also been raised about possibly unfair advantages that SOEs enjoy in global markets by virtue of their links to governments.

Among the most commonly cited among these is access to preferential financing for their international investments. Although it is difficult to prove empirically that SOEs do enjoy such advantages, a comparison of how SOEs and privately-owned enterprises (POEs) structure their cross-border M&A deals does point in this direction. For example, the average international deal size of SOEs is more than double that of POEs (Figure 6.9). This finding is not affected when controlling for industry or firm size and is consistent over time.[7]

Another important difference between the cross-border M&A deals of SOEs and POEs concerns the size of the equity stakes preferred by each type of firm. SOEs show a strong preference for taking partial stakes in their international targets, while for POEs 100% ownership is preferred (Figure 6.10). This finding is counterintuitive given that average SOE deal sizes are significantly larger than POE deal sizes; SOEs pay more for smaller stakes. What this shows is that SOEs ascribe higher valuations to their targets than POEs. While factors other than preferential access to finance, and therefore a lower cost of capital, might explain this finding, it is nonetheless what one would expect to find if indeed SOEs did enjoy preferential access to financing for their M&A deals.

Figure 6.9. **Average deal sizes of state-owned and privately-owned enterprises, 1996-2013**

(USD millions)

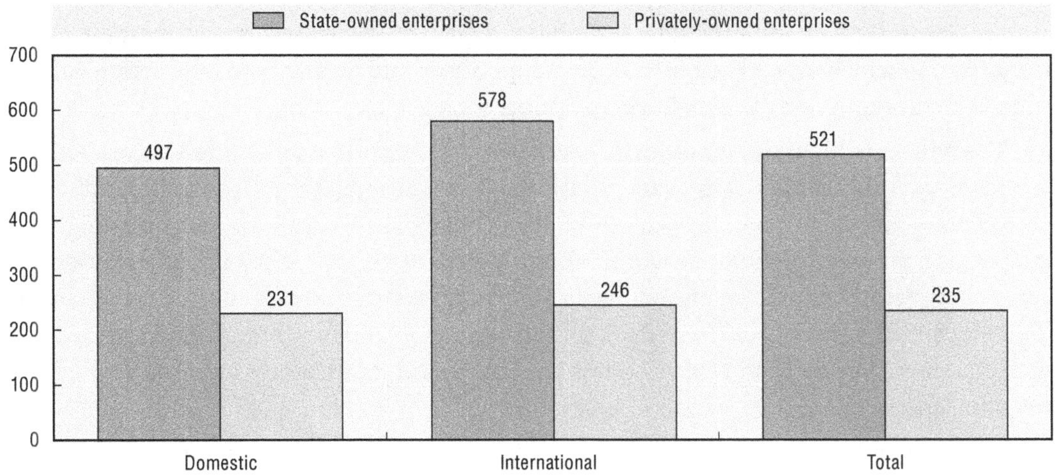

Source: Dealogic M&A Analytics database, OECD calculations.

StatLink http://dx.doi.org/10.1787/888933210026

Figure 6.10. **Deal characteristics: state-owned and privately-owned enterprises, 1997-2013**

(per cent)

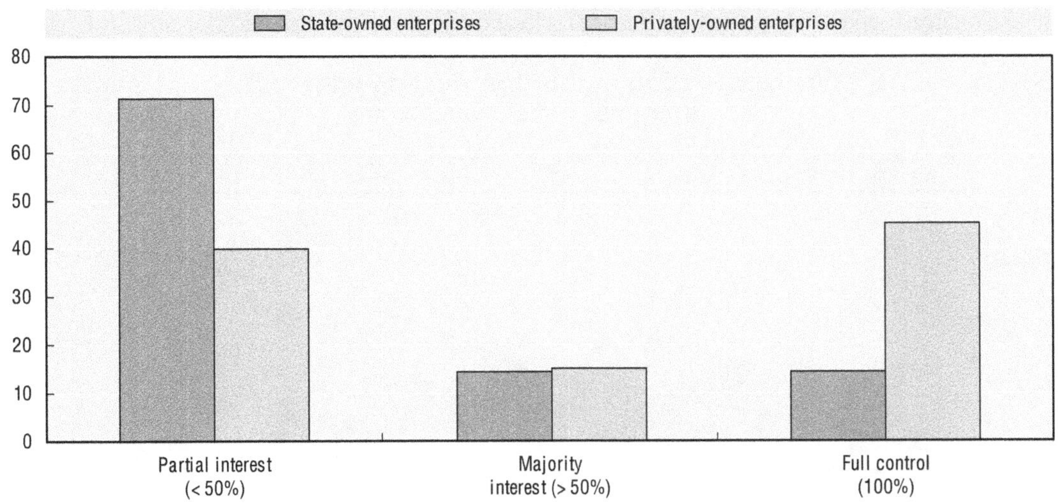

Source: Dealogic M&A Analytics database, OECD calculations.

StatLink http://dx.doi.org/10.1787/888933210034

The increased importance of SOEs as international investors in recent years could affect the outlook in two quite different ways. First, irrespective of whether in fact SOEs are competing unfairly in the global marketplace, the perception of unfairness could lead governments to impose restrictions on international investments by SOEs, now an important source of global investment. Second, if international investments by SOEs are grounded in policy-based support schemes (arising from differential policy treatment rather than real competitive advantages), one might reasonably expect that such policies will eventually be lifted in the face of persistent losses. Both of these considerations point to the downside for the outlook for cross-border investment by MNEs, at least in terms of the absolute amounts.

International co-operation in competition law enforcement is needed

More jurisdictions than ever are applying competition law.[8] Although laws and procedures vary across countries, different regimes around the world are remarkably similar. Common elements include: prohibitions against cartels; review of mergers based primarily or exclusively on their effects on competition; and an ability to take action against firms with market power that behave anti-competitively.

The widespread implementation of competition laws and establishment of competition enforcement authorities are extremely positive developments overall. Individual jurisdictions newly applying competition law, businesses based in longer-established competition jurisdictions and the world economy as a whole have all significantly benefitted from this development. Competition law is a key to preserving benefits of market operation at all steps in the global value chain. It protects the global value chain from the effects of restrictions on competition that raise market power and inefficiently increase costs down the value chain.

However, while international investment has increased dramatically since 1990, the enforcement of competition law has remained primarily a domestic exercise.[9] The increasingly cross-border dimension of business activities, together with the increase in the number of competition authorities creates additional complexity for cases with a multi-jurisdictional element (Figure 6.11). This complexity creates challenges for the effective and consistent enforcement of competition law. More importantly in the context of this chapter, in the absence of co-operation and consistent enforcement, international investors are faced with heightened uncertainty over their investment plans.

Figure 6.11. **More competition authorities dealing with more cross-border mergers and acquisitions**

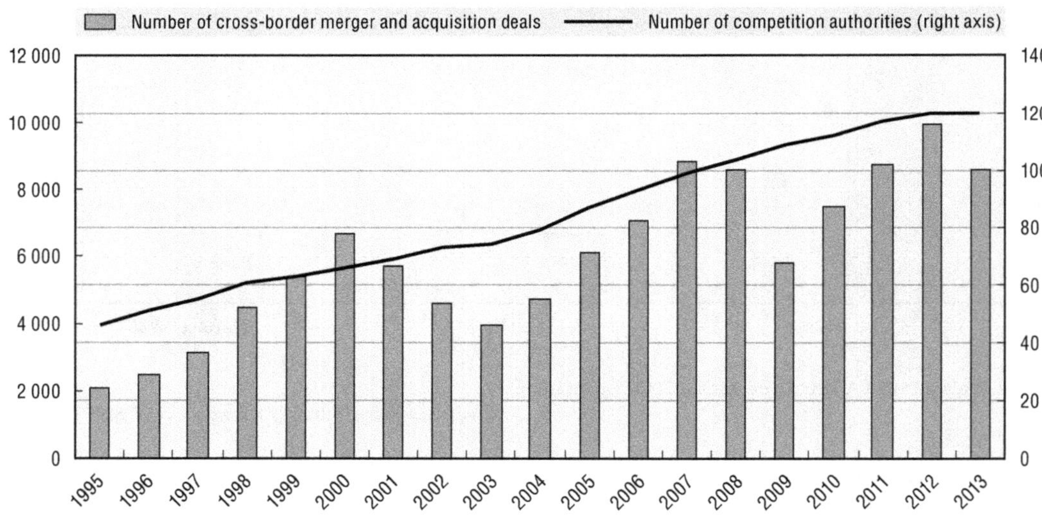

Source: OECD calculations based on Challenges of International Co-operation in Competition Law Enforcement, OECD (2014) *www.oecd.org/daf/competition/challenges-international-coop-competition-2014.htm*.

StatLink http://dx.doi.org/10.1787/888933210040

Cross-border mergers create scope for disagreement between competition authorities and can give rise to substantial costs when such disagreements occur. The implications for the outlook for cross-border investment by MNEs are twofold. First, the strictest standard for approving a merger will become the prevailing standard in many cases, potentially stopping mergers that would be approved by most jurisdictions even of truly global producers. This means that what most countries determine to be a pro-competitive or innocuous merger may be stopped by one authority having a different view. As more authorities evaluate mergers, it is more likely that one of them will form a different judgment, even from the same facts.

Second, the uncertainty created by a system in which any given cross-border M&A deal has to be reviewed by possibly dozens of different agencies, with different approaches and priorities, effectively raises the bar in terms of the willingness of firms to go ahead with deals, and may have a chilling effect on merger deal-making. To the extent that mergers enable sharing of good practices across borders, such efficiency enhancing effects of mergers would be limited.

Some support schemes for clean energy may lead to competitive distortions

In the past decade, governments have provided substantial support to clean energy that has benefited both domestic and international investment (OECD, 2015, forthcoming). Globally, policy support to clean energy amounted to USD 121 billion in 2013 (IEA, 2014). At least 138 countries had implemented clean-energy support policies as of early 2014 (REN21, 2014). Several countries have also supported clean energy by reducing barriers to international investment and trade, such as *de jure* restrictions on FDI and import tariffs.

Largely driven by policy support, new investment in clean energy increased six-fold between 2004 and 2011, reaching USD 279 billion in 2011, before declining in 2012-13. Solar and wind energy have received the largest share of new investment flows – USD 114 billion and USD 80 billion respectively in 2013. International trade and greenfield FDI have strongly contributed to the growth of solar and wind-energy sectors, as well as to the integration of these industries into global value chains. Both industries – and especially solar photovoltaic energy – are now characterised by the emergence of global production networks.

Since the 2008 financial crisis, however, the perceived potential of clean energy to support domestic growth and employment has led several OECD countries and emerging economies to design green industrial policies aimed at protecting domestic clean-energy manufacturers, especially in the solar photovoltaic and wind-energy sectors. In the post-crisis recovery context, policy makers have done so notably through setting local-content requirements. These typically require solar or wind developers to source a specific share of jobs, components or costs locally to be eligible for policy support or public tenders. Such requirements have been designed or implemented in solar and wind energy in at least 21 countries, including 16 OECD countries and emerging economies, mostly since 2009.

In a context of global value chains, local-content requirements have hindered global international investment flows in solar photovoltaic and wind energy. At the same time, they have had mixed or negative results in achieving policy goals such as local job creation.

The case of government support for clean energy highlights the potential for well-meaning government support programmes in new fields to cross the line, leading to distortions and, as in this example, restrictions on international investment. As mentioned at the outset, there is no evidence that governments have been veering towards protectionism in any sort of systematic way. However, as new technologies give rise to new industries, and as global value chains lead to new patterns of firm-level organisation across borders, protectionism in individual sectors can quickly give rise to spill-overs resulting in economic inefficiency and distortions on a global scale.

The level of outward investment from emerging market economies may be unsustainable

The extraordinary increase in international investment from the emerging market economies beginning around 2004-5 (see Figure 6.7) has often been lauded as a sign that investment globalisation is becoming more balanced. It has also created an expectation that an erosion of the parallel home-host/north-south distinction would bring about greater convergence on policy issues (since countries would no longer be seeing their interests uniquely from either a narrow host-country or home-country perspective).

However, the rapid rise of emerging market economies as sources of international investment (however measured) also gives rise to a question which has important implications for the outlook: does outward investment from emerging markets and China in particular represent a bubble?

One of the indications that points in this direction concerns the size of cross-border M&A deals. Just as previous booms have been led by surges in M&A activity in particular sectors, they have also been accompanied by sharp increases in average deal value (Figure 6.12). During each of the previous boom and bust cycles, the average value of cross-border M&A peaked at just under USD 150 million. Emerging markets (excluding China) have performed very much like the advanced economies in this regard since around 2004, reflecting the fact that they had not yet become important sources of outward investment at the time of the first international investment boom in 2000.

Figure 6.12. **Average cross-border merger and acquisition deal size, different country and country groupings**

(USD millions)

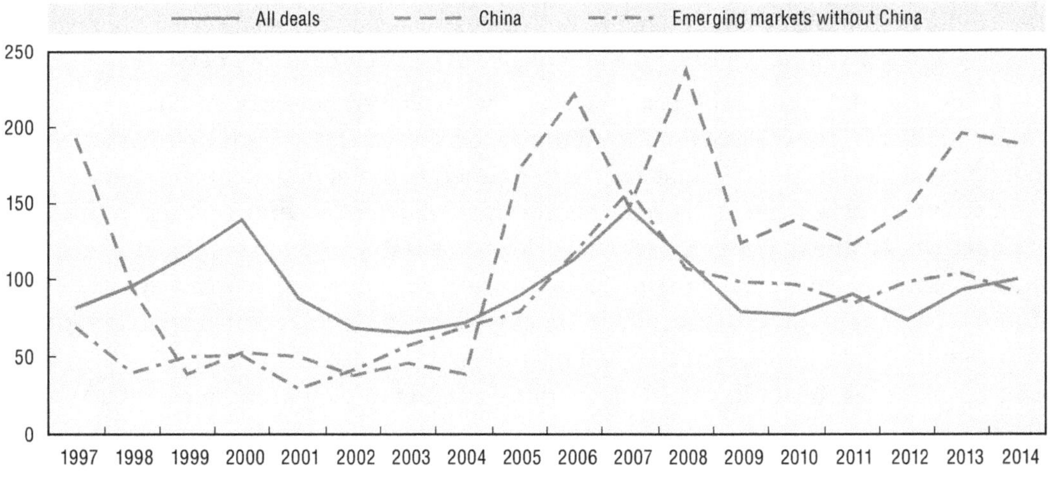

Source: Dealogic M&A Analytics database, OECD calculations.

StatLink http://dx.doi.org/10.1787/888933210056

China is represented separately in Figure 6.12. Up until 2004, China's average deal size wasn't much different than that of cross-border M&A from other emerging market economies and was generally lower than deals led by firms from the advanced economies. In the ten years since 2005, however, the average value of cross-border M&A deals by Chinese firms has been 76% larger than the world average. And in the last three years, they have been twice as large as the world average. Given that the turning point in previous MNE investment cycles has been marked by average deal sizes approaching USD 150 million, China's outward FDI has qualities which suggest that a correction is possible.

Another area of potential imbalance concerns the ratio of international divestment to cross-border M&A. As discussed in earlier sections on regional trends, international divestment has generally been on the rise in recent years, in particular for European countries, reflecting adjustments that firms are making in the organisation of their international operations to reflect major shifts in the world's economic centre of gravity, among other factors. The one important exception to this trend is found in the outward cross-border M&A from the emerging market economies (Figure 6.13).

Figure 6.13. **Outward international divestment as a share of cross-border merger and acquisition volumes, by country and country groupings**

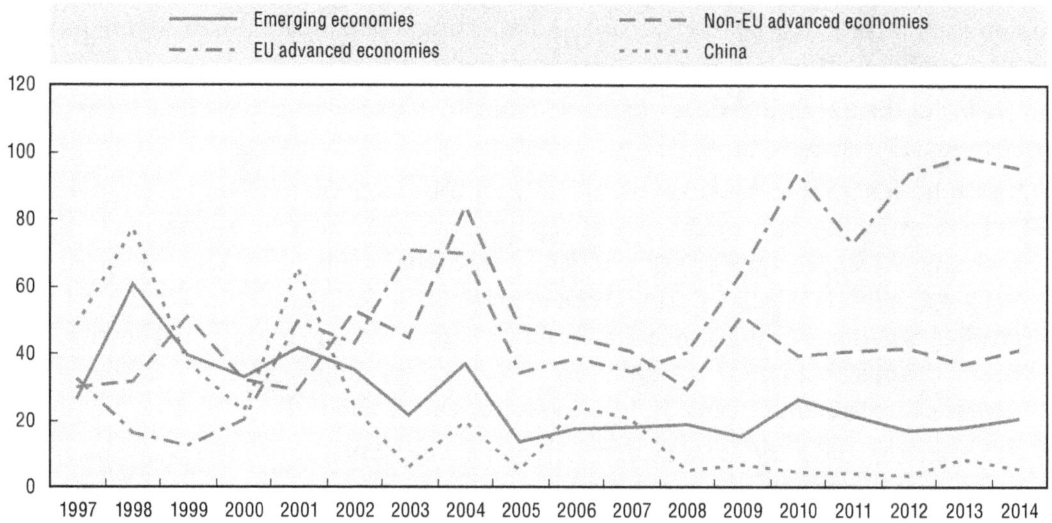

Source: Dealogic M&A Analytics database, OECD calculations.

StatLink http://dx.doi.org/10.1787/888933210063

Three distinct stories are apparent. First, the non-EU advanced economies currently have international divestment-to-investment ratios which at 42% are close to their historical average (43%). Second, the EU economies, having averaged 96% in the past 3 years, are well above their historical average of 55%. The international divestment-to-investment ratio of EU firms may begin to come down after three years of major structural adjustment in their international operations. Third, the emerging market economies have divestment-to-investment ratios below their historical average (27%) with a ratio of 21% in 2014.

Within this group, however, China again stands out as the main reason that the emerging market economies differ from the non-EU advanced economies. Since around 2008 international divestments by Chinese firms have been negligible, averaging 5%, well below a historical average of 22%. It seems implausible that Chinese firms will be able to sustain their current levels of international investment without at some point engaging in more international divestment more in line with the way most other firms are constantly reworking the architecture of their international operations.

In terms of the outlook, the sustainability of outward investment from China will be an important variable going forward. China accounted for 8% of total global cross-border M&A in 2014. There are currently three plausible channels through which one might expect China's outward cross-border M&A to shrink. First, the absolute value of its outward investment activity could be expected to slow down. Second, the size of deals by outward Chinese investors might at some point be expected to decline. Third, cross-border divestment by Chinese outward investors, currently also at unusually low levels, might also be expected to rise at some point.

Conclusions

One of the overarching themes of this chapter has been the re-organisation of the international business landscape in the wake of the global financial crisis. The emerging markets have become important sources of MNE investments while many advanced economies have declined, in particular in the European Union. The rising volume of international divestment relative to cross-border M&A, driven by asset sales by MNEs to domestic buyers, has been a global trend affecting all countries. In 2014, this form of investment de-globalisation reached a ten-year high.

Many of the trends and developments identified in this chapter have important policy implications. These include:

- A commitment to openness has undoubtedly contributed to the resilience of international integration in the face of the global financial crisis. Furthermore, previous FDI and international M&A booms in 2000 and 2007 were driven by financial bubbles in particular sectors. The levels reached during those booms should not be used as a benchmark for deciding whether current levels are 'normal'. Rather, an important policy lesson from these previous boom and bust cycles relates to the warning signals that sudden sharp increases in MNE investments in certain sectors can provide.
- Although the industry composition of cross-border M&A remains evenly balanced, investment from certain emerging market economies, in particular China, displays some of the hallmarks of previous bubbles, including extremely high growth rates, unusually high average deal values, and unusually low volumes of international divestment.
- Although governments have generally kept their markets open to international investment, policies in areas not directly associated with MNE investment have given rise to distortions and inefficiencies which could act as an unintentional brake on cross-border investment. Examples given related to the emergence of SOEs as an important new class of MNEs, the growing complexity of co-ordinating international M&A reviews and the harmful distortions to which support schemes for green energy have given rise. In cases such as these, the increasingly interlinked nature of the global economy has meant that distortions or inefficiencies that arise in one market are quickly transmitted to others.
- The policy implications of the apparent rise in investment de-globalisation are not yet clear. More empirical analysis is required. The key question is whether this is a transitory phenomenon or a long-term trend. The answer to this question will hold important implications for the ability of governments to formulate policy on a range of issues, including with respect to investment treaties, investment promotion, and efforts to promote deeper integration in global value chains.

Notes

1. FDI statistics and data on international M&A constitute two of the best sources of information on direct investments by multinational enterprises. Although not strictly comparable, these two series follow each other closely, only moving in different directions twice between 1997 and 2013. FDI statistics are provided by governments and are reported in every country's balance of payments statistics. Data on M&A are obtained from Dealogic's M&A Analytics database, a privately run database. An advantage of international M&A data over FDI data is timeliness.

2. About USD 130 billion of UK divestment in 2014 was due to Vodafone's sale of its stake in Verizon Wireless in the United States.
3. Australia; Canada; Hong Kong, China; Japan; New Zealand; Singapore; Switzerland; Chinese Taipei; and the United States.
4. Just over half of this international divestment was due to the USD 130 billion divestment of Vodafone's assets in Verizon Wireless in the United States.
5. The analysis in this section is based upon the same sample of emerging market economies covered in Chapter 2. See Annex 2.A1.
6. Trade follows the same cyclical patterns, but FDI displays stronger upward and downward overshooting effects.
7. Figures 6.9 and 6.10 are based upon a comparison of all SOE and POE deals worth over USD 5 million during the period 1996-2013.
8. The International Competition Network (ICN) now has 126 members from 111 jurisdictions.
9. The most notable exception to this is the European Commission's DG Competition, with competition powers across the European Union that are actively exercised on a regular basis.

References

CITI (2015), "M&A Catching UP", *Global Equity Strategist* (19 February 2015).

IEA (2014), *World Energy Outlook 2014*, OECD/IEA, Paris.

MSCI (2015), "MSCI ACWI Factsheet", February 2015, *http://www.msci.com/resources/factsheets/index_fact_sheet/msci-acwi.pdf.*

OECD (2015, forthcoming), *Overcoming Barriers to International Investment in Clean Energy*, OECD, Paris.

OECD (2015), "Interim Economic Assessment" 18 March 2015, *http://www.oecd.org/eco/outlook/Interim-Assessment-Handout-Mar-2015.pdf.*

OECD (2014), *International Co-Operation in Competition Law Enforcement*, OECD, Paris.

OECD (2008), *OECD Benchmark Definition of Foreign Direct Investment: Fourth Edition 2008*, OECD, Paris.

REN21 (2014), *Renewables 2014: Global Status Report*, Renewable Energy Policy Network for the 21st Century.

ANNEX 6.A1

Statistical tables and supplementary data

Table 6.A1.1. **Aggregate trends in cross-border mergers and acquisitions (M&A)**

USD billion

	1997	1998	1999	2000	2001	2002	2003	2004	2005
Cross-border M&A, global volume	**317,523**	**547,650**	**843,124**	**1,220,222**	**647,562**	**413,266**	**346,045**	**448,397**	**718,788**
Finance	30,707	49,663	64,791	125,418	89,480	34,316	60,823	72,402	89,154
Telecommunications	27,360	49,400	195,849	283,312	142,545	49,988	42,190	33,934	76,838
Cross-border M&A by non-listed SOEs	**8,362**	**5,894**	**26,329**	**34,289**	**17,605**	**21,089**	**6,276**	**13,077**	**20,858**
Cross-border divestment volumes	**98,409**	**125,305**	**197,216**	**285,773**	**269,840**	**191,642**	**189,215**	**326,783**	**269,510**
MNE-to-MNE cross-border divestment	54,276	56,345	121,804	133,304	156,977	91,998	71,666	108,009	130,667
MNE-to-domestic buyer cross-border divestment	44,133	68,961	75,412	152,469	112,862	99,644	117,548	290,068	138,842

	2006	2007	2008	2009	2010	2011	2012	2013	2014
Cross-border M&A, global volume	**1,022,809**	**1,683,335**	**1,322,405**	**646,672**	**768,937**	**1,009,952**	**735,400**	**804,154**	**868,192**
Finance	120,760	311,221	215,720	110,555	82,973	63,074	44,173	47,677	55,939
Telecommunications	127,217	90,655	46,211	39,179	69,073	67,092	37,714	106,658	95,414
Cross-border M&A by non-listed SOEs	**35,542**	**43,993**	**82,716**	**143,910**	**74,761**	**62,407**	**70,471**	**65,488**	**78,843**
Cross-border divestment volumes	**386,904**	**577,663**	**434,424**	**316,514**	**407,941**	**512,337**	**370,835**	**391,802**	**492,744**
MNE-to-MNE cross-border divestment	168,263	233,228	212,666	138,350	200,590	275,937	177,771	170,529	178,296
MNE-to-domestic buyer cross-border divestment	218,642	344,435	221,758	178,163	207,351	236,400	193,197	221,012	314,231

Notes:

"Cross-border M&A, global volume" covers all transactions in which the acquirer and the target are located in different countries.

"Finance" and "Telecommunications" sectors are defined according to the Dealogic M&A Analytics General Industry Grouping classification.

"Cross-border divestment volumes" covers all transactions in which the divestor and the target are located in different countries. If the acquirer and the target are also located in different countries, this constitutes an MNE-to-MNE transaction. If the acquirer and the target are located in the same country, this constitutes and MNE-to-domestic buyer transaction.

Source: Dealogic M&A Analytics database, OECD calculations.

StatLink http://dx.doi.org/10.1787/888933210473

Table 6.A1.2. **Regional trends in cross-border mergers and acquisitions (M&A)**

USD million

	1997	1998	1999	2000	2001	2002	2003	2004	2005	2006	2007	2008	2009	2010	2011	2012	2013	2014
European Union																		
Inward cross-border M&A	119,402	198,767	416,841	671,120	256,374	223,434	155,669	205,458	356,209	466,675	801,598	539,258	252,124	268,978	362,469	270,736	290,941	346,840
Inward cross-border divestment	43,969	50,152	119,927	127,347	86,287	106,591	86,710	196,939	127,344	172,475	275,676	207,345	101,017	145,197	199,817	116,338	95,259	142,844
Outward cross-border M&A	144,431	336,650	567,530	899,197	362,741	237,139	152,202	210,334	371,339	512,507	902,318	619,477	272,775	221,700	386,625	203,440	208,248	305,367
Outward cross-border divestment	47,437	54,749	70,055	181,427	180,637	102,702	108,089	147,420	128,495	199,159	312,505	250,154	175,596	208,589	282,956	190,334	205,659	291,527
Non-European Union advanced economies																		
Inward cross-border M&A	119,616	254,609	331,775	427,427	298,203	122,720	126,455	155,866	215,938	347,145	617,235	525,630	276,655	270,296	382,345	282,423	300,127	338,004
Inward cross-border divestment	40,542	64,539	59,919	124,408	153,640	62,168	65,193	154,463	88,538	108,337	187,460	112,543	118,923	111,258	144,234	129,676	122,408	228,598
Outward cross-border M&A	149,621	191,574	234,279	294,820	265,593	155,605	166,177	199,045	271,920	359,681	532,844	450,247	232,025	376,536	464,919	351,735	410,922	398,887
Outward cross-border divestment	44,746	61,194	119,243	95,119	77,361	82,010	74,558	167,421	130,470	162,039	218,930	133,725	119,686	148,972	190,510	147,023	151,800	165,733
Emerging market economies																		
Inward cross-border M&A	64,415	80,030	95,945	129,682	89,379	52,830	57,124	84,418	144,085	182,905	261,066	246,902	105,296	206,448	255,645	164,034	183,940	161,611
Inward cross-border divestment	11,875	9,807	16,439	36,999	27,853	21,621	33,672	44,877	44,511	80,816	115,182	87,697	88,261	133,284	164,560	108,769	149,285	97,963
Outward cross-border M&A	20,567	13,917	18,437	22,560	12,736	18,164	25,333	35,576	69,624	140,664	240,217	236,214	132,658	162,611	151,050	176,928	176,438	159,177
Outward cross-border divestment	5,476	13,917	18,437	22,560	12,736	18,164	25,333	35,576	69,624	140,664	240,217	236,214	132,658	162,611	151,050	176,928	176,438	159,177
Average deal size																		
All deals	**82**	**96**	**116**	**139**	**88**	**68**	**66**	**72**	**90**	**113**	**147**	**112**	**79**	**77**	**90**	**74**	**94**	**100**
China	193	94	39	53	51	38	46	39	173	221	147	237	124	138	122	145	196	189
Emerging markets without China	70	40	50	51	30	41	57	69	79	118	158	107	98	97	84	98	103	92

Notes: These regional breakdowns are based upon the sample of countries used in Chapter 2. In 2014 this sample of countries accounted for 97% of all inward cross-border M&A and 99% of all outward cross-border M&A.
"Inward cross-border M&A" covers all transactions in which the target is located in the region in question and the acquirer is located outside the region in question.
"Inward cross-border divestment" covers all transactions in which the target is located in the region in question and the divestor is located outside the region in question.
"Outward cross-border M&A" covers all transactions in which the target is located outside of the region in question and the acquiror is located inside the region in question.
"Outward cross-border divestment" covers all transactions in which the target is located outside the region in question and the divestor is located inside the region in question.

Source: Dealogic M&A Analytics database, OECD calculations.

StatLink http://dx.doi.org/10.1787/888933210485

OECD Business and Finance Outlook 2015

Chapter 7

Strengthening market-based financing of corporate investments

During the last ten years, corporations' use of capital markets has changed in a number of important ways. These changes have partly been driven by macroeconomic events that have affected traditional sources of funds and shifted some of the corporate debt from traditional bank lending to corporate bonds. They may also have been influenced by regulatory changes that have contributed to a decrease in the use of public equity markets by small and medium-sized enterprises. In a low interest environment, where institutional investors are pressed to meet their client obligations, corporations have also had to respond to investor campaigns for higher dividends and share buyback programmes.

Main findings

- Following a drop after the financial crisis, the number of shareholder campaigns has remained at a fairly stable level. Between 10% and 15% of all shareholder campaigns are focused on demands for buyback programmes and dividends.
- Since the financial crisis, the United States and Europe have both seen a marked increase in the issuing and outstanding stock of corporate bonds.
- Since 2008, companies from emerging market economies remarkably increased their use of capital market-based financing. Between 2000 and 2014, the total amount of money they raised through capital markets increased more than five times, reaching USD 458 billion.
- Further study is required to determine whether any regulatory initiatives may have contributed to a decrease in the number of small size companies that use public equity markets to raise capital.
- The profound changes in the functioning of secondary equity markets and trading practices over the last decade raise important policy issues with respect to ensuring level playing field among investors and efficient price discovery.

Introduction

Corporations' use of capital market-based financing has increased in importance for non-financial companies in the wake of the post-financial crisis period. This has largely been driven by a decrease in bank lending to non-financial companies and historically low levels of interest rates. At the same time, unintended consequences of re-regulation may have contributed to a significant decrease in the use of public equity markets by small and medium-sized enterprises in advanced economies. Concurrently, there have been a number of important developments in secondary markets, with respect to market structures, trading practices and investment strategies that challenge the existing policy framework.

What are companies doing and why?

Markets have favoured large share buybacks over capital expenditure

It is sometimes argued, that so called activist investors favour the short-term gratification of dividends and share buybacks over longer-term investment. The performance of such an investment strategy was tested in Chapter 2 and the results are reproduced in Table 7.1.

As shown in the table, an investment strategy based on selling high capital spending companies and buying low CAPEX and high buyback companies had a 6-year cumulative return of 50% in the United States, 47% in Europe, 21% in emerging countries and even 12% in Japan where activists traditionally play little role.

Table 7.1. **Which market investment strategy outperformed?**

Percentage gain

Infrastructure & General Industry

(buying the bottom quartile of companies CAPEX / (CAPEX + DIV & BUYBACKS) index and selling the top quartile)

	2009	2010	2011	2012	2013	2014	Cumulative
United States	0.56	1.70	16.18	11.98	3.84	15.55	49.82
Europe	-2.36	3.80	13.84	8.73	9.74	13.47	47.22
Japan	-7.27	0.45	9.63	9.29	2.17	-2.62	11.65
EMEs	-3.71	8.70	10.22	10.74	0.97	-5.52	21.40

Source: Bloomberg, OECD calculations.

StatLink http://dx.doi.org/10.1787/888933210490

A comparison between the performance of the S&P 500 Buyback Index, which measures the performance of the 100 stocks with the highest buyback ratios in the S&P 500 index, with the performance of the overall S&P 500 Index provides similar results. Over the last three years, the S&P 500 Buyback Index provided an annual return of 23.63%, which is significantly higher than the 16.94% annual return provided by the S&P 500 index.

Many explanations have been offered as to why companies make stock repurchases,[1] but two possible explanations are particularly important from a corporate governance perspective: investor activism and managerial remuneration systems.

Companies have been more willing to accommodate demands for buybacks and dividends in recent years.

Activist investors' attempts to influence companies' payout decisions have received a lot of attention since some of the largest listed companies recently have been subject to highly publicized investor campaigns. Figure 7.1 reveals a steady increase in recorded campaigns leading up to the financial crisis in 2008. Following a drop in investor campaigns after 2008, they have remained at a level of between 300 and 400 per year. This Figure also reveals that, although there has been a certain increase in the number of proxy fights, the dominant form of activism is 'other shareholder campaigns' which account for more than 70% of all campaigns since 2006. Other shareholder campaigns generally include activism, usually in the form of making communications and letters sent to management, made public by activist investors.

Figure 7.2 shows payout-related campaigns, which are defined as campaigns that are focused on a demand for buybacks and dividends. The data reveals that the annual average number of investor campaigns before and after the 2008 financial crisis has remained about the same of around 50 to 60 per year. There are nevertheless important variations between individual years. Following a significant increase between 2004 and 2007, activist campaigns peaked in 2007, dropped significantly after the financial crisis and, in 2014, were back at the 2006 level.

Payout-related campaigns accounts for between 11% and 16% of the total number of investor campaigns throughout the period. They were mainly carried out by sending letters to management or through other forms of public announcements and communication. They are less commonly carried out through proxy fights. In 2014, for example, the share of payout-related issues in proxy fights was 9% which was well below their share in 'other' shareholder activism campaigns (16%). The high costs associated with proxy fights may have discouraged activists from choosing this method.

Figure 7.1. **Investor activism trends by campaign type**

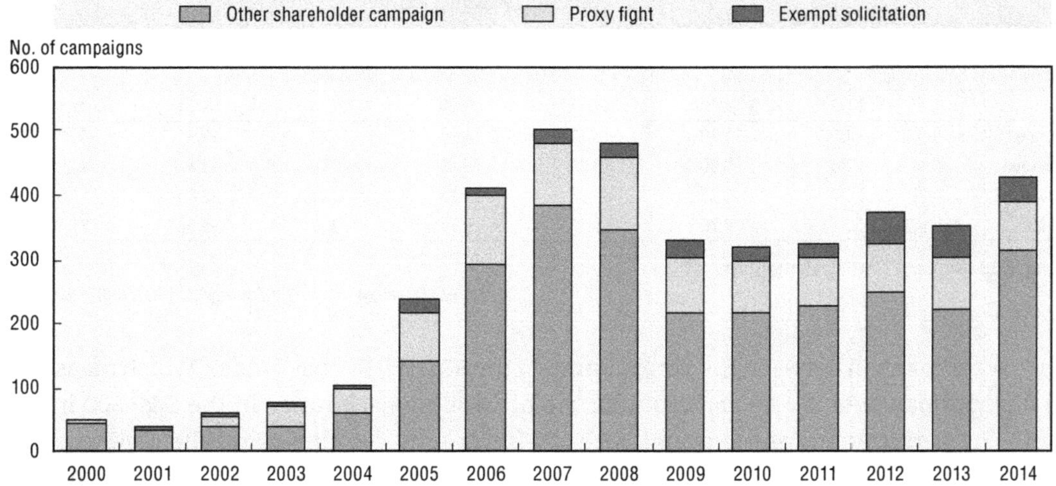

Notes: Other shareholder campaign includes corporate activism, usually in the form of making communications and letters sent to management, made public by activist investors. Under a proxy fight shareholders solicit the proxy or written consent of other shareholders in support of a resolution. An exempt solicitation is a campaign under which a shareholder can communicate its views to other shareholders without having to comply with US SEC proxy filing and disclosure rules. See the Annex 7.A1 for details on the data collection procedure.

Source: Factset, OECD calculations

StatLink http://dx.doi.org/10.1787/888933210078

Figure 7.2. **Payout-related investor activism campaigns**

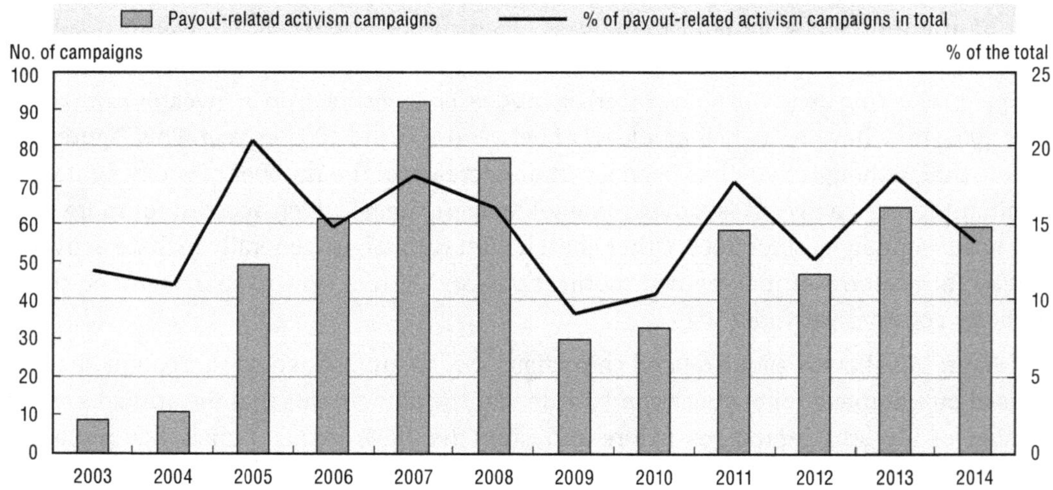

Note: See the Annex 7.A1 for details on the data collection procedure.

Source: Factset, OECD calculations

StatLink http://dx.doi.org/10.1787/888933210080

Manually extracted data from the synopses summarising the course of events around each campaign sheds light on companies' reaction to payout demands. Among 590 payout-related campaigns identified in the dataset, companies' subsequent action was explicitly stated in 313 (53%) of the cases. Figure 7.3 shows that out of those campaigns, the incidence of rejecting demands has always been small and there is also some indication that companies have been more willing to accommodate demands in the most recent 4 years.

Figure 7.3. **Company reaction after payout demands**

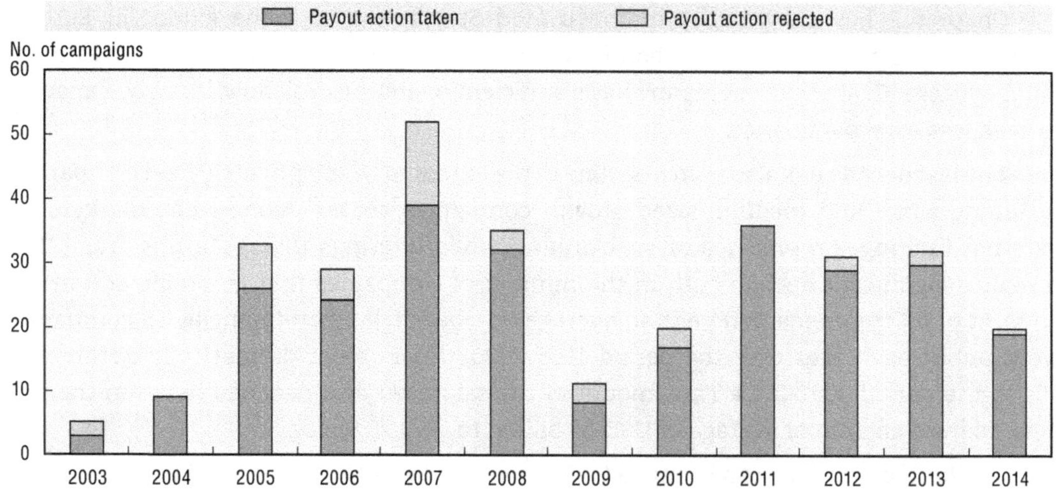

Note: See the Annex 7.A1 for details on the data collection procedure.

Source: Factset, OECD calculations

StatLink http://dx.doi.org/10.1787/888933219941

One factor that may lead to increased buybacks is when managerial remuneration is linked to earnings per share

In many countries, a large share of total compensation received by top executives is performance-based, usually in the form of stock and option grants or bonuses. According to Lazonick (2014), the 500 highest-paid US executives receive 42% of their pay from stock options and 41% from stock grants. Furthermore, 49% of US CEOs have their bonus structure tied to earnings per share (EPS) targets (Cheng et al., 2010). Given such a compensation scheme, managers may be tempted to use buybacks to temporarily boost their share price and also to reduce the number of shares outstanding to reach EPS targets.

Empirical evidence from the prior literature supports the idea that buyback activity is stronger in companies whose managerial pay is linked to EPS. Utilizing a CEO bonus database covering 1 423 US companies over the period 1993-2007, Cheng et al. (2010) find that when a CEO's bonus is linked to EPS, a stock buyback is more likely to occur and its magnitude tends to be larger. For such cases, share buybacks increase the bonus size by approximately 36%, on average.

Furthermore, companies are more likely to conduct buybacks when their EPS is less than but close to the EPS target that triggers a bonus. Young and Ying (2011) conduct a similar study but covering companies in the UK, where not only bonuses but also stock options or restricted stocks frequently depend on EPS performance through their vesting conditions. The study finds that the odds of repurchase for companies with an EPS-dependent pay are almost twice that for companies for which executive pay is independent of EPS.

Marquardt et al. (2011) differentiate between managers' decisions to conduct accelerated stock repurchases (ASRs) versus open market repurchases (OMRs). From the perspective of a myopic and EPS-motivated management, ASRs may appear more appealing since they allow for an immediate recognition of EPS benefits. The authors indeed find that companies are more likely to choose ASRs over OMRs when bonus pay is explicitly tied to EPS, when CEOs have a short employment horizon and when they are more entrenched.

Initial public offerings have declined in the United States and Europe

Chapter 2 has shown that in the United States, and to some extent in Europe, companies´ aggregate operating cash flows are more than sufficient to cover investment and buybacks. Given that a company has a sufficient operating cash flow, it can be expected to seek less external finance.

The last decade has also seen a decline in the extent to which privately held companies, including small and medium-sized growth companies access public stock markets for external funding. An analysis of such initial public offerings (IPOs) starting from 1995 reveals a significant decline both in the number of companies that go public and in the amount of IPO proceeds. Whereas an average number of 451 non-financial US companies went public each year over the period 1995-2000, this number dramatically declined to 104 in the period 2001-2014. The amount of capital raised also declined between the two periods from an annual average of USD 55 billion to USD 27 billion.

Similar observations can be made for Europe. The average annual number of listings by non-financial European companies more than halved from 343 in the 1995-2000 period to 160 in the subsequent period. The average amount of annual IPO proceedings also declined from USD 64 billion to USD 28 billion between the two periods.

Figure 7.4. **Initial public offerings by US and European non-financial companies**

(2014 USD billion)

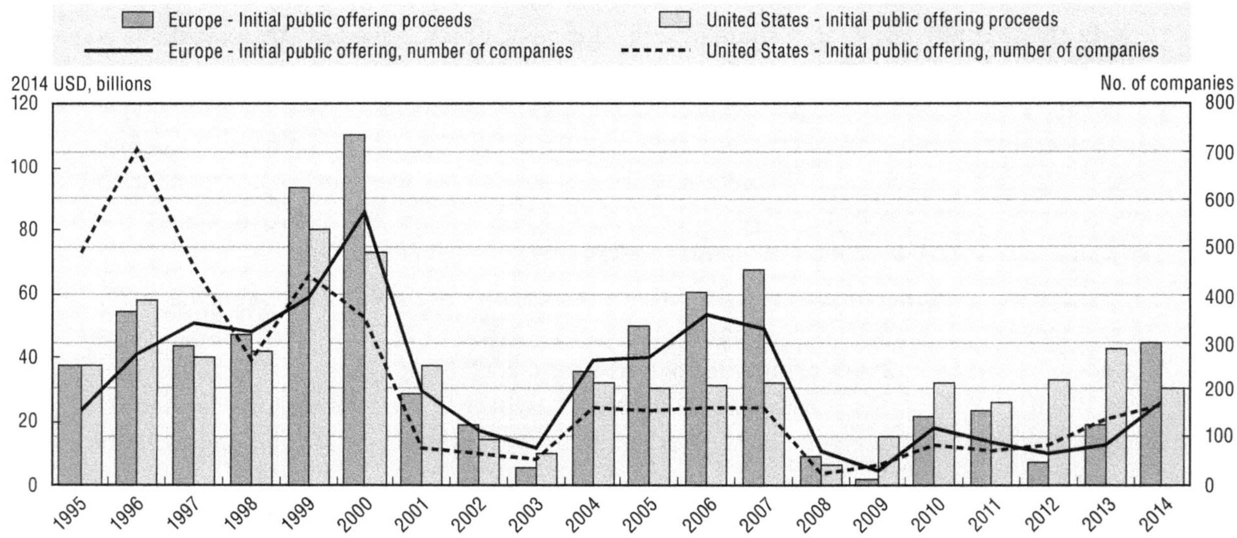

Source: Thomson Reuters, OECD calculations, see Annex 7.A1 for details.

StatLink http://dx.doi.org/10.1787/888933210090

But US and EU companies have taken advantage of low interest rates in bond markets

Looking at another part of the market for corporate finance, the relative abundance of operating cash flow has not prevented US and European companies from taking advantage of the corporate bond market. Corporate bond markets have become an increasingly important source of finance for non-financial companies since 2008. Two main factors seem to have contributed to this development: First, there was a decrease in bank lending to non-financial companies, due to the so-called deleveraging. Second, the historically low levels of bond interest rates have pushed companies to issue bonds to lock in the low costs of debt while it is still possible. Total outstanding amount of corporate bonds issued by non-financial companies reached USD 10.4 trillion in 2014 from a level of USD 5.5 trillion in 2007. Figure 7.5 illustrates, that as a result, the outstanding amount of corporate bonds issued by non-financial companies as a percent of GDP has increased significantly in both the US and Europe.

Figure 7.5. **Outstanding corporate bonds by non-financial companies**

(Percentage of nominal GDP)

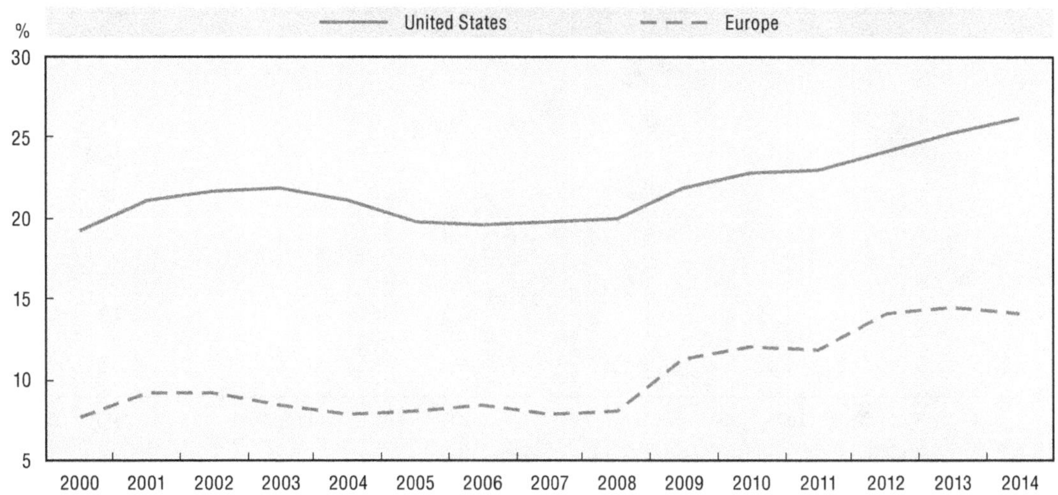

Source: Thomson Reuters, Bloomberg, OECD calculations, see Annex 7.A1 for details.

StatLink http://dx.doi.org/10.1787/888933210102

Based on a sample of almost six thousand corporate bond issues by US companies, Figure 7.6 presents the use of proceeds from corporate bonds as stated in the issuers' documentation related to the bond issue. Consistent with the findings in Chapter 2 regarding US companies' operating cash flows' adequacy for financing investment and payouts, the funding of buybacks and dividends has never been a dominant motive for issuing bonds. The percentage of bond issues in which the financing of buybacks or dividends is stated as a reason for the issue never passed the 10% mark, except for 2014 when this figure climbed to 17%. Similarly, the percentage of bonds issued to fund investment remained relatively low, with an average of 10% over the period observed.

Companies in emerging markets have relied more heavily on capital markets...

In Chapter 2, it was shown that especially after the financial crisis, emerging market companies' operating cash flow has fallen short of their investment needs. To finance the gap, these companies had to depend heavily on external finance. Figure 7.7 reports that non-financial companies in emerging market economies remarkably increased their use of capital market-based financing, from USD 73 billion in 2000 to USD 458 billion in 2014. The number of companies that raised funds has also significantly increased over the same period.

Chinese companies represent by far the largest increase in both absolute and relative terms among emerging market companies. From a nascent corporate bond market prior to 2008, Chinese issuers have during the last four years raised an average of almost USD 125 billion. This represents 42% of the total amount raised by non-financial companies in emerging market economies. Total public equity fundraising by Chinese companies also reached a record level of USD 142 billion in 2014, which made up 66% of total public equity raised by non-financial, emerging market companies in the same year.

Figure 7.6. **Use of corporate bond proceeds by US non-financial companies**

Percentage of total issues

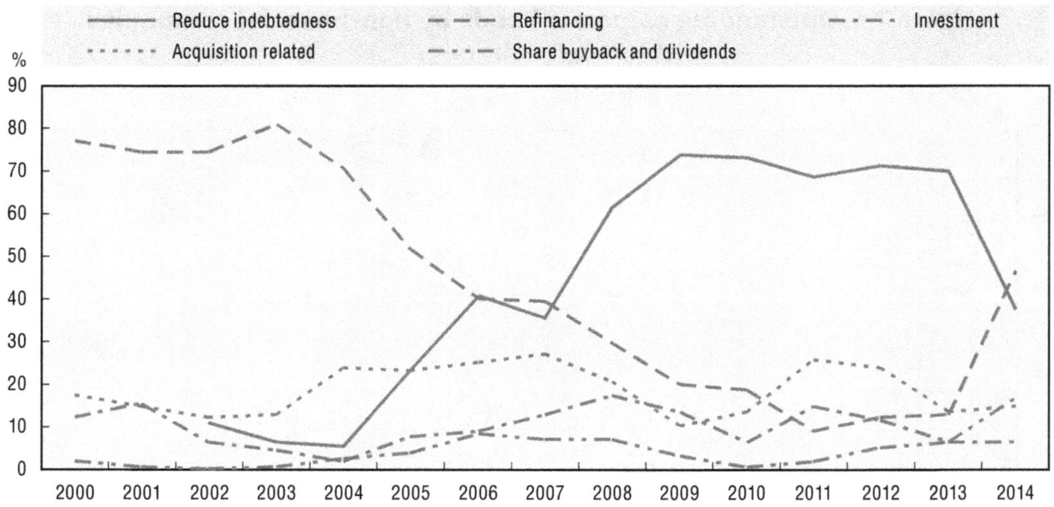

Source: Thomson Reuters, OECD calculations, see Annex 7.A1 for details.

StatLink http://dx.doi.org/10.1787/888933210117

Figure 7.7. **Capital market financing of non-financial, emerging market companies**

(2014, USD billion)

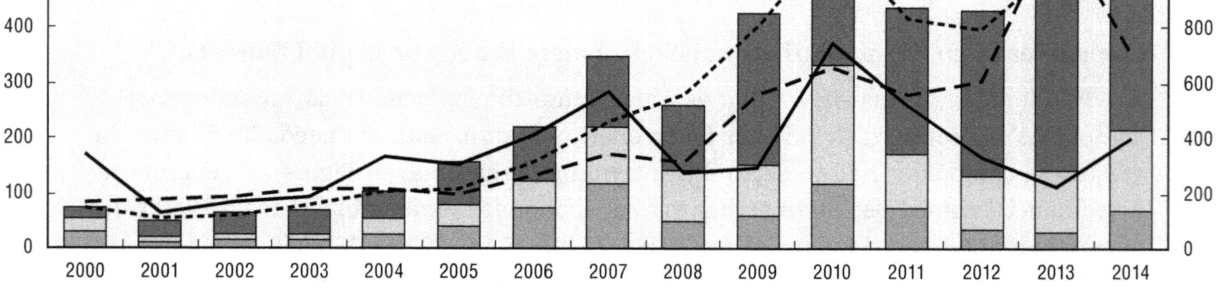

Note: The definition of secondary public offering or follow-on (SPO) covers all share issues of listed companies after an initial offer.

Source: Thomson Reuters, OECD calculations, see Annex 7.A1 for details.

StatLink http://dx.doi.org/10.1787/888933210129

An analysis of corporate bonds issued by non-financial companies in emerging markets at the breakdown of rating quality points to an increased risk appetite after the crisis. Although corporate bond issues by this group of companies were quite limited prior to the crisis, the amount of capital raised more than doubled from USD 118 billion in 2008 to USD 271 billion the next year. Furthermore, the share of non-investment grade bonds in the total amount raised increased from 3% in 2008, to 16% in 2014. However, there is some evidence of a cooling down of the emerging market corporate bond market. In 2014, total amount raised fell 39% from USD 396 billion to USD 243 billion.

Figure 7.8. **Corporate bond issuance by non-financial companies in emerging markets**
(2014, USD billion)

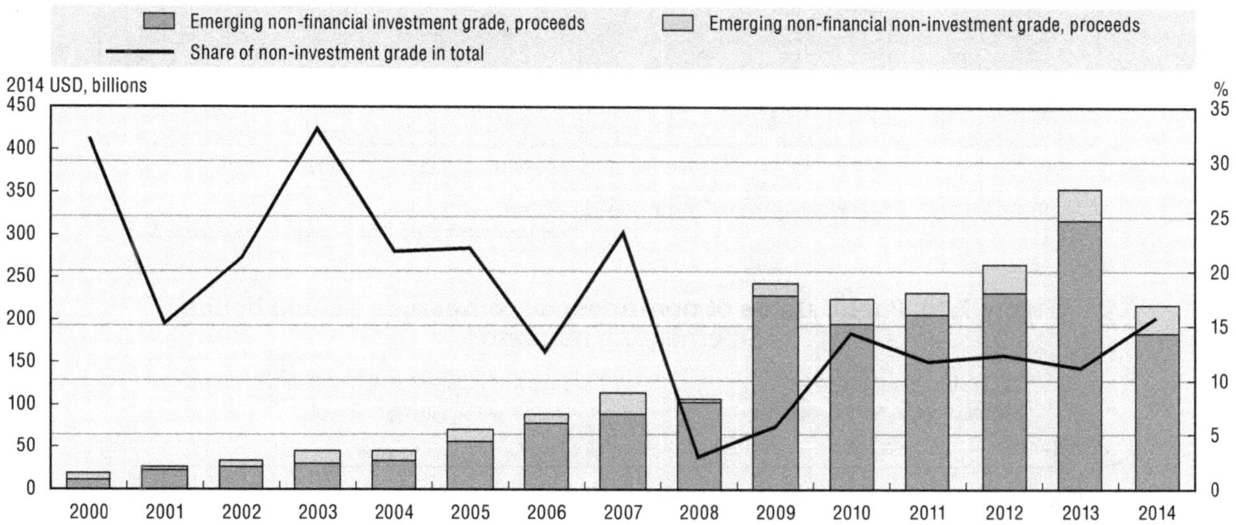

Source: Thomson Reuters, OECD calculations, see Annex 7.A1 for details.

StatLink http://dx.doi.org/10.1787/888933210138

...and their future refinancing needs will be high

Given the future refinancing needs of emerging market companies, a decreased investor interest in these markets may be problematic. Figure 7.9 shows that, as of end 2014, non-financial companies in emerging markets would, in the coming six years, have to pay down a total of USD 990 billion of bonds currently outstanding. This need for refinancing will be added to their need to find external finance for investment purpose. If the need for re-financing is coupled with a rise in interest rates, these companies will have to face a higher cost of borrowing.

Emerging market companies' dependence on external finance to fund their investment and to refinance their maturing bonds makes it even more important for these companies to have access to equity financing. Since equity capital has only a residual claim on corporate earnings, it can be used to finance investments with uncertain and long-term returns. In that respect, it contrasts with corporate bond financing, which provides funds to emerging market companies with an average maturity of 5.8 years. Furthermore, being a public company may in turn facilitate access to corporate bond markets. Figure 7.10 shows that between 60-70% of all corporate bond issuers in emerging markets are either public companies themselves or a subsidiary of a public company.

Figure 7.9. **Maturity profile of emerging market corporate bonds issued by non-financial firms**

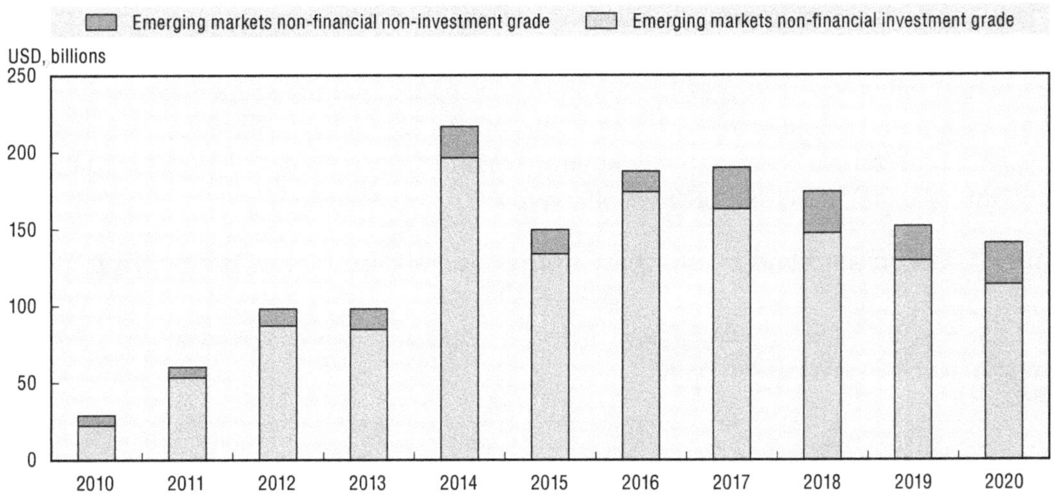

Source: Thomson Reuters, OECD calculations, see Annex 7.A1 for details.

StatLink http://dx.doi.org/10.1787/888933210141

Figure 7.10. **Public status of non-financial companies issuing bonds in emerging markets**

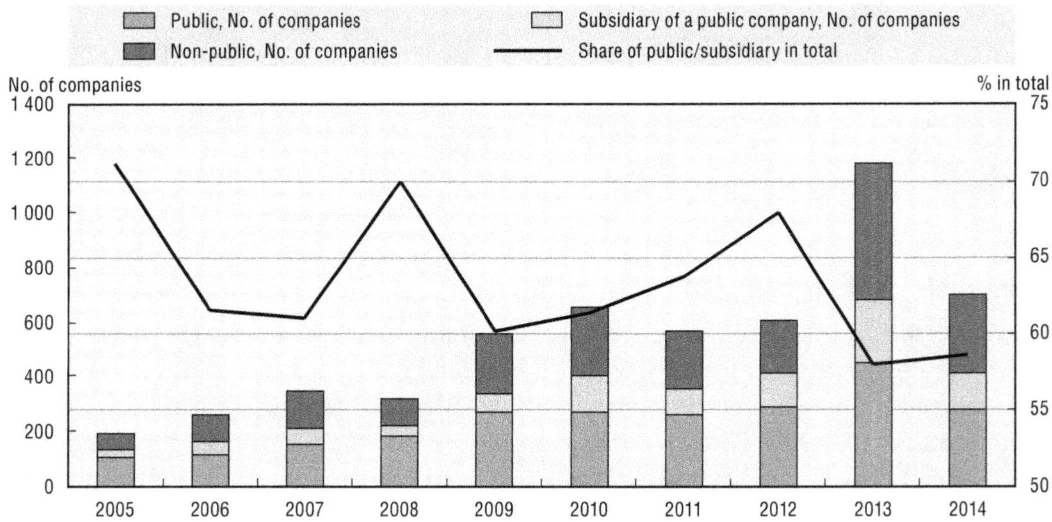

Source: Thomson Reuters, OECD calculations, see Annex 7.A1 for details.

StatLink http://dx.doi.org/10.1787/888933210152

Strengthening market infrastructure

Adequate dealer incentives are need to support markets for small company stocks

In contrast to the inherently liquid nature of large-cap stocks, small-cap stocks typically have an 'asymmetrical' order book where at any given point in time, there is not a large buyer to fulfil the order of a large seller (or vice versa). This asymmetric market structure generates the need for the existence of a market maker. The market maker can take the other side of the trade when no other willing buyer exists and assume the inventory risk with a view to sell the stocks at a premium when a willing buyer emerges. However, for the broker-dealers to play this market-making role, they should be adequately compensated for the costs incurred due to the capital they reserve, and the sales and equity research they carry out to support this function.

The reluctance of broker-dealers to make markets also reduces the time and capital they devote to equity research activity. Lacking the support of analysts in reducing the information asymmetry among their investors, small-cap companies' may see their cost of raising equity capital increase.

Figure 7.11. **The decline in small company initial public offerings in the United States**

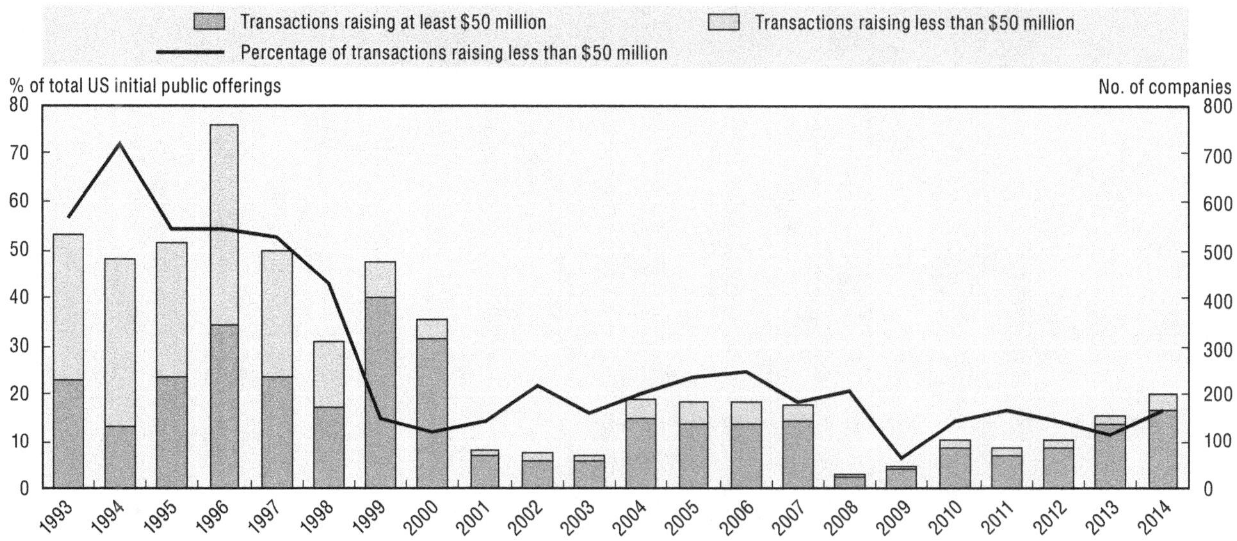

Source: Thomson Reuters, OECD calculations, see Annex 7.A1 for details.

StatLink http://dx.doi.org/10.1787/888933210162

Figure 7.11 plots the number of US companies tapping the IPO market at a breakdown of transaction size. In the 1993-1997 period, small companies constituted 58% of all IPOs on average. In the period that followed, small company IPOs dramatically declined and in 2014, they accounted for only 17% of the total.

As a response to the sharp fall in small company IPOs, the United States Congress enacted the JOBS (Jumpstart Our Business Startups Act) Act in 2012, aimed at easing the regulatory processes for small companies to go public and to remain listed. Concerns have been expressed from a variety of sources that decimalization, and the associated minimum price variations of one penny, may have had detrimental impact on the liquidity and trading of small-cap stocks. In addition, since summer 2014, the SEC has been preparing for the implementation of a targeted pilot programme that would widen the quoting and trading increments for certain small-cap stocks. The pilot programme's intention is to provide the means to further study and assess the impact of decimalisation on the market quality for small-cap stocks for the benefit of investors and issuers (SEC, 2014).

Although Weild et al. (2013) mainly focus on the United States, the authors also examine the IPO activity and average tick size in 25 additional jurisdictions. This comparative study reveals that countries whose markets offer higher aftermarket economic incentives (as measured by tick size as a percentage of share price) on small-cap stocks enjoy stronger IPO markets. Australia is one such country. Figure 7.12 shows that throughout the period,

Australia has sustained a strong small IPO market. In the period up to 2013, small company IPOs on average constituted 89% of the total number of IPOs. The decline observed in the last two years is largely attributable to a sharp increase in the number of large company IPOs, which reached a historical peak in 2014.

Figure 7.12. **Small initial public offering market in Australia**

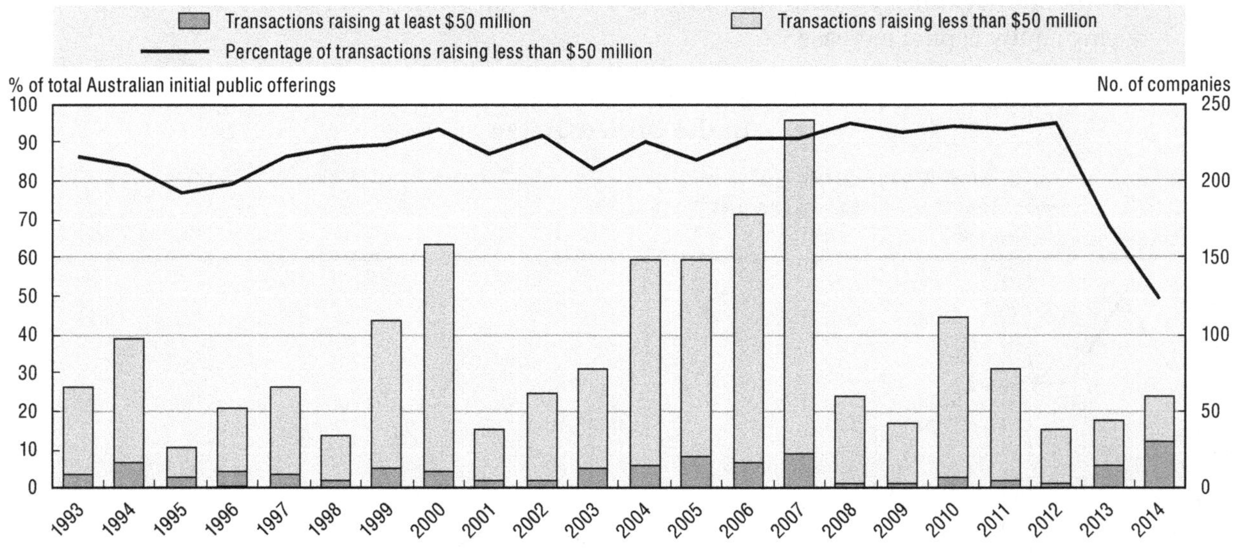

Source: Thomson Reuters, OECD calculations, see Annex 7.A1 for details.

StatLink http://dx.doi.org/10.1787/888933210178

Lack of support for small cap equites has affected the strategic behaviour of market participants

Given the lack of support for small-cap companies in equity markets, the IPO as an exit option for venture capital (VC) firms has fallen out of favour. Figure 7.13 presents the number of VC exits through an IPO as a percentage of the total in the United States stock markets[2] and the median offer amount when IPO is chosen as the exit strategy. Although prior to 1997, VCs exited their investments through an IPO 72% of the time, in the subsequent period this ratio sharply declined to 18%. Furthermore, the median offer amount, which ranged between USD 24-35 million in the first period, is USD 91 million as of 2013. These observations are consistent with the trend observed in Figure 7.11. Venture capital firms have to wait much longer now before they can cash out through an IPO and move to their next investment. While the time from first investment to IPO used to take around 4.5 years in the 1990s, it now takes 8.1 years.

Since the IPO route is blocked for many small companies that want to grow and for their venture capital investors, another exit alternative is to be acquired. However, the existence of the IPO market as a viable option allows companies to reach higher acquisition valuations.

The changes in market infrastructure have also caused institutional investors to adjust their investment strategies. Weild et al. (2013) argues that fundamentally-oriented institutions, which typically used to seek growth opportunities in micro-cap stocks, have left this segment in search of opportunities in more liquid larger cap stocks.

Figure 7.13. **Initial public offerings as a venture capital exit strategy**

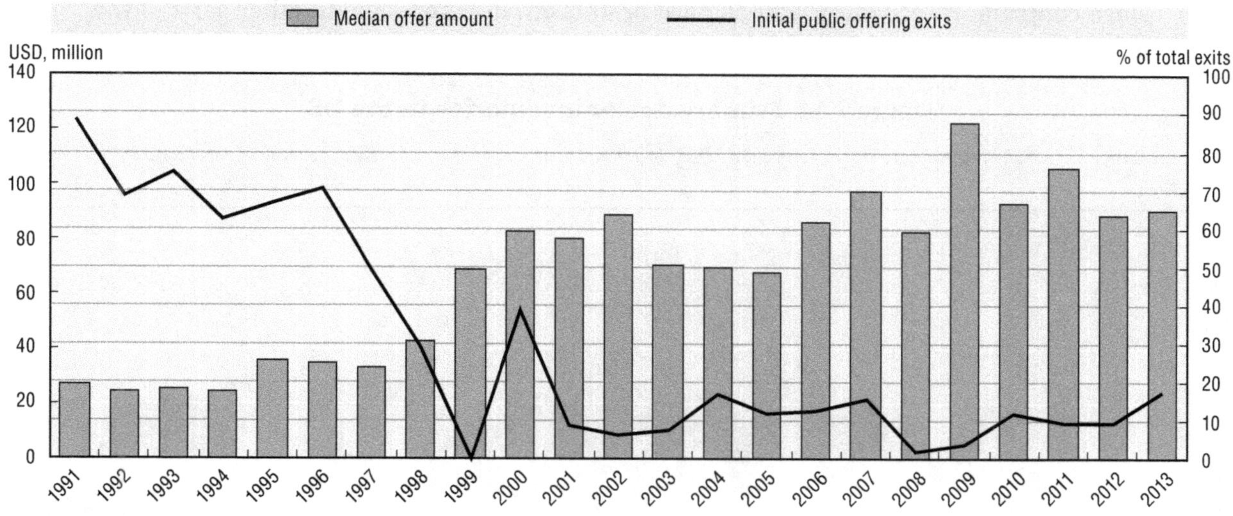

Source: 2014 National Venture Capital Yearbook

StatLink http://dx.doi.org/10.1787/888933210180

Dealer incentives have also worsened in corporate bond markets

In contrast to the secondary markets for public equity, which have long been transformed to electronic trading, over-the-counter trading still dominates the secondary market for corporate bonds. It is estimated that electronic trading accounts for only 24% of corporate bond trading volume in the US (TABB Group, 2014). The share of e-trading in European corporate bond markets is larger than its share in the US but is still rather low: As of 2012, this share stood at 29% of the total trading volume (McKinsey & Company and Greenwich Associates, 2013). On the other hand, in some emerging markets, institutional investors are required to execute all their trades on the exchanges. This requirement increases the share of electronic trading in those markets but has a limited impact on global volumes.

A primary reason for the continued dominance of dealers in the corporate bond market is the market's asymmetric structure. Given the large number of distinct corporate bonds outstanding at a given time, a counterparty willing to trade the same bond at the same amount is hard to find and a dealer has to take a market-making role. Therefore, as in the case with small-cap stocks, necessary conditions for this market model to work efficiently are the dealers' willingness and ability to play their intermediary role. Although dealers have traditionally been willing to bear the inventory risk in return for the profits they extract from bid-ask spreads, they have become increasingly reluctant in doing so since the recent financial crisis.

Data from Federal Reserve Bank of New York in Figure 7.14 demonstrate that primary dealers' inventories have experienced a sharp decline after the crisis. Compared to an estimated peak value of USD 38 billion in 2006,[3] dealers' corporate bond inventories are down to USD 7.7 billion as of February, 2015, corresponding to a remarkable 80% decline. This development may be partly explained by two regulatory changes; (1) Basel III that has discouraged banks from holding onto corporate bonds; and, (2) Volcker Rule that restricts banks in trading for their own accounts. It is unlikely that this trend is limited to the US since comparable regulatory actions have been taken in Europe and in other parts of the world.

Figure 7.14. **Primary dealer inventories in the US**

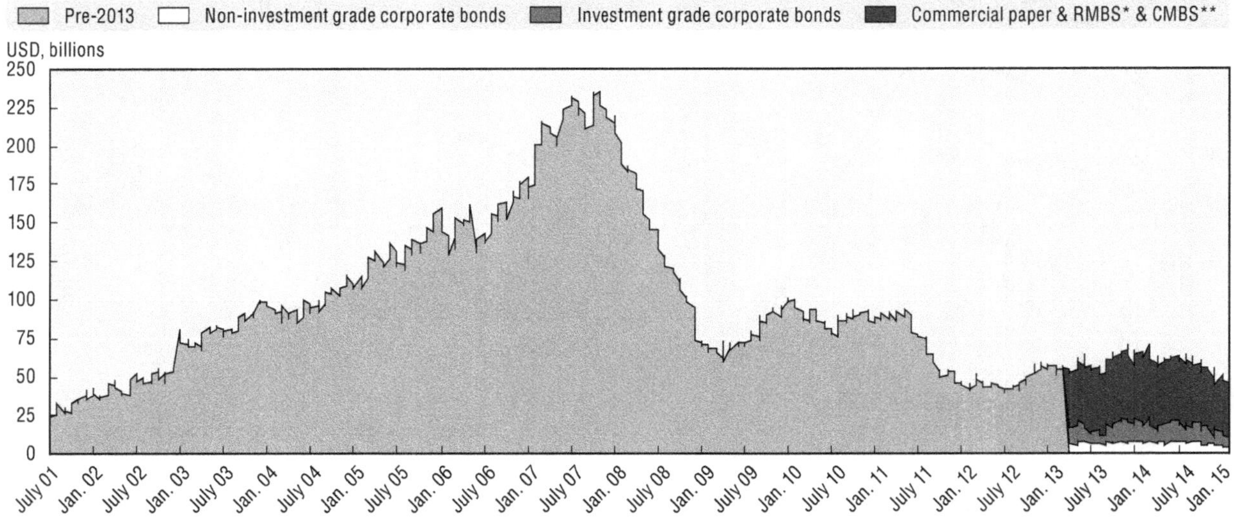

Note: *Residential mortgage-backed security, ** Commercial mortgage-backed security

Source: Federal Reserve Bank of New York

StatLink http://dx.doi.org/10.1787/888933219956

The decreasing interest in market making by dealers has encouraged new attempts to create electronic platforms for trading. It is expected that by 2016, 37% of corporate bond trading volume in the US will be executed via electronic trading platforms (TABB Group, 2014). This move from voice-based trading to electronic trading has benefited investors by a reduction in bid-ask spreads (Çelik et al., 2015).

If corporate bond dealers execute trades on an agency basis only or limit their market-making activities to bonds that are relatively liquid, then as a consequence, bond dealers would have little inventory risk. Dealers might reduce their support to the illiquid end of the corporate bond market, forcing the issuers of such bonds to offer more compensation to induce investors to hold their securities, increasing their cost of debt.

Market Axess Research (2013) shows that corporate bond liquidity monotonically increases with issue size. For instance, while the annualised turnover of issues with size less than USD 250 million is approximately 30%, that of issues with size greater than USD 1 billion exceeds 80%. It has been argued that a minimum issue size of USD 750 million is necessary to ensure future secondary liquidity of the issue (BlackRock, 2014).

As Figure 7.15 illustrates, issuance patterns have already evolved to large scale. The median issue size of bonds issued by US non-financial firms increased from USD 198 million in 2000 to USD 497 million in 2014. In contrast, issue size has remained relatively stable since the crisis, in other parts of the world. The recent increase in bond issue size in the US is quite similar to the trend observed in the US equity market at the end of 1990s. As a consequence, small and medium-sized companies, who cannot reach a critical issue size may either be excluded from important parts of the capital markets or see their cost of capital increase, as dealers will be reluctant to give market-making support for their securities.

Figure 7.15. **Average issue size, median issue amount**

(2014, USD million)

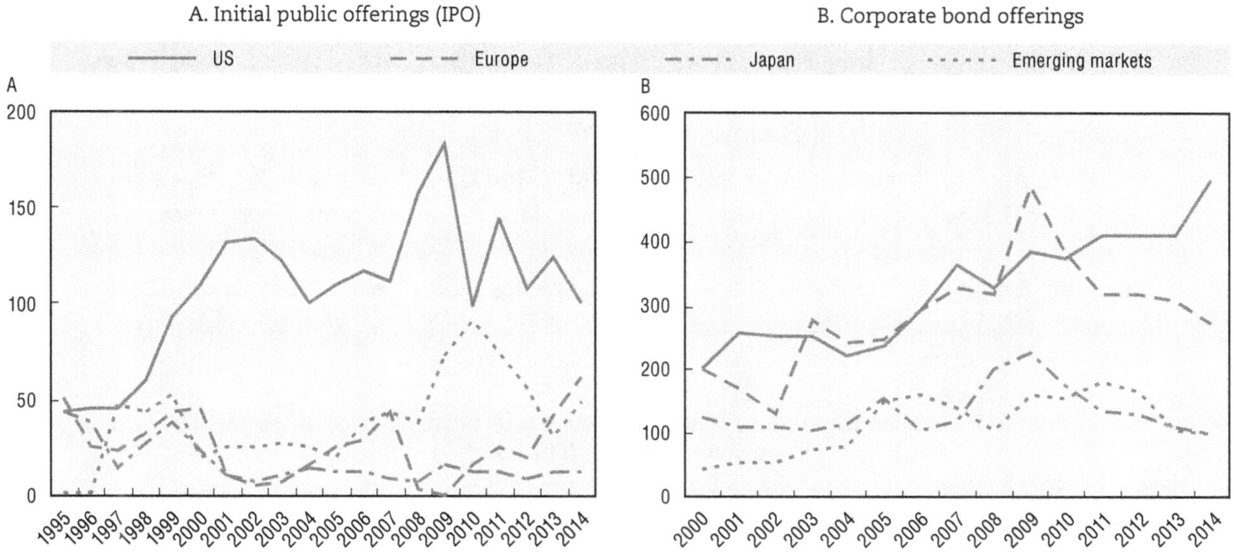

Source: Thomson Reuters, OECD calculations, see Annex 7.A1 for details.

StatLink http://dx.doi.org/10.1787/888933210198

Price discovery and the allocation of investments

The orderly functioning of secondary capital markets is critical both for capital formation and allocation. Companies' access to finance in primary markets through issuance of equity and bonds is therefore closely linked to the efficiency of the secondary market where these instruments are traded. Secondary markets also play a central role, through the price discovery mechanism, in the allocation of capital among different possible uses. An efficient and fair price discovery process is seen as a prerequisite for investors' confidence in the integrity of the markets, their incentives to identify and support long-term performance and ultimately for allocative efficiency.

Technological advancements and regulatory developments have led to profound changes in the functioning and structure of secondary markets over the last decades. The impact has been more pronounced for equity markets where traditional trading methods had been replaced by electronic trading already before 2000s. However, the growing importance of corporate bond markets and regulatory initiatives in the aftermath of the financial crisis, such as Basel III and the Volcker Rule, have given a new impetus to the discussion about the corporate bond market structure.

Fragmentation of markets raises important transparency issues

Since corporate bond markets are dominated by OTC trading, they are per definition highly fragmented, which makes it structurally difficult to find counterparties who are willing to trade a specific bond. Compared to 1990s, public equity markets are today also highly fragmented into traditional stock exchanges and non-exchange trading venues, such as alternative trading systems (ATS) in Canada and the United States, multi-lateral trading facilities (MTFs) in Europe and broker networks (IOSCO, 2011b). A high degree of fragmentation in security markets raises transparency issues - especially regarding the amount of trading in the dark.

Figure 7.16 illustrates that as of the third quarter of 2014, volume in the US equity market consisted of 55% of lit volume and 45% of dark volume. Dark volume consists of retail wholesalers (18%), dark ATS (15%), hidden exchanges (9%) and single dealer platforms (3%). TABB Group, providing these figures, defines dark pools as dark ATSs and single dealer platforms (Mostowfi, 2014). Overall, the US equity market is fragmented across 13 public exchanges and another 50 alternative venues (Foley, 2015).

Dark trading is relatively low in Europe and in the United Kingdom compared with the United States, but has been growing. In Europe, dark venues accounted for just over 6% of equity trading in October 2014. However, when data from all broker-run dark pools are included, that figure climbs to 11.2%, as estimated by Rosenblatt Securities (Detrixhe, 2014). Likewise, it is estimated that between 6 and 10% of UK equities by value are traded in the dark (Guthrie, 2014).

Figure 7.16. **Displayed and undisplayed trade volume in the US public equity markets (Q3 2014)**

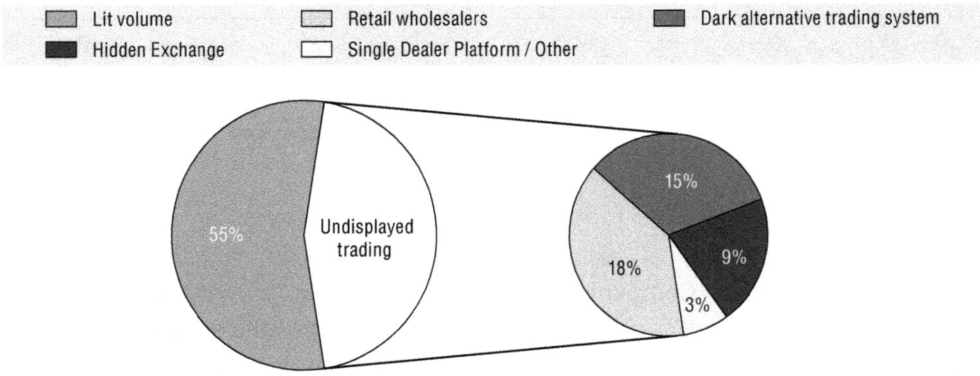

Source: TABB Group.

StatLink http://dx.doi.org/10.1787/888933210207

Dark pools have initially been established with the purpose of executing large trades without moving the price against the party placing the order by posting prices only after the deals are completed. However, in the recent years the share of dark pools in the total volume of equity trading has significantly increased. In the meanwhile, the size of trades executed in these venues decreased, moving them away from their original purpose. The average trade size in the top five dark pools in the United States was only 187 shares in May 2014 (McCranck, 2014).

Too much dark trading harms price discovery process and distorts allocative efficiency as the price observed in lit markets no longer reflects the true investor interest on the securities. Weaknesses in price discovery may also have a negative impact on secondary (follow-on) public equity offerings since the functioning of secondary public offering markets is closely linked to the efficiency of the price discovery process.

There have been some regulatory attempts to limit dark trading or cast some light on it. In Australia and Canada, for instance, trading in dark pools is now allowed only if it improves over the price offered on public exchanges. In June 2014, the US regulators started publishing aggregate information on trading volumes taking place on ATSs. However, this does not provide a complete picture since ATSs do not represent all dark trading venue volume (Bullock, 2014). On the other hand, in Europe, the directive on markets in financial instruments (MiFID 2) requires prices in dark pools to be determined with reference to a widely published price which is generated in another system and which is regarded by market participants as a reliable reference price. However, as lit pools are shrinking, the question arises as to where the breaking point is for using prices in lit pools as the reference for the large volume of trading taking place in dark venues. European Union, with rules to come into force in 2017, also intends to cap trading activity in dark venues and encourage orders to move back to lit exchanges. In this regard, each dark venue will be limited to 4% of EU trading in an individual stock, while overall activity on dark pools will be limited to 8% of total volume per stock. These caps will not apply to trades considered 'large-in-scale'.

High-frequency trading (HFT) adds to stock market liquidity but raises policy concerns

A major difference between secondary equity and bond markets is the level of trading activity observed in each. As Figure 7.17 illustrates, average daily trading volume in both the US and Japanese equity markets has always been much higher than that in the corporate bond markets. At year-end 2013, the total stock market capitalisation in the United States was USD 18 trillion and the total value of outstanding corporate bonds was USD 7.5 trillion. However, the average daily trading volume in the corporate bond market was around 20% of the average trading volume in the equity market.

An important, if not dominating, explanation for the dissimilarity in trading between corporate bond and equity markets is the inherent differences between the two instruments themselves. Another important factor behind the higher trade volume in equity markets is the dramatic growth of high-frequency trading (HFT) in these markets. Such trading practices do not play any important role in corporate bond markets.

The main features of HFT can be identified as proprietary trading using high-speed computers governed by sophisticated algorithms, applying co-location services in order to receive trading data just milliseconds before competitors, the use of individual data

Figure 7.17. **Average daily trade volume in the US and Japanese capital markets**

(USD billions)

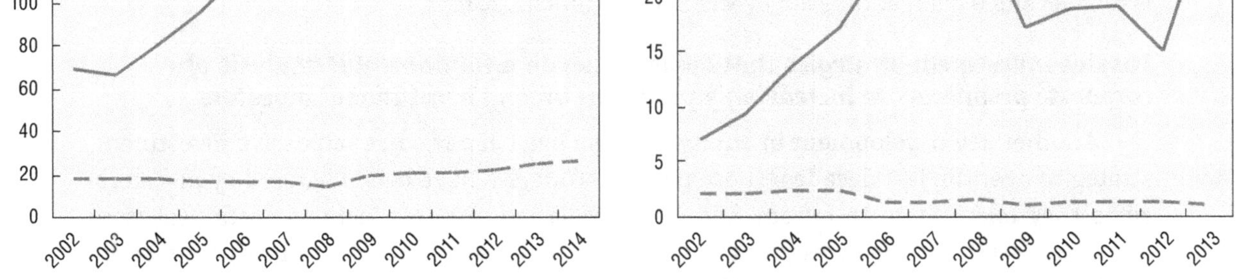

Notes: Data from the United States includes public and private placement (144A) corporate bonds. Japanese data include local currency straight bonds, asset-backed bonds, convertible bonds, bank debentures, and yen-denominated bonds issued by non-residents.

Source: The Securities Industry and Financial Markets Association (SIFMA), World Federation of Exchanges, Asian Development Bank (ADB) Asian Bonds Online

StatLink http://dx.doi.org/10.1787/888933210211

feeds that are offered for a fee by stock exchanges, very short timeframes for transactions, cancelation of orders shortly after submission and ending the trading day with a maximum flat position (SEC, 2010). A 2014 report by European Securities and Markets Authority (ESMA) reveals that in Europe HFT activity accounts for 76% of all orders, 49% of all trades and 43% of total value traded[4] (ESMA, 2014). With 48.5% of total equity volume, TABB Group estimates that the share HFT has in US equity markets is comparable to its share in Europe (Credit Suisse, 2014). The large share of HFT in equity markets has raised some policy concerns.

A common argument that HFT improves stock market liquidity and price discovery has been supported by a recent article by Boehmer et al. (2014), which investigates the effect of HFT in 42 equity markets. However, although the effect on liquidity is positive on average, the article finds that in the smallest tercile of stocks based on market capitalisation, price and volatility, greater HFT intensity actually reduces liquidity. Boehmer et al. (2014) also report that in terms of liquidity, HFT becomes less beneficial at times when market making is difficult.

From a corporate governance perspective, HFT can be seen as an investment strategy with a very short-term focus. The ambition is not to assess and trade on genuine information concerning the long-term performance of any individual company. Rather, the strategy is heavily based on short-term arbitrage opportunities that are often obtained by unique and fast access to trading information. Furthermore, the profits of HFT firms come at the expense of, among others, those who have spent resources to obtain information on firm fundamentals. If the returns to investing in information are reduced due to higher HFT activity and so investors that focus on fundamental analysis are crowded out, then equity prices will become less informative. Consequently, resource allocation will not be as efficient as it otherwise would (Stiglitz, 2014). In addition, it is argued that the crowding out of investors with a long-term focus makes the use of analyst reports superfluous especially for smaller companies, increasing the probability of mispricing and undermining the willingness of small companies to enter the public equity market (Doidge et al., 2011).

Another perception arising from HFT is fairness regarding the use of market data, since high-frequency traders generally make use of dedicated data feeds, which provide them with trading information ahead of the general public (Linton and O'Hara, 2011). In a recent study by Rogers, Skinner and Zechman (2014), it has been shown that such data advantage exists even in access to company filings. The study found that subscribers to the direct access feeds of companies' SEC filings received insider trading filings around 10 seconds before their public dissemination, a relatively long time in the HFT world. This issue has since been addressed by the SEC (Patterson, 2014).

Passive investment strategies that do not focus on a fundamental analysis of corporate prospects are increasingly prevalent among institutional investors

Another key development in equity markets has been the rise of passive investment strategies over the last decades. These passive strategies have been favoured by investors since they allow them to refrain from intermediation and transactions costs (Isaksson and Çelik, 2013). Passive investment strategies have also been prevalent in corporate bond markets since the main characteristics of a standard corporate bond with a par value that is paid back at maturity and regular payments up to the maturity of the bond makes it a suitable instrument for such strategies.

With the development of US exchange-traded funds (ETFs) in the mid-1990s, passive investment was taken to yet another level. These instruments were designed to be more tax-efficient, since they avoid capital gain taxes on the underlying assets being traded, until the ETF itself is bought or sold. Since their creation, ETFs have gained popularity as alternative investment vehicles for both passive and active investment strategies. They carry certain characteristics of mutual funds but are also tradable like shares on exchanges. Figure 7.18 presents the persistent and steep increase in the total market value of assets under ETFs, growing dramatically from USD 416 billion in 2005 up to USD 2.5 trillion in 2014.

Figure 7.18. **Global exchange-traded fund assets**

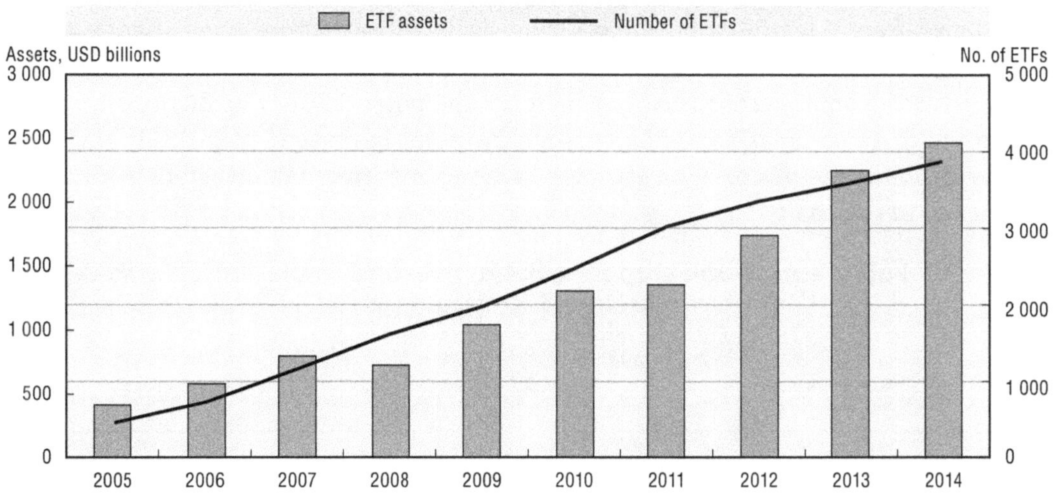

Source: ETFGI.

StatLink http://dx.doi.org/10.1787/888933210226

The investment chain has become larger and more complex

Figure 7.19 shows the distribution of outstanding public equity and corporate bonds across different investor categories in the United States, Japan and the United Kingdom as of year-end 2013. In all three countries, retail investors' share in corporate bond holdings is lower than their share in equity. While retail investors still play a relatively important role in the United States by holding 37% of outstanding public equity and 19% of outstanding corporate bonds, it is still a dramatic decrease compared to the mid-1960s when they held 84% of all public equity. Over the same period, direct shareholdings by retail investors in the United Kingdom have decreased from 54% to 11%.

Since flow of funds data used in the figure do not identify foreign investors' categories, which account for a significant portion of holdings in most markets, it is difficult to establish the total holdings of institutional investors at the national level. When only domestic investors are taken into account, traditional institutional investors (defined as pension funds, insurance companies and investment funds) together hold 36% of outstanding public equity and 44% of corporate bonds in the United States.

Since 2000, traditional institutional investors in OECD economies have more than doubled their total assets under management from USD 36 trillion in 2000 to USD 76 trillion in 2012. This trend represents a long-term structural shift in ownership of listed companies from direct ownership to intermediary ownership. This shift has been accompanied by a surge in new types of intermediary investors and investment vehicles, an increase in outsourcing of ownership and asset management functions, the emergence of new service providers and trading practices. Taken together, these developments have resulted in a longer and increasingly complex investment chain between savers and companies where different actors have different incentives in terms of investment strategies, business models and corporate governance priorities (Çelik and Isaksson, 2013).

In particular, the surge in outsourcing of asset management to external asset managers by large asset owners increases the risk that the ultimate savers' objectives become misaligned. Institutional investors have different business models, which arise from their different features and choices, such as liability structure, investment strategy, regulatory environment and fee structure. For instance, a business model of an asset manager with a short-term focus may increase the potential for misaligned incentives for long-term value creation. While outsourcing asset management in itself lengthens the investment chain, cross investments among institutional investors add to the complexity of the chain.

Figure 7.19. **Public equity and corporate bond investors in the United States, Japan and the United Kingdom (2013)**

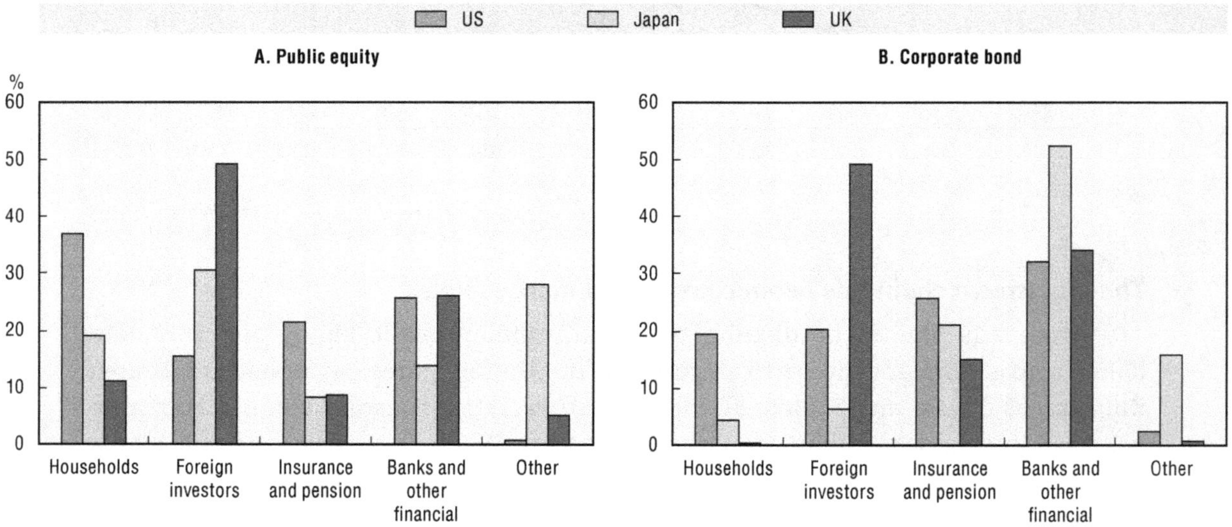

Notes: Equity data: The category Bank and other financial include mutual and exchange traded funds. Bond data: United States data include United States financial and non-financial corporate bonds and non-United States financial and non-financial corporate bonds. Japan data include external securities issued by Japan residents. United Kingdom data include long-term debt securities issued by United Kingdom monetary financial institutions (MFIs) and other United Kingdom residents.

Source: United States, Financial Accounts, Federal Reserve; Japan, Flow of Funds, Bank of Japan; United Kingdom, The Blue Book, Office for National Statistics.

StatLink http://dx.doi.org/10.1787/888933210230

Conclusions

Since 2000, the ecosystem of corporate finance has significantly changed in a number of important ways. In the wake of the financial crisis, bank lending to non-financial corporation has been in retreat in many advanced economies. For instance, in Europe it dropped by almost 15% (Çelik et al., 2015). At the same time, the fall in corporate bond rates has made it possible for some firms to replace bank borrowing by issuing bonds. The trend is particularly marked for non-financial firms, which in 2014 raised USD 1.6 trillion.

However, many companies have abandoned or stayed away from the stock market. The annual average number of new listings was 1 084 between 1995 and 2000. It dropped to 768 in the period 2001-2007, falling further to only 408 per year since 2008.

This has been partly due to the fact that the hurdle for smaller companies to access public equity financing has been raised. In real terms, the average size of public equity issues by non-financial US companies has doubled since the mid-1990s. This may partly reflect corporate governance reporting and compliance costs, but it also raises some concerns about the functioning of public equity markets. Further study is necessary to determine whether any regulatory initiatives have contributed to a decrease in the number of small size companies that use public equity markets to raise capital.

Stock exchanges have become profit maximising, publicly listed companies in their own right over the last 15 years. There has also been significant consolidation through mergers, both at national and international level.

Another important development is the growing size and importance of institutional investors, which have more than doubled their total assets under management since 2000. This has been accompanied by a surge in the variety of investors, asset managers, service providers and investment strategies. The most immediate effect is a longer and increasingly complex 'investment chain' where key actors may have different incentives. These incentives may create an environment in which investors and corporations adopt a short-term focus rather than a long-term value creation perspective. Therefore, it is crucial the policy framework supports sound, well-aligned incentives at every link in the investment chain.

Notes

1. The free cash flow hypothesis (Jensen, 1986) suggests that payouts to shareholders and an effective market for corporate control can serve to discipline managers by minimizing the cash at their disposal and so to reduce the opportunity for management to invest in value-destroying projects and to undertake excessive spending that can be better used in other parts of the economy. The signalling theory, on the other hand, argues that dividends and repurchases can be used to convey positive information known to managers but not known to investors in general (Miller and Rock, 1984). Based on payout data from 1972 to 2000, Grullon and Michaely (2002) put forth the substitution hypothesis, whereby companies use buybacks as a close substitute for dividends. Another motivation for buybacks that has been suggested in the literature is to avoid or to make up for the dilution that arises from the exercise of employee stock options (Kahle, 2002). Survey evidence from Brav et al. (2005) shows that managers time the market and accelerate buybacks when they believe that their stock is undervalued. The survey also reveals that managers are likely to carry out buybacks when they have run out of profitable investment strategies, when their stock's float is inadequate or when it is needed to offset for stock dilution.
2. The total number of VC exits corresponds to the sum of IPO exits and M&A exits. IPO exits are those done in the United States stock exchanges/markets with at least one United States domiciled VC investor. M&A exits are completed secondary sales and trade sales where the company was domiciled in the United States and had at least one US domiciled VC investor.
3. Note that prior to April 2013, The US Federal Reserve did not provide the primary dealer inventory data at the breakdown of corporate and non-corporate bonds. However, Goldman Sachs analysts have reverse engineered the longer term trend with respect to corporate bond inventories based on SEC filings and found that dealer corporate bond inventories reached their peak at about USD 38 billion in 2006 (Alloway, 2013).

4. ESMA estimates HFT activity under two different methodologies: (i) a direct approach based on the identification of HFT firms according to their primary business or the types of algorithms they use, and ii) an indirect approach based on statistics such as lifetime of orders or order-to-trade ratio. The figures that we report are the ones calculated with the latter methodology. The first methodology provides a lower bound to HFT activity, as it does not capture HFT activity by investment banks.

References

Alloway, T. and A. Massoudi (2013), "ETFs Under Scrutiny in Market Turbulence", *Financial Times*, 27 June.

Blackrock (2014), "Corporate Bond Market Structure: The Time for Reform is Now", BlackRock Investment Institute, September.

Blundell-Wignall, Adrian and Caroline Roulet (2015), "Infrastructure versus other investments in the global economy and stagnation hypotheses: What do company data tell us?", *OECD Journal: Financial Market Trends*. DOI: *http://dx.doi.org/10.1787/fmt-2014-5js4sbd025d6.*

Boehmer, E., K.Y.L. Fong, and J. Wu (2014), "International Evidence on Algorithmic Trading", *http://ssrn.com/abstract=2022034.*

Brav, A., J.R. Graham, C.R. Harvey, and R. Michaely (2005), "Payout Policy in the 21st Century", *Journal of Financial Economics*, Vol. 77, No. 3, pp. 483–527.

Bullock, N. (201), "Financial Regulators Probe Dark Pools", *Financial Times*, 16 September.

Çelik, S. and M. Isaksson (2013), "Institutional Investors as Owners: Who Are They and What Do They Do?", *OECD Corporate Governance Working Papers*, No. 11, OECD Publishing. *http://dx.doi.org/10.1787/5k3v1dvmfk42-en.*

Çelik, S., G. Demirtaş and M. Isaksson (2015), "Corporate Bonds, Bondholders and Corporate Governance", OECD Corporate Governance Working Papers, No. 16, OECD Publishing. *http://dx.doi.org/10.1787/5js69lj4hvnw-en.*

Cheng, Y., J. Harford, and T. Zhang (2010), "Bonus-driven Repurchases", *Working paper*, *https://oupd.ou.edu/dam/price/Finance/CFS/paper/pdf/Bonus_driven%20_Repurchases.pdf.*

Credit Suisse (2014), *Equity Research Report*, 22 April.

Detrixhe, J. (2014), "Dark-Pool Trading Sets Records in Europe as Rules Change", *Bloomberg*, 3 December, *http://www.bloomberg.com/news/articles/2014-12-03/dark-pool-trading-sets-records-in-europe-as-rules-change.*

Doidge, C., G.A. Karolyi and R.M. Stulz (2011), "The U.S. Left Behind: The Rise of IPO Activity Around the World", *National Bureau of Economic Research Working Paper*, No. 16 916.

ESMA (2014), "High-frequency Trading Activity in EU Equity Markets", *http://www.esma.europa.eu/system/files/esma20141_-_hft_activity_in_eu_equity_markets.pdf.*

Foley, S. (2015), "Big Fund Managers Form New Dark Pool Equity Trading Volume", *Financial Times*, 19 January.

Grullon, G., and R. Michaely (2002), "Dividends, Share Repurchases, and the Substitution Hypothesis", *The Journal of Finance*, Vol. 57, No. 4, pp. 1649-1684.

Guthrie, J. (2014), "Big Bourses Take on Dark Pool Competitors", *Financial Times*, 9 November.

IOSCO (2011a), "Development of Corporate Bond Markets in the Emerging Markets", Emerging Markets Committee of the International Organization of Securities Commission in Colloboration with the World Bank Group, IOSCO, Madrid.

IOSCO (2011b), Regulatory Issues Raised by the Impact of Technological Changes on Market Integrity and Efficiency, IOSCO, Madrid, *www.iosco.org/library/pubdocs/pdf/IOSCOPD361.pdf.*

Isaksson, M. and S. Çelik (2013), "Who Cares? Corporate Governance in Today's Equity Markets", *OECD Corporate Governance Working Papers*, No. 8, OECD Publishing. *http://dx.doi.org/10.1787/5k47zw5kdnmp-en*

Jensen, M.C. (1986), "Agency Cost of Free Cash Flow, Corporate Finance and Takeovers", *American Economic Review*, Vol. 76, No. 2, pp. 323-329.

Kahle, K. (2002), "When a Buyback isn't a Buyback: Open Market Repurchases and Employee Options", *Journal of Financial Economics*, Vol. 63, No. 2, pp. 235–261.

Lazonick, W. (2014), "Profits without Prosperity", *Harvard Business Review*, September 2014, *https://hbr.org/2014/09/profits-without-prosperity*.

Linton, O. and M. O'Hara (2011), "The Impact of Computer Trading on Liquidity, Price Efficiency/Discovery and Transaction Costs", The Future of Computer Trading in Financial Markets, Working Paper, Foresight, London, *www.bis.gov.uk/assets/foresight/docs/computer-trading/11-1276-the-future-of-computer- trading-in-financial-markets.pdf*.

MarketAxess Research (2013), "Bond Turnover: The Long and Short of It", 5 September, *http://www.marketaxess.com/research/blog/single.php?permalink=bond-turnover-the-long-and-short-of-it-2013-09-05*.

Marquardt, C., C. Tan, and S.M. Young (2011), "Accelerated Share Repurchases, Bonus Compensation, and CEO Horizons", *2012 Financial Markets & Corporate Governance Conference*, *http://ssrn.com/abstract=1972680*.

McCranck, J. (2014), "Report Sheds Light on Activity in the U.S. Dark Pool Trading", *Reuters*, 2 June.

McKinsey & Company and Greenwich Associates (2013), "Corporate Bond E-Trading: Same Game, New Playing Field".

Miller, M.H. and K. Rock (1985), "Dividend Policy under Asymmetric Information", *The Journal of Finance*, Vol. 40, No. 4, pp. 1031-1051.

Mostowfi, S. (2014), "US Equity Market Structure: Q3-2014 TABB Equity Digest", 4 December, *http://www.tabbgroup.com/PublicationDetail.aspx?PublicationID=1597*.

National Venture Capital Association (2014), Yearbook 2014, prepared by Thomson Reuters.

Patterson, S. (2014) "Lawmakers Expressed Concerns About System That Can Give an Edge to Rapid-Fire Traders", *The Wall Street Journal* 26 December 2014. Available from : *http://www.wsj.com/articles/sec-plans-to-fix-flaw-in-electronic-distribution-system-1419621428*.

Ramaswamy, S. (2011), "Market Structures and Systemic Risks of Exchange-Traded Funds", *BIS Working Papers*, No. 343.

Rogers, J.L., D.J. Skinner, and S.L.C. Zechman (2014), "Run EDGAR Run: SEC Dissemination in a High-Frequency World", *Chicago Booth Research Paper*, No. 14-36, *http://ssrn.com/abstract=2513350*.

Securities and Exchange Commission (SEC) (2010), "Concept Release on Equity Market Structure", SEC, Washington, DC.

Securities and Exchange Commission (SEC) (2014), "SEC Announces Pilot Plan to Assess Stock Market Tick Size Impact for Smaller Companies", SEC, Washington, DC, SEC Release No. 34-72460, available at *http://www.sec.gov/rules/other/2014/34-72460.pdf*.

Stiglitz, J.E. (2014), "Tapping the Brakes: Are Less Active Markets Safer and Better for the Economy?", *Presented at the Federal Reserve Bank of Atlanta*, 15 April, *https://www0.gsb.columbia.edu/faculty/jstiglitz/download/papers/2014_Tapping_Brakes_pub.pdf*.

TABB Group (2014), "TABB Estimates 37% of US Corporate Bond Market will be Executed Electronically by 2016, up from 24% Today", 29 January, *http://www.businesswire.com/news/home/20140129006145/en*.

Weild, D., E. Kim and L. Newport (2013), "Making Stock Markets Work to Support Economic Growth: Implications for Governments, Regulators, Stock Exchanges, Corporate Issuers and their Investors", *OECD Corporate Governance Working Papers*, No. 10, OECD Publishing.

Young, S., and J. Yang (2011), "Stock Repurchases and Executive Compensation Contract Design: The Role of Earnings Per Share Performance Conditions", *The Accounting Review*, Vol. 86, No. 2, pp. 703-733.

ANNEX 7.A1

Methodology for data collection and analysis

Public equity data

Initial public offering (IPO) and secondary public offering (SPO) data are based on original OECD calculations using data obtained from Thomson Reuters Thomson One New Issues Database. IPO and SPO data exclude Real Estate Investment Trusts (REITs), closed-investment funds, over-the-counter (OTC) markets and unit/trust offerings.

The IPOs of companies that were listed in an organised market after the IPO but currently traded in OTC markets are included. SPO covers all share issues of listed companies after an IPO. The country breakdown was carried out based on the domicile country of the issuer. Issuance amounts are in 2014 USD adjusted by US GDP deflator.

Corporate bond data

Corporate bond data are based on original OECD calculations using data obtained from Thomson Reuters Thomson One New Issues Database. Primary corporate bond data exclude sukuk bonds, convertible bonds, preferred shares and bonds with an original maturity less than 1 year or an issue size less than USD 1 million. Tranches under the same bond package are counted as a single issue.

Outstanding amounts are calculated based on annual net issuance amounts. Actual call date data obtained from Bloomberg were used in net issuance calculations. The country breakdown was carried out based on the domicile country of the issuer. Issuance amounts are in 2014 USD adjusted by US GDP deflator.

Activism data

Data on campaigns initiated by activist investors are obtained from the SharkRepellent.net through Factset database. Factset tracks activist campaigns that have targeted the companies incorporated in the US. Activist campaigns against non-US incorporated companies are only tracked if the investor is part of the SharkWatch50 list, which is a compilation of 50 significant activist investors identified by the database.

Campaigns related to investment funds, trusts, REITs and SPACs and campaigns with a missing synopsis field have been excluded from the analysis. The final sample covers 3,928 activist campaigns announced over the period 2003 to 2014. To identify buyback- and dividend-related campaigns and the subsequent company reaction, the synopsis fields of the campaigns whose synopsis includes one or more of the payout-related keywords were read. Unless the response of the company to the activist campaign is explicitly stated in the synopsis, the subsequent firm action is classified as "unrecorded".

ANNEX 7.A2

Statistical tables and supplementary data

Table 7.A2.1. **Corporate bonds issuance**

	USD billion														
	2000	2001	2002	2003	2004	2005	2006	2007	2008	2009	2010	2011	2012	2013	2014
World	**2,044**	**2,327**	**1,976**	**2,710**	**2,820**	**2,803**	**3,591**	**3,532**	**2,800**	**3,133**	**3,130**	**3,059**	**3,556**	**3,463**	**3,580**
Non-financial	716	1,037	708	854	719	667	928	992	900	1,615	1,326	1,339	1,714	1,805	1,613
Financial	1,328	1,290	1,268	1,855	2,101	2,136	2,663	2,539	1,901	1,518	1,804	1,720	1,842	1,659	1,967
Investment grade	1,959	2,199	1,875	2,496	2,593	2,620	3,335	3,275	2,739	2,885	2,702	2,708	3,068	2,896	3,012
High yield	85	128	102	214	227	183	256	256	61	248	428	351	488	567	568
Advanced economies	**1,985**	**2,233**	**1,895**	**2,586**	**2,683**	**2,614**	**3,306**	**3,212**	**2,580**	**2,671**	**2,645**	**2,542**	**2,929**	**2,794**	**3,026**
Non-financial	694	992	667	803	668	586	827	860	779	1,342	1,070	1,073	1,417	1,403	1,365
Financial	1,291	1,241	1,228	1,783	2,015	2,028	2,479	2,353	1,800	1,329	1,575	1,469	1,512	1,391	1,661
Investment grade	1,912	2,114	1,805	2,397	2,477	2,470	3,086	3,014	2,529	2,446	2,280	2,241	2,509	2,298	2,526
High yield	73	119	91	189	206	144	220	198	51	225	365	300	420	497	501
Emerging markets	**59**	**93**	**81**	**124**	**138**	**189**	**285**	**319**	**221**	**462**	**486**	**517**	**627**	**669**	**553**
Non-financial	23	44	41	52	51	81	102	133	120	273	256	266	296	401	247
Financial	36	49	41	72	86	108	183	187	101	189	229	251	330	268	306
Investment grade	47	84	70	99	116	150	249	261	211	439	422	467	560	598	486
High yield	12	9	11	25	22	39	36	58	10	23	63	51	67	71	67
United States	**812**	**1,001**	**793**	**916**	**889**	**791**	**1,095**	**1,227**	**742**	**743**	**799**	**764**	**1,000**	**1,060**	**1,066**
Non-financial	304	526	350	400	326	264	387	448	346	502	538	517	697	709	677
Financial	508	475	443	516	564	527	708	779	396	241	261	247	304	351	389
Investment grade	755	897	714	760	740	681	943	1,072	702	590	526	554	686	763	805
High yield	57	104	79	156	149	111	152	155	40	153	272	210	315	298	261
Europe	**882**	**893**	**804**	**1,290**	**1,418**	**1,428**	**1,783**	**1,564**	**1,359**	**1,410**	**1,257**	**1,196**	**1,266**	**1,110**	**1,347**
Non-financial	263	283	191	270	213	197	313	273	286	612	311	312	463	433	464
Financial	620	610	613	1,020	1,204	1,232	1,470	1,291	1,073	798	946	883	802	677	883
Investment grade	873	886	798	1,266	1,381	1,404	1,732	1,534	1,350	1,351	1,192	1,127	1,190	951	1,136
High yield	10	7	7	25	37	24	50	30	9	59	65	69	75	160	211
OECD Total	**1,973**	**2,222**	**1,892**	**2,561**	**2,675**	**2,607**	**3,304**	**3,211**	**2,567**	**2,666**	**2,632**	**2,536**	**2,896**	**2,791**	**3,005**
Non-financial	685	984	669	799	672	590	829	868	778	1,347	1,076	1,081	1,412	1,413	1,380
Financial	1,288	1,238	1,222	1,762	2,003	2,017	2,475	2,343	1,789	1,319	1,556	1,455	1,483	1,378	1,625
Investment grade	1,897	2,103	1,799	2,372	2,472	2,465	3,084	3,014	2,519	2,438	2,265	2,235	2,467	2,299	2,502
High yield	76	120	93	189	203	142	220	197	48	228	367	301	428	493	503

Notes: Corporate bonds issuance data are obtained from Thomson Reuters New Issues Database. Data exclude convertible bonds, preferred shares, sukuk bonds and bonds with an original maturity less than 1 year or an issue size less than USD 1 million. The country breakdown was carried out based on the domicile country of the issuer. Issuance amounts are in 2014 USD adjusted by US GDP deflator.

Source: Thomson Reuters, Bloomberg, OECD calculations.

StatLink http://dx.doi.org/10.1787/888933210506

Table 7.A2.2. **Initial public offering issuance**

USD billion

	2000	2001	2002	2003	2004	2005	2006	2007	2008	2009	2010	2011	2012	2013	2014
World	**279**	**120**	**83**	**66**	**154**	**181**	**274**	**319**	**104**	**118**	**287**	**153**	**102**	**138**	**225**
Non-financial	260	95	60	44	128	147	203	247	73	97	202	138	92	112	184
Financial	20	26	23	22	26	34	70	72	31	21	85	16	10	26	41
Advanced economies	**241**	**107**	**62**	**43**	**120**	**119**	**147**	**144**	**45**	**37**	**128**	**72**	**59**	**91**	**141**
Non-financial	222	82	42	31	100	104	124	125	22	30	81	64	54	80	112
Financial	19	25	20	12	20	15	23	19	23	6	47	8	4	12	29
Emerging markets	**38**	**13**	**21**	**23**	**34**	**62**	**127**	**176**	**58**	**81**	**158**	**81**	**44**	**46**	**84**
Non-financial	37	13	18	13	28	43	80	122	51	67	121	74	38	32	72
Financial	1	0	4	10	6	19	47	53	7	14	38	7	6	14	12
United States	**80**	**47**	**27**	**13**	**43**	**37**	**38**	**34**	**28**	**17**	**36**	**28**	**34**	**47**	**46**
Non-financial	73	37	15	10	32	31	31	32	7	15	32	26	33	43	30
Financial	7	10	12	3	10	6	6	2	22	2	4	2	2	4	16
Europe	**118**	**43**	**19**	**9**	**40**	**56**	**73**	**77**	**10**	**4**	**24**	**29**	**10**	**25**	**57**
Non-financial	110	29	19	6	36	50	61	68	9	2	22	23	7	19	45
Financial	7	14	1	3	4	6	12	10	1	2	2	6	2	6	12
OECD Total	**228**	**105**	**55**	**40**	**117**	**121**	**143**	**139**	**49**	**32**	**106**	**69**	**60**	**93**	**139**
Non-financial	210	80	39	28	94	105	120	118	25	27	78	61	55	82	110
Financial	18	25	16	12	22	16	23	22	24	5	28	8	5	11	29

Notes: Initial public offering (IPO) data are obtained from Thomson Reuters New Issues Database. Data exclude Real Estate Investment Trusts (REITs), closed-investment funds, over-the-counter (OTC) markets and unit/trust offerings. The IPOs of companies that were listed in an organised market after the IPO but currently traded in OTC markets are included. The country breakdown was carried out based on the domicile country of the issuer. Issuance amounts are in 2014 USD adjusted by US GDP deflator.

Source: Thomson Reuters, OECD calculations.

StatLink http://dx.doi.org/10.1787/888933210510

Chapter 8

Pro-competitive policy reform for investment and growth

Promoting competition was declared to be a priority by the G20 in 2014, recognising that it is market competition between firms that provides them with an incentive to reduce costs and develop new and better products. The economic evidence shows that some of the most effective structural reforms to promote growth are those increasing product market competition. On the other hand the most damaging restrictions on competition often arise from protected state-owned enterprises (SOEs) or from regulatory policies that unnecessarily limit competition. Since state ownership is becoming more significant in the world economy, it is increasingly important to ensure that SOEs face similar competitive conditions, on equal terms, as do private sector firms. Identifying and redesigning the most damaging regulations can be difficult and, in many cases, politically challenging. Quantification of benefits and accounts of other countries' experiences can help explain and gain political support for reforms. Some cases are described here.

Main findings

- In the absence of competition, firms face little incentive to innovate and to invest to improve productivity growth. Inefficiency resulting from weak competition could be an important factor in weak economic growth overall.
- Government restrictions on competition, for example through protecting incumbent state-owned firms or through regulation or undue financial advantages, can be particularly damaging to innovation, investment and growth.
- State ownership is becoming more important in the global economy, mainly because of the increased share of emerging economies with large state-owned sectors, particularly (but not only) China. The scope for anti-competitive distortions from this source is therefore increasing, unless state-owned enterprises can be subjected effectively to competition, and to effective systems of corporate governance.
- For regulatory distortions, the devil is in the detail: reform at the 'big picture' level of removing formal barriers to entry may not be enough. Growth-enhancing reform needs to work through the large stock of specific regulations that have anti-competitive effects if it is to be effective.
- Removing such restrictions to promote growth need not result in short-term costs. Some deregulatory initiatives to promote competition, such as liberalising trading hours (for example, lifting restrictions on Sunday trading) can generate new employment opportunities and economic expansion.

Introduction

In its Brisbane Declaration of 2014, the G20 explicitly identified the link between the quality of a country's competition policy framework and its investment performance: "Fostering competition is critical for our economies. Well-designed competition policy, effective enforcement of competition law, and competition-based economic reforms promote higher investment and employment."

This chapter calls attention to the overwhelming evidence in support of the G20's statement about the benefits of competition policy for investment and growth. Strengthening competition should therefore be a crucial component of any strategy for economic growth, particularly if what is needed is a recovery from a period of anaemic demand. Two important priorities are (1) ensuring a level playing field between state-owned enterprises (SOEs) and those privately owned so that SOEs are not insulated from competition; and (2) avoiding poorly designed regulations in product markets, particularly where their intention is to achieve non-economic (e.g. social) objectives. The evidence arises from econometric analysis of firm-level data, through sector-level studies to comparisons of national policy. This link between competition and firm productivity arises in advanced OECD economies as well as in fast-growing emerging economies, especially in Asia, that are often held to exemplify an alternative growth model based on state protection.

The effects of competition and competition policy

More competition leads to better productivity performance

Joseph Schumpeter said, "Without development there is no profit, without profit no development". Does Schumpeter's statement mean that firms should be protected from competition, to give them the incentive or the retained earnings to invest? There is ample evidence that the answer is no: policies that successfully stimulate competition favourably affect macro-economic outcomes.[1] Most convincingly, detailed firm-by-firm and even plant-by-plant analysis demonstrates that suppliers facing more competition have higher productivity and faster productivity growth. One of the largest studies, (Disney, Haskell and Heden, 2003) using data on 140 000 separate businesses in the UK, concludes "Market competition significantly raises both the level and growth of productivity." Another, analysing data on 500 German firms (Januszewski et al., 2002), confirms the existence of a positive link between productivity growth and competition. Furthermore, sectoral studies confirm that this effect also applies to the Japanese (Sakakibara and Porter, 2001) and Korean (Baek, Kim and Kwon, 2009) experiences of economic growth, despite the widely-held belief[2] that these countries followed a different development model involving protection from competition. In particular, Michael Porter and his co-authors have convincingly demonstrated that it was those sectors in Japan that had least protection from imports that were the successful world-beaters, while the protected sectors (such as aircraft manufacturing) failed.

As productivity growth is the main component of *per capita* GDP growth, this micro-level analysis makes a solid and convincing case that competition boosts growth, at least in the long run. Other strands of the academic literature demonstrate that firms subject to competitive constraints invest to innovate, and thereby increase productivity both through reductions in costs and the creation of new products.[3] Figure 8.1 illustrates the relationships. Policies that allow more effective competition in markets lead to higher productivity growth. This occurs mainly through better performing firms displacing weaker ones: investing, innovating and expanding, although there is also an effect to improve existing firms, through stronger managerial incentives. Effective macroeconomic adjustment mechanisms should generate the aggregate demand needed to make returns on capital attractive enough to encourage new investment that permits freed labour

Figure 8.1. **A pro-competition policy framework can boost economic growth**

StatLink http://dx.doi.org/10.1787/888933210247

resources to be effectively employed. Overall, this leads to both higher industry-wide productivity growth, directly and indirectly through more efficient supply chains, and effective use of available manpower. These, in turn, increase overall economic growth.

Government restrictions, such as regulations that limit the number of suppliers in a market or distort the ability of producers to compete, are particularly likely to harm productivity. Studies based on the OECD's Product Market Regulation (PMR)[4] indicators provide some evidence of the harmful effect of anticompetitive regulation at national level. For example, there is a statistically significant negative correlation between the level of product market regulation and the change in multi-factor productivity when comparing two time periods. Figure 8.2 from a paper by OECD researchers (Arnold, Nicoletti and Scarpetta, 2011) illustrates this:

Figure 8.2. **Product market regulation and productivity acceleration**

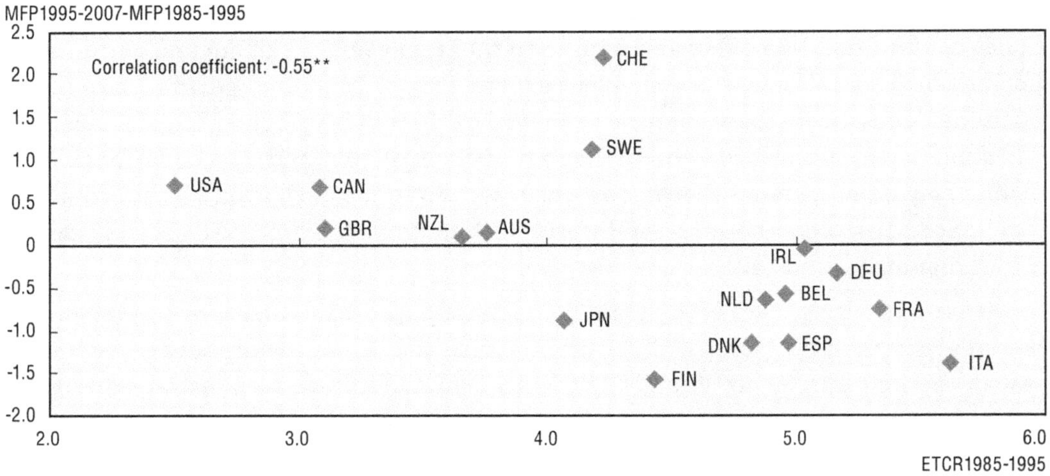

Source: Arnold, Nicoletti and Scarpetta (2011).

StatLink http://dx.doi.org/10.1787/888933210255

The PMR Index includes not only measures of regulations affecting private sector firms, but also indicators of state involvement in markets more generally, including through direct ownership of SOEs.

Far from promoting investment or growth, then, government regulation protecting firms from competition is likely to stifle it. If companies put their efforts into seeking government protection from competition (foreign or domestic) they will have less ability and incentive to innovate. Schwab and Werker (2014) look at profits expressed as mark-ups and find that countries with higher mark-ups in manufacturing grew more slowly. The effect can be strong enough to overcome the 'catch up' advantages of poorer countries, suggesting that when the least developing economies liberalise and open up their industries, they can grow rapidly towards convergence with OECD economies.

This helps answer a question that policymakers in emerging economies sometimes pose: if China, India and others grew so fast before introducing competition law,[5] how can anyone claim competition law is necessary – or even good – for growth? One answer is that very rapid growth in very low income economies is possible as long as basic conditions for business success – such as reasonable protection of property rights – are in place. Industries can expand rapidly taking on low-skilled labour, and might have rather low productivity but nonetheless contribute substantially to GDP growth. However, later on the presence of inefficient firms can become a significant drag on the economy. To move to the next level of economic development, effective competition is needed – for example to eliminate the 'fat tail' of inefficient firms found in China by van Reenen et al (2011). Effective competition policy could be an important part of moving to the next phase of development, when the gains available to the lowest-income economies have been exhausted.

Flexible product markets contribute to macroeconomic adjustment

But what of the short term? Are these long run gains achieved only at the expense of short-term pain, for example as firms experiencing productivity gains shed labour? If so, might governments be justified in retaining restrictions on competition during downturns, at least temporarily? Industries often seek such 'temporary' protection, whether from domestic or foreign competition.

A major problem with this is that, in practice, temporary relief often becomes permanent, as firms face very few incentives to improve while under state protection (and every incentive to devote resources to lobbying for extensions). But is there nonetheless an argument in principle for weakening competitive pressures in hard economic times, to prevent irreversible losses of capacity? Or (a slightly different point) perhaps competitive markets might be good for *long-run* growth of capacity and productivity, but should they be reined back when the interest is instead in strengthening a *cyclical* expansion, for example following a macroeconomic shock?

Evidence is somewhat mixed, but OECD researchers' analysis of structural reform in product and labour markets suggests that any losses arising from more competitive product markets are transitory, at the worst. For example, Cacciatore et al (2012) finds that pro-competitive product market reform stimulates GDP immediately, but can lead to some increase in unemployment, typically for a period of one to two years. This is perhaps unsurprising, if the labour-shedding effects of increased competition are immediate, while the gains from new entry and from smaller competitors expanding capacity take some time to emerge. Similarly, updating earlier work by Duval *et al* (2007) to take account of the recent recession, Sutherland and Hoeller (2012) conclude that less regulated product markets reduce the time required for recovery from a macro-economic shock (particularly supply shocks). There is a rather complex link with labour market reform, for example Cacciatore et al (2012) finding that product and labour market reforms act as substitutes for one another (product market competition becomes more important in the absence of flexible labour markets), in contrast to Bassanini and Duval (2009), who find that they are complements (reforming both policies produces larger gains than the combined effect of reforming one but not the other).

One potentially illuminating source of evidence on the effects of competition law and policy on recovery is provided by different responses to the downturn of the 1930s. Few countries actively enforced competition laws as early as the 1930s, but one of the few that did – the United States – took a policy decision to roll back its antitrust enforcement in the depths of the depression. The National Industrial Recovery Act (NIRA) of 1933 legalised cartels in participating sectors, as part of a deal in which price-fixing was exchanged for agreements to maintain wages and employment. Thus, in contrast to the priorities suggested by the studies of product and labour market reform described above, the US Government deliberately sought to reduce product and labour market flexibility. During the 1930s, the collapse in prices that the United States experienced was not continuous or monotonic at a time when output fell more than 30% below trend. This is an outcome to which the NIRA seems to have contributed, reinforcing the effect of positive demand-side factors on prices once the recovery gathered pace.[6] As Romer (1999) noted "By preventing the large negative deviations of output from trend in the mid-1930s from exerting deflationary pressure, it prevented the economy's self-correction mechanism from working. Thus, the NIRA can be best thought of as a force holding back recovery, rather than as one actively depressing output."[7]

Promoting market competition to increase growth

Pro-competitive structural reforms could raise aggregate output by about 9% in the OECD area

As Figure 8.3 illustrates, analysis by the OECD using the PMR Index suggests that product market reform has very significant potential to raise GDP in most economies: by as much as 30% in some large emerging economies.

Figure 8.3. **Potential GDP gains by 2060 from product market reform**

(%)

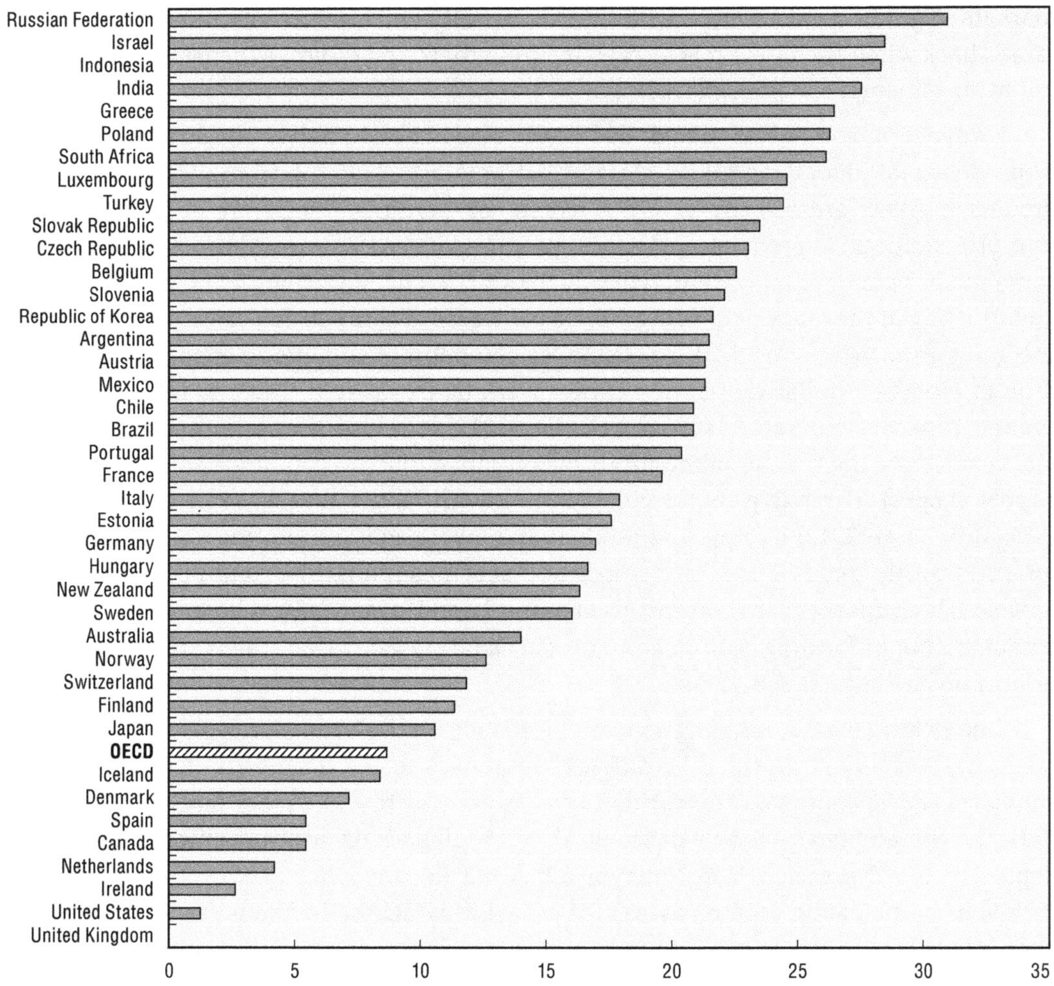

Source: OECD Economic Outlook, May 2013.

StatLink http://dx.doi.org/10.1787/888933210269

Regulatory constraints on competition, and other forms of state intervention, including state ownership, can prevent efficient market competition. The removal of these inefficiencies can itself directly result in increased output, but more importantly create a more dynamic economy for sustained economic growth over the longer term, particularly when more competitive markets in upstream sectors result in cost savings and quality improvements for downstream firms. It is often these upstream firms supplying essential inputs – network and infrastructure industries as well as financial institutions – that are subject to state controls and regulations, as we now discuss.

State-owned enterprises are increasingly important in the global economy

In the mature economies SOEs[8] are not particularly prevalent. OECD studies indicate that they typically account for around 3 per cent of economic activity and employment. However, their importance goes beyond this because they tend to be concentrated in a few areas – notably the network industries – on which the entire private business sector depends for its downstream competitiveness. Furthermore, the recent financial crisis has further transferred a number of financial institutions to temporary state ownership and/or control, including in countries (e.g. the Netherlands, United Kingdom and United States) that were believed to have abandoned state ownership of systemically important enterprises.

However, the main reason for the renewed concerns about competition from SOEs arises from the growing importance of a number of emerging economies that still have large SOE sectors. A few years ago the OECD estimated that SOEs account for around one third of the economic activity in China and Russia, and about one quarter in India[9] (e.g. OECD, 2009a, and OECD, 2009b). Most of these countries have active privatisation programmes, but over the last decade their economic growth rate has outstripped the pace of privatisation, so their SOEs are increasingly important in the global marketplace.

As of 2014, 22 of the world's largest companies have the state as a majority or major shareholder.[10] Table 8.1 provides a 'league table' of the largest 25 state-invested non-financial companies according to the most recent Forbes 2000 ranking. OECD governments are more strongly represented among the (majority or partial) owners of large enterprises than would perhaps have been expected. Ten of the top-25 enterprises are found in the OECD area, almost all of them domiciled in European countries. Among the other 15, more than half are controlled by the Chinese government. In OECD and emerging economies alike the predominant sectors are telecommunications services and the extraction and processing of hydrocarbons.

State ownership of financial institutions is concentrated in much fewer countries. Apart from a couple of North and West European banks, large state-invested financial institutions are almost entirely found in emerging economies. Among the largest of 25 such financial institutions fifteen are Chinese, including twelve banks and three insurance companies.

But they appear to be insulated from competition, which could be holding back growth

This growing importance of SOEs in the global economy has given rise to concerns. The relative inefficiency of SOEs has been documented by a number of empirical studies, although there is less consensus on whether the inefficiency is intrinsic or reflects public policy objectives with which these enterprises have been charged.[11] This raises the risk that SOEs could crowd out more efficient enterprises from the market place, if their government owners favour them to compensate for that inefficiency.

Table 8.1. **Top companies with government involvement*, 2014 (USD billion)**

Rank	Company	Sector	Domicile	Market value	Sales	Assets
3	PetroChina	Oil & Gas Operations	China	202.0	328.5	386.9
9	Volkswagen	Auto & Truck Manufacturers	Germany	119.0	261.5	446.9
11	Gazprom	Oil & Gas Operations	Russia	88.8	164.6	397.2
16	China Mobile	Telecommunication	Hong Kong, China	184.6	102.5	192.8
17	Sinopec-China Petroleum	Oil & Gas Operations	China	94.7	445.3	228.4
18	Petrobras	Oil & Gas Operations	Brazil	86.8	141.2	319.2
21	Rosneft	Oil & Gas Operations	Russia	70.0	142.6	229.4
25	ENI	Oil & Gas Operations	Italy	90.9	152.7	186.6
32	EDF	Electric Utilities	France	75.8	100.4	353.9
33	Statoil	Oil & Gas Operations	Norway	89.2	105.2	146.0
38	NTT	Telecommunication	Japan	61.0	110.7	189.3
43	Enel	Electric Utilities	Italy	53.2	106.3	226.2
61	Saudi Basic Industries	Diversified Chemicals	Saudi Arabia	94.4	50.4	90.4
64	CNOOC	Oil & Gas Operations	Hong Kong, China	67.2	43.0	102.7
74	China Shenhua Energy	Diversified Metals & Mining	China	57.6	42.8	80.4
77	Ecopetrol	Oil & Gas Operations	Colombia	83.6	37.7	68.5
78	EADS	Aerospace & Defence	France	56.9	78.7	128.6
87	France Telecom	Telecommunication	France	39.0	54.4	118.3
88	Deutsche Telekom	Telecommunication	Germany	71.2	79.8	162.8
92	China Telecom	Telecommunication	China	37.4	52.3	89.7
102	Deutsche Post	Air Courier	Germany	45.4	73.1	48.9
111	SAIC Motor	Auto Manufacturers	China	24.7	88.3	56.4
112	Oil & Natural Gas	Oil & Gas Operations	India	46.4	29.6	53.8
116	PTT PCL	Oil & Gas Operations	Thailand	26.7	92.5	54.8
124	China Unicom	Telecommunication	Hong Kong, China	31.6	48.0	87.5

* Public sector ownership at least 10% by either the national or sub-national level of government. Financial institutions are not included.
Source: Forbes© Global 2000.

StatLink http://dx.doi.org/10.1787/888933210529

An earlier OECD study examined the possible consequences for competition in the markets for goods and services and concluded that the main concerns include equal treatment in the areas of cost of finance, regulatory and tax treatment and private participation in the public procurement process (OECD, 2012). SOEs can be provided with incentives to behave more efficiently in two ways: their internal corporate governance can be reformed to provide more commercialorientation, and the external environment can be reformed (with or without privatisation) to create more competitive markets.

This section employs firm specific data to investigate the performance of SOEs and other companies with strong government investment, to illustrate the likely effect of greater competition. We take a sectoral approach, as the differences between sectors (especially comparing utility and network industries to other sectors) can often swamp the differences between public and private performance measures within sectors. Using the *Forbes© Global 2000* list of companies from 2014, SOEs are compared with private firms in five sectors where state ownership is perceived to be particularly widespread: oil and gas, mining, air transportation, power generation and telecommunications.[12]

During the past few decades the pace of privatisation of SOEs around the world has continued apace, albeit with a significant slowdown during the recent financial crisis. The privatisation of SOEs has generated large revenues for many governments and, perhaps even more importantly, it has provided a potential solution to the problem of inadequate SOE performance such as, transparency, "agency problems"[13] and governmental interference. In the aftermath of the crisis, as privatisation schemes regain popularity, important questions remain for both researchers and policy makers, such as the effect of privatisation or reforming of SOEs on their profitability and operating margins.

Profitability

Using the available information this section assesses the impact of ownership on the financial performance of SOEs. Three indicators are used to measure profitability: (i) return on total assets (ROA), which is defined as total profits (net income) divided by total fixed assets; (ii) return on shareholder funds, essentially identical to return on equity (ROE) which is defined as total profits divided by total shareholder funds; and (iii) return on capital employed (ROCE), which is defined as total profits divided by total shareholder fund plus non-current liabilities.

Figure 8.4. **Financial performance by ownership[1] and sector between 2000 and 2013**

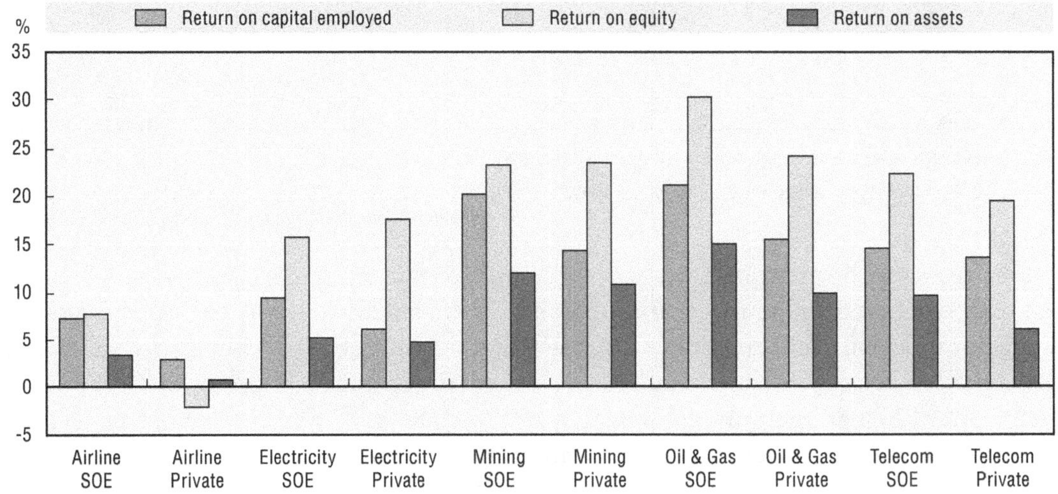

1. Private and State-owned Enterprise (SOE)

Source: OECD calculations based on Bureau Van Dijk publishing (BvDEP).

StatLink http://dx.doi.org/10.1787/888933210277

Figure 8.4 provides an overview of the profitability of SOEs and private firms across sectors. Remarkably, in the airline industry the average profitability of private enterprises over the last decade appears to have been negative or close to zero. Conversely, state-owned airlines have earned a modest return on their investments. Generally, with respect to the return on assets and return on capital, the performance of SOEs is higher than private companies. Only in the case of electricity is there by some measures (though not including ROA) a higher degree of profitability in the private sector.

Indicators of operating margins

This section compares price-cost margins (PCM) across firms[14], as well as other indicators of operating margins. Margins can be taken as an indicator of market power, which is often related to the degree of market concentration in a sector, although measurement difficulties mean that any such conclusions should be treated with caution.

The results generally show a clear pattern of higher margins for SOEs than for private firms, sector by sector. This is similar to the pattern of results for profitability indicators and could reflect less competition for state-owned firms.

Table 8.2. **Comparison of price-cost margins (PCM) and other margin indicators by sector from 2000 to 2013**

	Average of EBITDA* margin	Average of gross margin	Average of profit margin	Average of PCM
Airline	**11.2**	**36.6**	**1.9**	**0.02**
Private	8.8	29.7	0.9	0.01
SOEs	16.1	49.3	3.8	0.03
Electricity	**31.1**	**52.9**	**14.8**	**0.10**
Private	27.9	53.3	12.9	0.03
SOEs	37.2	52.2	18.4	0.22
Mining	**30.4**	**41.1**	**19.5**	**0.02**
Private	31.1	41.3	19.4	0.02
SOEs	27.9	40.7	19.7	0.01
Oil & Gas	**30.9**	**45.7**	**18.3**	**0.02**
Private	32.9	47.4	17.5	0.01
SOEs	26.4	41.7	20.1	0.05
Telecom	**36.2**	**63.7**	**12.8**	**0.05**
Private	33.8	61.0	9.5	0.04
SOEs	40.3	69.4	18.7	0.07
Grand Total	**30.5**	**49.6**	**15.3**	**0.05**

* EBITDA: Earnings before interest, tax and depreciation allowance.

Source: OECD calculations based on Bureau Van Dijk publishing (BvDEP).

StatLink http://dx.doi.org/10.1787/888933210537

In the case of air transportation there are overall lower EBITDA margins,[15] gross margins [16]and profit margins[17] than in other industries. This may well reflect the greater degree of international competition in this sector affecting both private firms and SOEs, than in other sectors in which markets are essentially domestic. Even so, there is a clear indication of higher operating margins where the state is a significant owner, as well as some indications of greater market concentration (i.e. higher PCM).

The telecom sector has generally highest margins as compared to other sectors. This finding is perhaps unsurprising: the telecom sector was the scene of significant technological evolution as well as rapidly growing penetration of fixed lines, mobile and internet services during this period. However, as the costs of funding the expansion were correspondingly high, this did not (as demonstrated above) result in abnormally high rates of return. In the telecom sector as well the gap between margins in SOEs and private firms is non-trivial. In the electricity and mining sectors, the difference between private firms and SOEs is not compelling, although on the whole earnings margins tend to be higher when the state is involved.

Regulations can be repealed or reformed to allow competition to work

Frequently the strongest barriers to competition do not arise from the direct state control of economic activity, but from unnecessarily anti-competitive regulations. Not all regulations are anti-competitive, but those that are will harm the economy, for the reasons set out earlier. Some such regulations will be necessary, but often they will arise to protect a favoured interest group, or will simply be poorly designed – unnecessarily restricting competition to further a social goal that could instead be achieved by working with, rather than against, the market. It is within the power of governments to tackle these regulatory impediments to growth directly. In a series of publications, OECD has developed the evidence base to support the use of its Competition Assessment Toolkit (Box 8.1), which assists governments to identify the harmful effects of anti-competitive regulations and propose alternatives.

Box 8.1. **The OECD's Competition Assessment Toolkit**

The OECD's Competition Assessment Toolkit is a structured methodology to help governments identify and change policies that unnecessarily prevent, restrict or distort competition

The approach is derived from the understanding that competition authorities have gained about effective competition in markets, in their work to identify, assess and remedy possible breaches of competition law. It applies that approach to regulatory constraints, bringing the rigour that is needed when investigating possible breaches of law in an adversarial environment, in which analysis has to be able to stand the test of formal legal challenge. The OECD's intention is to provide officials who are not competition experts with the guidance and tools needed to carry out such analysis, when assessing policies.

This involves three stages of analysis. An initial screening phase should identify which laws and regulations have the potential adversely to affect competition. The Toolkit provides a checklist against which to asses this question. Then, regulations identified as potentially problematic are assessed in depth, to see if in fact competition is restricted to a significant degree. The Toolkit provides methods and real-world examples to guide this process. Finally, if a significant effect is found, the investigator should identify the objective of the regulation and consider whether this same objective could be achieved by redesigning the regulation so that it does not have this effect (or consider simply abolishing the regulation if the adverse effect is large and there is no feasible alternative design).

The OECD does not advocate deregulation in all circumstances. Governments need to regulate markets to pursue many different social and economic goals. The Toolkit helps inform the decisions they take on whether and how to regulate.

The Toolkit is currently available in two volumes, in 17 languages. A third volume – the Operational Manual, providing step-by-step guides to specific techniques, with a particular emphasis on quantifying the effects of the regulations under analysis – will be published in 2015.

Source: *www.oecd.org/competition/assessment-toolkit.htm.*

The OECD was asked to use the Toolkit to assess policies for anti-competitive effects in Mexico, in a sequence of projects from 2008, in Greece in 2013 and 2014 and most recently in Romania, starting in 2015.

The Toolkit provides a flexible methodology that can be applied to a wide range of problems, some of them idiosyncratic to the economy under investigation, others of more general applicability. Two examples of analysis from the OECD's Toolkit work that seem particularly likely to promote productivity growth and economic expansion are provided below.

Example: liberalising Sunday trading would promote employment

Firstly, restrictions on trading hours act as a direct constraint on economic activity. Analysis conducted by the OECD (Genakos and Danchev, 2014) strongly suggests that – for example – liberalising Sunday trading is likely to increase employment. 30 European countries were considered. An index of Sunday regulation was constructed which covered the period from 1999 to 2011. Over this period a number of countries liberalised Sunday trading rules, at least to some extent, while others continued with a policy of not allowing

Sunday openings. The changes over time in the differences across countries permitted an assessment of how the change in policy affected the countries that adopted it compared to those that did not.[18]

Economic outcomes were measured from panel data covering prices, expenditure and per capita income, employment and the number of firms, for three products (food; clothing & footwear; and household furnishing, equipment and maintenance) and sixteen retail sectors.[19] The three products represent goods with different durability and thus purchase frequency (non-durable, semi-durable and durable, respectively).

The countries that deregulated were the 'treated' group, while non-reforming countries (that did not change their regulation) were the 'control' group. Due to the inclusion of sector-country and time fixed effects, the impact of regulation on the dependent variable (for example, prices or expenditure) was identified from countries that changed their Sunday trading regulation. It measures the effect of regulation in reforming countries, compared to the general evolution of the same variable in non-reforming countries.

The results indicated that both employment and output increased in European countries as a result of liberalising Sunday trading. That is, new firms were attracted into the sectors, increasing employment and sales, but also existing firms took on more staff and saw their business grow. This outcome confirmed the evidence provided by economic studies published previously (Burda and Weil (2005), Goos (2004), Gradus (1996), Pilat (1997), and Skuterud, 2005), but it goes one step forward because it looks at a large number of countries while the existing studies are all based on data from individual countries.

Example: opening industries to foreign ownership can promote competition and investment

Most competition-enhancing reforms simply lower barriers to entry, allowing additional competition to arise from wherever it may, whether domestic or foreign. However, some barriers to entry specifically discriminate against foreign producers. Tariffs and non-tariff barriers to trade are obvious restrictions on product market competition, which have been extensively studied by economists. Restrictions on foreign direct investment (FDI) can also serve to limit competition. As well as constituting a barrier to entry, such restrictions can be particularly harmful as they make technology transfer and the catch up benefits of FDI unavailable, or at least more difficult and costly to obtain, particularly for countries behind the technological frontier.

Mexico provides a case in point. In its work with the Government of Mexico to identify and remove barriers to competition in a number of key sectors (OECD and Comisión Federal de Competencia, México, 2012) the OECD has identified interactions between restrictions on FDI and other regulatory restrictions on competition that produce poor economic outcomes. The Government of Mexico has taken steps to reform this regime.

Since Mexico historically had one of the most restrictive regimes for FDI in the OECD, it is unsurprising that FDI inflows were lower than would otherwise have been expected, particularly to sectors facing explicit prohibitions or limits on foreign ownership. However, the indirect effects of these restrictions from their impact on competition are also important.

Figure 8.5. **Evolution of OECD index of Sunday trading liberalisation across 30 European countries[1,2]**

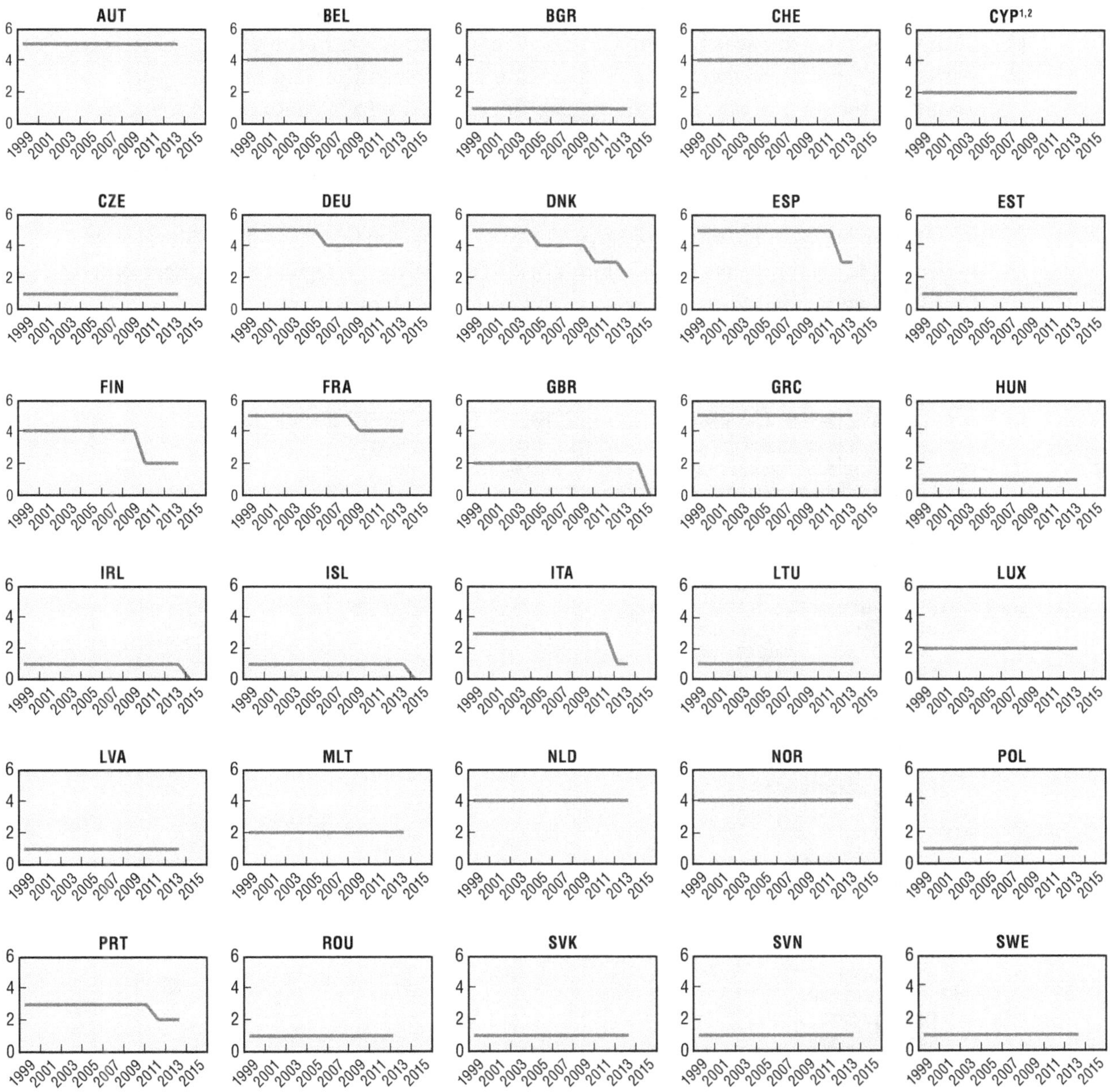

Notes: The figure presents information on the evolution of Sunday trading regulation indicator across 30 European countries with indicator 1 being the least restrictive and indicator 5 the most restrictive.

1. Note by Turkey

The information in this document with reference to "Cyprus" relates to the southern part of the Island. There is no single authority representing both Turkish and Greek Cypriot people on the Island. Turkey recognises the Turkish Republic of Northern Cyprus (TRNC). Until a lasting and equitable solution is found within the context of the United Nations, Turkey shall preserve its position concerning the "Cyprus issue".

2. Footnote by all the European Union Member States of the OECD and the European Union

The Republic of Cyprus is recognised by all members of the United Nations with the exception of Turkey. The information in this document relates to the area under the effective control of the Government of the Republic of Cyprus.

Source: Genakos and Danchev (2014) estimates based on Sunday trading regulation indicator constructed using information from the OECD PMR indicator on regulation of shop opening hours and legislation search in secondary sources on timing and extent of reforms.

StatLink http://dx.doi.org/10.1787/888933210289

Mexican consumers pay more for many services than consumers elsewhere in the OECD and, to take a non-price related example, penetration of both mobile and fixed-line telephone services was slower than in other countries in the region (OECD, 2011). At least part of the reason for this was the uncompetitive market structure of the telecoms market, the restrictions on foreign ownership in fixed-line services and related services (such as TV, preventing the offer of so-called 'triple-play' services). The Peña Nieto Government has significantly reformed the rules affecting competition in the telecoms market, removing barriers to FDI and creating a new telecoms regulator with enhanced powers to tackle abuse of monopoly. This forms part of the Pact for Mexico, which has reformed many important sectors of the economy, most notably energy. The OECD's interim update of its PMR indicator for Mexico in 2014, found that these reforms will move Mexico's regulatory stringency in telecoms from worse than the OECD average, to a better score than average.

Figure 8.6. **OECD Foreign Direct Investment Regulatory Restrictiveness Index**

(Open = 0; completely closed = 1)

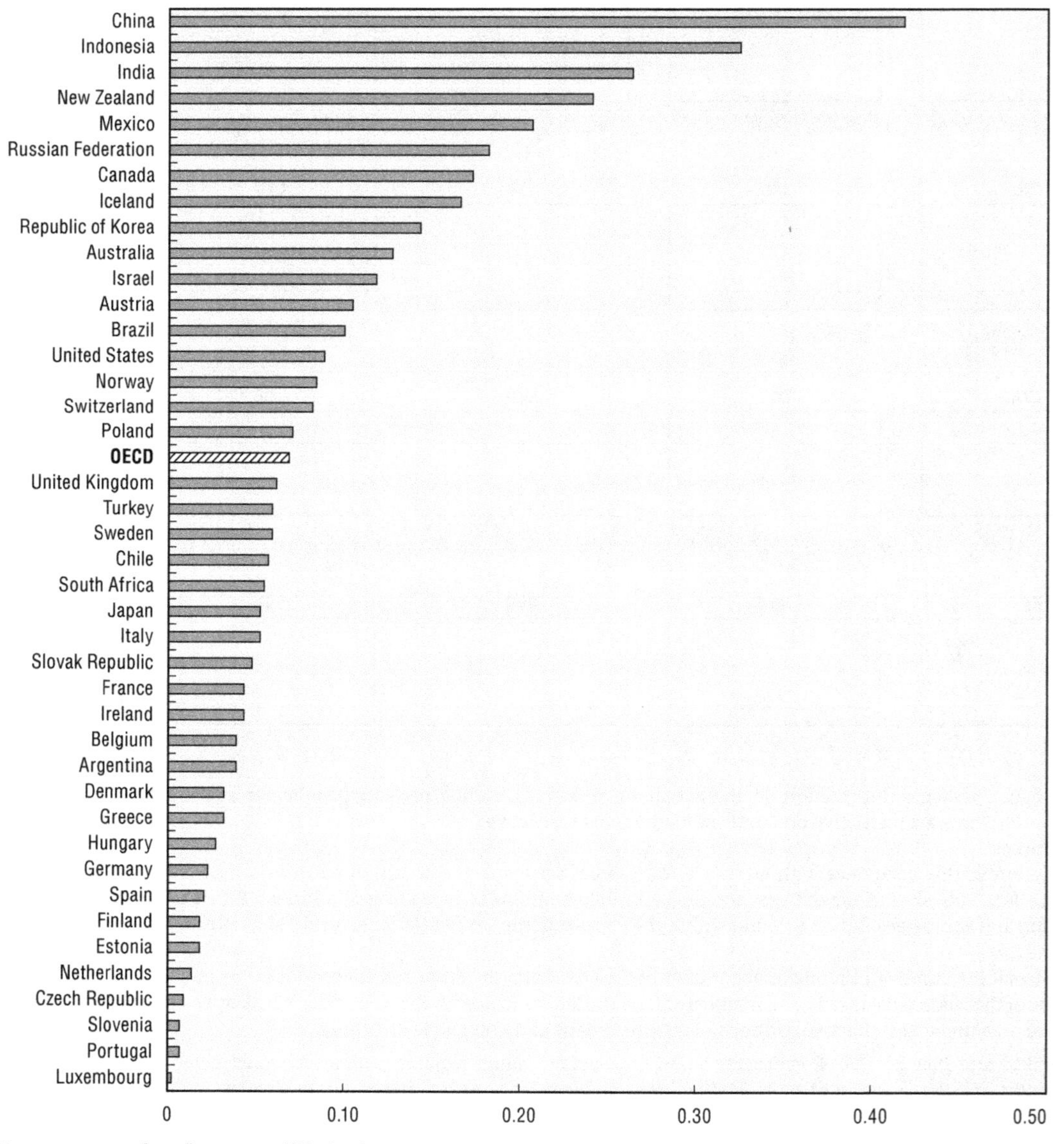

Source: www.oecd.org/investment/fdiindex.htm.

StatLink http://dx.doi.org/10.1787/888933210299

In air transport too, barriers to entry remain. An OECD study demonstrated that fares were significantly lower on routes with low cost carrier participation,[20] but this participation remains constrained – especially for domestic routes – by a 25% cap on foreign ownership. Restrictions such as non-market allocation of slots at Mexico's main airport reinforce this problem.[21]

Conclusions

Remarkably, almost all G20 countries now have some form of competition law, often based on very similar objectives and economic approaches, despite the very different political and economic structure and history of each of these countries. The contrast with the late 1990s – when big emerging economies resisted incorporation of competition policy into negotiations on the Doha round as a Western imposition on their systems – is very striking. India's Competition Commission recently fined a large state-owned company for breach of competition law,[22] for example, while in China companies take private action in the courts using the competition laws.[23] Some jurisdictions continue to develop their laws – and especially their practices and procedures, which vary much more than do the substantive terms – but there is a strong degree of consensus on the basic approach. The main challenge in competition law is to achieve better international co-ordination, so that global firms do not face multiple overlapping and possibly inconsistent investigations (Capobianco, Davies and Ennis, 2014). This would be a useful step forward now; but as globalisation continues the need will become pressing.

One area where the G20 countries differ considerably is in how strongly the state intervenes in product markets, and how well their regulations are designed to avoid restricting competition. To meet their more immediate need for growth in a time of weak demand, the G20 countries all could take significant steps to improve competition in markets affected by restrictive regulations or other forms of distortive *state* intervention, including any favoured treatment of state-owned enterprises. Table 8.3 summarises recent OECD policy recommendations to the G20 countries in this area.

Table 8.3. **Summary of OECD recommendations to G20 countries in areas of competition and trade**

	Australia	Brazil	Canada	China	Germany	European Union	France	India	Indonesia	Italy	Japan	Korea	Mexico	Russian Federation	South Africa	Spain	Turkey	United Kingdom	United States
States Strengthen competition in network industries			✓		♦	✓				♦				♦	✓		✓		
Reform/simplify product market regulations						♦			✓									♦	♦
Reduce barriers to competition in the services sector		✓			✓	✓										✓			
Reduce barriers to foreign ownership/investment/trade	✓		✓			♦		✓			✓	✓	✓	✓					
Reduce regulatory barriers to competition							✓			✓		♦	✓		✓				
Reduce state control over economic activity or public ownership			♦	✓										✓					
Reform planning regulations																		✓	

Note: ✓ refers to priorities identified in OECD *Going for Growth* series and ♦ refers to OECD *Economic Survey* recommendations for individual countries.

Source: OECD (2014d).

StatLink http://dx.doi.org/10.1787/888933210541

Reforms of this sort can be politically difficult. Typically, the losers from such reforms are a small group of suppliers, including state-owned incumbents, with a strong interest in preserving their existing protected positions. The gains will almost always outweigh these losses, but those gaining might have a much quieter political voice – consumers and the population at large all standing to make a small individual gain, or potential new entrants, whose voice is never heard over existing incumbents.

As the evidence set out here suggests, however, policymakers should be prepared to take on this political challenge. Pro-competitive reforms do not necessarily or always involve short-term pain for long-run gains.

Notes

1. The effects of competition are set out in an OECD Factsheet (OECD, 2014b).
2. See for example Chang (2011) for a recent example.
3. The effect of competition on innovation is complex, and the literature is summarised in the OECD (2014). Most recent empirical studies suggest an inverted U-shaped relationship, so that moderate competition is associated with the highest rates of innovation. In general competition policy is concerned not with making already competitive markets more competitive, but rather with intervention to prevent or correct monopoly and its abuse, so this finding is unlikely to diminish the beneficial effects of pro-competitive policies in practice (and the empirical literature on policy effects bears this out).
4. For more information on PMR see *www.oecd.org/economy/growth/indicatorsofproductmarketregulation-homepage.htm*.
5. Both China and India adopted competition law only after 2000 (although India had previously possessed some rather ineffective 'fair trading' provisions).
6. Weinstein in Brunner (1981).
7. Taylor (2002, 2007) finds a 10% reduction in output due to NIRA, and notes in Wright and Zeiler (2014) "What would have happened had the NIRA never been passed? The economy would almost certainly have recovered more quickly. Once the banking crisis had permanently ended and Roosevelt devalued the dollar, [...], the recovery appeared to be self-sustaining. Had the NIRA not interfered with this progression, the term "Great Depression" might not have come into existence." Another, controversial, study - Cole and Ohanian (2004) – also finds a very large effect but this study has been strongly challenged, for example by Krugman (New York Times, 27 September 2011). In a subsequent study of differential competition policy responses to the crisis, Cole and Ohanian (2013) also find that pro-cartel policies in fascist European economies delayed recovery.
8. Throughout this section 'SOEs' refers not only to companies that are majority-owned by the state but also to companies where the state is the largest shareholder and owns a stake of at least 10%.
9. In smaller, resource-dependent emerging economies the share is often larger due to predominant state ownership of their mining and petroleum companies.
10. Among the largest 100 financial institutions, 25 are owned or controlled by the state. In the case of non-financial enterprises the share is 20 out of 100.
11. In the 1980s and 1990s a number of academic studies analysed pre and post-privatisation performance of previously state-owned enterprises in and generally concluded that the transfer of ownership raised productivity. More recent studies have focused on the efficiency of SOEs in continued state ownership in emerging markets (e.g. Lee et al., 2012).
12. To analyse the performance and the financing structure of these firms, firm-level information was extracted from an OECD corporate database using Bureau Van Dijk publishing (BvDEP) that contains financial and ownership information for over 44 million companies across the world. The OECD corporate database has in the past been used for analysing a variety of issues such as productivity growth, export performance, innovation and international investment literature. The company information in the OECD corporate database includes firm-specific details that should not change from one year to another, such as the company name, its city and country, as well as the core sectoral industrial activity of the firm (with four-digit NACE rev. 2 codes). The financial information is broken down into two major components: the firm's balance sheet and

the profit and loss account reported for given time periods. The account is complemented by information on value-added, the cost of employees and export turnover, on a non-systematic basis.

13. The term agency problems usually refers to a conflict of interest between a company's management and its owners, but may also refer to conflicts of interest between majority and minority shareholders.

14. $$PCM = \frac{Value\,of\,Sales - Inventories - Payroll - Cost\,of\,Materials}{Value\,of\,Sales + Inventories} = \frac{Value\,added - Payroll}{Value\,added + Cost\,of\,Materials}$$

See Domowitz et al., (1986) for the more detailed equations and assumptions.

15. $$\text{The EBITDA Margin} = \frac{Operating\,profit\,/\,loss(EBIT)}{Operating\,revenue(turnover)}$$

16. $$\text{The Gross Margin} = \frac{Gross\,profit}{Operating\,revenue(turnover)}$$

17. $$\text{The Profit Margin} = \frac{Profit\,/loss\,before\,tax\;\&\,extra\,items}{Operating\,revenue\;(turnover)}$$

18. This estimation framework constitutes a cross-sectional time series analysis, assessing the effects of pro-competitive policy interventions. By studying several different cases (such as different geographical markets), in only some of which a change occurred, other factors that affect outcomes can be controlled for, without explicitly modelling them, if they can be assumed to have common effects across the sample.

19. Where a 'sector' refers to a four-digit NACE classification, using the Statistical Classification of Economic Activities in the European Community.

20. OECD and Comisión de Competencia, México (2010).

21. See OECD Airline competition roundtable discussion *www.oecd.org/competition/airlinecompetition.htm*.

22. See for example *http://articles.economictimes.indiatimes.com/2014-12-23/news/57349955_1_fair-trade-norms-competition-commission-possible-anti-competitive-practices*.

23. *www.chinalawvision.com/2014/12/articles/competitionantitrust-law-of-th/private-aml-enforcement-is-catching-up-its-public-counterpart/*.

References

Arnold, J. M., G. Nicoletti and Scarpetta, S. (2011), "Regulation, Resource Reallocation and Productivity Growth", *European Investment Bank Papers*, 16(1), 90-115.

Baek, C., Y. Kim and H. Kwon (2009) , "Productivity growth and competition across the Asian financial crisis: Evidence from Korean manufacturing firms", *Center Economic Institutions Working Paper Series*, No. 2009-12.

Bassanini, A. and R. Duval (2009), "Unemployment, institutions, and reform complementarities: re-assessing the aggregate evidence for OECD countries," *Oxford Review of Economic Policy*, Oxford University Press, vol. 25(1), pages 40-59, Spring."

Benham, L. (1972), "The effect of advertising on the price of eyeglasses", *Journal of Law and Economics*, 337-352.

Bertrand, M., E. Duflo and S. Mullainathan (2004), "How Much Should We Trust Differences-in-Differences Estimates?", *Quarterly Journal of Economics*, 119, 249-75.

Bouis, R., O. Causa, L. Demmou, R. Duval, and A. Zdzienicka (2012), "The Short-Term Effects of Structural Reforms: An Empirical Analysis", *OECD Economics Department Working Papers*, No. 949.

Burda, M. and P. Weil (2005), "Blue Laws", unpublished working paper, *www.philippeweil.com/research/blue2.pdf*.

Brunner, K. (1981), *The Great Depression Revisited*, Springer, Netherlands.

Cacciatore, M., R. Duval and G. Fiori, (2012), "Short-Term Gain or Pain? A DSGE Model-Based Analysis of the Short-Term Effects of Structural Reforms in Labour and Product Markets," *OECD Economics Department Working Papers* 948, OECD Publishing.

Capobianco, A., J. Davies and S. Ennis (2014), "Implication of Globalisation for Competition Policy: The Need for International Co-Operation in Merger and Cartel Enforcement", available at *http://papers.ssrn.com/sol3/papers.cfm?abstract_id=2450137.*

Card, D. and A.B. Krueger (1994), "Minimum Wages and Employment: A Case Study of the Fast-Food Industry in New Jersey and Pennsylvania", *American Economic Review*, 84, 772-793.

Chang, H. (2011), *23 Things They Don't Tell You About Capitalism*, Penguin Books.

Cole, H. L., and L. E. Ohanian (2013), "The Impact of Cartelization, Money, and Productivity Shocks on the International Great Depression", *National Bureau of Economic Research Working Paper*, No. w18823.

Cole, H. L., and L. E. Ohanian (2004), "New Deal policies and the persistence of the Great Depression: A general equilibrium analysis", *Journal of Political Economy*, 112(4), 779-816.

Disney, R., J. Haskel and Y. Heden (2003), "Restructuring and productivity growth in UK manufacturing", *The Economic Journal*, 113(489), 666-694.

Domowitz, I, R.G. Hubbard and B.C. Petersen (1986), "Business Cycles and the Relationship between Concentration and Price-Cost Margins", *The RAND Journal of Economics*, 17(1).

Duval, R., J. Elmeskov and L. Vogel (2007), "Structural policies and economic resilience to shocks", *OECD Economics Department Working Papers*, No. 567.

Hellenic Statistical Authority (2011), "Labour Force Survey" (database), *www.statistics.gr/portal/page/portal/ESYE.*

Evenett, S. (2003), "Competition Law and the Investment Climate in Developing Countries. A contribution to WDR 2005 on Investment Climate, Growth and Poverty", Case study commissioned by the Department for International Development, UK.

Genakos C. and S. Danchev (2014) "Evaluating the impact of Sunday trading devaluation", *OECD Competition Working Paper*, available at *www.oecd.org/officialdocuments/publicdisplaydocumentpdf/?cote=DAF/COMP/WP2(2014)1&docLanguage=En.*

Goos, M. (2004), "Sinking the Blues: The Impact of Shop Closing Hours on Labour and Product Markets", *Centre for Economic Performance Discussion Paper Series*, No. 664 (December).

Gradus, R. (1996), "The Economic Effects of Extending Shop Opening Hours", *Journal of Economics*, 64, 3, 247-263.

Januszewski, S. I., J. Köke and J. K. Winter (2002), "Product market competition, corporate governance and firm performance: an empirical analysis for Germany", *Research in Economics*, 56(3), 299-332.

Kerdrain, C., I. Koske and I. Wanner (2010), "The Impact of Structural Policies on Saving, Investment and Current Accounts", *OECD Economics Department Working Papers*, No. 815.

Kobayashi, B. and T. Muris (2013), "I Can See Clearly Now: Lee Benham, Eyeglasses, And The Empirical Analysis Of Advertising And The Effects Of Professional Regulation", *Competition Policy International* Vol 9 No. 1.

Lee, I.H., M. Syed and L. Xueyan (2012), "Is China Over-Investing and Des it Matter?", *IMF Working Paper* 12/277.

Nickell, S. (1996), "Competition and Corporate Performance", *Journal of Political Economy*, 104(4), 724-746.

Nicoletti, G. and S. Scarpetta (2003), "Regulation, Productivity and Growth: OECD Evidence", *Economic Policy*, 18(36), 9–72.

OECD (2014a), *OECD Competition Assessment Reviews: Greece*, OECD Publishing, Paris, DOI: *http://dx.doi.org/10.1787/9789264206090-en.*

OECD (2014b), "Factsheet on how competition affects macro-economic outcomes", *www.oecd.org/competition/factsheet-macroeconomics-competition.htm.*

OECD (2014c), "Focus on Inequality and Growth, *www.oecd.org/els/soc/Focus-Inequality-and-Growth-2014.pdf.*

OECD (2014d), "How can competition contribute to the G20 commitment to raise GDP by at least 2%?", *www.g20australia.org/sites/default/files/g20_resources/library/How%20can%20competition%20contribute%20to%20the%20G-20%20commitment%20to%20raise%20GDP%20by%20at%20least%202%25.pdf*

OECD (2012), *Competitive Neutrality: Maintaining a Level Playing Field Between Public and Private Business*, Paris.

OECD (2011), "OECD Review of Telecommunication Policy and Regulation in Mexico", *http://dx.doi.org/10.1787/9789264060111-en.*

OECD (2010), "Competition Assessment Toolkit *www.oecd.org/competition/assessment-toolkit.htm.*

OECD (2009a), "State-Owned Enterprises in China: Reviewing the Evidence", Occasional Paper.

OECD (2009b), "State-Owned Enterprises in India: Reviewing the Evidence", Occasional Paper.

OECD (2007), "Taxi Services: Competition and Regulation", OECD Competition Committee Roundtable, *www.oecd.org/daf/competition/sectors/41472612.pdf.*

OECD and Comisión Federal de Competencia, México (2010) *A Competition Policy Assessment of the Domestic Airline Sector in Mexico and Recommendations to Improve Competition, www.oecd.org/daf/competition/45049588.pdf.*

OECD and Comisión Federal de Competencia, México (2012) *Eliminación de restricciones a la participación extranjera en México - Evaluación de los beneficios potenciales en algunas industrias, www.oecd.org/daf/competition/IEDreporteOCDECFC.pdf.*

Pilat, D. (1997), "Regulation and Performance in the Distribution Sector", *OECD Economics Department Working Papers* 180, OECD Publishing.

Rauch, F. (2013), "Advertising expenditure and consumer prices", *International Journal of Industrial Organization*, 31(4), 331-341.

Romer, C. D. (1999), "Why did prices rise in the 1930s?", *The Journal of Economic History*, 59 (01), 167-199

Sakakibara, M., and M. E. Porter (2001), "Competing at home to win abroad: evidence from Japanese industry", *Review of Economics and Statistics*, 83(2), 310-322.

Schwab, D. and E. Werker, Profits and Economic Development (3 April 2014). Harvard Business School BGIE Unit Working Paper No. 14-087. Available at SSRN: *http://ssrn.com/abstract=2409251 or http://dx.doi.org/10.2139/ssrn.2409251.*

Skuterud, M. (2005), "The Impact of Sunday Shopping on Employment and Hours of Work in the Retail Industry: Evidence from Canada", *European Economic Review*, 49, 8, 1953-1978.

Smith, A. (1776), "An Inquiry into the Nature and Causes of the Wealth of Nations".

Sutherland, D., and P. Hoeller (2013), "Growth-promoting Policies and Macroeconomic Stability", *OECD Economics Department Working Papers* 1091, OECD Publishing.

Taylor, J. E. (2007), "Cartel Code Attributes and Cartel Performance: An Industry-Level Analysis of the National Industrial Recovery Act", *Journal of Law and Economics*, 50(3), 597-624.

Taylor, J. E. (2002), "The output effects of government sponsored cartels during the New Deal", *The Journal of Industrial Economics*, 50(1), 1-10.

Urzúa, C. M. (2008), "Evaluación de los efectos distributivos y espaciales de las empresas con poder de mercado en México", *Mexican Federal Competition Commission*. Available at: *www.oecd.org/daf/competition/45047597.pdf.*

Van Reenen, J. (2011), "Does competition raise productivity through improving management quality?", *International Journal of Industrial Organization* 29, 306–316.

Wright, R. E. and T. W. Zeiler (2014), *Guide to U.S. Economic Policy*, CQ Press 1483386317.

ORGANISATION FOR ECONOMIC CO-OPERATION AND DEVELOPMENT

The OECD is a unique forum where governments work together to address the economic, social and environmental challenges of globalisation. The OECD is also at the forefront of efforts to understand and to help governments respond to new developments and concerns, such as corporate governance, the information economy and the challenges of an ageing population. The Organisation provides a setting where governments can compare policy experiences, seek answers to common problems, identify good practice and work to co-ordinate domestic and international policies.

The OECD member countries are: Australia, Austria, Belgium, Canada, Chile, the Czech Republic, Denmark, Estonia, Finland, France, Germany, Greece, Hungary, Iceland, Ireland, Israel, Italy, Japan, Korea, Luxembourg, Mexico, the Netherlands, New Zealand, Norway, Poland, Portugal, the Slovak Republic, Slovenia, Spain, Sweden, Switzerland, Turkey, the United Kingdom and the United States. The European Union takes part in the work of the OECD.

OECD Publishing disseminates widely the results of the Organisation's statistics gathering and research on economic, social and environmental issues, as well as the conventions, guidelines and standards agreed by its members.

OECD PUBLISHING, 2, rue André-Pascal, 75775 PARIS CEDEX 16
(21 2015 01 1P) ISBN 978-92-64-23261-7 – 2015

www.ingramcontent.com/pod-product-compliance
Lightning Source LLC
Chambersburg PA
CBHW080536250926
51846CB00016B/1139